SECRET
COMMANDOS

BEHIND ENEMY LINES WITH THE
ELITE WARRIORS OF SOG

JOHN L. PLASTER

Simon & Schuster

NEW YORK   LONDON   TORONTO   SYDNEY

SIMON & SCHUSTER
Rockefeller Center
1230 Avenue of the Americas
New York, NY 10020

For information about special discounts for bulk purchases,
please contact Simon & Schuster Special Sales:
1-800-456-6798 or business@simonandschuster.com

Designed by Paul Dippolito

Manufactured in the United States of America

1   3   5   7   9   10   8   6   4   2

Library of Congress Cataloging-in-Publication Data
Plaster, John L.
Secret commandos : behind enemy lines with the elite warriors of SOG / John L. Plaster.
p.   cm.
Includes index.
1. Vietnamese Conflict, 1961–1975—Commando operations—United States.
2. Vietnamese Conflict, 1961–1975—Regimental histories—United States.
3. United States. Military Assistance Command. Studies and Observations Group—History.
4. Ho Chi Minh Trail—History.   I. Title.
DS558.92.P547   2004
959.704'38—dc22   2004042821
ISBN 0-684-85673-5

Acknowledgments

A book containing this amount of detail is possible only with the generous assistance of many people, especially fellow SOG veterans. The names of those I interviewed will be found in the text, and I sincerely thank all of them. Many others helped, too, including Steve Sherman, whose voluminous SOG files aided in confirming many facts; Jack Kull likewise helped me find declassified annual SOG reports; Roxanne Merritt, director of Fort Bragg's JFK Special Warfare Museum, was helpful, as always; Joe Caver, director of the USAF Historical Research Agency archives at Maxwell Air Force Base, Alabama, responded to my every request; Jimmy Dean of the Special Forces Association helped me find old comrades, as did my old SOG recon friend, Brendan Lyons; during repeated trips to Fort Bragg, former One-Zero Ron Knight and his wife, Sandra, opened their home to me; CCN Hatchet Force veteran Chuck Pfeifer did likewise when I visited New York City; Cathy Chance spent hundreds of hours transforming my taped interviews into useful transcriptions; photo credits accompany each picture, but for these I especially thank SOG veterans Frank Greko and Ted Wicorek, along with photo technicians Roger Kennedy, Charles Farrow, and Douglas Black; my editor at Simon & Schuster, Robert Bender, never wavered in his support, encouraging me at the moments when I most needed it; and, of course, my lovely bride, Gail, provided inspiration. I must also acknowledge some unknown people—the helicopter crewmen, fighter pilots, and Forward Air Controllers who braved enemy fire to extract me and my teams from sometimes grave situations. Without them this book would not exist.

To today's U.S. Army Special Forces soldiers,
who continue the great tradition of MACV-SOG

Contents

Preface
xi

Maps
xii

Author's Note
1

PART ONE
Fort Bragg
3

PART TWO
Recon
25

PART THREE
Covey
267

Afterword
345

Index
351

Preface

Larry Trimble held the pen and pad, sitting there in the Bamboo Lounge with his recon buddies, Jim Lamotte and Ricardo Davis. They'd been drinking most of the day and felt the glibness that comes with alcohol. But they still weren't getting it quite right.

On a week-long break between missions behind enemy lines on the Ho Chi Minh Trail, this afternoon the three Green Berets reckoned it was time their unit, SOG, had a motto—but it had to say it just right, had to capture the flavor of taking on deadly risks to bring back intelligence under circumstances some people might find suicidal. It was hard to explain, even to themselves, the euphoria after each mission, and the gambler's daring that stirred them to go again. Camaraderie held them together, for there was no fanfare for their covert actions. It had to say that, too.

As the night mellowed and the balls of discarded paper piled up, they almost had it—a few more changes, then, yes! That was it, that explained it! Larry Trimble read it aloud:

> *You've never lived till you've almost died.*
> *For those who fight for it,*
> *Life has a flavor*
> *The protected will never know.*

Lamotte and Davis agreed. It was perfect.

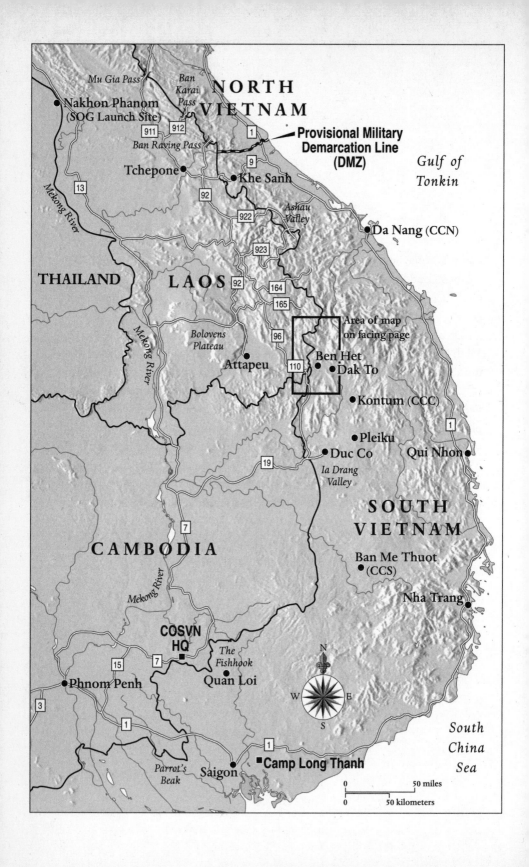

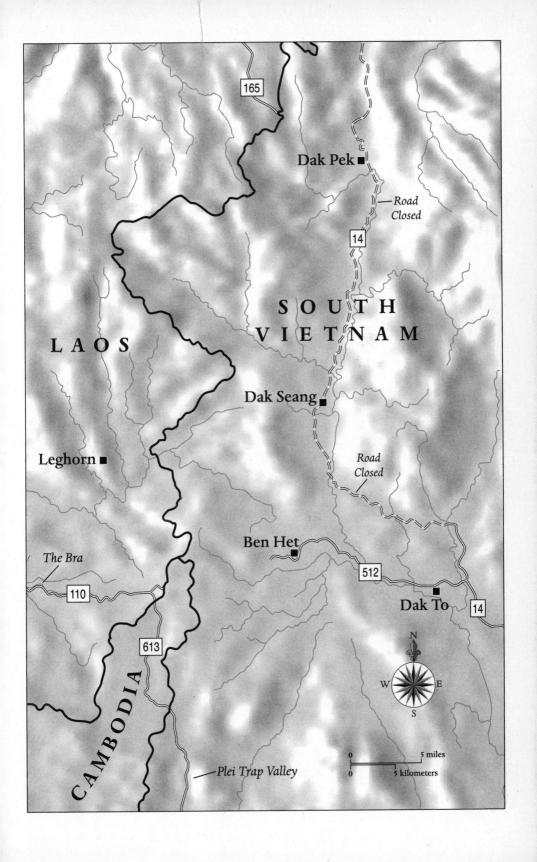

I have fought a good fight,
I have finished my course,
I have kept the faith.

2 Timothy 4:7

SECRET
COMMANDOS

Author's Note

There was a chill in the northern Wisconsin air, that October afternoon of 1998. Bayfield County's apple harvest was underway, and colorful leaves converted my roadway into a sublime cathedral through which I drove to the Iron River post office. On Main Street, I waved to neighbors who as readily waved back. Inside her tiny office, the postal clerk, Peggy, handed me a small package.

Postmarked, Quantico, Virginia, it was from FBI Special Agent Barry Subelsky, a friend and—like me—a former Green Beret. This was curious—I hadn't expected anything from Barry. After an hour running errands, I drove home with the box on the seat beside me. Retrieving it from my truck, I opened it to find an old cassette tape and Barry's note: "John, here's a recording of radio messages, apparently a recon team in trouble in Laos. Where and when isn't certain."

He'd recently found the tape among some forgotten Vietnam War memorabilia. Barry couldn't remember how he got it. "Maybe you can tell from the jargon," he continued, "if this was SOG," meaning the Studies and Observations Group, which ran top secret missions along the Laotian Ho Chi Minh Trail. He'd been stationed at Ben Het, a remote camp near the border, so that was entirely possible.

Digging around, I found an old cassette player, slipped in the tape, sat back, and pushed "play."

A radio voice called breathlessly, *"Prairie Fire! Prairie Fire!"*—SOG code words for a team in such terrible straits that they were about to be overrun.

The voice raised the hairs on my neck.

Then came a calmer voice, *"This is Delta Papa-Three . . ."*

It was my own voice.

And I realized exactly what this recording was. I turned off the lights, and sat in the dark, listening.

It was, I knew, 29 January 1971, the day we lost David Mixter and almost lost his teammates, Pat Mitchel and Lyn St. Laurent. That was Pat's voice calling, "Prairie Fire! Prairie Fire!"

Recon Team Colorado's eight men had been hit by a North Vietnamese forty-man platoon near a major enemy supply road in Laos. But ten miles away, Recon Team Hawaii, with my old teammates Les Dover, Regis Gmitter, and John Justice, also had been hit and declared a Prairie Fire Emergency. I could not go to the aid of both teams. Hearing my own voice, it was as if I was back there, when there was no time, but I had to make decisions.

And live with them.

Closing my eyes, listening to the lead gunship, Panther 36's radio voice, I could actually see his Cobra gunship down on the deck, dodging green tracers to fire rockets and strafe. Then the White Flight (rescue) Hueys were driven off by ground fire, and we'd brought in A-1 Skyraider attack planes.

It was all on the tape, exactly as it had happened.

I could not sleep that night.

The memories were fresh again, of that operation, of many operations, inspiring a thousand other recollections that swept across me—anguish, humor, fear, pride, and memories of the fine men I'd known and served beside. They were hilarious days, horrifying days, unforgettable days.

The years had passed, but my memories of those men seemed as fresh as on the day it all had happened.

PART ONE

Fort Bragg

Chapter One

Like many young men graduating high school in 1967, I went directly into the Army, much as our father's generation had done during World War II. In blue-collar, northeast Minneapolis, it was assumed that you served your country; the only question was whether you waited to be drafted for two years, or enlisted for three, choosing what you wanted to do. Along with several gung ho classmates, I followed the latter course, enlisting for Airborne-Infantry—paratroopers.

After Basic Training that sweltering summer at Fort Campbell, Kentucky, we were shipped to the pine forests of Fort Gordon, Georgia. There, in a cluster of Quonset huts called Camp Crockett, we trained to be Airborne-Infantrymen, bound for Vietnam and elite units, such as the 173rd Airborne Brigade, 101st Airborne Division, and the 1st Air Cavalry. In addition to lots of instruction on patrolling, weapons, and small unit tactics, we underwent tough physical training. Soon we found ourselves running five miles each morning in heavy jump boots, followed by hours of physical exercise. Our trainers, themselves Vietnam Airborne veterans, cut no slack. We expected none.

All that running and calisthenics later enabled us Camp Crockett graduates to skate through Jump School at Fort Benning, Georgia, while most Airborne trainees struggled and one quarter washed out. Then we got our great payoff—we jumped from airplanes, just like the World War II paratroopers we'd grown up admiring. Descending gracefully onto the Fort Benning drop zone among those billowing canopies, I forgot about all the harassment and physical agony. I loved being a paratrooper.

One morning, in our final week of Jump School, a rugged figure in a green beret appeared. He just stood there, watching our company while we underwent morning exercises. Afterward, he addressed us; anyone interested in volunteering for Special Forces could meet with him that evening. My neighborhood buddies had had enough training—I was the only one of them to go with twenty-five other Airborne students to listen to the Special Forces sergeant.

Unlike any other job in the Army—such as an infantryman or military policeman—you could not enlist to be a Green Beret. To be considered for Special Forces, the recruiter explained, you had to be a qualified paratrooper, with an intelligence test score high enough to attend officer candidate school, and meet the Army's highest physical fitness standard. All of us met these requirements, but there was still a special aptitude test, the recruiter explained.

Could I be a Green Beret? The Green Berets were gods. Only one year earlier, in 1966, the largest selling 45-rpm single was not recorded by the Beatles or the Rolling Stones—it was "The Ballad of the Green Berets," sung by Staff Sergeant Barry Sadler. Before that, the Vietnam War's first Medal of Honor had gone to Roger H. C. Donlon, a young Special Forces captain, while Robin Moore's novel *The Green Berets* had hung on the *New York Times* best-seller list for more than a year. Only five years earlier, over the protests of Pentagon bureaucrats, President John F. Kennedy had authorized the green beret to these superb warriors, declaring their headgear "a symbol of excellence, a badge of courage, a mark of distinction in the fight for freedom."

During my childhood in Minnesota, I'd heard Scandinavian neighbors speak in awe of the Norwegian Resistance and their inspiring fight against the Nazis. I read books about them, and the French Resistance. Such gallant guerrilla fighters had shown that small groups of dedicated men operating behind enemy lines can have effects far beyond their numbers—just like America's Special Forces. And now, as a freshly trained paratrooper, I had a chance to volunteer for the Green Berets—at least maybe.

Originally, Special Forces accepted only experienced soldiers—at least twenty years old, with a minimum rank of specialist four. Heavy casualties in Vietnam had compelled lowering the age to nineteen, and the rank to private first class, neither of which I met. I was only a private, and three months past eighteen. "But I'll be nineteen by the time I finish training," I tried to persuade the recruiter.

The Green Beret sergeant looked me over, then announced, "You can take the Special Forces Qualification Test with the others. Let's see how well you do." Designed by RAND, a defense think tank, this was the strangest test I'd ever taken, resembling the opening scene in the TV series *Mission: Impossible,* with tape-recorded instructions, exotic scenarios, photos to study, then a series of questions offering only imperfect answers. I could not tell how well I'd done.

The next afternoon, the Special Forces sergeant called back eight of us. I had a 477 out of 500, the highest score in our group. I was in—I had a chance to earn a green beret. An hour after graduating and pinning on our silver paratrooper wings, I said goodbye to my neighborhood buddies, and boarded a chartered bus for the 450-mile drive to Fort Bragg, North Carolina.

It was after dark when I awoke to see the bus headlights illuminating a sign—"Headquarters Company, Special Forces Training Group." At Basic Training we'd been greeted by shouting drill instructors; at Camp Crockett's Airborne-Infantry school it was more screaming drill instructors; at Fort Benning the black-hatted Airborne cadre had shouted and dropped us for push-ups. How much worse would it be here?

Momentarily, the headquarters company door opened, out strolled a lone Special Forces sergeant first class with a clipboard. The eight of us trotted dutifully before him, but he just let us stand in a cluster while he pulled out a pipe.

After puffing it to life he announced, "We've kept the mess hall open for you. Stow your duffel bags inside the hallway. After chow, I'll issue you bedding. Any questions?" His tone was relaxed, almost friendly. Until now, we'd been housed in World War II–era wooden barracks or crude Quonset huts, with forty men bunked in large open rooms. Here at Fort Bragg the sergeant ushered us into modern brick buildings resembling college dormitories, with just eight men per room. Our quarters were immaculate, with brightly painted walls and tiled floors.

Yes, Special Forces was different. Now we'd have to prove ourselves in the six weeks of Phase One, the initial and most difficult portion of SF training.

Where would we start? Learning to master explosives? Sabotage? Raids?

"To accomplish your missions," an old master sergeant told us during orientation, "you must be both a warrior *and* a teacher. Therefore, the first subject that will make or break your future in Special Forces is MOI—methods of instruction."

What! A teacher? We wanted to kill the enemy and blow things up. Instead, we faced a whole week of MOI. "If you cannot learn to teach," the master sergeant warned, "there's no room for you in SF." He was serious.

That first week was devoted to teaching skills, instructed by the sharpest group of Non-Commissioned Officers (NCOs) I'd yet encountered in the Army—bright, devoted, well spoken, and just rough enough around the edges to make them Special Forces. All were combat-seasoned with plenty of firsthand experience to make teaching points.

Our most unforgettable instructor had to be Sergeant First Class Morris Worley. Recovering from serious combat wounds, rather than convalesce at home Worley sat in a chair in front of us, lecturing on effective teaching techniques. Despite his clumsy cast and bandages covering much of one leg and his face, he never even hinted he was in pain, though we could see ugly red scars beneath his right sleeve from which his hand hung stiff and almost unusable.

He struggled to write on the blackboard, but did so legibly, pretending it was entirely normal.

Unknown to us, each morning another instructor, Sergeant First Class Bob Franke, helped Worley dress, then put him in the back seat of his car and drove him to our classroom. Before we arrived, Franke and a third instructor, Sergeant First Class Bob Jones, put Worley in a chair, then carried him to the podium.

Truly, Worley was a man of humility and indomitable spirit—and, we learned one day, of great courage. During a break, a fellow student told us Worley had been awarded the Distinguished Service Cross, America's second highest heroism award, just below the Medal of Honor. Worley had been in something called, the student thought, SOG. None of us knew what those letters stood for, and when one student asked an instructor, all he got was an angry glare. Whatever SOG was, we were not to inquire about it.

That week of MOI opened our eyes to the reality of Special Forces. One morning Worley noted, "Montagnard tribesmen can only reason up to an arithmetic value of three—'One-two-three-many.' How," he challenged us, "do you teach him that an M-16 has a twenty-round magazine?" Yes, we had to pull off our boots and show him fingers and toes.

Or, you're to teach a class on the M-72 Light Antitank Weapon, and you won't get your first M-72 air-dropped for another week—What do you do? We handcrafted a model from wood, string, and wire, and instructed on that. From hand-making our training aids to using a sandbox and pine cones to teach tactics, our instructors encouraged improvisation and field expedients. For our final test, each of us had to teach a class to the instructors (acting as foreign guerrilla students), with one playing the role of interpreter, further complicated by a few invented "cultural taboos" that we would discover only during our class. It was hilarious to figure out our guerrillas were offended by a pointed finger, or the word "the," but the lesson was well learned.

A few men failed, and that was the last we saw of them. For the rest of us, it all made more sense now—of course, to be Special Forces we had to be teachers.

The rest of our Phase One training focused on Unconventional Warfare—landing behind enemy lines to recruit, train, and lead local guerrilla bands, and through them create intelligence networks and organize underground railways to assist downed pilots and escaped POWs.

We learned much from the World War II experience of the OSS, the Office of Strategic Services, a quasi-military U.S. secret agency, whose veterans went on to found both the Central Intelligence Agency and U.S. Army Special

Forces. Just like the OSS, we studied how to survey an aircraft landing site in an occupied country, set up encoded marker lights, then quickly move away with the arriving supplies and personnel before enemy security forces reacted. Or how to hold a message aloft on wire and poles, to be snatched up by a low-flying airplane. To communicate with our agent network, we employed a dead letter drop—a concealed message left at an agreed-upon spot, so we'd never have to meet face-to-face.

If the Soviet Union invaded Western Europe, dozens of Special Forces teams would parachute behind Russian lines—to recruit Czechs, Poles, East Germans, Lithuanians, Latvians, even Russians—and especially ethnic minorities—to create an immense resistance movement throughout Eastern Europe. Already, our instructors hinted, more than adequate stockpiles of weapons, radios, and supplies had been secretly cached from Norway to the Swiss frontier of Germany so that still more Special Forces teams could stay behind as the Russian invaders surged westward, adding dozens of additional teams in their rear, and thousands more guerrillas.

To fulfill this role, the twelve-man Special Forces A-Team was structured to operate autonomously for extended periods. Led by a captain with a lieutenant assistant, the A-Team's ten NCOs possessed an ideal combination of technical skills—two medics, two communications men, two weapons men, two demolitions men, and two operations and intelligence men to plan training and operations. Not only did this mean an impressive force multiplier—500 foreign combatants for the investment of twelve Green Berets—but it put these local guerrillas in direct support of the U.S. armed forces. What better way to integrate a guerrilla movement into U.S. military operations than to have it trained and led by Americans, communicate with American forces, and coordinate their operations? It was brilliant.

During the fourth week of Phase One, everyone's attention switched to Vietnam, where the news was not good. Two North Vietnamese divisions had encircled the U.S. Marines at Khe Sanh, who were pounded day and night by heavy incoming fire. Then came the Tet '68 Offensive, an unexpected country-wide attack and temporary seizing of most major towns in South Vietnam. And especially ominous, for the first time in the war, enemy tanks struck, overrunning the Special Forces camp at Lang Vei, only six miles west of Khe Sanh. This was close to home—there were NCOs in Training Group who knew the Green Berets at Lang Vei, or had even served there themselves. There was genuine doubt about the direction the war was taking.

Grim as this sounded, at Training Group there still were light moments.

One morning, the acting first sergeant of our company, Sergeant First Class Ernie Fant, was pacing before the morning formation when he noticed one man lacking the requisite pistol belt and canteen.

"Just where is your pistol belt, trooper?" Fant demanded.

Of course he'd lost it or forgotten it somewhere, but that would have been admitting a foolish mistake—for sheer originality, utter genius under stress, this guy deserved an award. Standing at perfect attention, he responded, "The moles took it."

Fant didn't know what to say. He eyed that young trooper up and down in amazement. "Moles?"

The young soldier lifted his hands to his mouth and flexed his fingers sideways, the way a little furry mole digs. "You know, Sergeant, *moles*."

Fant fought back a smile. "Well, do you s'pose the moles will bring it back?"

"I sure hope so."

He got away, clean, and everyone admired him for it, including Fant.

By now, a month later, we had only one more week of Phase One to go, then the worst would be over. Just a seven-day field exercise—why, we could skate through that as easily as we'd skated through Jump School at Fort Benning, we thought. Then, during a cigarette break, a grizzled master sergeant told us, "We only want men who really want to be in Special Forces."

In the early 1960s, he recalled, the 77th Special Forces Group faced a reduction, with his company finding it had only fifteen slots for thirty NCOs. "So the sergeant major took us behind headquarters to a sawdust pit used for parachute training, and told us, 'The last fifteen of you in that pit, you'll stay in Special Forces. The other fifteen, the ones who end up outside the pit, you'll go over to the 82nd Airborne Division.'

"Twenty minutes later," he concluded "we knew who really wanted to be in Special Forces. By the end of next week, we'll know which of you really want to be here."

A hint of what was coming was a detailed inspection of our gear just before we left. The instructors went through our pockets, through our rucksacks, even unrolled our dry socks, to ensure we carried no food. Then we rode to Pope Air Force Base, donned parachutes, and climbed aboard a C-123 transport. Well after dark, we jumped into Camp Mackall, a separate training base that adjoins Fort Bragg.

After forming up on the drop zone, we force-marched a few miles—to "escape" enemy security forces—then established a perimeter in thick forest. This was no campout, but a tactical situation in which we pulled perimeter security and practiced noise and light discipline. But we had at least eight hours sleep, so it didn't seem very difficult.

At dawn, we met the NCO who ran Camp Mackall, Sergeant First Class Manuel Torres, a matter-of-fact sort who neither cajoled nor cursed us. Either we would meet his standards and become Green Berets, or fail. It was up to us. To put us in the right mood, he began with a "stroll" on the Torres Trail, a quarter-mile of waist-deep swamp that we trudged in full rucksacks. Filthy, soaked, and winded, at the end we were greeted by instructors with spit-shined boots, a knife-sharp crease in their starched fatigues, and a clean green beret. Rotated twice per day, the instructors always looked parade ground sharp, in contrast to the students' steadily declining appearance. Their instruction was excellent, especially classes on raids, patrols, and ambushes, using bare dirt as a chalk board and a tree limb as a pointer.

Our survival instructor, an old Cajun chicken thief, covered everything from serious skills to amusing animal lore. City boys were fascinated by how he put a live chicken to sleep: Fold the bird's head under a wing, grip her firmly and rotate the bird in a slow, arm's length circle, then gently sit her on the ground and release your grip—the bird would sit there, perfectly asleep, until he clapped his hands. To hypnotize the chicken, the old Cajun sergeant held the bird's beak to the dirt, then drew a line with his fingertip, from the beak outward about four inches, over and over, slower and slower, until the chicken's pea-brain became so mesmerized that everything beyond that dirt line faded into oblivion. The bird just stared, bug-eyed, until the sergeant clapped his hands.

"You know why they call SF 'snake eaters'?" he asked. "Back in '62, when JFK come down here, our committee gave the demo-stration. One a my sah-gants, he hold up the rattlesnake, ready to cut it up for dinner, an' Pres-dent Kennedy, he say, 'What do yah do when you got no knife?' An' that sahgant, he just bite that snake's head clean off, yessir! An' duh Pres-dent, he just laugh and laugh. That sahgant, he promoted next day, yessir! Ever since, we be 'snake eaters.'" He stuck his chest out.

It was all very funny. Then he handed us lunch—live chickens and rabbits. From then on, we no longer received canned C rations—all our food was on-the-hoof. If we couldn't start a fire, or proved too slow skinning, gutting, and cooking our rabbit or chicken or goat, we simply did not eat. And if you didn't like it, the instructors offered, "Just quit and you'll have all the delicious fried chicken you can eat!"

Initially when there was downtime we had talked about women. Now we talked about food, only food—barbecued ribs, thick juicy steaks, you name it. For Charlie Pesten and me, this grew into a blueberry pie obsession. When we weren't ambushing or marching or digging, Charlie and I fantasized over blueberry pie, taking turns describing our mother's recipes, recalling memories of berry picking, and deciding upon the perfect ice cream complement.

We also studied land navigation, beginning with an old Special Forces instructor who delicately poked a map with a needle-sharp pencil. "That's where we are," he indicated with such precision that, literally, *he pinpointed the spot where we stood,* pointing to the landmarks and terrain features by which he'd reckoned so exactly. After his class we attempted to mimic his precision on our compass azimuths and pace counts as, day and night, we trudged through swamps and waded swift streams to find specially numbered 55-gallon drums on what was as much an obstacle course as a compass course. An all-too-easy 5 percent error in direction or pace count led you to the wrong barrel—a few wrong barrels and you were washed out. Just as we began to achieve some success, the instructors added time pressure—bring back the right barrel number, *and* be back before the deadline! This was another make-or-break skill because a Special Forces soldier often operates alone on unfamiliar terrain, requiring excellent land navigation skills.

Our instructors dealt a constant dose of mental stress and physical exhaustion, but not a drill sergeant's in-your-face shouts and silly harassment, which don't actually mimic combat conditions. No, these imaginative Green Beret NCOs simulated combat to make the stress sensible; for instance, when a road surveillance team employed sloppy camouflage, instead of screaming profanities and dropping the soldiers for push-ups, the instructor shouted, "You've been spotted!" The resulting wild dash to the rally point, then quick march with rucksacks up and down hills to escape taught us the unforgettable consequences for being spotted. Stupid tactics, discipline infractions, bad field craft—each transgression instigated an aggressive enemy action that wore us down while teaching us tough lessons and inspiring the weak at heart to quit.

Whenever the going got especially tough, the instructors all but bribed us to quit. "Hot food," they'd offer, "cold sodas—it's yours if you want it. Just quit." Or, an instructor would indignantly advise, "You don't have to put up with this bullshit. I'd quit if I was you." For many trainees, quitting was the simple solution. Good riddance. As for the rest of us, we'd have starved, gone without sleep, died, to wear the green beret. Our creed became, "You may kill us, but you cannot make us quit."

One evening my team foolishly allowed a barbecue atmosphere to overtake us while roasting a goat, and our chuckling drew an instructor's attention. "Air raid!" he screamed and tossed an artillery simulator. We had to rush off, tearing away raw goat flesh, which we munched as we ran, leaving the carcass behind.

Food and sleep deprivation, combined with almost constant marching and climbing, quickly wore down men's social veneer. What was left was our soul, which the instructors incessantly tempted with offers of comfort, food, and rest. We began to lose track of time, finding our team again plodding through the waist-deep mud on the Torres Trail until each leg felt like it weighed 100 pounds, and we couldn't remember what infraction put us there.

It became especially difficult to stay awake when pulling your hour on guard while your teammates slept. And that led to my team's worst night in Phase One. With only one more day to go, a teammate on guard duty failed to challenge an approaching instructor; he'd probably fallen asleep but wouldn't admit it, and the instructor himself wasn't sure. The angry instructor led him and the three men closest to him—including myself—to a small clearing illuminated by the full moon. "Four good men were killed tonight," he seethed, "because this man failed to do his fucking job. Do you know what you have to do now?"

He studied our blank faces. "You're going to bury your dead." With his heel he scraped a square on the ground. "You'll dig six feet deep, six feet wide, and six feet long." Each of us knew that with our small entrenching tools we'd be digging all night. The guilty man quit on the spot. Maybe he thought he was helping us by taking responsibility, but that left only three of us to dig—and the instructor wasn't backing down. He'd return at dawn to inspect the grave.

There was no use crying about it. My teammate Bill Copley suggested that two men dig and one man rest, rotating on the half-hour. It was steady work, all night long, but we kept going with the knowledge that there was just one more day—by this time the following night, we'd be aboard Hueys flying back to Fort Bragg.

We finished a half-hour before sunrise, but we'd expended far more energy digging than we'd replaced in those half-hour naps, so we were more exhausted than ever. There was just one more day, one final exercise, we kept telling ourselves. With the end of the ordeal in sight, we were tapping into reserves of spirit and body to keep going.

That final exercise was a night raid to rescue POWs. All day we marched toward the POW camp, then performed recons, and after dark infiltrated to within sight of it. At midnight, all eight trainee teams converged to assault the camp, which we achieved to the satisfaction of our instructors. Then we split and made our separate ways to the landing zones, where helicopters would lift us back to Fort Bragg.

My team made that two-mile march in only an hour, arriving there at 0125 hours, a full fifteen minutes before the choppers were due. Lying in the bushes, I dreamt of hot food, a cold beer, a shower, then clean sheets. Life was good—we'd made it! We would be Green Berets!

Then headlights appeared and we pushed our faces to the ground to avoid being seen. A two-and-a-half-ton truck halted nearby and out stepped Sergeant First Class Torres. He walked directly to where we lay. "Your helicopters have been shot down," he announced. "You must walk out."

I wanted to scream. I'd squeezed through the pain, the exhaustion, inadequate food, sleep deprivation, pushed myself to make it to today—*and it wasn't over!* One man began to weep. "Of course," Torres offered, "you can quit. I'd understand, that's OK. We have hot chow in the truck." Several men from another team already were in there, eating and smoking cigarettes.

Like my teammates, my enthusiasm was spent, leaving only cold resolve to die or succeed. We would not quit—you can kill us but you cannot make us quit. No one on our team took up Torres's offer.

On our map, Torres pointed to a destination twenty-two kilometers away—about fifteen miles cross-country, through swamps and streams. The intervening ground was patrolled by instructors and 82nd Airborne soldiers riding jeeps. Get caught by them, and we'd be brought back here to start again. "Be there by noon if you want to wear a green beret," Torres warned. "One minute late is a fail." He drove away.

We had ten hours, meaning 1.5 miles per hour, cross-country, with no allowance for breaks. Our acting team leader, a staff sergeant, had our only compass and map, so he got us headed in the right direction. Instead of bypassing obstacles, his unimaginative straight-line route sent us directly through deep washouts, swamp, and thick undergrowth, which wore us down and slowed us. The last straw came when he had us ford Big Muddy Creek at a terrible spot where the current almost swept us away. Barely dragging himself from the water, he sheepishly admitted that he'd lost our only compass in the water. Without announcing it, his spirit spent, he quit.

How could we possibly find our way? Another trainee, Jim Godwin, took the map and studied it. "We can follow the landmarks," he suggested, an idea seconded by Sergeant Cletis Sinyard, a combat veteran of the 1st Air Cavalry. We'd travel landmark to landmark, staying close to roads—they'd be our compass—and somehow we'd evade the 82nd Airborne troops trying to hunt us down. The odds were terrible but there was no other option and no time for talk.

We were off.

I'd never been so exhausted in my life. At times I had to tell my legs to move. As quickly as we sat down for a break, we'd fall asleep. I began hallucinating, talking to a bush I imagined was a teammate. Then the helmet tied on my rucksack came loose and kept slapping my leg but I couldn't concentrate enough to retie it. I threw it away. Whenever we heard jeeps on the roads, we'd lie down and instantly fall asleep, yet somehow someone always got the rest of us up, and we kept moving.

Time was a blur, though it flowed swiftly. One moment it was 9:00 A.M., then another moment it was 11:30, and we only had thirty minutes left. We jogged that final mile with rucksacks, and arrived at the rendezvous with three minutes to spare. Then I was gobbling down a C ration can of ham and lima beans, the most delicious meal I'd ever eaten.

For the next hour we watched others straggle in, collapse, and weep— they'd given it their all and come up short. But there was nothing they could do. The standard was the standard, and Torres enforced it.

Only once did Torres waver, I later learned from a buddy who went through another Phase One cycle. When a team arrived totally spent less than a minute after noon, Torres learned they had carried a sick teammate, and left him behind only when they reached a road where medics could find him. They'd done their absolute damnedest; these were the kind of men who should be in Special Forces. Yet the standard was clear. "I'll tell you what," Torres offered. "It's forty-five kilometers (twenty-seven miles) back to Smoke Bomb Hill. You can climb aboard the trucks and ride back with us, and that's the end, you're terminated. But if you walk out, I'll still give you a go." Totally drained, their feet blistered, bloody, and swollen, three gave up.

But two determined-to-the-death men put one wobbly leg in front of the other, and started to walk toward Fort Bragg. The trucks pulled away. They walked a hundred yards to a curve, and there waiting for them was Sergeant Torres and his jeep. "Get aboard, Green Berets," he announced. And off they rode.

The following Monday, about twenty-five of us, less than half our original class, stood formation in front of the JFK Center Chapel. Upon order, we removed our Army baseball caps and threw them away. Then, to the order "Don berets," we placed green berets on our heads, knowing our lives would never be the same. There were still months of training ahead of us, but, as the old master sergeant had said, now we knew who really wanted to be in Special Forces.

Our graduation speaker, the Training Group sergeant major, kept his words few and his point clear: "A green beret is a hat. It's hot in the summer and it's cold in the winter, and it doesn't have a bill to keep the sun out of your eyes. You do not want to be a green beret, you want to be a Special Forces soldier. And that means a lot more than any hat you may ever wear."

Later that day, we lined up outside Training Group headquarters to be interviewed personally by the commander, Colonel George Callaway, and learn whether we'd train to be medics, commo specialists, weapons men, or demolitions men. Most of us wanted Weapons School, so we could fire dozens of exotic U.S. and foreign firearms. This was also the shortest speciality course, getting you out of training and into a real assignment the quickest. I'd crammed from *Small Arms of the World*, memorizing weights, lengths, and cyclic firing rates of all sorts of weapons. I told the man behind me, Glenn Uemura, a Hawaiian who'd carried our heavy .30 caliber machine gun during Phase One, "When the colonel hears what I have to say, he's sending me straight to Weapons School!"

Indeed, I presented my case well, despite Callaway being the first full colonel I'd ever spoken to. He listened to everything I had to say, nodded thoughtfully, then announced, "I think you'll make a much stronger commo man, with all that weapons knowledge. You're going to Commo School." And that was it. Glenn Uemura, too, was going to communications training, along with Jim "Mule Skinner" Pruitt, Jack Damoth, and Bill Copley, with whom I'd dug that six-by-six-by-six grave. Two thirds of our Phase One class went to commo, which just happened to fill all the vacancies in the next commo course.

Uemura, predictably nicknamed "Pineapple," became my closest comrade in commo training, which turned out to be much more technically difficult than we'd anticipated. Not only did we have to learn all the complexities of radios and custom-made antennas, but we had to master sending and receiving Morse code, and encryption techniques. Like any other part of Special Forces training, academic failure here meant termination.

All day long, five days a week, we listened to tape recordings of Morse code "dits" and "dahs" overlaid with a human voice reciting words of similar syllable lengths. This word association system, invented by a civilian, Judson Cornish, matched a voice saying *A-long* with the tapped dit-dah for A, and *Brake Cyl-in-der* (dah dit-dit-dit) as B, and so on. As the course progressed, the Morse code volume steadily increased, and the human voice faded from our earphones. By the end of eight weeks, the human voice was gone, and we could send and receive code to Special Forces standards.

During Morse code training, one sound booth was occupied by a middle-aged master sergeant from the 3rd Special Forces Group. A qualified weapons man, what was he doing there? "Oh, I'm a team sergeant, nothing going on for a month, so I thought I'd come over here and learn Morse code." He couldn't have had more than three or four years left in his career, yet here he was, struggling through mentally agonizing code school, with a bunch of twenty-year-olds. A basic ethic of Special Forces, he explained, was to train and to learn. Training never ended. If you knew more than your teammates, your job was to teach them, and vice versa. I noticed that he constantly carried a paperback book tucked in his back belt, like many another Special Forces sergeant. All these NCOs were inveterate readers—from Zane Grey to Aldous Huxley, from Caesar's *Conquest of Gaul* to Heinlein's *Stranger in a Strange Land*. Mostly Southern boys and largely self-taught, Special Forces NCOs, I found, were quick studies, to be intellectually underestimated at great peril. Only in Special Forces might you find a dirt-poor Mississippi boy who spoke fluent French, had graduated from a CIA lock-picking course, and was attending night school to earn his graduate degree in history from Duke University.

One night during Morse code training, while passing our company day room, I noticed a throng of men watching TV. President Lyndon B. Johnson had lost the New Hampshire primary, and now we watched him announce that he wouldn't seek another term. As a conciliatory gesture to Hanoi, he ordered a partial bombing halt, ending air attacks against two thirds of North Vietnam. U.S. planes were now restricted to the southernmost panhandle, where supply roads led to Laos and the Demilitarized Zone. A few men thought this might end the war; most, including all the older SFers, thought it was a wasted gesture, that Hanoi would exploit it to the hilt and give nothing in return. They were proved correct.

Our communications training continued, unaffected by political developments. We learned how to operate most radios in the Army system, plus a few others unique to Special Forces. Chief among the latter was the AN/GRC-109, designed during World War II for use by secret agents. Its two waterproof black boxes—each the size of a bread loaf—could be powered by anything from flashlight batteries to the hand-cranked generator included in its air-dropped kit. Its Morse code signal could bounce off the ionosphere and transmit halfway across the world.

Every time we transmitted on the AN/GRC-109, we cut a wire antenna of different length according to the metric length of our signal frequency. To calculate this length, we learned algebraic formulas. After mastering this, we learned about all kinds of antenna variations so we could fine-tune for a particular frequency, or reduce its size, or, importantly, make its output directional to minimize the chances of the enemy finding our team by triangulating our signal.

Signal security became our most important subject, whether learning how to encrypt messages or how to avoid enemy radio direction finding. The greatest vulnerability for a force operating behind enemy lines, we learned, is its connections with the outside world, against which an enemy will mount his greatest detection effort. *Find the radio, and you've found the team! Break his code and you'll know his plans!*

Therefore, we learned how to mask our radio signal by exploiting topography—transmit from a deep ravine or valley whose long axis points toward your receiving station. The earth will absorb the 345 degrees of radio waves emitting right, left, and to your rear, so an enemy intercept station must be along that narrow 15 degrees to your front in order to catch your signal.

An instructor told a humorous tale of an SF team on exercise in Germany that drove an American radio intercept station crazy. The signal intercept unit pretended the Green Berets were Soviet commandos, to be triangulated and attacked. Ingeniously, the SF commo men connected their transmitter to the barbed wire fence that surrounded the intercept station. Inside, the signal technicians could not understand what was wrong—according to their instruments, *the team's transmitter was everywhere!* Desperate, they phoned other intercept stations to help them fix the transmitter's location. All of them perfectly fixed the site right at the signal intercept station. The intercept team had to ante up cases of cold beer before the Green Beret commo men would explain how they'd done it.

In message encryption, we learned how to employ various grids of letters and numbers to scramble a message or substitute for letters. Then there were book codes, in which the sender and receiver agree upon using a certain book—the Bible, a Shakespeare play, an obscure book of verse. Then each Morse code message would refer to a particular page and line as the encipherment grid. With enough computer time, a sophisticated enemy could crack a book code or the various scrambled and substituted codes by comparing millions of possible solutions until they began to see understandable sentences. Therefore, these offered only limited security.

The most secure encryption, we learned, resulted from one-time pads, which use randomly generated letters to preclude any kind of pattern. As its name implies, each pad was used only once, then destroyed. So long as the encipherment employed random letters, no amount of computer analysis could find a pattern and crack the resulting messages.

Finally, we learned about duress codes, something we hoped we'd never need. A duress code is a word or group of letters that a radio operator slips into a message to let a receiving station know he's sending the message under duress—*I've been captured, a gun is to my head, so beware of what I report or request from you.*

The twelve-week commo course wrapped up with a week-long field exercise. Students divided into four-man teams, backpacking their radios into the spectacular mountains of Pisgah National Forest. Three times a day, each team erected a custom wire antenna, then tapped out an encrypted Morse code message to Fort Bragg, some 250 miles away.

While we attended the communications course, other Special Forces students were being trained as weapons men, demolitions specialists, and medics. The entire weapons course was held right at Fort Bragg. The demo men trained there and at Fort Belvoir, Virginia, where Army engineer instructors taught them as much about building things as blowing them up. Special Forces medic training, by far the most academically demanding, put its students through training at Fort Bragg and Fort Sam Houston, Texas, where their green berets sometimes brought them into disfavor with conventional Army officers.

During one training cycle at Fort Sam Houston, the Special Forces medics were stuck in the post's least desirable barracks, an isolated building across the street from post headquarters. The SF guys suspected they were isolated to keep their mischief in check. They ignored the affront, but could not ignore the room-jarring explosion each morning at 0600 hours when an MP honor guard fired a 37mm howitzer in front of post headquarters. The post commander— who conveniently lived miles away—thought this an inspiring way to start the day, and cared not one hoot about the effect on those Green Berets across the street.

Eventually, the medics took matters into their own hands. Expropriating a bucket of golf balls from a local driving range, the Green Beret medics stuffed an old mop head down the howitzer's bore as wadding, then poured in the balls. When the MP honor guard next fired the gun—KABOOM!—the golf balls shattered almost every window in the post headquarters building. There was hell to pay, but no one was able to prove a thing. And it did end the early morning explosions.

Whether medics, weapons men, demo specialists, or commo men, after finishing our respective speciality training we had a few weeks of downtime before we all got back together for the last portion of SF training, Phase Two. Of course, we couldn't be left to our own devices, so the Training Group cadre generated make-work details to keep us out of trouble.

Every morning, just after the 0800 hours formation, those of us awaiting Phase Two were greeted by a master sergeant with a clipboard, who issued assignments to clean out classrooms, or paint walls, or sweep parking lots, or pick up pine cones. By the third morning, my classmate Bill Copley arrived at formation with a push broom; while the master sergeant was assigning details, Bill started sweeping the sidewalk, gradually working his way around the corner of the building. He was gone. He spent the rest of the day sitting in the nearby woods, reading a book. Several of us later duplicated Copley's feat, a practice we called "ghosting"—making yourself invisible, disappearing. As long as we stayed out of trouble, the Training Group cadre didn't try very hard to find us.

The most extreme case of ghosting had to be a guy from Boston who had two months to wait for the next medic course. To stay busy, he was told to monitor coal furnaces in a dozen old buildings on Smoke Bomb Hill. During his first morning's rounds he came upon a civilian employee doing exactly the same thing. So he went home to Boston and every few days phoned a buddy at Fort Bragg. He was never missed.

For most of us, though, a few days of ghosting and we were ready for something challenging, so we volunteered to be aggressors for the current Phase One class, supporting Sergeant Torres and his Camp Mackall instructors. Some fifteen of us trucked out to Mackall, where we lived under the stars, far from the formalities of Training Group, led by three older NCOs who'd just finished Weapons School—Sergeant First Class David Higgins, and Staff Sergeants Ricardo Davis and Earl Savage.

Day and night we were the bad guys making life difficult for Phase One students who, just like us three months earlier, were encouraged to quit whenever the going got tough. It wasn't nearly so tough for us, as aggressors, though we ate the same food as the students. By now it had become second nature to dress and roast chickens and rabbits on an open fire. When my buddy Walter Horion and I cooked, we even coated our birds with the barbecue sauce we brought along.

One evening, sitting around the fire, we speculated on where we'd be assigned after graduation. Everyone wanted combat with the 5th Special Forces Group, the Green Beret unit serving in Vietnam. Many 5th Group men were assigned to A-Camps, remote outposts where a twelve-man Special Forces A-Team recruited, trained, and advised Vietnamese peasants or Montagnard hill tribesmen. Most A-Camps overlooked the border or sat astride major infiltration routes, where they became burrs under the enemy's saddle. Some of the heaviest Special Forces fighting had been defending besieged A-Camps.

Another possibility was serving in a Mike Force, or Mobile Strike Force. Led by a nucleus of Green Berets, these companies and battalions of Chinese Nungs or Montagnards were America's counterpart to the British Gurkhas. Developed as reaction forces for A-Camps that had been attacked, they'd become conventional light infantry, fighting as much as any American unit in the war. It was not unusual for an NCO to command a 100-man Mike Force company, and when short of officers, NCOs ran the whole battalion. Imagine, a Green Beret sergeant first class commanding as many combat troops as a U.S. Army lieutenant colonel!

Project Delta, too, was a coveted assignment, running reconnaissance in some of the enemy's most heavily defended enclaves in South Vietnam.

Sitting around the fire, one man started to weigh which of these would be the best assignment, when a voice cut him off.

"That's not all there is," Ricardo Davis interrupted. "There's something else." An amiable New Mexico native with an easygoing spirit, Ricardo had already done one Vietnam combat tour, with the 101st Airborne Division. While waiting for Hueys to lift his company from an airfield near the Laotian border, he said, he'd witnessed something very odd, like nothing he'd seen in Vietnam. "These guys got off some unmarked helicopters. They were dressed in North Vietnamese uniforms. And they carried silenced weapons—British Sten guns. I saw 'em myself."

"Well," another NCO asked, "who were they?"

"I don't know. But I'm sure they were SF."

Another man added that during weapons training he'd heard vague references to men running for days on end deep behind enemy lines, even getting B-52 bombers in support. These things were so closely held we couldn't tell how much of it was real. No one knew exactly who these secret operatives were, or where they were, or how to get to that unit. But we'd all heard fourthhand accounts, incredible stories of wild missions and names like Mad Dog Shriver, Moose Monroe, Billy Waugh, Jason T. Woodworth, Skip Minnicks. There wasn't a man in Special Forces who hadn't been told Mad Dog's amazing rejoinder when an officer had radioed him, concerned because his encircled team might be overrun. Shriver replied, "No, sweat. I've got 'em right where I want 'em—*surrounded from the inside.*" Six weeks earlier, Skip Minnicks and Major George Quamo had led two dozen men into Lang Vei, the Special Forces camp overrun by tanks, and had rescued the survivors. These were legendary deeds, and legendary men.

All of this had something to do with SOG—but we could not even find out what those letters stood for. It remained a great mystery.

Peace talks had begun in Paris, but at Fort Bragg we were too busy in Phase Two to pay much attention. Reassembled now as qualified medics, weapons men, demo men, and commo men, we were led by already qualified SF NCOs acting as team sergeants. In Phase One we'd been trained as guerrillas; now, in Phase Two, based on the "it-takes-a-rat-to-catch-a-rat" philosophy, we would be trained for counter-guerrilla operations.

The weeks flowed swiftly, and soon we were parachuting into North Carolina's Uwharrie National Forest for our week-long final exercise. This culminated in my team simulating the destruction of a major highway bridge. Although we escaped clean, the exercise controllers turned us over to the aggressors, so their military intelligence interrogators could practice on us, and we'd have some experience at resisting interrogation.

There was no real torture, per se, but we were softened up by being kept in small cages, or forced to kneel in a pit full of water for hours. At one point, an interrogator laid a handkerchief over my face and slowly poured a canteen of water across it, giving the uncomfortable sensation that I was drowning. Within a day, we were liberated by another A-Team, then just a forced march and that was it. Training was finished.

After the graduation ceremony in the JFK Center headquarters auditorium, many of us posed for family photos beside the just installed Special Forces memorial stone, dedicated on 4 July 1968 by actor John Wayne. As brand-new Special Forces soldiers, we hoped to prove worthy of its simple inscription: "In Tribute to the men of the Green Beret, United States Army Special Forces, whose valiant exploits will ever inspire mankind."

About half our men immediately received orders for Vietnam, to the 5th Special Forces Group. The rest of us were sent to other groups, though we knew it would not be long before we, too, would be off for Southeast Asia. I was assigned to the 7th Special Forces Group, only a few blocks from my Training Group barracks.

That summer of 1968, the 7th Group seemed a holding force—half the men were just back from a Special Forces tour in Vietnam, expecting another tour; and the rest of us were awaiting orders for our first tour in Vietnam. We trained, and cross-trained in other specialties, but Vietnam was always on our minds.

By mid-September my patience was gone. I could wait no longer. A senior NCO had given me a Pentagon phone number used by old hands when they wanted a Special Forces overseas assignment. I dialed it from a phone booth. A woman with a pretty Southern accent and a friendly voice answered. Mrs. Billy Alexander listened sympathetically, then promised to do her best to get me to Vietnam.

Sure enough, less than a month later I had orders to the 5th Special Forces Group. I couldn't believe it was that easy! I could have kissed her.

On the eve of the 1968 presidential election, I was home on leave when President Johnson ordered a complete halt to bombing inside North Vietnam, an accommodation to spur Hanoi's Paris negotiators into serious discussions, and to boost election prospects for Vice President Hubert H. Humphrey. Hanoi gave nothing in return.

On election night, I was in the Hall of States at the Leamington Hotel in Minneapolis, Humphrey's national campaign headquarters. Admitted by a ticket from my father's labor union, all night I drank free liquor, ate free food, and listened to Peter, Paul and Mary. I couldn't have cared less about politics— it all seemed a great lark. But it was a historic occasion, and I listened there in the ballroom to Humphrey's concession speech, wondering what the future would bring.

Three weeks later, I was at Fort Lewis, Washington, among thousands of replacements shipping out for Vietnam, everyone from cooks to helicopter mechanics and infantrymen. Organized into 150-man planeloads, we faced a three-day wait before our charter flight departed, during which time the Fort Lewis cadre would keep us out of trouble with endless trash pickups and point- less formations. As we formed for yet another keep-busy detail, a Green Beret sergeant first class stepped before our 150-man formation and called authorita- tively, "All Special Forces personnel! Fall out for PT!" A Fort Lewis NCO ob- jected, so the Green Beret sergeant offered, "Anyone else want some physical training, just fall in right here. We're starting with a five-mile run, then an hour of Army Drill One."

No one else joined the nine of us standing in our own little formation.

"Attention!" the Green Beret sergeant ordered. "Right face! Forward march!" No sooner were we out of sight than he commanded, "Halt! Left face! At ease." He grinned. "OK guys, you're on your own."

So we avoided the silly make-work, instead hanging around bars and coffee shops until our plane departed. Then it was a twenty-hour flight to Vietnam, during which we Green Berets sat together, wondering where we'd be as- signed. Several men wanted to be in the Mike Force, a couple others wanted to try out Project Delta, and one said he'd try to go back to the same A-Camp where he'd served an earlier tour.

I thought about that mysterious outfit Ricardo Davis had mentioned, the guys who wore enemy uniforms and carried silenced weapons. The mysteri- ous guys called SOG.

PART TWO

Recon

Chapter Two

Was there really a SOG? You sure couldn't tell looking around Nha Trang, the seaside resort town where the 5th Special Forces Group was headquartered. No office bore that title, and SOG was not listed anywhere among 5th SFG elements. Maybe it really was a myth—after all, I'd never seen or heard any confirmation of those whispers at Fort Bragg. After two days of snooping around, I got nowhere.

Even worse, I hadn't volunteered for any other unit, such as the Mike Force, so an in-processing clerk told me I'd been designated for the 5th Group's Signal Company. The eight men I'd arrived with would go their separate ways the next morning, and I'd be stuck in Nha Trang as a rear echelon radio operator. I detested the prospect.

That evening, I sat in the NCO club, complaining about my plight. Then, as fate would have it, in strolled Bill Gabbard, a teammate from Phase Two who'd been in Vietnam about three months. Over drinks we recalled the exciting adventures we'd talked about back at Fort Bragg. Then Bill's companion, an SF sergeant, nodded an "OK" to him, a gesture that caused Bill to slide his chair closer to the table and lower his voice. "John, do you want to do the real shit? The shit you came into SF to do?" Of course I did. "Go to CCN," he advised. "Don't ask, we can't tell you. *Just go to CCN—Command and Control North.*"

"Well, at least tell me what it's like."

"Oh, it's dangerous, dangerous as shit," his companion interjected. "But it's really a good deal. You're going to get killed anyhow. May as well come up to CCN and get a good deal out of it."

That cinched it. The next morning I attempted to volunteer but it was too late. The in-processing clerk passed out assignment slips to the nine of us, mostly mid-grade NCOs, along with my old friend from Training Group, Glenn Uemura, and an African-American weapons man, Reinald Pope. Both their slips said, "CCN." Mine read, "Signal Company."

"Does everyone have an assignment?" the clerk asked. I palmed the assignment slip, then raised my hand. "I didn't get one," I lied, "but I'm supposed to go to CCN, with Uemura." Hurriedly, he scribbled "CCN" on a piece of paper, handed it to me, and that was that.

So instead of Signal Company, I was processed for CCN, whatever that was.

Glenn and Reinald knew as little about CCN as I did. Like me, they'd been advised to volunteer without knowing where or what it was. The following morning, we boarded the strangest C-130 transport plane I'd ever seen. Nick-named a "Blackbird" because of its distinct black and forest green paint scheme, the plane's nose bore a folded yoke, part of a special apparatus for ex-tracting secret agents from the ground. Its U.S. insignia were painted on re-movable metal plates, so they easily could be taken off. Inside the C-130, the cargo compartment's forward third was curtained off with a warning: TOP SECRET. Squeezed into the remaining seats was a smorgasbord of passengers— Chinese, Vietnamese, Americans in civilian clothes, armed and unarmed Green Berets, and nondescript Asians whose nationality I could not even guess.

An hour later, we touched down at the sprawling Da Nang airbase, the busiest military airfield in the world. Then we rode aboard an open truck onto the CCN compound, past several armed guards and a RESTRICTED AREA sign that forbade photography. Situated on a sandy beach on the South China Sea, CCN's barbed wire compound measured about two square blocks, overshad-owed by 1,000-foot-high Marble Mountain jutting from the sand a quarter-mile away.

Still, no one told us anything. The CCN administrative NCO assured us that all our questions would be answered in the morning.

Thus, there was quite a sense of anticipation the next day when Uemura, Pope, and I sat in a CCN conference room dominated by a wall-size red curtain boldly labeled TOP SECRET. We could not tell what was on the other side. Min-utes dragged by.

Then the CCN commander arrived in all his magnificence, garbed in a black windbreaker over jungle fatigue pants and shower shoes, his head topped by a green beret. From his lips he pulled a cigarette holder, tapped off an ash, and announced, "Hi. I'm Jack Warren."

With practiced flair, Lieutenant Colonel Warren swept aside the top secret curtain, then watched our amazed faces as reality sunk in. It was a large map. Examining it, I looked for familiar South Vietnamese place names, but they were way, way over on the right edge. In a few seconds, I understood—*this was a map of southern Laos.*

"Gentlemen," Colonel Warren continued, "welcome to Command and Control North."

He pointed his cigarette holder to a grease-penciled box on the map, at least a dozen miles inside Laos. "We have a recon team here monitoring truck traffic on Highway 922." Not far away, he tapped two other boxes. "This one is watching a river ford over the Xe Kong River. And these guys are looking for a regimental base camp, so we can hit it with a B-52 strike."

Down south about 100 miles, where Laos ended at the border with Cambodia, another five teams were in place, having inserted from a CCN forward operating base at Kontum, in the Central Highlands of South Vietnam.

This program, Warren boasted, was the first in American military history in which a prolonged special operations effort was supported exclusively by air—for insertion, extraction, and fire support.

"Mostly," he explained, "we gather intelligence." But when the opportunity presented itself, "We do to them what they do to our troops in South Vietnam." This meant that CCN teams mined enemy roads, ambushed units, and called air strikes on hidden bases. "We make them pay a price for each pound of supplies they bring south, for each mile they travel the Ho Chi Minh Trail."

Ho Chi Minh Trail? I'd seen press photos of Vietcong coolies pushing bicycles and assumed the enemy hand-carried supplies along small footpaths. This map displayed an intricate highway system—a spiderweb of red lines depicting hundreds of miles of road—maintained not by peasant guerrillas but by many thousands of North Vietnamese regulars—the North Vietnamese Army, NVA—using heavy engineering equipment. Some 10,000 trucks rolled nightly on the Trail. The scale of it astonished me. Hanoi's troops had pushed the Laotian inhabitants out of an area the size of Massachusetts, then occupied it as if it were their own territory. From there they were supporting and running the whole war in South Vietnam. "Last year alone," Warren noted, "the enemy brought 235,000 men down the Trail."

Into the sanctuary of this neutral territory, along with Cambodia down south, entire enemy divisions withdrew for safety and rest between battles in South Vietnam. Once across the border there, they were immune from American ground action, Warren explained. "Except by us." For diplomatic reasons above my level of comprehension, the U.S. government had chosen to disavow these cross-border missions, so they were classified top secret and officially denied. The North Vietnamese insisted they had no troops in Laos or Cambodia, so the United States did likewise.

Dedicated Special Forces soldiers, not one of us even looked to each other or whispered. If those were the conditions under which we must fight, we accepted it.

"You will not keep a diary or journal," he ordered. "Your letters are subject to censorship. You are forbidden to tell anyone outside here what you are doing. We train Vietnamese and Montagnards, that's all. On paper we belong to the 5th Special Forces Group. In reality, we work for SOG, that's the Studies and Observations Group, down in Saigon. Even that relationship is classified secret, so if anyone asks, you don't even know what SOG is. Any questions?"

I had to keep from laughing. As hard as I'd tried to find SOG, I had stumbled into it without even realizing it. Pope, Uemura, and I each signed a nondisclosure agreement, committing us to keep the secrets of SOG or face ten years in federal prison, a $10,000 fine, or both. That done, Colonel Warren shook our hands, wished us well, and left as quickly as he'd appeared.

So, there really was a SOG. And now I was in it. Excitement swept over me. As I walked across the CCN compound, I kept seeing in my mind movie images of the Norwegian Resistance ambushing German convoys and disappearing into the friendly forest. This was going to be great!

A voice behind me called, "Hey, so now you know!" It was Bill Gabbard, grinning. I grabbed his hand and thanked him for getting me to CCN.

In Bill's team room, I was drawn to a silencer-equipped British Sten gun hanging over his bunk. I hefted it and observed, "This confirms it." Bill looked to me curiously. "Back at Bragg, a guy named Ricardo Davis told me he'd seen guys in NVA uniforms carrying silenced Sten guns. Sure enough, this is the unit."

Gabbard chuckled. "And a hell of a coincidence, 'cause Ricardo Davis is here, too. He's on Recon Team Copperhead, with Jim Lamotte." Another friend from my commo course, Jim "Mule Skinner" Pruitt, was on Recon Team Asp. Special Forces was a small world.

Bill and I spent the afternoon firing his Sten gun down on the beach, watching its 9mm slugs splash into the waves, but so quiet you couldn't hear it above the rolling surf. After chow, we sat in the NCO club, where Bill offered valuable advice, like, "Only drink in bars with chicken coop wire inside the windows." Why? "So grenades can't be thrown through the glass." That made sense. "And when staying at House 22," CCN's safe house in downtown Da Nang, he continued, "always take a top bunk."

"In case a grenade rolls in the door?"

"No!" Bill laughed. "So the guy in the top bunk can't puke on you."

Gabbard walked me back to my room in the transient billet, where Glenn Uemura and Reinald Pope already had climbed into their bunks. I sat on my bunk, and noticed bullet holes in the plywood wall. Pope pointed to a dozen more holes and asked, "Say, did some fool fire a weapon in here?"

Bill's smile evaporated. "Sapper attack."

"Sappers?" For the first time I noticed brown stains in the floor—old blood-stains, big ones.

"North Vietnamese commandos," Gabbard explained. "A hundred of 'em came across the beach, hit the camp back in August. They blew guys up in their bunks with satchel charges or shot 'em when they ran out the doors. That's why a lot of us ended up here, replacements for those guys."

We slept uncomfortably that night, in other men's deathbeds.

Dawn brought Christmas Eve day, and a promised meeting with the CCN sergeant major, who would give us our individual assignments. We never met him. Instead, we repacked our bags and caught another C-130 Blackbird; along with a staff sergeant from Da Nang we'd been reassigned to the CCN forward operating base at Kontum.

By noon, the populous coastal plain was far behind us, replaced below by an endless carpet of jungled hills, the Central Highlands of South Vietnam, home to the country's mountain—or, in French, *Montagnard*—hill tribesmen. Soon, we touched down at Kontum airfield, rolled past a wrecked World War II–era C-46 transport plane, there since God knows when, then the pilot reversed engines, and we taxied to a waiting flatbed truck. Uemura, Pope, the staff sergeant, and I climbed onto the flatbed while a forklift transferred freight. That's how we rode through Kontum city, sitting atop cargo boxes, an M-16 rifle I'd drawn at Da Nang resting in my lap.

The capital of Kontum Province, with perhaps 10,000 population, Kontum had architecture that reminded me of a Mexican border town, except many buildings still bore bullet pockmarks from the heavy fighting of the Tet Offensive, when 600 North Vietnamese Army soldiers had been killed here. As our truck passed civilians along the unpaved streets, I kept my M-16 ready, alert for anything. But there was no real threat.

We had to drive two miles south of Kontum to reach CCN's Forward Operating Base Two (FOB-2), like the Da Nang compound, about two square blocks of single-story, mostly clapboard buildings. FOB-2 straddled Highway 14, Kontum Province's main north–south road, which cut the compound into halves. Each half was encircled by a perimeter of outward-facing sandbagged bunkers, then three rows of stacked barbed wire.

At the east gate, we were halted by security guards who inspected our truck's underside for bombs hidden by VC terrorists. Then we were waved inside, into an ant heap of humanity. We passed Vietnamese soldiers in red berets and camouflage uniforms, then more Vietnamese in plain uniforms bearing no rank. Men with darker skin, apparently Montagnard tribesmen, squatted in a circle, smoking cigarettes. Still more Vietnamese, identifiable as helicopter crewmen by their gray flight suits and aviator sunglasses, walked toward the helipad where five H-34 choppers sat. I saw dozens of Vietnamese women—cleaning women and cooks in white blouses and black pajama pants with conical straw hats, or other women in more fashionable silk Ao Dai tops, marking them as higher-caste clerks and nurses. There was a hustle in this place, and purpose in everyone's walk.

Just ahead, Special Forces NCOs and officers clustered around a cement block building, the Tactical Operations Center, their clean uniforms and shined boots a sure sign of staff duty.

Then as we climbed from the truck and grabbed our bags, I noticed three Green Beret NCOs with scruffy boots talking to nine dark-skinned Montagnards, all of them heavily armed, their web gear draped with live grenades and loaded magazine pouches. Beyond them stood a single-story clapboard building, a sign hanging over its door, "Recon Company."

Moments later, the four of us were standing before the FOB-2 sergeant major's desk, while he delivered a predictable welcome. After finishing, he asked our assignment preference; Pope, Uemura, and I all requested recon. As quickly, he announced, "OK, you're in recon company." He looked to the staff sergeant who'd flown in with us. "And you, Sergeant?"

Sweat had formed on his forehead. "I can best serve the unit, I think, Sergeant Major, in the Communications Section. I have experience as a commo supervisor."

"We can use a commo chief. We'll give you a shot."

Relief swept over his face. For the remainder of his year at Kontum, he so fastidiously stayed in the underground Commo Center that I hardly ever saw him again.

Our in-briefing here at Kontum wasn't nearly as dramatic as Lieutenant Colonel Warren's had been in Da Nang, the major difference between the two compounds being the cross-border areas in which these SOG units operated. As the FOB-2 operations captain explained, CCN forces based at Da Nang and Phu Bai roamed the DMZ and southern Laos from about forty-five miles northwest of Khe Sanh southward for perhaps 100 miles, to where Laotian Highway 165 entered South Vietnam. Our Kontum-based FOB-2 forces picked up Laos from Highway 165 southward, then extended another fifty miles into Cambodia.

Thus, from Kontum we were penetrating a 100-mile front of Laos and Cambodia, to a depth of about eighteen miles to the west, an area half-again the size of Rhode Island.

South of our area of operations, we learned, another SOG unit, CCS, or

Command and Control South—based in Ban Me Thuot—ran missions into Cambodia.

The U.S. State Department demanded a higher level of deniability for operations in Cambodia because its ruler, Prince Norodom Sihanouk, had convinced much of the world his country was truly neutral, despite the presence of many thousands of North Vietnamese and Vietcong soldiers. This political sensitivity increased our restrictions: SOG teams going into Cambodia had to be sterile, that is, armed with foreign weapons and untraceable gear, and no matter how dire your situation, no tactical air support would come to your aid. You were practically on your own.

There was no debate; these were the rules and we accepted them.

The combat forces at FOB-2 were made up of recon teams—of which we had about eighteen fully manned, though twenty-four were authorized—and three Hatchet Force companies. Each recon team was assigned three Americans and nine native soldiers, although the team leader likely took only six or eight men on most missions. Teams at Kontum were named for states—Recon Team Ohio or Recon Team Texas—while those at Da Nang were named for poisonous snakes and those at Ban Me Thuot for tools. Kontum's 100-man Hatchet Force companies were organized much like Mike Forces, with a nucleus of four Green Berets leading each forty-man Nung or Montagnard platoon, adding three more Americans to lead each company of three platoons. Recon teams almost always operated independently, with five or six constantly on the ground in Laos and Cambodia. The larger Hatchet Force companies and platoons, however, required extensive helicopter support, reducing how often they could be fielded.

After the briefing, Pope, Uemura, and I carried our bags to the recon company office where the first sergeant, Lionel "Choo-Choo" Pinn, chewed on his unlit cigar and grumbled to himself. As the wreathlike patch on his right shoulder attested, Pinn, a large, half-Seminole veteran, had served in World War II with an Airborne-Ranger battalion. His Combat Infantryman's Badge, sewn over his right shirt pocket, bore two stars, meaning he'd seen combat in three wars—World War II, Korea, and Vietnam.

Since Sergeant Pope was older and already an NCO, Pinn could deal with him, immediately assigning him to a team. But Glenn Uemura and I were young, not even sergeants yet, and Pinn wasn't sure where to send such tenderfeet. In Glenn's case, the problem solved itself when the team leader of RT Hawaii, Sergeant First Class Bill Delima, heard that a fellow Hawaiian from Hilo had arrived. He scooped up Glenn like a long-lost brother, and off they went to their team room.

While Pinn mulled over my team assignment, he told me to go unpack and draw my field gear from supply. That proved a snap because the supply sergeant was Dave Higgins, who'd been on aggressor duty with me at Camp Mackall. Dave already had served on the Hatchet Force, then came here to supply. He couldn't do enough to help, fixing me up with all my standard gear, plus SOG's unique off-the-books items, such as a black windbreaker like Colonel Warren had worn, along with a special SOG knife, a Swiss Army knife, and a commercial Seiko wristwatch. As Higgins told me, those were mine to keep, courtesy of SOG.

I'd completely forgotten it was Christmas Eve until I walked into the NCO club and discovered the crazy culture I'd fallen into. Despite Kontum's out-of-the-way location, these resourceful Green Berets had recruited a major band, the Surfaris, famous for their top ten hit "Surfer Joe." Just about every one of our 225 Green Berets was squeezed into an NCO club half the size of a basketball court where the rock band's amplified music shook the roof. How could this little club possibly afford the Surfaris? Simple, we sold quality liquor to underage U.S. 4th Infantry Division soldiers and other Americans in defiance of official rationing rules. Therefore, while the typical Vietnam NCO club was a plywood and tin firetrap, ours looked like a nice Stateside cocktail lounge, complete with handmade teak furniture flown back from Taiwan aboard a SOG C-130 Blackbird. In addition to a first-class stereo system, we even offered flush toilets, an unheard-of luxury in Vietnam.

Peering through the heavy cigarette smoke, I couldn't believe the variety of attire. In one corner, an eccentric NCO in a camouflage tuxedo swapped stories with friends, while in another corner a drunken pilot danced on a table, wearing only cowboy boots, a helmet, and a pistol belt arranged so his holster covered his crotch. Other men wore everything from cutoff jeans to bowling shirts. A lot of booze had already been consumed, and the night was still young.

When finally I got a beer and found a seat, it was beside several Vietnamese women, one of whom spoke with a heavy whiskey voice. Known as "Helen," she patted my knee and smiled. "You new guy," she said, "you cherry boy." An NCO behind her called above the loud music, "Hey, Helen, show him your pussy!" Exactly as asked, she hefted her skirt to her naked waist, threatening, "My monkey gonna catch you!" I backed away, only to be tongued in my ear by another Green Beret, which caused a cluster of recon NCOs to snicker at my shocked reaction. They had me marked as a new guy. At their urging I downed a few shots of liquor, but they kept up the harassment until I tongued the ear of the man who'd tongued mine. After that we all listened to the Surfaris' renditions of Beach Boys hits and Johnny Rivers songs—"Secret Agent Man" was especially well done, eliciting enthusiastic cheers.

The partying might have gone on much longer, but about midnight someone emptied an M-16, full-auto, not far from the club, instigating a full alert. When that klaxon sounded, the club emptied in ten seconds, everyone scrambling to get his weapon and go to his assigned alert locations. The shooter turned out to be an inebriated Montagnard, who'd fired his weapon in the air to celebrate Christmas. The club didn't reopen.

It was difficult sleeping those first nights, difficult adapting to the heat, adapting to mortars firing illumination flares, and adapting to 175mm guns two miles away at Firebase Mary Lou, whose concussion rattled my building each time they fired.

Then there was the Cobra alarm clock. Every morning, around 0700, my mind detected a distant buzz that grew and grew until a noisy WHOP-WHOP-WHOP-WHOP! roared overhead, a pair of Cobra gunships buzzing the compound. Momentarily six Huey helicopters joined them, then all landed on our helipad for the pilots to attend the FOB-2 daily mission briefing.

Those first days passed slowly. Like every first sergeant in the Army, Lionel Pinn felt obliged to keep his soldiers busy, so while I awaited my team assignment he sent me over to help our club manager recover from the Christmas party. The manager, an immense sergeant first class, "Big Bob" Barnes, could have been an NFL defensive lineman, but, I learned, he had been a recon team leader.

Big Bob had once slipped into an NVA battalion bivouac area and stolen a 100-pound Chinese-made radio set—complete with codebooks—by just hefting it over his shoulder and running off with it. The problem was, few men wanted to go to the field with him, concerned that were he wounded, they couldn't carry him. Eventually that stark reality ended his recon days, putting him here, in the club.

But that recon background made Barnes a better club manager, because he understood the stress-relieving antics of men just back from combat. I watched a half-dozen drunken men stumble into the club demanding drinks—it was hardly 11:00 A.M.—but Barnes served them, and then ignored them when they attempted to guzzle flaming shots of brandy, setting themselves and their clothes on fire. Instead of threats or shouts, he just waved his hand and explained, "Aw, they're just recon guys on stand-down. Don't pay 'em no heed."

"Stand-down"—a week to unwind after each mission—was one of CCN's privileges.

On my way back to the recon company office, I paused as an eight-man recon team—three Americans and five Montagnard tribesmen—filed out the front gate, headed for the chopper pad. Led by a Montagnard, or Yard, as they were known, in NVA uniform carrying an AK, they were an imposing sight: Except for two indigenous soldiers with grenade launchers, the rest bore CAR-15s, the folding stock, submachine gun version of the M-16, and lots and lots of ordnance. Just looking at the way they walked and carried their weapons I could tell they were damned good. I wished I was going with them.

In the recon company orderly room I found First Sergeant Pinn and our company commander, Captain Edward Lesesne, a very impressive Special Forces officer. Already on his second SOG tour, he was as much a gunfighter as any of the NCOs. A few months earlier, when recon men grumbled that it was becoming too dangerous to snatch enemy prisoners from the Ho Chi Minh Trail, Captain Lesesne didn't criticize or cajole them—he accompanied a team into Laos and snatched an NVA himself, SOG's first Laotian prisoner in nine months. Prior to his SOG service, Lesesne had been on the classified Special Forces mission in Bolivia that led to the capture and execution of Cuba's infamous revolutionary Che Guevara.

Lesesne had good news. "First Sergeant Pinn and I have assigned you to Recon Team New Mexico. They're in training right now, because the assistant team leader is gone to school. The team leader is on his way over here to meet you." At last, I was a full-fledged recon man.

Specialist Five Larry Stephens, my new team leader, arrived, shook my hand, and led me away. Like me, Stephens was a commo man, but months in the FOB-2 commo section had added unwanted pounds to his frame. He was glad that now, with me aboard, he had a complete team.

Our RT New Mexico team room measured maybe ten feet by twenty, enough to accommodate the three Americans, while our nine Vietnamese were housed separately, in their own team room, about 100 yards away. After helping me move in my gear, Stephens explained, "Our third man, Billy Simmons, is down at One-Zero School." This was a SOG course, named for the recon team leader's code number—One-Zero. The most prestigious title in SOG, recon team leaders were always called One-Zeros, and commanded automatic respect.

Likewise, an assistant team leader had a code number—the One-One. On RT New Mexico, the absent Sergeant Billy Simmons was the One-One. And me? I held the third slot as One-Two, or radio operator, the newest man, stuck with carrying the heavy team radio, a PRC-25. But I didn't mind that one bit, now that I was on a team.

Stephens explained that each recon team had indigenous soldiers of the same ethnic group—Chinese Nungs, or Montagnard tribesmen, or, as we had, Vietnamese. Our men were not soldiers but mercenaries, hired and paid by SOG, which also got them a draft deferment. SOG duty was more dangerous than service in the Army of the Republic of Vietnam (ARVN), that is, the South Vietnamese Army, but our men received much higher pay, better living conditions, and less regimentation than the ARVN.

When I met them, our nine Vietnamese mercenaries seemed a cheery lot, smiling a great deal, which they apparently thought compensated for their lack of English. I found myself doing the same, nodding and smiling to demonstrate goodwill, but completely unable to communicate until I learned to speak through the team interpreter. I managed not to offend anyone, so at least initially I thought I was doing all right.

It was my proudest moment thus far in Special Forces, that next morning, to stand formation with RT New Mexico. Just before formation, First Sergeant Pinn's stereo blared with Kate Smith's "God Bless America," then he marched out before us and called, "Atten-shun!"

Our recon teams stood in files, with the One-Zero at the head. I was behind Stephens when he saluted and called, "Recon Team New Mexico, present!" Behind me stood our nine Vietnamese, in order of their mercenary rank. After all the teams had reported, Pinn called, "At ease," stuck his cigar back in his mouth, and began his administrative announcements.

Only eight teams stood formation that morning. I was surprised to notice that some One-Zeros were not their team's highest-ranking man. Ralph Rodd, for instance, One-Zero of RT Colorado, had to be five years younger and one stripe shorter than his One-One, behind him. Here in SOG, rank did not determine leadership; experience and ability meant far more than the stripes or bars a man wore.

I was also struck by how few Green Berets and how few teams actually comprised recon company. There were then six teams in the field, plus four teams on stand-down, which combined with the teams here in formation yielded eighteen total teams. These fifty-four Green Berets were targeted across a 100-mile-wide stretch of the Cambodian and Laotian border, an area occupied by at least 40,000 North Vietnamese soldiers. So much was expected of so few.

Yet these small numbers were deceptive, for these ranks concentrated some of the finest talent in American special operations. RT California under the lanky One-Zero Joe Walker constantly ran the toughest targets in Laos, because SOG headquarters knew he'd succeed where others might fail. I envied Glenn Uemura, standing there with RT Hawaii, a first-string team led by Bill Delima, with Lonnie Pulliam, a former Florida state trooper, as One-One. RT

Delaware, with One-Zero Joe Van Diver and One-One Robert Van Hall, could take on any target, as could RT Kentucky, led by Robert "Squirrel" Sprouse, or RT Wyoming with One-Zero Jon Davidson and One-One Craig Davis.

The rest of us were teams that hadn't yet proven themselves—like RT New Mexico—or teams recovering from losses, or a few teams that fell somewhere in between. There wasn't a set pecking order, but everyone pretty well knew the best teams by their results. Still, any target behind enemy lines could prove hazardous beyond expectations, so every team had to be ready for the toughest situation.

After formation, the Americans gathered around the recon company training NCO, Sergeant First Class Robert Howard, the most impressive man I ever met in Special Forces. Physically imposing, he stood just six feet, but every ounce of his 170 pounds was solid muscle, backed up by an attitude that didn't take much lightly. Already on his third tour in Vietnam, he twice had been recommended for the Congressional Medal of Honor, only to have it downgraded to a Distinguished Service Cross and a Silver Star.

Despite his well-known combat prowess, he spoke humbly, matter-of-factly, in a smooth Alabama accent, as he reviewed that day's training with the One-Zeros. Most team leaders had planned range firing, or tactical exercises in the nearby jungle, some of which sounded suspiciously like sleeping under the trees. That didn't much bother Howard. "Oh, if y'all screw off, don't worry 'bout Bob Howard catchin' you. No, sir, the NVA's gonna kill you, then you'll know you should'a trained harder." He squinted an ironic grin, looking much like Clint Eastwood playing Dirty Harry. But Howard wasn't playing.

More than anything, he was pleased because he'd been the acting recon company first sergeant until Lionel Pinn had arrived a week earlier. Though Howard was now the training NCO, he knew this was only temporary, and he'd soon be back where he preferred to be, in combat.

RT New Mexico, by contrast, would not soon be in combat. Larry Stephens had me and the Vietnamese grab our weapons and web gear, and we spent the morning walking along a dirt road and through a friendly Montagnard village.

From time to time, we reacted to simulated enemy contacts by jumping for cover and pretending to fire back. Stephens sweat profusely, halting our training several times to drink water. During a break, I examined Stephens's custom-made web gear, five canvas claymore mine bags he'd had a local seamstress sew in a circle, with a tie in the front. He could carry lots of magazines and grenades, he showed me. But the rig didn't seem very rugged.

Training would be better, Stephens promised, when Billy Simmons got back from One-Zero School. An extra week or two of training with Simmons, and we'd be ready for our first target.

That afternoon a passing NCO knocked on our team room door and hollered, "A team's coming in—got shot out!" He didn't hang around, just left straightaway for the helipad. Stephens was gone, so I wasn't sure what I was supposed to do. Another passing NCO saw me standing in the door, waved, "C'mon," so I followed him.

By the time we got to the helipad, there must have been 100 men up there, looking to the west, where a flight of Hueys was slowing to land. I turned my face from the flying dust, then looked back to see a recon team climb from a chopper. They looked drained, physically and emotionally, with dirty, unshaved faces and twisted, sweaty hair. The One-Zero's face hung a ghostly pale beneath smudged camouflage stick. Dried blood streaked across his fatigues.

Bob Howard wrapped an arm around his shoulder, and a dozen One-Zeros surrounded him, put a beer in his hand, and patted his back. In the background, I felt awkward, like a gawker at an accident scene. I asked the man beside me, "What happened?"

"Scherdin is missing," he said. He meant Private First Class Bob Scherdin, a young Green Beret from New Jersey, the other American on this mission. Their team had made contact with a vastly more numerous enemy force. The NVA had hotly pursued and almost overrun them, hitting them so hard that Scherdin, the One-One, became separated. A Montagnard, Nguang, saw him fall, hit by an AK slug in his right side; he tried to help him but Scherdin only groaned and couldn't lift himself. Then an AK round hit Nguang and he had to leave or die. It was surprising anyone had escaped.

The mood in the club that evening was gloomy. Then, at sunset, a USAF forward air control (FAC) plane overflew the Laotian hill where Scherdin had gone missing and heard an emergency radio beeper but no voice contact. It could have been the enemy using Scherdin's radio to lure a rescue force into a trap. Or it might be Bob Scherdin, unable to speak, grasping for his last chance to live.

The next morning a throng of us watched as a forty-man Hatchet Force platoon filed past us, on their way to the chopper pad. They were going to try to locate and rescue Scherdin. Among them, a foot taller than the Montagnards, walked Bob Howard in a floppy jungle hat, accompanying them as their acting platoon sergeant. When it was time to go after a fellow recon man, you simply could not hold Howard back. Walking with Howard was a youthful, blond-haired lieutenant, Jim Jerson, the platoon leader. Following them were Sergeants Jerome Griffin and Robert Gron—two squad leaders—and First Lieutenant Terry Hamric, who'd volunteered to go along.

It would be a momentous day.

About mid-afternoon, 30 December 1968, as they climbed the hill toward Scherdin's last known location, the enemy tripped a horrible ambush. Every half-hour, someone came into the NCO club with another update.

Lieutenant Jerson is almost dead . . . Howard has been badly wounded, too, but he managed to save Jerson . . . The enemy has used a flamethrower on our men . . . The shattered platoon is barely holding together . . . Lieutenant Hamric is wounded, too . . . Just before dark, Howard got the survivors into a defensive perimeter . . . They can't last until morning . . . Howard called gunfire from an AC-130 Spectre gunship right across their position.

The Hatchet Force seemed trapped. Then a bold move got them out: Under the light of air-dropped flares, Hueys from the 189th Assault Helicopter Company—the "Ghost Riders"—made a midnight extraction, getting away before the enemy could react. Still, the cost was high: Though Howard had done his all to save Lieutenant Jerson, the young officer died in the medevac hospital in Pleiku. About twelve Montagnards had been killed or seriously wounded. Howard was badly wounded and hospitalized at the 71st Evacuation Hospital in Pleiku. Lieutenant Hamric had been hit, too.

The same day they came out, the recon company commander, Captain Lesesne, sat down and wrote up Bob Howard for the Medal of Honor. He described how Howard had been hit beside the mortally wounded Jerson, knocked unconscious, lost his weapon, and awoke to see an NVA incinerating the area with a flamethrower. Weaponless, Howard forced the enemy back with a hand grenade, then found a workable M-16. The firing became so intense his M-16 was hit by an AK, then he had to fight off the enemy with a .45 caliber pistol. Despite his own serious wounds, Howard dragged the badly wounded lieutenant down the hill, killing more NVA on the way. Then he assembled the survivors for a final fight against numerically superior NVA, and at the most desperate moment, Howard called AC-130 Spectre gunship fire across his own position.

This being the third time Bob Howard had been recommended for the Medal of Honor, Lesesne was certain he would receive it. The biggest question in Lesesne's mind was, would Howard come back to Kontum, or be medevaced back to the States? Would we ever see him again?

As for Bob Scherdin, the missing recon man—we still knew nothing of him, and never would.

It wasn't scheduled or announced, but the next night everyone knew to be at the club for the closest thing we had to a memorial service, a ritual unique to SOG. I sat with my One-Zero, Larry Stephens, watching and drinking a beer. The mood began understandably somber, with small groups of men drinking and talking of the lost men. Then the liquor began loosening tongues; friends and teammates recalled what a fine man Jerson or Scherdin had been, only to be met by a human insight into why, also, each was equally a true son-of-a-bitch. Everyone laughed. Eventually someone proposed a toast to some aspect of Jerson's or Scherdin's character, or some funny thing he'd said, then everyone stood, raised glasses, and called, "To Bob," then, "To Jim."

And then, recon company commander Captain Lesesne announced, "Let's sing 'Hey, Blue.' " Everyone stood. Lesesne sang alone at first: "I had a dog and his name was Blue, Bet you five dollars, He's a good dog, too." The room echoed to all the other voices, singing the chorus, "Hey, Blue—You're a good dog, you."

These tough old Special Forces soldiers fought back tears, some gave up and let it flow, others became too choked up to sing. As Lesesne began the next verse, tears fell from men who didn't give a damn who saw them. "Old Blue died, and he died so hard, shook the ground in my backyard."

Everyone sang, "Hey, Blue—You're a good dog, you."

Lesesne's eyes filled, too, but he continued, "Link by link, I lowered the chain, and with each link, I called his name." Then followed an extraordinary oral history of SOG, name after name, verse after verse, a long roster of the men killed or missing in action, but not forgotten by comrades. At last, that sad litany reached its end, and the final verse was sung, "Copley, Scherdin, and Jerson, too. Hey, Blue, You're a good dog, you."

Copley? It sounded like they'd sung *Copley!*

I turned to Stephens. "That was Copley—*Bill* Copley?"

"Yeah," he confirmed. "Lost on his first mission. A few weeks ago."

My stomach twisted. Bill Copley, with whom I'd spent that long night digging a hole during Special Forces training. His recon team had been hit by a large NVA force in Laos. In the initial burst of fire an AK round had hit him in the left shoulder, exiting in the middle of his back. His One-Zero carried him, then stopped to treat him and found his face ashen with no sign of life. With Bill apparently dead and the enemy about to launch another assault, his teammates were forced to evade, leaving his body behind. Bill was only nineteen years old.

I drank as heavily as any of the others that night, thinking about Bill being MIA and hoping never again to have to sing "Hey, Blue."

I asked an older recon man, "Is it always like this? Losing guys one at a time. Doesn't it ever let up?"

He shook his head at my greenness. "What makes you think we don't lose *whole teams?*"

Given this level of casualties, only a regular flow of volunteers could keep our teams operational. Hardly a week after I arrived more replacements came in, including an outstanding young weapons man who seemed ideally suited for recon, John St. Martin. Elite service ran in his family; John's father had been a U.S. Navy Underwater Demolition Team man in World War II, and taught his son boxing when he was only nine. A competitive athlete in his hometown of Upland, California, St. Martin had lettered in football, while also playing basketball and baseball. He liked a challenge and fit right in on RT New York, just down the hall from my team room. We became instant friends.

My training with RT New Mexico continued, progressing from simulated live fire to actual shooting at our own range, about four miles south of Kontum. Called the Yard Camp because one of our Montagnard Hatchet Force companies was based beside it, the range was rustic by Stateside standards, but unencumbered by range regulations. We fired anything we wished, exactly as we wished.

I got a chance to handle and fire Stephens's CAR-15—the shortened version of the M-16 with collapsible stock—the only one on our team. It was instant love. For balance, pointing, and just plain handiness, the CAR-15 was far superior to the M-16, but there were not enough CAR-15s to go around. As a brand-new team, we were lucky even Stephens had one.

As we loaded into our truck, another team rolled up—Joe Walker and RT California. A well-established team, every one of Joe's Americans and Montagnards packed a CAR-15 except his two M-79 grenadiers. Watching them handle their weapons and line up in a tactical file, I could appreciate their experience and training. More than just a team in name, RT California displayed a smoothness in control, almost a harmony—as if every man understood what he should do each moment without having to say one word. I had not seen that among us on RT New Mexico.

When RT California reacted to contact, they smoothly peeled off, each one covered by at least one other man, all their automatic fire well controlled in three to five round bursts. Then, Walker aimed an antitank rocket launcher, an RPG, a Soviet-made weapon captured from the North Vietnamese. An ear-splitting explosion and backblast sent the football-size RPG rocket in a shallow arc, to detonate 100 yards away. There, a yellow flash and a tremendous blast shook the ground as powerfully as three hand grenades detonating. It was quite a firepower display.

Yes, Joe Walker's RT California was a force to be reckoned with. Perhaps, with enough training and practice, RT New Mexico could equal them.

As we drove back into FOB-2, a figure in hospital pajamas stood at the recon company door talking to Captain Lesesne. He bore several bandages and looked exhausted, but it really was him—Bob Howard was back.

Fearing that Army doctors might ship him to Japan for recovery, Howard had gone AWOL from the hospital, then hitchhiked aboard a Huey back to Kontum. He trusted our own Special Forces senior medic, Louis Maggio, to remove the dead tissue around his wounds and pull his stitches, so why did he have to be in a hospital? As soon as he could find a fresh set of jungle fatigues, he announced, he'd be back on duty.

What a morale boost. All of us looked up to Howard. He was the gallant knight whose shining example inspired all the young squires. Humble and never boisterous, he so well shielded his wife and two daughters from his combat exploits that it was a complete surprise when they had accompanied him to a Fort Bragg formation in mid-1968 to watch the commanding general pin eight medals on his chest, including five Purple Hearts and a Distinguished Service Cross. He was now on his third Vietnam tour, each with a six-month extension. Why so much time in 'Nam? "I guess it's because I want to help in any way I can," Howard explained. "I may as well be here where I can use my training; and besides, I have to do it—it's the way I feel about my job."

With that kind of inspiring example, I took it in stride that afternoon when I learned our team had been targeted for a mission. Despite our One-One, Billy Simmons, being off at One-Zero School, and my own inexperience—and repeated promises that we would not be scheduled for an operation until we were ready—Larry Stephens and I were told to go to the Tactical Operations Center (TOC) for a mission briefing.

On the briefing room map, a grease pencil line traced a six-kilometer box—about four miles by four miles—identifying our target in southeast Laos. "Your mission," said Major Frank Jaks, the FOB-2 operations officer, in a faint Slavic accent, "is *area recon.*" This meant we were to explore the area and report any enemy presence.

According to intelligence, that presence might be considerable. Laotian Highway 110 cut through the north side of our box, and a few antiaircraft positions had been reported earlier by pilots who'd been fired upon. At least one NVA battalion—500 to 700 men—was believed to be in our general area. Had their exact location been known, it would have been hit by a B-52 strike.

It was the enemy's ability to reinforce that most concerned us. Elements of two NVA infantry regiments—the 27th and 66th—plus two artillery regiments—a total of 7,000 NVA—were believed to be no more than a thirty-minute vehicle ride from our target.

On the positive side, if we got in deep trouble we could declare a Prairie Fire Emergency, and we'd have priority for air support in Laos, diverting dozens of fighters our way. Were we captured or to have to explain our presence in Laos, an intelligence officer said, "Your cover story is, your team is looking for a missing C-123 that vanished west of Ben Het Special Forces Camp. You are unaware you're across the border."

After the briefers finished, I asked Major Jaks, "What about civilians, sir?"

He looked at me as if I were out of my mind. "There are *no* civilians out there, it's all NVA, all enemy," he snapped. "And you'd better look out, young man, or they will kill you." His directness surprised me, but I would learn that Major Jaks's opinions were always to be taken seriously. No stranger to war, he'd begun fighting as a teenager in the Czech Resistance in World War II, and was already on his third tour in Vietnam. We had no further questions.

The following day, Larry Stephens flew a visual recon of our target aboard an Army O-1 Bird Dog reconnaissance plane, but when he returned he didn't have much to report. Whatever the enemy had in our target was too heavily camouflaged to be seen from the air.

One day later, we were again in the Tactical Operations Center, this time for One-Zero Stephens to give his briefback—explaining how we'd accomplish our mission—to the FOB-2 commander, Lieutenant Colonel Roy Bahr. It was the first time I'd seen Bahr, who previously had been the CCN Forward Operating Base commander at Khe Sanh until the Marines withdrew and the base closed the previous spring.

So little was known about our target that there wasn't much Stephens could plan. He focused his briefback on our insertion, which he intended to accomplish in a one-ship landing zone.

To his way of thinking, the smallest possible LZ was preferable because it was less likely that the enemy would have it covered. The quickest way to get in there was to land the entire team on one Huey—which limited us to six men. Therefore, he was bringing himself, me, and four Vietnamese. He indicated a rough scheme for exploring the area, and that was it. Lieutenant Colonel Bahr found no fault with his plan.

After that, we drew rations and ammo and issued them to our Vietnamese. Stephens inspected their packed rucksacks to make sure each man had his claymore mine. Then he looked through their magazine pouches to see that all were fully loaded.

On our last night at FOB-2, I stayed out of the club and went to bed early. It was hard getting to sleep.

The following morning after breakfast, Stephens and I went to recon company and put all our personal effects—ID cards, dog tags, wallets, and Geneva Convention cards—into a manila envelope, sealed it, and handed it to First Sergeant Pinn to be locked in the unit safe. Watching that safe door swing shut gave me an unsettling feeling, the first time that the words "covert" and "deniable" lost their abstractness.

Then I put my heavily loaded web gear over a new set of jungle fatigues—devoid of patches and name tapes, sterile for the mission—shouldered my rucksack, grabbed my M-16, and joined the rest of the team. Together we walked to the helipad, as I'd watched other teams do since the day I'd arrived at Kontum.

We climbed aboard the lead Huey, from the Pleiku-based 189th Assault Helicopter Company, a brightly painted Grim Reaper on its nose. Momentarily, the pilots returned from the FOB-2 daily briefing, climbed in, and began cranking the main rotor. Their every action interested me, because—despite eighteen months of Basic, Infantry, Airborne, and Special Forces training—I'd never before been aboard a helicopter. As quickly as they came off the Bell assembly line, Hueys went to Vietnam, not to Fort Bragg or Fort Benning.

The whining turbine spun the rotor faster and faster, then the bird lurched up a bit, vibrated, lurched again, and—*smooth*—we were hovering above the ground, feeling afloat. Just five feet off the ground, the pilot turned us around, into the wind, then dipped his nose, and all six of our Hueys took off as one, climbing effortlessly away, northwest, toward Dak To and Laos. Our escort birds, four Charlie-Model Huey gunships—the Cougars—rose behind us, then joined us in formation. Five H-34 Kingbee helicopters—flown by Vietnamese crews—brought up the rear. Amazingly, inserting our little six-man team was today's sole job for this whole aerial armada of fifteen helicopters.

Sitting beside Stephens in the open Huey door, I watched the countryside whisk by as we flew to Dak To. Our aircraft passed directly over a Montagnard village, its communal longhouse with upward-soaring roof reminding me of cathedral spires.

The interior of our Huey had been stripped of seats except for those occupied by the two door gunners, who each had a pedestal-mounted M-60 machine gun before him with hundreds of rounds of belted ammo. We sat on the aircraft floor, while to our backs were rolled-up aluminum ladders and rucksacks packed with 100-foot ropes. Called McGuire rigs, the ropes could be dropped through the jungle treetops to extract recon men even when there was no LZ.

In only about twenty-five minutes the Dak To runway took shape before us. Our long line of helicopters descended, then landed on one side of the field, next to three buildings in a small barbed wire compound. Ours were the only helicopters here, but the base had been teeming a year earlier, when the 173rd Airborne Brigade and the 4th Infantry Division had fought one of the war's toughest battles in the facing hills. Now, only an American engineer battalion remained at Dak To, along with a U.S. Army emergency medical bunker.

The launch site sat behind RESTRICTED AREA signs, guarded by a recon team that was also available for emergency rescues. The team rotated weekly. In addition to being a rearming and refueling site for our helicopters, Dak To was a standby location for teams and aircraft to wait for the call to take off, only ten minutes from the Cambodian and Laotian frontiers.

While we waited, a USAF forward air control plane flew across the border with a SOG Green Beret on board, monitoring the teams already on the ground, and coordinating the insertion of additional teams. Code-named "Covey," he was looking for a suitable insertion LZ, which might take hours if weather was a problem. This morning the weather looked fine. We expected to launch in less than an hour.

While Stephens waited for Covey's call in the commo shack, I looked into a jeep's mirror and applied camouflage stick. I had never been more elated. All my Special Forces training, all that preparation, had been leading to this moment, to my first operation. I had no consciousness of danger, only eagerness to get on with it, the greatest adventure of my life. As advised by an old-timer, I drank as much launch site water as I could, preserving my own full canteens for the mission.

I was rechecking my gear for the tenth time when I noticed another Huey land just outside the launch site. Two men in sterile fatigues with loaded rucksacks and full field gear stepped off the bird and walked toward us, causing Larry Stephens to run from the commo shack and wave happily. In a moment he brought them over and introduced the first man as my teammate, Sergeant Billy Simmons. We shook hands heartily. The other man, Staff Sergeant Charles Bullard, was Billy's best friend and had been his teammate at One-Zero School. Bullard had volunteered to come along on our mission.

Simmons explained that a C-130 Blackbird had brought them back from One-Zero School an hour ago. When they'd learned we were at Dak To, they grabbed rations and ammo and got on this Huey to join us. This couldn't be better, it seemed. Our team was reunited, and we had the freshly trained Simmons and Bullard to help make up for my inexperience. We would launch momentarily.

Then Stephens went over to the lead Huey pilot, who was spooning a can of C ration peaches. This wasn't Stateside, so the pilot didn't pull out a pencil and paper to calculate his load limit. He just looked around at the eight of us, eye-balled our bulging rucksacks, and said, "Nope." Stephens dickered with him for a minute, then the young aviation warrant officer nodded.

I heard Stephens's voice tell me, "You can't go." I couldn't believe it! He con-tinued, "The chopper would be overloaded." I tried to argue but the decision had already been made. "You can go next time," Stephens promised. I accepted his call. He was One-Zero.

Then Covey radioed for a launch.

While the pilots and door gunners prepared for takeoff, we quickly trans-ferred my PRC-25 radio into Bullard's rucksack. I walked them to the Huey and wished them well, shaking each man's hand. When their helicopter lifted away I waved. Soon, their long line of choppers disappeared into the western sky and the distant green hills of Laos.

I sat around the rest of the day at Dak To, then flew back to Kontum, em-barrassed to have camouflage stick on my face, feeling like I hadn't been chosen for sides in baseball. At the recon company office I retrieved my manila enve-lope, then went back to the team room, alone. I washed the camouflage off my face, then heated a C ration from my rucksack. Lying in my bunk, I drifted off to sleep, disgusted that my teammates were out there, in Laos, on a mission, and I was sleeping on clean sheets.

Late the next morning, a runner told me I was wanted at recon company. Sure as hell, I thought, First Sergeant Pinn has cooked up some project to keep me busy. I dreaded it.

But when I walked in, Pinn, Howard, and Lesesne stopped talking, and turned to me. Pinn chewed his unlit cigar. Their faces hinted stress. Then Cap-tain Lesesne said, "Covey couldn't raise Recon Team New Mexico this morn-ing." I wasn't sure what he was trying to say. "A Bright Light team is on the ground right now."

I had to ask, "What's a Bright Light team?"

I should have heard the slamming of a vault door, or perhaps the chuckle of the Reaper. As it was, I wasn't sure what Lesesne was trying to say. Had some-one been wounded? Were they running with the NVA in pursuit? I looked to their faces.

I heard Howard's voice but I barely understood what he said. "They were killed, John. Stephens, Bullard, and Simmons—they're all dead. The Bright Light team is the rescue team, bringing out their bodies."

It was too much. I'd just been at Dak To with them. We'd had a whole team, this couldn't be! How? Then the full realization swept over me. *I was the sole survivor of Recon Team New Mexico. But for the lift capacity of a Huey helicopter on a warm day, I would have been dead, too.*

That evening, the returning Bright Light team provided further details. My teammates had been pounded by a barrage of rocket-propelled grenades, RPGs—the kind of rocket Joe Walker had fired at the Yard Camp range—wounding all three Americans. Then assaulting NVA riddled them with AK slugs at point-blank range. Not one of my teammates even got off a shot—they didn't stand a chance.

The Bright Light team had found them the same way NVA trackers had, by following the trail they'd unwittingly left from their insert LZ to the spot where they'd died.

There was no helipad to go to, no one to see or talk to, nothing to do. Their bodies were already en route to Graves Registration in Pleiku, to be prepared for shipment back to the States. And, I learned, their families would be told they'd died in combat inside South Vietnam, not in Laos, to conform to State Department deniability rules. That's how all SOG casualties were reported.

Most of the next day, I sat alone in our empty team room. I felt relieved when a lieutenant arrived to inventory and pack Larry Stephens's and Billy Simmons's personal belongings. Unable to watch, I left. In the RT Delaware team room, One-Zero Luthor "Luke" Dove found a letter from Charles Bullard's girlfriend saying she was worried he was going to be killed. She'd begged him to be careful.

That night in the club I seemed in a trance when Captain Lesesne led us again as we sang "Hey, Blue." Then came the gut-wrenching moment when we added the last stanza and those three names—"Stephens, Simmons, and Bullard, too. Hey, Blue, You're a good dog, you."

Before I could weep I wandered outside, lit a cigarette, and looked up at the moon. I'd read somewhere that the Greeks believed that as long as someone remembers you, you are immortal. Aloud, I vowed I would never forget my teammates, never, though I had hardly known them.

Then I let go and wept as hard as anyone else.

You could say they died from bad luck or bad field craft, but I thought they died from too little time, not enough chance to learn from mistakes—in SOG, just one mistake and you could be dead. Larry Stephens never was able to benefit from experience. I broke down again.

But Stephens, Simmons, and Bullard wouldn't want this blubbering. I had to get tough, starting now, tonight, this minute. Their deaths made no sense, no sense—unless I learned from their loss. The trackers had got them. What could I do differently? Despite their training, they weren't ready. I've got to make myself ready, I've got to learn, to listen, to absorb. I knew nothing, I had to admit that to myself. Lessons to learn? I didn't even know the right questions. All my previous training was only a foundation. Basic Training, Airborne Infantry, Jump School, Special Forces—they had hardly touched upon the life-and-death skills I needed now.

I knew *nothing*.

I must learn how to evade hundreds of armed pursuers out to kill me, learn how to outwit human trackers and dogs. And I had to master my weapons.

Or the NVA would kill me, too, just as Major Jaks had warned. At that moment I understood as I'd never understood before, my naïveté washing away like the tide carrying away beach sand. I would never again liken SOG to the Norwegian Resistance or to any movie I'd ever seen. My mind-set was there, it was all clear. I knew what I had to do.

There was so much to learn.

Chapter Three

Not since the French and Indian War had Americans roamed such complete wilderness to combat a numerically superior foe. To prevail in these conditions demanded long-forgotten skills—tracking, counter-tracking, stealth, stalking, concealment, bushwacking. And since the job was not simply to survive, but to accomplish missions *and* survive—in that priority—only the highest order of field craft would do.

The skills were identifiable, yet there were no applicable field manuals, no books, no training films, not even lesson plans. As a longtime One-Zero noted, "You can't find this stuff in 'the book,' because *we're writing 'the book.'* "

Then where could I learn?

Much of this priceless knowledge, I discovered, was offered up daily in the world's finest tactical classroom, our NCO club. Almost every night, some recon One-Zero arrived in the club, fresh from a narrow escape, an ingenious ambush, a bold raid, to sit among his comrades over a drink and recount his unvarnished experience, blow by blow.

After RT New Mexico was lost, I found myself in limbo, awaiting another team assignment, so I spent every evening in the club, soaking up these firsthand combat experiences. While I sat there quietly listening, a just-back One-Zero would arrange beer cans, glasses, and ashtrays to represent a hill or an LZ, or scrawl his team formation on a cocktail napkin, then vividly describe his most recent gunfight to his recon colleagues.

Each account generated a lesson, giving me something to emulate or avoid. For instance, one team leader advised, "When climbing a ridge, pause and listen *before* you're within grenade range of the top." That morning he'd climbed just such a hill, discovering the hard way that a hidden trail lay up above. The NVA heard his team breaking brush and lobbed grenades down on them. A fresh bandage attested to the price this lesson had cost him.

Supplementing their highways, One-Zero Squirrel Sprouse explained, the NVA maintained a network of high-speed foot trails. Typically six feet wide and perfectly flat, these trails linked enemy encampments or paralleled highways to leave the roads clear for truck convoys. "If a high-speed trail is in use," he told me, "they keep it so clean, it looks like they took a broom to it."

Another One-Zero warned, "Stay off their trails. Surveil them, ambush them, but don't travel on them unless you're looking for trouble—'cause you'll sure as hell find it."

And when you're surveiling a trail, a One-Zero advised, "Never look into a passing NVA's eyes." This bordered on superstition, he admitted, but there were too many cases where eyes met and bullets flew. No, it was safer not to look in their eyes.

Getting off a shot even a split second before the enemy fired, another One-Zero said, could save your life. "Make it a habit," Joe Walker counseled, "everywhere you look, shift your muzzle that way. If something's interesting enough to draw your eye, it's interesting enough to draw your muzzle."

One-Zero Richard "Moose" Gross said that doing obvious things would get you killed. When hundreds of pursuing NVA chased his team into the heavily jungled bend of a river, the team appeared trapped there. Instead of awaiting the inevitable, his six men low-crawled into a seemingly open field, and hid in a fifteen-foot-wide patch of knee-high brush. The NVA searched everywhere *except* that spot—after all, it was too small to conceal a recon team.

Sergeant First Class Barry Keefer needed just one glance at an NVA to record fabulous intelligence. "Look close at him," he said. "How fresh is his haircut? That'll tell you how disciplined his unit is. Is he carrying his weapon like he's used to it? That says whether he's rear echelon or hard-core infantry." It was all logical, yet keenly insightful. "If he doesn't have a rucksack, and his weapon is slung on his shoulder, he's based nearby and just walking from here to there. A loaded rucksack—probably not based nearby. If he's carrying his AK alert, at port arms, he's hunting for your team, so watch the hell out."

Most One-Zeros didn't look tougher, bigger, or older than other men. But they were gods in SOG because their courage, resourcefulness, and tactical judgment had been tested against masses of North Vietnamese. It was their wits that got them through, making their slightest observation worth heeding. These men usually had six months or more running recon, but it wasn't time that distinguished them so much as the number of missions they'd run. For in this unforgiving environment, a man with ten missions didn't know ten times as much as a man with one mission—he knew a *hundred* times as much. On average, by the time a man was a One-Zero, he had about eight missions under his belt; given SOG's high casualty rates, add five more missions and he was a senior One-Zero and almost a statistical anomaly; by the time he had twenty missions behind him, it was a wonder that he was still alive.

There was no naïveté among this bunch—luck played a role once in a while, one team leader explained, but fully 95 percent was common sense, good tactics, solid training, and the One-Zero's force of personality. *He made it work.* It's like stand-up comics—one polished comedian *makes* a joke funny, while another guy falls flat delivering the identical line. Beyond experience and personality, a One-Zero had to be able to improvise, to react creatively—even intuitively—to a changing or incomplete situation or even to a total surprise.

Even sharing all these qualities, different One-Zeros displayed different leadership styles. Some were very aggressive—attack the enemy before he attacks you, no matter his size—fight your way through and run like hell! Others might be more cautious, employing stealth rather than boldness. Each team's combat style reflected its One-Zero. RT California was bold and combative because Joe Walker was; RT Colorado's Ralph Rodd was quiet and intellectual, and loved outfoxing the enemy to reach a heavily patrolled road; another team captured NVA prisoners because their One-Zero liked to get right in the enemy's face. The more I recognized these tactical styles, the more I saw the ideal as a balance. Despite the contradiction, a recon One-Zero had to be part wolf and part jackrabbit—selectively bold or cautious—but few men can agilely switch back and forth. With crystal clarity, I saw that small unit missions succeeded when the right men led them. It's that simple.

Staff Sergeant Joe "Gladiator" Walker was a stunning example.

By the time I arrived at Kontum, Joe already had spent eighteen months running recon inside South Vietnam with the 5th Special Forces Group's Project Delta, then came to CCN and ran recon cross-border for another year. Gangly with horn-rimmed glasses, Joe presented an unimposing figure, looking like an engineer or maybe a schoolteacher. But behind his energetic eyes, he was constantly conceiving mayhem. Give him a box of laundry soap and he'd start figuring out how to fashion a weapon from it. Unemotional, a matter-of-fact sort, he was liable to stand over a dead NVA and critique the error that got him killed. This man of unshakable equanimity one night lay beside a Laotian highway, motionless, while a passing enemy soldier paused to urinate on his head. Joe didn't even flinch, just let that warm urine splash in his hair.

Walker loved tactics, constantly finding new ways to integrate weapons with his team, from the RPGs I'd seen him fire, to a 60mm mortar, even sawed-off machine guns. "If you move properly and the NVA see you in a controlled, team formation," Walker believed, "they probably won't stay and fight." Some people criticized Joe because occasionally he'd quick-march on a highway in broad daylight to lose trackers. "People can condemn the hell out of me for that," Joe responded, "but I'm still here."

One night, instead of just observing a convoy roll past on Highway 110, he dropped incendiary grenades rigged with six-minute time delay detonators into the trucks' cargo compartments. Between Walker's grenades and a later air strike, he knocked out more than fifteen trucks—and the enemy never knew he was there.

Walker's boldness was too much for several of his assistant team leaders. More than once, upon returning from a mission, his One-One told him, "That's all the excitement I'll need in this life," and quit. Another time, Bob Howard recounted, Walker took along a new man because no one else would give him a chance. The new guy accidentally fired an M-79 grenade launcher, bouncing its round off the ground, glancing off Joe's right hip and into a tree, where it exploded. Walker requested an immediate emergency extraction— not for himself, despite the painful blow that left him limping, but for the new man. Or else he would kill him.

Despite his audacity, Walker's tactical judgment was sound. While SOG teams usually could count on lavish air support, for example, Walker advised, "Never start a fight that you can't win with everything you have right now."

It was in the NCO club that I heard many secondhand accounts of the legendary Sergeant First Class Jerry "Mad Dog" Shriver, then running recon down at our sister SOG installation, CCS, in Ban Me Thuot. My favorite Shriver story wasn't a combat account, but an incident that occurred while he was on standdown in Saigon. Not one to be concerned about rules, Shriver just wandered around the city and one night found himself in an off-limits area after curfew. Two MPs spotted his tall, thin frame walking along a street and waved him over. The senior MP announced, "Sarge, you're under arrest. You're going to have to come with us."

Shriver offered no resistance. He so readily climbed into their jeep that they didn't bother to handcuff him. Then, realizing he was Special Forces, one MP ordered, "All right, give me your gun." Accordingly, Shriver handed him a .38 caliber revolver he'd carried concealed in a shoulder holster. At the MP station, the lanky Green Beret was booked and led to a cell while a desk sergeant put his personal effects in a manila envelope.

The next morning a SOG officer arrived to sign for the curfew violator. Momentarily Shriver appeared, looking none the worse for a night in lockup. The SOG officer signed a prisoner release form, then asked, "Where are his things?" The MP desk sergeant handed over the envelope containing Shriver's personal flotsam and the unloaded revolver. "No," the major emphasized. "The *rest* of his things."

The MP sergeant didn't know what he was talking about. Then Shriver spoke up, "Oh, sir, I got it all right here." He lifted his jungle fatigue shirt, disclosing two .45 automatic pistols, four hand grenades, a Gerber fighting knife, and brass knuckles. The shocked desk sergeant only muttered as Shriver scooped up his revolver, nodded, and walked away.

SOG's finest One-Zeros—men like Mad Dog—were occasionally honored for some great feat with the covert war's ultimate recognition, a personal meeting with the commander of U.S. forces in Vietnam. Flown to Saigon, they met face-to-face with General William Westmoreland, or later, General Creighton Abrams, to brief him on the One-Zero's latest operation. Master Sergeant Dick Meadows, one of SOG's original recon legends, had twice briefed Westmoreland, who gave him a direct commission. He was now *Captain* Dick Meadows, commanding the CCN recon company at Da Nang. Bob Howard, too, had been carried to Saigon on a C-130 Blackbird to meet the war's top general, so these things still could happen.

Such grand possibilities, however, occupied few men's daydreams. There were plenty of hard, cold realities to keep their attention. For me, the number one subject was trackers, whether human or canine.

A wise One-Zero assumed trackers were constantly prowling behind him and acted accordingly. If you continued in one direction too long, One-Zero Bill Hanson cautioned, a tracker can figure out where you'll cross one of his trails, which you don't even realize lies ahead. "They'll get some NVA out there and lie along that trail, waiting in ambush." Therefore, Hanson advised, change your direction at least hourly and do your best to avoid leaving a detectable trail. A team's One-One, walking at the rear of the file, helped by sterilizing the backtrail, erasing signs of the team's passage. But if the One-Zero thoughtlessly maneuvered his men across muddy ground or down a steep hillside, he made sterilizing almost impossible.

Every three steps or so, that One-One had to turn around and look and listen for trackers. When a tracker was detected, the One-One could shoot him with a variety of suppressed submachine guns, like Bill Gabbard's Sten gun. Or evade the tracker by leaving a false trail on soft soil and hopping away on rocks as Geronimo's Apache braves did in the Arizona desert. "Remember," Hanson emphasized, "you control where the tracker goes, so it's not tough to lead him into an ambush or a mine."

Tracker dogs inspired a special anxiety. For that bark ignited primordial fear that death was approaching, led by a carnivore's senses. But, I learned, a tracker dog's yelp was actually advantageous, like a human tracker shouting, "Here I come!" Now you *knew* you were being shadowed, and could react by spraying tear gas powder, or creating false trails or ambushing.

The greatest danger was a silent human tracker who managed to follow a team all the way to where they put up for the night, as had happened to my RT New Mexico comrades. After they settled down, the tracker had hours to bring in a whole NVA unit—perhaps a company of 100 men—who could blast you with RPGs, then assault and finish you off.

There was still another kind of tracker, RT Ohio One-Zero Floyd Ambrose told me. This kind followed you but hung back beyond your vision, and shouted or made noises or fired signal shots. "It's nice to think you're evading them," Ambrose explained. "But they're actually driving you in a certain direction, right into a blocking force."

I asked, "How can you tell?"

"They're making too much noise, and the direction you're forced to go seems to be toward a likely trail—look out! They'll also try to herd you along a ravine, against a cliff or a wide river, any place to funnel or trap you." During RT Ohio's most recent mission, he recalled, "They purposely made noise to steer us toward an ambush. So we turned around and attacked them."

Ambrose was convinced RT New Mexico had been hit by an elite NVA counter-recon unit, their version of Special Forces. Trained and organized especially to hunt and kill SOG teams along the Ho Chi Minh Trail, counter-recon soldiers displayed markedly better marksmanship, tactics, and field craft than ordinary infantrymen. They were our nemesis, our deadliest foe.

"But they'd rather take us alive," Ambrose reported, and this, too, he didn't doubt, because he'd personally witnessed it. A few months earlier, while his team was briefly encircled by NVA, a voice called on a megaphone, imploring his Montagnards to turn over the Americans. "Give us the Yankees, and you can go free," the voice promised.

Ambrose grunted. "*And just by chance* this fucking NVA officer is carrying a megaphone. You think NVA officers stroll along the Ho Chi Minh Trail carrying megaphones? And they were on us quick, just after we landed. *They had to know we were coming.*"

It sounded paranoid, but to men like Ambrose, who'd regularly operated outnumbered behind enemy lines, it was entirely rational. "Listen," Ambrose joked, "it's only paranoia if someone *isn't* really trying to track you down and kill you." His humorous retort became a slogan scrawled on FOB-2 walls, though his point was genuine: Several times a team's entire American complement was lost, but its indigenous soldiers escaped and walked out or were picked up days later.

This possibility of treachery seemed real when a team had an experience like RT Arizona's. The One-Zero, Lieutenant Jim "King Arthur" Young, along with One-One Mike Wilson and One-Two John St. Martin—on his first mission—were inserting on a landing zone in Laos when they suffered a freak accident.

Eagerly exiting their helicopter, St. Martin landed atop Lieutenant Young, knocking him down and breaking his arm. They never went to the wood line, but immediately called back the helicopter to extract them. As they climbed into the hovering chopper, heavy fire erupted from a small rise just to their front. "They were waiting for us!" Young realized. "If St. Martin hadn't jumped on me, we'd probably have been dead." Their heavily damaged chopper barely made it back to the Dak To launch site.

Another critical subject for an apprentice such as myself was how to escape all those pursuing NVA, who sometimes numbered in the hundreds. Several times a week, an FOB-2 team made contact and escaped, often killing dozens of NVA without sustaining a single friendly casualty.

"Think of it like doors slamming shut just as your team runs through them," explained a One-Zero. "Shoot at those guys, knock a few of 'em down, then get moving again before they can flank you. If you're slow, a door slams and it's too late to jump through—now they have you surrounded, and you have to fight for your life. You must keep moving. If you keep moving, you stand a chance."

And what if you can't move? The final option was to grab the nearest defensible terrain, stack magazines and grenades, and fight it out. That's when you declared a Prairie Fire Emergency, when you were in danger of being overrun and needed priority air support right away. Hopefully enough helicopter gunships and fighter-bombers could get there fast enough to kill the enemy or push them back. Then the helicopters could extract you.

Having listened to two weeks of combat anecdotes and lessons learned, at last I had a fair grasp of our recon mission, enemy tactics, and our operating environment, and I'd met nearly every One-Zero at FOB-2. My availability and enthusiasm were conspicuous, and about six teams had open slots. Yet not a single One-Zero emerged to ask me to join his team. I began to wonder, was this some kind of shunning?

In a subtle way, I could see, some One-Zeros were superstitious—I alone had survived, my three comrades were dead. The designation RT New Mexico had been erased off the manning board, and I lived in a ghost team room. Was I a harbinger of misfortune? An unlucky penny? One-Zeros knew only too well that sometimes even when you did everything right, you still suffered a calamity—things happen beyond your control, that 5 percent luck a One-Zero had called it. Did anyone really want to tempt fate when already he bore such burdensome danger? Exactly the shunning I sensed now had happened already to Specialist Five Frank Belletire.

Three months earlier, when my classmate Bill Copley had come up missing in Laos, RT Vermont was tasked to search for him. But the team One-Zero was away on leave, and his One-One, First Lieutenant Jim Birchim, had no other American teammate. Brand-new to recon, Frank Belletire volunteered. Belletire had never even met Birchim until they boarded their insert helicopter.

For three days they searched but found no sign of Copley, though they heard NVA talking and moving. Then they were ambushed and an exploding grenade wounded Lieutenant Birchim, throwing him so violently that he broke his ankle. Despite his own wounds, Belletire placed covering fire for Birchim to get a head start; the enemy caught up and they had to shoot their way out. The team was scattered, leaving only two Montagnards with the Americans.

Then Belletire brought in fighters with cluster bombs danger-close, only twenty-five yards away, and the NVA fell back. It was almost dark when a Huey hovered on the treetops, 100 feet above, to drop them four ropes with McGuire extraction rigs. One got hung up in the trees, so the four of them would have to ride three rigs. Belletire got each Yard into his own padded McGuire rig seat, then climbed into the third seat. Lieutenant Birchim sat on his lap.

After lifting them vertically through the trees, the chopper flew into a terrible tropical storm, so terrible that in the dark the pilots could not find Dak To airfield. Thus, they flew an hour and a half with the men dangling 100 feet in a furious storm. When the chopper finally landed at FOB-2, the men on the helipad found Belletire covered with ice, unconscious, shaking, with terrible rope burns across his hands. Lieutenant Birchim was gone. Sometime during that flight, despite Frank's superhuman effort to hold him, Birchim had fallen 3,000 feet, only God knew where.

Lieutenant Birchim's widow received his posthumous Distinguished Service Cross.

Though everyone respected Belletire's courage and stood in formation to watch him receive a Silver Star, not a single One-Zero offered to give him another chance. He sensed that some men even avoided sitting with him in the club. He spent a month in the communications section fixing radios. Then One-Zero Floyd Ambrose said to hell with what anyone else thought and invited Belletire to join him on RT Ohio. Belletire proved himself an excellent recon man, and RT Ohio ran consistently successful missions.

It turned out I'd waited long enough. After a recon company morning formation, I was called in to see Bob Howard. Standing next to his desk were two

African-American NCOs. The slighter of them looked me over, stroked his chin some, then extended his hand. "Hi," he said, "I'm Ben Thompson, RT Illinois." He nodded toward the taller NCO. "This is my One-One, SFC Jim Stevenson."

"He's willing to give you a shot," Howard said. "OK?"

Of course!

Walking to the RT Illinois team room, Thompson filled me in. His companion, Stevenson, was rotating home, returning to his first love—jazz. An accomplished pianist, Stevenson hadn't played for a year. Ben Thompson was halfway through this, his second combat tour; he'd spent a previous year with the 101st Airborne Division. His code name was Cobra, but that didn't mean he was blindly aggressive. "Just so you understand," Thompson emphasized, "my goal is to always get everybody back." That sounded fine to me.

That afternoon I met our nine Vietnamese teammates, who nodded, shook my hand, and pronounced their names. Vietnamese invert the order of their names—like an American calling himself "Doe John." My best attempt to say their names elicited only smiles. The effort was mutual: I overheard them practicing, "Plah-stur," and soon they were calling me "Truong Si Plah-stur," though I'd not yet made sergeant.

Ben counseled me to be tactful when correcting the Vietnamese. Losing face was a terrible insult for them. If a serious correction was needed, he'd handle it himself. The one thing they did that rubbed me wrong was their denigration of Montagnards, whom they look down on as inferior. The analogy to racism in America had not gone unnoticed by Ben, but he had a practical attitude. "Don't judge 'em," he advised. "That's just the way they are. They don't know any better."

Within a few days, Stevenson left and we received our third American, a young medic who'd just recovered from a serious gunshot wound, Sergeant George W. Bacon III. One of the smartest men I ever met and a fine athlete, George's medical skills were a great bonus; he could treat serious wounds, and taught me life-saving beyond mere first aid, such as how to tap a vein for an IV. Further, this remarkable man spoke fluent Vietnamese, useful for communicating with our soldiers, and for learning what bargirls said about us when we went downtown. It said a lot for his character that George insisted, since he'd arrived last, that he should be One-Two, which meant he would carry our heavy radio. To our surprise, Ben said he preferred carrying the radio himself, so he wouldn't have to relay messages through any radio operator.

Our first training involved crossing danger areas, such as trails or streams or clearings, places where we might be ambushed or stumble into the enemy. It went smoothly, with our point man, Hai, halting, extending his left hand and sweeping it slowly left and right to signal a trail; then, Ben and one M-79 man stepped on either side of Hai to cover him; Hai jumped across, did a quick check of the other side and gave us a thumbs-up; the rest of us hastily followed, each covering right or left as he crossed. It took only thirty seconds, attesting to Ben's leadership and the team's experience.

After that it was "string" training, slang for extraction by McGuire rig. Along with several teams, we took turns riding these rope rigs dropped from a Huey hovering 100 feet over our helipad. Simulating an extraction from a tiny jungle opening too small to land a chopper, we climbed into four six-foot rope loops covered with canvas padding, then rose vertically and flew away. The rig's only safety feature was a wrist slip-loop. Because several men had slipped out and fallen to their deaths from McGuire rigs, most of us preferred to wear a Swiss seat—a harness tied around the waist normally used for rappelling—which we snapped onto the line, instead.

That was how George and I and two Vietnamese rode, our arms locked as the chopper lifted us straight up. Almost right away we slipped apart and began swaying into each other. It was quite a ride, something like riding a hot air balloon without the balloon. For five exhilarating minutes we flew 2,000 feet above Kontum, the wind rushing past us, and our Swiss seats pinching off blood flow to our legs. Slowly descending back to the helipad, we swung like giant pendulums until men on the ground grabbed us. We couldn't stand up for five minutes.

That week of training gave me a chance to know our Vietnamese teammates better. Lam was assigned an M-79 grenade launcher, a single-shot weapon that fired an egg-size exploding warhead. He didn't like the M-79, but Lam was such a fine shot that Ben made him carry it. Our other grenadier, Trung, was impetuous, with a tendency to be too big for his britches. Loi, armed with an M-16, was a "Saigon cowboy," whose self-confidence exceeded his abilities. Quang was almost as much a cowboy as Loi, with a penchant for tailored uniforms and black flight suits. Our shortest man, Huynh, stood just four foot five and constantly smiled, showing off his gold teeth. Then there was Binh, a believer in Chinese medicine, whose remedies combine superstition with ancient science. One day Binh caught a large scorpion at FOB-2, and rushed downtown to sell it to his Chinese *Bac Si* (doctor), pocketing $50 for its venom.

Hai, our indigenous team leader, walked point, the most dangerous job. On paper, his position carried the most authority but the real power rested in our interpreter, Suu. Our highest-paid mercenary due to his language skill, Suu was very intelligent and perhaps twenty-five years old, yet, like many Vietnamese men, he could have passed for a teenager. Adept at leveraging his role of speaking for the Americans, I sensed that when it suited his purposes, his translations went well beyond what we had said. There was always something a bit crafty, almost duplicitous about Suu and I never felt entirely comfortable around him. I couldn't quite put my finger on it. Still, we didn't depend entirely upon Suu, communicating to our Vietnamese through pidgin English, such as, "No can do," "You come now," "Numbah One," and "I see."

Like RT New Mexico, RT Illinois lacked CAR-15s except for the One-Zero's. Since I couldn't get my own CAR-15, I opted for a suppressed Swedish K 9mm submachine gun, the perfect weapon, I thought, for a One-One. It was so quiet a snapping finger sounded louder and much more accurate than Bill Gabbard's Sten gun. Firing that Swedish K daily, within a week I could place a two-round burst into a tin can at twenty-five paces. Now I was ready to eliminate trackers—one of my major responsibilities—or to disable an NVA with one or two well-placed shots so we could take him prisoner. In SOG's world, this was a recon team's greatest achievement, "snatching" a prisoner from behind their lines, earning instant respect all the way to the SOG commander in Saigon.

It wasn't easy. Snatching meant ambushing the enemy along a heavily used road or trail, where he naturally concentrated; you never knew how many more NVA were nearby or even following the ones you'd just engaged. Indeed, there might be hundreds more within earshot.

That's what happened to Joe Walker's RT California one afternoon in Laos. Lying in ambush beside a road, Walker watched four NVA march past as if on a parade ground, in step, AKs on their shoulders, helmets perfectly aligned. "They looked like little West Point cadets," Walker thought. After they passed, he stepped out and whistled. They turned and foolishly tried to grab their AKs; everyone on RT California fired one shot, killing them instantly. Walker had begun searching their pockets for intelligence when, not 200 yards away, a whole company—100 NVA—rushed from a hidden bunker area, screaming and firing. "We ran like hell for a day and a half," Walker recounted. "They were really after our ass."

But sometimes those enemy masses could be green troops, unready for combat, with quite different results. This was the case when RT Texas One-Zero David Gilmer attempted a prisoner snatch with One-One Clarence Long and One-Two Richard Nowak. In a steep valley, he set up along a fresh trail in hopes of capturing a prisoner. No one else was to fire unless absolutely necessary, he instructed. Only Gilmer would initiate fire. Minutes later, an NVA with an AK appeared, escorting two men carrying loads on their backs. He let them pass.

A moment later, here came three more, again two porters and one armed escort. They, too, walked past. Gilmer began counting. Soon 150 men had passed—all as threes—and more were coming. Wisely, he canceled the ambush and just kept counting.

Then, *KAA-BOOOOOM!* An RT Texas Yard detonated a claymore mine and now there'd be hell to pay! Here came three more NVA! Gilmer shot them, turned to evacuate his team—and here came three more NVA. He shot them, too. And here came three more. Panicked green troops, they could only do as last told, and kept walking the trail toward Gilmer. It was a shooting gallery. Over and over, three more NVA arrived and Gilmer kept shooting them. By the time RT Texas withdrew, Gilmer had fired fifteen twenty-round magazines and before him lay a staggering fifty NVA dead and dying, lives as foolishly wasted as if they'd been lemmings throwing themselves off a cliff.

With these experiences in mind, Ben designed an ambush around my suppressed Swedish K, with George Bacon and myself snatching one NVA while the rest of our team stood ready to fight off any reaction force. We drilled this over and over until we could set up the ambush in less than three minutes, and then shoot, seize, and escape with a prisoner in just two minutes.

After ambush practice one day, George looked me over in my web gear and shook his head critically. I had everything I needed, he agreed, but it just wasn't laid out well. A student of scientific method, George had developed a doctrine that can best be called, "function dictates location." That evening he opened my eyes to the smartest way to organize my gear for combat, laying it all out on our team room floor.

In my pockets went survival items, such as a signal mirror, miniature smoke grenades, morphine injectors, compass, and signal panel. This way, he said, I'd never separate myself from these.

Next came my web harness with fighting gear—ammunition, grenades, knife, handgun, and gas mask. Standard pouches were too small and restrictive; George replaced these with much larger pouches designed to carry canteens. Magazines went on my left side because I reloaded left-handed, keeping my right hand on my weapon. Grenades stowed on my right so I could grasp one right-handed, pull the pin with my left, then lob right-handed. In the tropical heat we needed four canteens—two balanced on opposite hips and two more in my rucksack pockets. Behind my neck he taped a can of serum albumin, a blood expander given intravenously to counter severe blood loss; a suspender held a Swiss seat for rappelling or coming out on strings. To signal air strikes or extraction helicopters I added assorted smoke and white phosphorus grenades. "Never carry green smoke," George advised. "Pilots can't see it against the foliage." By sweat and regular usage, eventually the canvas pouches conformed to my body's shape, becoming a second skin.

Into my rucksack went those things I didn't need at a second's notice, such as a claymore mine, explosives, rations, more canteens, extra grenades, and a spare PRC-25 radio battery. I always carried a light antitruck mine—an extra five pounds. On George's advice, I slid my banana-shaped SOG machete into the forward slit of my rucksack, carrying it flat against my spine for protection from shrapnel. Our rucksacks held no grooming items—no toothpaste, no toothbrush, soap, or shaving gear—and no tarp or tent or poncho to shield your body from tropical downpours, only a paper-thin Vietnamese sleeping bag that compressed to the size of a cigar box. Priority was ammunition, then signal and survival gear, water, and food, in that order. Teams often ran out of food for a couple days, but twenty seconds without ammo meant certain death.

By the time I'd reassembled my web gear it was the heaviest load I'd ever borne. First, my suppressed Swedish K submachine gun—with thirteen thirty-six-round magazines. *Already that's twenty-five pounds.* Add the rest of my web gear—canteens, grenades, gas mask, handgun—plus survival gear in my pockets. *The burden had risen to fifty pounds.* To grow accustomed to the load, each day in training we wore our web gear fully loaded. My legs quickly built up, but it was a burden to add the rucksack—*another thirty pounds.* Thus, a recon man's total load was roughly eighty pounds—half his weight—not to bench-press a few times but to carry all day long, up and down jungle hills, through streams, while moving stealthily or outrunning enemy soldiers.

Now my gear was squared away, our training had been excellent, I'd mastered my Swedish K, and RT Illinois was functioning as a team. In recon company, our status went "green." We could expect a mission anyday.

Then Maggie arrived.

I'd gone into the club for a drink with Glenn Uemura and his RT Hawaii One-Zero, Bill Delima, when the door swung open and there stood the grinning Martha Raye—comedienne, actress, singer, and dancer—attired in jungle fatigues with a green beret and a lieutenant colonel's oak leaf. This one-woman USO show seldom stood onstage, preferring to entertain face-to-face. Most stars visited Vietnam for a week or two but Maggie came for months. By the time she dropped by FOB-2, she'd been in Vietnam more than two months on her sixth unpublicized tour.

Recognizing Delima from a previous visit, she plopped down at our table.

Drinking from a bottomless vodka-7, she made time for everyone. She told me about her childhood, growing up in the 1920s, the daughter of vaudeville stars. Their sole luxury was a Pierce-Arrow limousine that they drove all over the country; that car was her home, her playground, her pumpkin carriage when she played Sleeping Beauty. During World War II she'd known all the stars, all the great generals, and shared anecdotes about everyone from Douglas MacArthur to George M. Cohan. Her career high point had been the 1940s and 1950s and she reflected the unabashed patriotism of that era.

When one man lamented America not standing behind us, Maggie jumped to her feet, waved her finger at him, and snapped, "Listen here, you whining son-of-a-bitch! *I'm here, I'm American, and I support you.* Cut out that sniveling crap!"

Everyone stood, cheered, and chanted, "Mag-gie! Mag-gie! Mag-gie!"

Then she sang "Going Out of My Head" with no accompaniment, just her great voice.

Afterward she gave us her Bel Air address. "You're all welcome," she said and meant it. "God bless all of you." She kissed each of us and left for Da Nang. What a classy lady.

The next morning Ben Thompson received our warning order: RT Illinois had a mission.

That afternoon, the last week of February 1969, Ben, George, and I attended a briefing in the Tactical Operations Center. Our target was designated November-One, a six-kilometer square of Laos, some twenty-five miles northwest of the Dak To launch site. There was little fresh intelligence such as agent reports or radio intercepts to indicate whether any NVA were there. Learning that was our mission.

The next day Ben flew a visual recon over November-One aboard an Army O-1 Bird Dog spotter plane, detecting a few trails but not much more. Three days flashed past in training and live fire shooting drills. Then George and I listened while Ben briefed back his plan to our FOB commander, Lieutenant Colonel Bahr, who nodded his approval.

Then it was the eve of our insertion. Ben took George and me to the club, not for drinks but to talk to Staff Sergeant Howard "Karate" Davis, the Special Forces NCO who would ride with the USAF forward air controller the next morning to insert us. Since our supporting FAC unit was code-named "Covey," which was each FAC's call sign, Karate's job was called "Covey Rider." In SOG, where One-Zeros were gods, these Covey Riders had to be Holy Spirits. Knowledgeable of both dangers and opportunities—and experts on Air Force ordnance—each Covey Rider possessed shrewd judgment and tactical dexterity. It was a Covey Rider who brought in the fighters and gunships to save you when all hope seemed lost; it was a Covey Rider who led the helicopters to resurrect you from near death; it was a Covey Rider whose voice might be the last you heard in this life.

In the club, Karate Davis waved us to his table. Still in his flight suit from a long day of flying, he nursed a beer, his animated eyes projecting friendliness and optimism beneath a prematurely gray crew cut. Karate agreed to select an insertion LZ in the southeast corner of our target area, since Ben hadn't found a suitable LZ during his aerial recon.

Seeing that I was new and had never before directed an air strike, Davis assured me it was simple. "When you're in contact, just give me an azimuth and a distance. Remember. Just an azimuth and a distance." As a visual reference, so our position could be seen from the air, he insisted, toss a white phosphorus grenade. "That white smoke mushrooms through the canopy, right now, clear as a bell. Forget colored smoke—use WP." Ordinary colored smoke took minutes to reach the 100-foot-high treetops, I learned, delaying an air strike; by then, the smoke may have dissipated and couldn't be seen, or drifted downwind, misidentifying your location and causing a bombing accident. I would always follow Karate's advice, despite the great danger of white phosphorus: the coffee-mug-size grenade bursts into a thousand particles, which burn at 2,000 degrees when exposed to oxygen. One grape-seed-size particle could burn completely through an arm or leg. Your only hope was to smother it with mud to cut off the oxygen. Were an enemy rocket fragment or AK slug to puncture a WP grenade on your web gear, instantly you'd be covered with flaming particles, a truly horrific way to die. Despite that danger, I'd always carry a WP grenade on my suspender, and just hope for the best.

"Let's get some sleep," Ben suggested, and we turned in.

After a full breakfast we drew maps, signal codebooks, and top secret "black propaganda" items to plant behind enemy lines. The latter included several loose rounds of sabotaged AK ammunition—code-named "Eldest Son"— which would destroy a rifle and kill or injure its shooter when fired. Should we kill any NVA, these loose rounds were to be inserted in their magazines so other NVA would recover and fire them. Also, we were to plant a forged handwritten Vietnamese-language letter called a soap chip; cleverly written, the psychological warfare experts in Saigon believed it would leave any reader inescapably depressed.

By 0830 hours the eight of us were on the helipad, boarding the Hueys to the launch site. It was eerie landing at the Dak To launch site. Almost a month had passed since I'd been there with RT New Mexico. I felt a chill when I walked across the spot where I'd waved goodbye to Stephens, Simmons, and Bullard, but kept my mind occupied talking with George, making final adjustments on my gear, and applying camouflage stick.

About 1:00 P.M., Karate Davis radioed: The weather was perfect and he had a pair of fighters en route to cover our insertion. It was time to launch.

As their rotors began cranking, American and Vietnamese helicopter crewmen donned body armor and flying helmets. I climbed aboard the lead Huey with Ben and Hai, our point man, and Suu, our interpreter. George and three more Vietnamese boarded the number two bird. This day I felt excited. My stomach churned with butterflies, sitting in that Huey doorway, knowing that in twenty minutes I might be shot dead, or this helicopter might plunge afire through the treetops.

As the Huey lifted up, I swung my legs to force myself to relax, giving an optimistic thumbs-up to the launch site and Bright Light team. They returned the gesture. Then our bird's nose dipped and we lifted away westward, followed by a long line of Hueys and Kingbees. Four Cobra gunships climbed up beside us. Our door gunners inserted belts of ammo into their machine guns.

Our formation flew past mile-long strings of craters where B-52s had carpet-bombed the valley floor below Ben Het Special Forces Camp, the final outpost before Laos. Built on three bulldozed clay hills, the camp jutted above complete greenery, an orange beacon rising from the jungle. Then Ben Het faded behind us, and with it faded all civilization.

Ahead I saw nothing—no sign of man, no distinct landmarks—just thickly jungled hills. In this mass of north–south ridgelines, one was the border but it would test anyone's map-reading skills to know which. These mountains, the Chaine Annamatique, rose as high as the Appalachians, lushly forested with bluffs towering over wild rivers. Here and there, nomadic mountain people had cleared a patchwork of slash-and-burn fields to plant crops. But they were long gone and their fields grown over. Everywhere, I saw bomb craters. Where they'd fallen in bottomland, they'd filled with water that shimmered in sunlight as we passed.

Then, off in the distance, through the misty Laotian haze, materialized a half-mile-wide orange ribbon that starkly contrasted its lush surroundings. As we approached, it resolved into detail—clay-colored bomb craters and landslides—miles and miles of them, thousands, along the east–west Highway 110. In some spots the road had been so heavily bombed that there were just overlapping craters—not a single tree, not even a blade of grass still grew.

This was the Ho Chi Minh Trail.

Seeing it so clearly got to me—not one visible sign of man anywhere, yet this well-maintained highway attested to thousands of enemy hidden below. To venture beneath these trees would be like diving into the sea to swim among schools of sharks. But that's where we were going.

Our aerial procession turned north toward target November-One. I felt thousands of eyes watching us. *There's no cover, they can hear our helicopters! It's taking forever! Why don't we go down! We're so naked, everyone can see us for miles! Let's go down! Get down!* In those final minutes before landing, every recon man felt anxiety welling up inside. You were at the mercy of powers beyond your control; you only wanted to get away from that noisy chopper, get on the ground, get in control again.

Above us, Covey and a pair of A-1 fighter-bombers circled. Then, at last, two Cobra gunships were on the deck, trolling near our LZ to see if they drew ground fire.

Momentarily our two Hueys spiraled downward, losing altitude so quickly that the air pressure blocked my hearing. I pinched my nose tight and blew, popping my ears, and saw we were so low the bastards must be aiming at us. As the treetops sailed past, I swung my Swedish K back and forth, alert to return any sudden burst of ground fire. Humidity surged and sweat streamed from my face. Then we cleared the last treetops, the Huey flared, and we descended into a small LZ.

I looked to the left door, where Ben stood on the helicopter skid. When he gets off, everyone gets off; if he doesn't get off, we stay on the aircraft. There's no time to explain the decision; we just do it. At six feet, he jumped, and then we all jumped and rushed for the wood line ahead of the nose, as Ben had directed. No one looked back as our bird lifted away.

In the jungle, secure in our tight circle of bodies, I began to breathe easier. Clear of the aircraft, my weapon in my hands, again I could influence my own fate. Momentarily, another Huey arrived, landing George and the rest of the team. Then it was gone and we could hear clearly.

For ten minutes we lay there silently, watching and listening, hearing only the distant buzz of Covey's engines. Then Ben whispered a "Team OK" into the radio handset, and Covey's engines, too, faded away, leaving only the sound of insects and chattering monkeys.

We were on our own, deep behind enemy lines, in Laos.

Ben looked to our point man, Hai, then pointed north, our direction of march. Hai nodded, turned, and we were on our way. While they filed off, I fluffed up the foliage where we'd lain, to thwart trackers. As the One-One, I was "tail gunner," the last American in our file.

We blended well into the triple canopy jungle, whose first layer incorporated bushes and short trees just above our heads; a second canopy grew to the height of average American trees, adding perhaps 30 percent more overhead foliage; then climbing spectacularly above that, to perhaps ninety feet, rose the third canopy. Combined, they shielded the jungle floor from aerial observation, minimized any wind, and sealed the humidity inside. We sweated profusely, constantly.

While we walked, Ben cradled the radio handset on his suspender, close to his ear, the volume so low he alone could hear a radio call. For navigation we drifted in the direction of unfolding interest as it revealed itself—moving in one general direction, but keeping close track of where we were. For security, Ben varied our direction every hour, after a ten-minute listening break.

All day, we never spoke and rarely whispered, relying upon gestures and facial expressions and hand and arm signals. An open raised palm meant *halt,* but closing the palm into a fist meant *Freeze!* A shrug meant "I don't know." Soon, I saw, our language differences had little effect in the jungle because we communicated as our ancestors had, before verbal language existed.

One bad habit I faced was letting my mind drift into a favorite song or old TV episode. By constantly focusing on tiny tasks—like examining each spot an NVA might lurk, picking the next place to rest my foot, selecting the best cover from AK fire—I countered this inattention, until I focused on the here and now. As Joe Walker had advised, my Swedish K's muzzle followed my eyes. And every three steps or so, I turned around, looked and listened for trackers, just as Bill Hanson had recommended.

That first day we found no sign of the NVA.

A little before 5:00 P.M., Ben began looking for our RON—our rest overnight—position. Selecting the right place to put up overnight meant the difference between life and death, as RT New Mexico's fate had shown. Ben was exacting in this. First, we button-hooked—doubled back in a wide circle—to watch our backtrail for ten minutes to ensure no trackers were shadowing us. Then he led us in a new direction, into the densest brush he could see, on a downhill slope. Halfway down—beyond the range of anyone tossing grenades from the top—we traversed the hill sideways another fifty yards, then all eight of us squeezed into a spot so small that the enemy couldn't imagine we could hide there. That was our RON.

In five minutes, we'd put out six claymores—electrically detonated mines that fired hundreds of steel balls in a shotgun pattern, propelled by C-4 explosive—running the control wires back into the RON. Army guidelines said to emplace a claymore no closer than fifty feet due to its backblast; we put ours on the reverse side of trees just twenty feet away, so a searching NVA couldn't cut the wires or turn the mines around on us. If the NVA closed in on us, we'd first throw grenades—the enemy couldn't tell in the dark where grenades came from—then blow claymores. Only as a last resort would we fire our weapons, because muzzle flashes would pinpoint our location.

Crammed so close I could touch the men on my right and left, I slipped out of my rucksack and began encrypting our daily situation report for Ben. Using a one-day code sheet akin to a one-time pad, I picked from randomly generated three-letter substitutions for words and short phrases, like "XRS" to mean "no enemy," and "YGF," "seen today." Ben reviewed it, then read it over the radio to Covey, whose engines buzzed in the distance. Karate Davis wished us well, then flew away for the night. After that Ben shut down the radio. We were on our own until dawn.

I unfastened my web gear and draped it behind me, so all I had to do was sit up and it was on. Dinner was cold rice, C ration meat, and canned fruit. After that, I opened my rucksack to remove a sweater and thin sleeping bag, immediately closing it so I was ready to go. In the cool dampness of dusk, I pulled on my sweater, wrapped the bag around my shoulders, and lay my head on my gas mask. My Swedish K lay six inches from my hands. A little after dark I was asleep, and slept straight through except for my one-hour tour on watch.

All of us were up and alert before daylight, which, unlike sunrise in the States, leaped from a hint of dawn to full daylight as suddenly as someone pulling a sky-wide curtain. By then, we'd already rolled up and stowed our sleeping bags, ready to go. We sat facing outward, watching our claymores, eating cold rice, just listening and waiting for Covey's morning radio check. Not until that tenuous lifeline returned would we venture from our RON.

Soon, we heard Covey's engines, Ben radioed a quick, "Team OK," and it was time to go. In five minutes we'd recovered and packed the claymore mines and off we went. I hung back to erase evidence of our RON, disguising where we'd buried C ration cans. So many little plants had been crushed that a careful search would have revealed our presence. I did the best I could.

That morning, we continued heading roughly north, and continued finding no sign of the NVA. To keep my mind occupied, I adopted an old squirrel hunting technique I'd learned in Minnesota. Instead of scanning the area immediately around me—by which time squirrels would be long gone—I looked as far ahead as I could see, pushing my focus to the limit of my vision. With each step—as more terrain unfolded—I pushed my visual sense farther ahead, to the very edge of my field of view. Maybe I'd see an NVA five seconds before he saw me—but that's all I needed.

At noon, we stopped for lunch, but also this was "Pok Time," Vietnamese siesta, when they rested from the midday heat. Until 1:30 or 2:00 in the after-noon, all NVA movement stopped; if your team moved and generated noise, instantly they'd know you were Americans. And, lying back resting, they'd be making little or no noise. It was safest to honor Pok Time, to do as they did.

A little before two, we picked up our claymores and moved out. We hadn't gone 100 yards when we encountered our first trail. After crossing it, using the danger-area-crossing technique we'd practiced, Ben put us in a perimeter and went back to photograph it. George, Hai, and I covered him. It was not in use, George showed me, pointing to leaves and debris on its surface. Ben pulled his compass, shot a quick azimuth, then we crept back into the jungle.

All three of us meticulously wrote up the trail in our notebooks, including its grid coordinates, width, condition, overhead foliage, and exact axis. So long as one American survived, a complete record of our discoveries would survive the mission.

By now we'd crossed one major ridgeline and a dozen intervening slopes, so Ben wanted to fine-tune our grid location. He radioed Covey and ten minutes later the little Air Force O-2 was circling 2,000 feet above us, looking for the mirror George was flashing toward him. "Bingo!" Luke Dove, now a Covey Rider, called, and then he gave us our exact location. We didn't have to pop smoke or make a single noise. That mirror really impressed me.

An hour after Covey left, Hai, our point man, made a teepee with his hands—the signal for hooches. Ben halted us. We listened for ten minutes but heard nothing. Ben kept on his own rucksack—it held the radio—but had the rest of us remove rucksacks, to silently creep forward. I'd tiptoed only a dozen yards when the jungle opened into a man-made clearing, all the underbrush cut away but the overhead foliage left intact. About seventy-five yards across, it contained a dozen bamboo and palm frond houses.

Fanning right and left, we advanced tactically to clear it, then left three men on the far side as security while we examined it more closely. Some 100 NVA had lived in the hooches, with slit trenches and underground bunkers to pro-tect them during air strikes. Inside one large bunker—apparently a dispen-sary—we found empty North Korean penicillin bottles, which we took to bring back. Ben estimated that the hooches, yellowed by age but not in disrepair, were three months old.

While Ben shot photos, George and I plotted the camp's coordinates and drew a quick sketch showing its dimensions and the locations of trenches and bunkers and hooches. Then we were gone, having paused only ten minutes.

That night, our RON was similar to the first night, on the side of a steep hill. After Covey left, we shut off the radio. But this night was not without incident.

About 8:30 P.M., we heard approaching airplane engines. Sitting up when the sound drew near, we got a glance as it passed, flying so low we could look straight out at it. It appeared to be a C-47 twin-engine transport, blacked out but so close we could see instrument panel lights glowing on the pilot's face. At dawn we entered the plane in our notes, including its azimuth and estimated speed.

That morning we discovered a fresh trail. We lay in ambush for two hours, ready to attempt a prisoner snatch, but not a single NVA came by. Then Ben led us a safe distance away to pause for Pok Time.

By 4:00 P.M. we were climbing yet another hill when I made the mistake of grabbing a bamboo tree. A fine brown powder sprinkled across my arm and instantly I was scratching and cursing myself. Nature's perfect itching powder, it sent me convulsing in unrelenting itching.

Then a Vietnamese voice shouted not 100 yards uphill. We froze. My itching ceased. More voices called out, almost laughing, at ease. We heard the sound of chopping and spadework.

The NVA were building a base camp up there, Ben concluded. What should we do? Crawl up there, watch them, and report it tonight? Ben lifted his radio handset, hailing Covey, then whispered, "We need an air strike."

A half-hour later, while the voices and work continued 100 yards away, George lay on his back in a bomb crater to signal Covey with the mirror while I covered him. Momentarily the throaty roar of two heavy reciprocating engines joined Covey, and that got the NVA's attention. Their voices became agitated, shouting warnings to one another. "One hundred meters, 350 degrees, on top the hill," Ben explained into the radio. Karate's O-2 went into a shallow dive, fired a marking rocket on the hill, and the NVA silence became overwhelming.

Then two diving A-1s groaned to a high pitch, and their 20mm cannons sprinkled all across the hilltop. There was no reaction. They circled around, made their second pass, and all the machine guns in the world opened fire. At least a company was up there, 100 men rattling away with AKs and light machine guns, but they had no effect on the A-1s, which added napalm this time.

On about the fifth pass, I watched a tumbling aluminum cylinder fall through the trees, thinking, "That's coming at us." I smelled petroleum—saw the napalm igniters go off—then WHOO-OOMPF!—flames flashed, singeing my eyelashes and setting Ben's rucksack afire. It seemed god-awful close, but how much worse it must have been to be in that 100-foot fireball, where the enemy soldiers were. They kept firing, and the A-1s kept bombing and strafing, now adding cluster bombs, which exploded with the rhythm of popping popcorn, each pop an exploding baseball-size bomblet. We did not hear their screams but the NVA must have suffered heavily.

The enemy never saw us, yet they had to realize they'd been discovered by a ground team; they'd be looking for us. We crept away.

Ben became extra cautious. Though we were out of water, he would not travel to the only nearby stream for fear the incensed enemy might look for us there. He was extra fastidious in selecting our RON, too. That night we heard no enemy.

The next day, despite our great thirst, Ben would not go near the stream. Due to come out that afternoon, we'd just have to grunt through it without water. By early afternoon we were looking for a suitable extraction LZ. Ben passed up the first one because it was too obvious, too large, and therefore possibly covered by antiaircraft guns.

It was 3:30 P.M. by the time we reached a suitable LZ, one that seemed too small to land a Huey. Indeed, it wasn't usable until we chopped bamboo and thin brush on its edges, which we didn't start until Covey said the helicopters were on their way. While our Vietnamese chopped, Ben had me look at a tree whose branches hung over the LZ. "Can you blast that?" It was sixteen inches wide, softwood. "Yes," I decided, speaking through parched lips. We all were suffering from dehydration and it had become hard to swallow.

"Well, rig it but don't blow it until the choppers are almost here." George and I prepared the charges from C-4 explosive and a claymore mine while Ben talked to Covey.

When Ben nodded, I pushed the firing device and *boom!* My main charge shattered the base, then the high charge kicked the falling tree sideways, away from the LZ. As the smoke cleared, bingo—there was our Huey. The pilot descended expertly into our hole, so tight that halfway down he swung the tail boom to clear a tree branch. He hovered at twenty feet while the door gunners kicked out aluminum ladders, covering us with their machine guns. Slinging my Swedish K over my back, I scrambled up the swaying ladder. George got there first, then pulled me aboard.

As we lifted away it was pure elation, that great danger receding with the humidity below us. In seconds we were safe, a pleasant wind rushing past. It was great to be alive. Covey had alerted the Dak To launch site that we'd been out of water, so the crew chief had brought along a five-gallon water can; George and I took turns, laughing and lifting it to our lips and gulping like there was no tomorrow. By the time we landed at Dak To, we had to vomit.

But we felt great.

Chapter Four

An hour later, as our Huey descended to the FOB-2 chopper pad, I was surprised to see it swarming with people. All of recon company—forty or more men—seemed to be there. But why?

Momentarily we landed, climbed out, and a One-Zero I hardly knew shoved a cold beer in my hand and patted my back. Other men, from a dozen teams, patted everyone's back, passed out beer, and shook our hands. Bob Howard was there, and First Sergeant Pinn and Captain Lesesne. And Lord, did that beer taste great! Our Vietnamese chugged ice cold Coca-Colas.

Each returning recon team was welcomed back this way, I learned, with the turnout of recon company's Americans. We may be on different teams, but we're all in this together, is what it meant. Looking around that helipad, I'd never felt such a bond.

Afterward we dropped off our rucksacks in the team room, then an intelligence analyst led us to the Tactical Operations Center for a preliminary debrief. We described our most critical finds—the NVA we bombed, the empty hooch area, and the airplane that flew past us in the dark. The analyst immediately teletyped these to Saigon. Details could wait until our formal debriefing tomorrow.

Then it was a hot shower, followed by a T-bone steak dinner with all the trimmings—another tradition for returning recon men. After that, we had drinks in the club, where Ben recounted our mission to a handful of interested listeners; there'd have been more, but we hadn't been in any gunfights. Ironically, the most successful recon mission—gathering intelligence without discovery—can seem almost routine.

That night, climbing into clean sheets proved a sensual luxury. I slept soundly.

The formal debrief took all of the next morning as the analyst walked us through our mission, squeezing every possible detail from us. He carefully recorded each trail, added the empty base camp to the SOG database, as well as the new base camp site we'd bombed. Even though the bombing must have killed dozens of NVA, our estimate of twenty-five enemy dead was just a passing statistic—SOG never developed a body count mentality. Collecting intelligence mattered more than killing the enemy.

It turned out our most valuable intelligence was an item we only casually recorded—that blacked-out airplane. During World War II, we learned, the Soviet Union had built a licensed version of the American C-47 as the Ilyushin 718, and later supplied it to Hanoi. A Mike Force unit fighting outside Ben Het had reported a transport plane and parachutes at night, only to be called crazy or mistaken, but now we'd confirmed their intelligence. Critical supplies, perhaps medical, had been air-dropped by the North Vietnamese Air Force.

The following day our team began a one-week stand-down, seven whole days to unwind with no formations, no duty, no set hours, nothing. After a week in the jungle carrying heavy loads, we'd been physically drained, but our mental exhaustion was even greater. That incessant tension—constantly alert, constantly watching, constantly hiding, and constantly listening but never once speaking in a normal voice—knowing the slightest error meant likely death or disappearing forever. The psychological toll had been far greater. We needed that week.

We could have traveled anywhere in South Vietnam, riding a SOG C-130 Blackbird to Saigon or Da Nang, for instance, where SOG maintained safe houses with free lodging. But Ben and George weren't the partying type, so we stayed right there at FOB-2. Mostly, I lay around, reading books during the day and socializing in the club at night. George worked on a Montagnard language dictionary he was writing, played Simon & Garfunkel records, and wrote letters to his family in Old Lyme, Connecticut. Each morning, the three of us went to a shantytown outside the FOB-2 gate for Chinese soup. Sitting on flimsy stools and feeding ourselves with communal spoons kept in a tabletop jar, we downed many a ten-cent bowl of beef broth with noodles, chopped greens, and hot peppers. Whenever we left, the old mamasan wiped off our spoons nice and clean and stuck them back in the jar for the next patrons.

RT Ohio was on stand-down, too, so I partied one day with Floyd Ambrose and his One-One, Frank Belletire. Nicknamed "Pigpen" because of his personal cleanliness habits, Floyd started us drinking beer in his team room at ten in the morning. We had a good buzz going by the time we shifted to the club two hours later, where we found some guys from RT Maine nursing drinks and playing Monopoly. Another guy, off RT Nevada, was bent over at the back door, vomiting, having chugged a whole bottle of Cold Duck to win $5.

Inside of two minutes, Floyd had pushed together three tables, seated everyone at them, and cranked up the jukebox with an assortment of country-western hits. Floyd did like a good party. The RT Nevada man was still in a daring mood, so he challenged all of us to consume a cocktail of his choosing. Why not? He brought back a trayful of scotch and grapefruit juice, which sounds worse than it is. We downed them handily.

Then Floyd suggested, "Let's have a recon cocktail." Hell yes, everyone roared. Then we asked him its contents.

It began with an assortment of liquor mixed in a beer pitcher—vodka, gin, rum, scotch, bourbon, brandy, schnapps, beer, and wine. Floyd swirled it around, sniffed it, then added a pinch of his belly button fuzz—"Just for flavor," he explained. He handed it to the guy from RT Nevada, who didn't think twice, just tipped it back, then passed it to me. It was strong, I found, but it wasn't that bad. I took a swig. Momentarily, it was back in Floyd's hands, he took his drink, but clearly he was not satisfied. "This wasn't stirred properly," he announced, opening his fly and sticking his penis in the pitcher, swirling the liquid around.

Again, the RT Nevada lad took his swig, then added another ingredient—he spat in it and passed it to me. All eyes watched me down a mouthful, then, to continue the tradition, I spat in it, too. Everyone followed suit, giving Floyd quite a drink when his turn arrived. He took his chug, but had to exact revenge. Old Pigpen dumped an overloaded ashtray in the pitcher and shoved it over to the RT Nevada man, who looked down at the soupy mixture with floating ashes and cigarette butts, building up the courage to lift it to his lips.

Then Bob Howard walked in. Howard asked, "Anyone here seen Sergeant Keefer?" No one had, but the RT Nevada man, a daring sort, held up that disgusting concoction and offered, "Sergeant Howard, would you like to try our recon cocktail?"

Without blinking, Howard took the pitcher, heartily downed twice as much as any one of us, handed it back, and walked away. Like it was nothing. Not even a word. And unlike us, he was cold sober. It was magnificent.

The rest of the day we sang recon songs, swapped war stories, and toasted lost comrades. It was the drunkest I'd been since arriving at FOB-2.

The last night of stand-down, I was sitting on my bunk writing a letter when George Bacon returned from the shower room, wearing only a towel around his waist. In the light of an overhead bulb I noticed something on his shoulder and had to look hard to figure out what it was. It was a scar, the worst I'd ever seen, looking as if someone had ripped out a handful of flesh, then twisted it shut. He noticed my stare. "An AK," he explained.

"Khe Sanh?" I asked.

George forced a smile but I could see there was no humor here. "No. That was 23 August."

Twenty-three August! I recalled the bullet holes and the bloodstained floor in my room in Da Nang. This was a date that became famous, 23 August 1968. On that night, at CCN's Da Nang compound, more Green Berets were killed and wounded than in any incident in the history of U.S. Army Special Forces. Though it was a night he'd have rather not relived, George told me the story.

"That morning I'd flown to Da Nang," he began, "for a promotion board." With nothing to do in the afternoon, he walked down to the beach, where recon men on stand-down were sunning themselves, listening to Merle Haggard songs, fishing with hand grenades, and paddling around in rubber rafts. The atmosphere was resortlike, this beautiful beach among sprawling American bases and a big PX just down the road. "You just wouldn't think the enemy was around there."

That night he was up late working on his dictionary of Montagnard in the Bru dialect. It was a tedious task: The Bru tribe had no written language, so George had to sound out each word phonetically, in English, then translate the sounds into written Vietnamese, with definitions, cross references, and synonyms. He turned in about midnight.

Across the CCN compound, in an officers billet, that night's staff duty officer, Captain Chuck Pfeifer, was trying to rest. A Hatchet Force company commander, Pfeifer was recovering from a bad bout of malaria, and in Da Nang's sweltering humidity he tossed and turned, unable to sleep, though both his roommates were snoring steadily. Earlier that evening, the U.S. Marine duty officer at an adjacent Marine air facility had warned him that Communist troops were in the area. That was why Pfeifer had insisted that CCN's nightly security patrol—performed by a recon team—take along an M-60 machine gun when they climbed the adjacent Marble Mountain.

Later they would thank God for Pfeifer's insistence.

At midnight the club closed. A half-hour later all was quiet. One A.M. passed peacefully, then two. But on CCN's 300-yard-wide beachfront at 2:30 A.M., there were bobbing dots among the crashing waves, dots that grew until they took shape as human heads swathed in camouflage scarves.

A dozen figures scrambled from the waves. Then another dozen, and another and another. By the time all had made it ashore, they numbered some 100 soldiers from North Vietnam's Special Operations Brigade, a sister unit to the counter-recon groups hunting SOG men in Laos. Called sappers, these were Hanoi's most elite commandos. Their bodies greased to squeeze through fences, they wore only loincloths or khaki shorts and carried AKs, grenades, hand-thrown RPGs, and woven baskets containing demolition charges. Each charge held five pounds of high explosives, enough to make toothpicks of a flimsy wooden hooch.

While most of the sappers lay still, some crawled beneath CCN's perimeter lights to cut breaches in the head-high barbed wire. Inside they were met by a cook's helper who'd insinuated himself on the CCN compound to spy for them. Everything was ready. They had only to wait for the supporting mortar attack.

Captain Pfeifer still tossed and turned on his sheets. He heard a distant *boom-boom*—a mortar firing. The Marines were firing illumination, he thought. Then—*KA-KA-KA—KA-KA-KA-KA!* AK fire! Right in camp!

Pfeifer grabbed his Browning 9mm pistol and peered through his screened window—there stood an NVA with a satchel charge, three feet away. Pfeifer shot him through the head. As quickly, another sapper jumped to Pfeifer's door, blasting away with an AK. "Get under your bed!" he shouted to his room-mates, pumping five shots through the door, enough to dissuade anyone from coming in.

In a nearby billet, Sergeant Major Richard Pegram, Jr., who'd helped rescue survivors at the overrun Lang Vei Special Forces Camp in February and later survived wounds at Khe Sanh, stepped cautiously from his door, almost bumping into a waiting NVA. Pegram was shot dead.

Another Lang Vei rescuer, Staff Sergeant Howard Varni, died at almost the same instant over in the recon company area. Master Sergeant Charles Norris and Staff Sergeant Talmadge Alphin, Jr., who'd survived near-death just three months earlier when the launch site at Kham Duc was overrun, died, too; both gunned down by sappers.

One Green Beret awoke to feel a sapper's AK muzzle touch his head—as it fired, he knocked the barrel aside, the muzzle blast ripping off a finger. He threw the sapper across the room, seized his own CAR-15, and shot the man dead. Bleeding badly, he rushed outside.

All this was swirling around George Bacon, who hardly even knew the lay-out of the Da Nang compound. "I rolled out of my bunk, grabbed my M-16, and jumped out the door," he recounted. Throwing himself on the sand, he tried to make out sappers but it was almost impossible since most Americans, like George, were in their shorts, attired identically to the enemy. Uncertain where or what to shoot, George just lay there.

On top of nearby Marble Mountain, the CCN recon team leader hefted his M-60 machine gun, dashed a few yards, then he could see them—100 yards below, an NVA mortar crew prepared to quick-fire their weapon. The One-Zero hosed them down, riddling their bodies with tracers until they stopped moving. There would be no further mortar fire.

But down below the fight continued. A sapper squad reached the CCN communications bunker. One NVA tossed an explosive charge inside, killing three Americans instantly and knocking out all the telephones and radios.

Meanwhile, in almost simultaneous explosions and bursts of gunfire, five sergeants first class died—Don Welch, Albert Walter, Tadeusz Kepczuk, Donald Kerns, and Harold Voorheis. At the sound of a grenade bouncing in his hallway, Sergeant First Class Pat Watkins, Jr., grabbed a .45 auto pistol. After the grenade exploded, Watkins peeked into the hallway where an NVA was igniting a demolition charge. He shot him dead, seized the man's AK, and ran outside, pressing the distinctive weapon to his body lest someone shoot him as a sapper.

Nearby, a young American lieutenant jumped from a doorway only to be shot by a waiting sapper. Badly wounded, he spotted two sappers in a shadow waiting for more Americans to come out. Lacking his own weapon, the lieutenant heroically shouted warnings to other Green Berets, who shot the lurking gunmen.

In another building First Lieutenant Paul Potter wasn't so lucky. He was the only officer to die that night, though twelve other officers were wounded.

Captain Ed Lesesne, the visiting FOB-2 recon company commander, didn't even have a weapon when an AK slug hit an officer in his room. Another officer ran out the door only to be shot by a hidden sapper. Then a sapper rolled a grenade in the room, but it didn't go off. That was enough for him. Lesesne dove out the door. He wasn't shot.

Still in his billet, Captain Pfeifer was ready to chance a run for it when the door swung open and a roommate yelled, "Grenade!" Pfeifer pulled his mattress over himself, then the concussion blew him completely out the door. He found himself barefoot, still beneath the mattress, his body torn by grenade fragments. Around him he saw nothing but carnage; in the light of burning buildings, American dead and wounded were sprawled everywhere, and everywhere it seemed, NVA sappers ran through the shadows.

Young men died that night: Private First Class William Bric III, Specialist Four Anthony Santana, and Sergeants James Kickliter and Robert Uyesaka. Old soldiers died, too: Master Sergeant Gilbert Secor, a Special Forces medic who'd won a Silver Star for the Lang Vei rescue, along with Master Sergeant Rolf Rickmers, the Hatchet Force first sergeant from FOB-4.

One sapper whipped a long cord around his head as if whirling a sling, spinning an RPG to arm it. An American shot him dead before he could toss it.

Another sapper ran down a plywood sidewalk ready to throw a grenade when a SOG recon man gunned him down. All night he lay there, cradling that live grenade, and all night his still form was shot over and over.

From a nearby hooch, First Lieutenant Robert Blatherwick rushed out into a hail of enemy fire, shooting one sapper and making it safely to cover. In a momentary lull he carried away a badly wounded comrade to the relative security of an undemolished barracks.

Then three Green Berets made it to a mortar pit and began firing illumination, bathing the camp in eerie yellow light and stark shadows. Robbed of darkness, the sappers settled in where they were, lying low in shadows, under buildings and behind walls.

George Bacon crawled through dancing shadows toward better cover, drawing bursts of AK fire that cracked over his head and threw sand on him. He lay still for an eternity until he saw two figures ever so slightly silhouetted in the flare light. With two quick shots he hit both of them, but his muzzle flashes drew return fire. He had to lie still and hope nothing hit him.

Captain Lesesne still hadn't found a weapon and dared not call out for one. He found a knee-high sand dune against a small shed. Working ever so slowly, he pushed his legs into the dune and covered himself with sand. He hoped no sapper stepped on him.

Nearby, a tremendous explosion shook the ground. A sapper carrying a lit demolition charge had been shot, vaporizing in one furious flash.

Bacon spotted a man moving through a shadow but he didn't fire, fearing he might be a friendly indigenous soldier. Slowly he eased up on one elbow to see him better—a bullet slammed viciously into his right shoulder, knocking him unconscious.

From under his mattress, Pfeifer scrambled back into his hooch, pulled on trousers, then grabbed hand grenades and two M-16s. "Two are better than one," he told himself. Ignoring his own wounds, he wrapped a towel around a wounded lieutenant's head, then advised him to stay hidden in the room. Pfeifer decided to go hunting.

Slipping out, he came upon Sergeant Major Jim Moore; together they crept to the next hooch to check on Pfeifer's Hatchet Force lieutenants. They found that a sapper had burst in and sprayed the room, hitting all three officers. First Lieutenant Travis Mills had been badly gut-shot, another lieutenant had been hit in the groin, and Lieutenant Blatherwick had already gone to find help to get the wounded men to the dispensary. Seeing they were taken care of, Captain Pfeifer and Sergeant Major Moore went back outside to help other trapped Americans who desperately needed rescue.

From where he'd buried himself in the sand, Captain Lesesne heard people taking cover only a few feet away—he dared not even turn his face to see who it was. AKs and CAR-15s and M-16s fired intermittently, and Lesesne still hadn't found a weapon.

Meanwhile, Lieutenant Blatherwick had grabbed the dispensary's medical jeep and, driving with total abandon, raced across the compound past astonished enemy sappers to carry wounded men to safety and medical treatment. Oblivious to the fire he was drawing, the courageous young officer made repeated runs to rescue men and snatch them from harm's way. Probably a dozen men's lives were saved that way.

Continuing his search with Sergeant Major Moore, Captain Pfeifer reached the CCN mess hall, where several NCOs already had dug in and were exchanging fire with sappers. "There's a whole bunch of bad guys pinned down over there by the TOC," one man explained, pointing to the Tactical Operations Center, forty yards away. Then Pfeifer couldn't believe his eyes. From another direction, an unarmed American waved to the sappers and called out, attempting to surrender. The naive man raised his hands to show no offensive intent, then stood in the open. The sappers shot him dead.

Chuck Pfeifer watched him fall and thought, They just killed this guy. What are we going to do? The problem was the enemy's cover—they were sheltered behind the thick sandbagged walls that protected the TOC, where no M-16 or machine gun fire could get them, yet the NVA could cover a vast area, preventing the evacuation of many wounded men. A onetime football player at West Point, Pfeifer was confident he could heave grenades right in their laps, he told Sergeant Major Moore. Then an AK round smashed Moore's arm—the enemy had spotted them and poured fire their way.

Pfeifer's hastily organized squad returned fire. With two men pulling pins and handing him grenades, Pfeifer let each one cook for two seconds, then lobbed it expertly, letting loose a barrage of air bursts ten feet above the NVA positions—BOOM!—BOOM!—BOOM!—BOOM! The effect was devastating. Half the sappers died, the others fell back.

Refining and repeating the tactic, Pfeifer's men advanced and kept the enemy's heads down with heavy fire while the West Pointer heaved another grenade barrage, arcing them to detonate just above their heads, despite their cover behind a building. In minutes the Americans had recaptured the TOC, by which time Pfeifer had thrown more than fifteen grenades and probably killed as many NVA.

With the way clear, at last men were able to reach Bacon, who'd lain there an hour in terrible pain, unable to move. With help he could walk but the pain overwhelmed him; the AK slug had shattered his collarbone, blowing out a cupful of flesh and bone through the ugly exit wound in his back. A pressure bandage eased the bleeding.

Nearby, several men led the wounded Sergeant Major Moore toward the dispensary while Pfeifer pounded on the heavy TOC door until someone unlocked it from inside. It was Lieutenant Colonel Jack Warren, the CCN commander. "Come with me, Pfeifer," he announced. "We're going to walk the perimeter."

In the pale dawn's light, skirmish lines of Americans advanced methodically through the compound, clearing each room, each roof, each crawlspace to root out enemy holdouts. They found sapper bodies in ones and twos everywhere. Each body had to be checked. Americans, living and dead, were pulled from shattered buildings; unarmed men who'd lain low all night climbed from their hiding places, Captain Lesesne among them.

Walking the perimeter with Lieutenant Colonel Warren, Pfeifer saw too many familiar faces among the bodies. He paused before one lifeless form, that of a recon man who'd already pulled his last mission, scheduled to rotate home the next day. The sight so enraged Warren that he cursed and emptied his CAR-15 in one long burst at Marble Mountain.

At the dispensary they found bedlam, blood everywhere, overworked medics rushing to save dozens of lives while volunteers held IV bottles. The bodies of just-dead men were slipped into body bags. Even the CCN surgeon, Captain Roary Murchinson, had been wounded. On one stretcher, George Bacon patiently waited his turn for treatment, knowing his wound was serious but probably not lethal; he wished he hadn't been hit so badly so he could help.

Lieutenant Colonel Warren stared at the long rows of dead and wounded men, muttering to himself, over and over, "I can't believe, I just can't believe, can't believe it." Captain Pfeifer walked away.

By now Pfeifer was beyond anger or sadness. He trudged numbly into the club, sat down, poured a shot of Jack Daniel's, and opened a beer. The jukebox played "Angel in the Morning" but the irony was beyond his frazzled mind. He downed the shot, chasing it with a Budweiser. Then one of his Vietnamese Hatchet Force soldiers dashed in, calling, "VC! More VC!"

Pfeifer grabbed his M-16. "Where?"

"In shithouse!"

Pfeifer trotted to the latrine and peppered twenty rounds through its wooden door. He changed magazines, edged forward and—*KA-WHOOM!*—the sappers suicidally detonated an explosive charge, throwing Pfeifer to the ground and knocking the wind from him. In the billowing dust of the demolished latrine, he saw one sapper near death, tauntingly glaring at him—Pfeifer shot him three times. Then he shot the sapper's dead comrade. And for good measure he wandered across the compound, shooting every sapper body he found.

Outside the dispensary, finally it was Bacon's turn. A medical jeep carried him to the naval hospital in Da Nang.

In those three hours of confusion and carnage, one out of every three Americans at the CCN compound—*sixty-four men*—had been killed or wounded, and another sixteen indigenous soldiers had been killed. Thirty-eight North Vietnamese commandos had been killed and nine captured—all of them wounded. Intelligence later determined they'd entered the sea through a nearby fishing village, then simply waded through chin-deep water to reach CCN.

The human toll cannot be conveyed by statistics. Though not the worst injured, Bacon required repeated surgeries and five months of convalescence and physical therapy before he joined us at FOB-2. Yet in the bedridden months he had to think about that night and the twisted gob of pink flesh in his back, George never lost his lightheartedness.

He smiled. "It really screwed up my suntan," he finished. "That's all."

Stand-down was over. The next morning RT Illinois's status changed to green, but instead of being scheduled for a regular recon mission, we were slated for a week of Bright Light duty—standing by at the Dak To launch site, ready to go after downed pilots or a recon team in trouble. As with any other mission, we'd have one week to prepare.

Ben Thompson asked us, "You ever rappel from a helicopter?" George had rappelled several times but I'd never rappelled at all. The only way to reach a downed aircraft often was to rappel directly onto it from a hovering helicopter. This was a mission-essential skill.

All available helicopters were needed for operations, but that didn't stop Ben. Our team hiked two miles to the Kontum bridge, where he lashed our line to a rail so we could rappel onto a sand bar in the Dak Bla River. The rappelling procedures were simple, from how you tied the rope Swiss seat around your waist to how you snapped the metal carabiner link onto the line. Equally though, a simple mistake could get you killed. I paid undivided attention.

After several descents onto the sandbar, we got into our full field gear, complete with rucksacks and weapons; during my next descent, my top-heavy rucksack turned me upside down while the additional weight made it almost impossible to brake. Ben and George stopped laughing long enough to keep me from landing face-first in the sand. After a few more descents, I could rappel as well as any man on the team.

While Ben laid on supplies—especially extra ammo—and George outfitted his medic's aid bag, I began practicing with the M-60 machine gun I'd use for Bright Light duty. A very reliable, belt-fed gun, the M-60 unfortunately was not well suited for firing on the move; it was butt-heavy and poorly balanced, and a 100-round assault bag canted it left and down. The only way to shoot it well, I found, was to attach a top sling and carry a half-size, fifty-round belt—then I could make that gun cook!

By midweek, Ben had integrated my M-60 with our immediate action drills—standardized exercises in which our entire team reacted to enemy fire, either to break contact by shooting and peeling away, or by focusing our fire and assaulting through the enemy. Since half my 1,000 rounds of machine gun ammo would be distributed among teammates, they even practiced passing me 100-round belts.

There was lots of first aid training, too, instructed by George, so that any one of our Vietnamese could apply pressure bandages or rig a quick stretcher by cutting bamboo poles and sliding them through sleeves tucked inside a buttoned shirt. We reviewed how to inject morphine, then how to load an unconscious man in a Hanson rig—a nylon strap harness developed by FOB-2 recon One-Zero Bill Hanson—to extract him on ropes dropped from a helicopter.

We fired almost every day and, just like the rappelling training, I could see the shooting practice building confidence in all our men, including myself. If we had to fight our way in to rescue someone, we'd need that confidence as much as the skills behind it.

Late that week, Ben recalled the tree I'd blown down on our extraction landing zone, and asked me to experiment with explosives so I could pre-rig tree-cutting charges for Bright Light duty. I went to the supply office, where again I found Dave Higgins, an old friend from Fort Bragg, who again proved totally cooperative. "John," he declared, waving a hand, "just help yourself to whatever you need from the shed."

What a shed he had! I'd only heard of such exotic demo devices—time pencils, acid delay detonators, booby trap devices, whole cases of dynamite, C-4 plastic explosive, det cord, thermite grenades, tear gas powder, assorted mines, electric and nonelectric blasting caps. *And it was all mine!* There were no nosy safety officers, no limits, no restraints—just the exhortation to be creative. Recon men usually were.

Rigging tree charges was a snap using C-4 and det cord; I placed each completed charge in a claymore mine bag, then rigged it so you didn't have to remove the charge, just tie the canvas bag to a tree using cloth slings from ammo bandoliers, which proved faster and more reliable than taping the charge. With

George's help, I demonstrated to Ben and our Vietnamese teammates that we could prepare a tree for demolition in less than a minute.

The final day we spent cleaning weapons, packing, inspecting gear, and testing our radios. That night I slept soundly, knowing we were ready.

Descending into Dak To the next morning, Ben pointed northwest from our Huey to the orange clay hills of Ben Het Special Forces Camp, nine miles away. All I could make out was rising dust, but Ben's experienced eye understood. "That's incoming," he shouted above the whine of our Huey's turbine. "They're shelling Ben Het."

It was no surprise. For two months SOG recon teams had monitored the steady growth of enemy forces in Laos, west of Ben Het, until elements of two NVA infantry regiments—the 66th and 24th—crossed the border to encircle the camp. Meanwhile a third regiment, the 28th, was interdicting the only road to Ben Het, Route 512, which originated right here, at Dak To. To hamper aerial resupplies, a regiment of antiaircraft guns—everything from 12.7mms to 37mms—was arrayed south and east of Ben Het's airfield. The shells we saw falling were courtesy of the NVA's 40th Artillery Regiment, whose 85mm guns were shelling Ben Het and its airfield from the bomb-free safety of "neutral" Cambodia. The Ben Het fighting was the largest enemy offensive since the siege at Khe Sanh a year earlier.

Although our launch site lay beyond the range of Cambodian-based artillery, the North Vietnamese correctly saw Dak To and its airfield as a critical support base. Enemy artillerymen, outfitted with portable 122mm rocket launchers, roamed the facing hills, pounding Dak To almost daily.

Hardly had our choppers shut down when a loud whooshing-whistle screamed across the sky—KA-RUUMP!—a flash and blast 800 yards away. "Incoming!" someone shouted. Instantly the pilots raced back to their birds, jumped aboard—another whooshing-whistle—another KA-RUUMP!—only 600 yards—rotors spun—KA-RUUMP!—300 yards away—the choppers scrambled skyward.

Meanwhile, all of us at the launch site had crammed into two small sandbagged bunkers. For a few seconds it was thrilling, like a passing summer thunderstorm. Then I realized the ear-splitting explosions were shifting closer, I couldn't move, couldn't go deeper, and couldn't shoot back. There was nothing we could do except pray that a rocket didn't hit our bunker. Weighing almost 120 pounds, a single eight-foot rocket generated a blast comparable to an American 105mm howitzer, enough to flatten a wood frame house back home. Or to blow our bunker sky-high.

Then it stopped. There was no "all-clear," just the absence of another explosion and the sound of our returning helicopters. Venturing out, we could see our Cobra gunships strafing a ridge five miles southwest, sending the enemy rocketeers running. None of us had been hit and none of our choppers damaged, typical for a long-range rocket attack against an area target.

Inside the barbed wire launch site compound stood just two buildings, a simple radio shack from which the launch officer communicated with Covey and FOB-2, and a canvas-topped hooch for the Bright Light team. While the launch officer and his radio operator set up, we unloaded our gear and got settled in the hooch.

We would take over from RT Maine. This was their last day of Bright Light. Led by One-Zero Marvin "Monty" Montgomery, with One-One David Baker, RT Maine would go back to Kontum with the choppers this evening, so they'd already removed their gear from the hooch to make room for us. We unrolled our sleeping bags on canvas cots, then carefully arranged our equipment like firemen positioning gear for quickly responding to an alarm. The concept was the same, with minutes making the difference between life and death—rush to the choppers, brief onboard, and go get somebody out of a heap of trouble. For today, we were a backup to RT Maine; we'd do almost nothing, though we were ready to go into combat with thirty seconds' notice.

As of that morning we had six recon teams on the ground in southern Laos, the maximum number believed prudent to deploy, given the support aircraft we had at Dak To and the distances to the teams. One team was RT Hawaii, my friend Glenn Uemura's team. Led by One-Zero Bill Delima, with Glenn as the One-Two radio operator, they had a new lieutenant, Gregory Glashauser, as One-One. This was their second day in Target Juliet-Nine, the hottest target in southern Laos, the kind of target a top team like RT Hawaii could expect. Just after dawn Covey had obtained a "Team OK" from each of the teams. With no one slated for extraction, and none at Dak To to insert, both we and the aircrews were just standing by in case someone got into trouble.

Accustomed to waiting at Dak To, some helicopter crewmen busied themselves tossing horseshoes, while others slept in the shade beneath their tail booms, and others just sat there, munching C rations or playing checkers or reading. They appeared to be lounging around, not a worry in the world—but their aircraft doors and canopies were propped open, seat restraints laid out for quick donning, helmets perched atop the seats, and machine gun trays up, ready for loading. Like us, they were ready to go in seconds. And like us, they were all volunteers, the best men their units had to offer.

Army helicopter pilots, unlike Air Force, didn't need a college degree; many were scarcely out of high school, gutsy twenty-year-old warrant officers, too young, perhaps, to be daunted by the everyday dangers of flying for SOG. No youthful SOG aviator put it so well as Mike Taylor, a Huey pilot in the 57th Assault Helicopter Company, who attempted to explain aerial tactics to a visiting Marine colonel. "We stay as high as we can as long as we can," Taylor told him, "then we get as low as we can, as quick as we can." The colonel replied, "Those tactics sound suicidal." "No, sir," Taylor explained, "the tactics are sound—the *mission* is suicidal."

Gunship pilots shared the Huey pilots' flying acumen and fatalism. Cocky, fearless youths—"old" gunship pilots were a ripe twenty-four—their 361st Attack Helicopter Company birds were the first helicopters over an LZ, scanning for signs of NVA, daring the enemy to fire. Nicknamed the "Pink Panthers," their Cobras sported the pink cat in tophat made popular in the Inspector Clouseau movies, though their performance was hardly comical. Turning tight circles on the treetops, their combination of agility and light ordnance—four pods of 2.75-inch rockets, a 40mm grenade launcher, and a minigun—proved ideal to support a team in contact or to suppress ground fire when escorting Hueys. It was not uncommon to deliver Cobra fire within fifty meters of a team, even twenty meters for minigun fire.

That first day of Bright Light, a Huey crew chief took a few minutes to show me his aircraft, from the instrument panel to the extraction rigs, machine guns, and intercom system. It all made more sense to me after that—except I still didn't understand how these guys could fly through antiaircraft fire, day after day, noisy sitting ducks in the open sky. "The happiest I am," I told him, "is when I get off that bird, and get away in the jungle. You have to be nuts to fly in and out of hot LZs like you do."

"We're nuts?" he responded. "You guys are *fucking crazy* to get *off* the helicopter!"

Well, we were all probably a bit unbalanced to do what we were doing.

Ben spent much of the day in the radio shack with the RT Maine One-Zero, monitoring the radios, while George talked to another Special Forces medic, Sergeant Joe Parnar. A fellow New Englander and a medic course classmate, Parnar had arrived with us as the chase medic, that is, one of the medics assigned to our FOB-2 dispensary, who rode aboard a designated Huey, ready to administer emergency treatment to any casualty. Say a team had a severely wounded man—the chase medic would ride his extraction Huey and work on him the whole time it took to fly back to Dak To. Once there, nurses and doctors from a 4th Infantry Division emergency treatment center could take over or the chase medic could ride with the injured man all the way to the evacuation hospital in Pleiku, an hour away. This immediate treatment by a knowledgeable Special Forces medic frequently meant the difference between life and death.

Because chase medics often rode into hot LZs to extract injured men, they frequently displayed heroism of a high order. Parnar was no exception. While flying, he earned three Purple Hearts, a Silver and a Bronze Star, plus the Soldier's Medal. Yet that wasn't enough, the Boston native told George. "I'd rather be running recon with you guys," he said. "That's where the real action is."

By now it was mid-afternoon, the hottest part of the day. I strolled over to watch the Cobra pilots pitching horseshoes. Behind me a voice shouted, "*Launch! Launch!*" It was the launch officer; someone was in trouble. The aviators dropped their horseshoes and made a dead run for their cockpits, jerking off the rotor blade tie-downs on the way. I ran to George at the radio shack door, and together we listened silently to the radio inside, hearing Covey's side of a tense conversation with a recon team. As the Cobras lifted away, Ben whispered, "A team's in contact. One man's hit bad. They're pinned down, can't move."

My first thought was my buddy Glenn Uemura. I asked, "Is it RT Hawaii?"

Preoccupied, the launch site officer ignored me. Behind us, RT Maine One-Zero Monty Montgomery, One-One Baker, and three Yards were tying into rope Swiss seats, ready to rappel directly into the surrounded team. Monty was taking just five men. Rather than have RT Illinois reinforce his Bright Light team and land on a large LZ a half-mile way, he wanted to get in faster and closer, especially with daylight down to a few hours. It was dangerous as hell.

Twenty-five miles away in Laos, RT New Hampshire was fighting for its life. Though One-Zero Jim Ripanti had outmaneuvered tracker teams and whole platoons of searchers for three days, that afternoon he'd run out of luck. In a quick exchange of fire, Lieutenant Ripanti had been hit in the chest by an AK, and his One-One, Staff Sergeant George Fails, was badly shot through both legs. A Montagnard, too, had been wounded seriously and could not walk. Ripanti refused first aid and attempted to direct the defense but he was on the verge of death; unable to walk, Fails took over the radio from their One-Two, Sergeant Mike Kinnear, who became a one-man fire team, crawling and shooting wherever the NVA massed to assault them.

When RT Maine's Huey arrived overhead, Monty, Baker, and their three Yards stepped out on the skids, ready to rappel—then a sudden eruption of ground fire drove their bird away, hitting it twice. On the ground, Fails directed Cobras and a pair of A-1s, then the Bright Light Huey returned. This time Monty's men instantly kicked off, reaching the ground before enemy fire found their helicopter.

By then Lieutenant Ripanti had been lying still for some time. He was dead, Montgomery could see. While Kinnear and his Yards held off the enemy, Monty and David Baker rendered first aid to Fails and the badly wounded Yard, then placed them and Lieutenant Ripanti's body in extraction harnesses. Momentarily a Huey appeared overhead, dropped ropes, and lifted out the body and two wounded men. Heavy Cobra fire prevented the enemy from downing the Huey, but Monty realized they couldn't attempt that again—by now the NVA knew exactly where the helicopters must hover. Unburdened by casualties, he decided they would fight their way through encirclement to reach a sit-down LZ.

Back at Dak To we were in the dark. The Covey Rider—focusing on air strikes and the team in contact—still hadn't told us which recon team had been hit. It seemed a superfluous detail for unessential recipients. All we knew for sure was that at least one badly wounded American was en route to Dak To.

The Dak To radio crackled with a Huey pilot's tense voice, "White Lead is inbound, need a stretcher and medics." Again I feared it was Glenn Uemura. The launch site lieutenant turned to me, "Get a stretcher, get out there, pronto."

While George ran for a doctor in the 4th Division medical bunker, I dashed off, found a stretcher, waved over three of our Vietnamese to help me, then sped to the landing Huey; I ran as fast as I could but I dreaded getting there.

The wounded man was not Glenn. It was Lieutenant Jim Ripanti, huddled in a fetal position, his jungle shirt dark with blood. "You'll be all right," I hollered over the grinding turbines. It took the doorgunner and myself to shift Lieutenant Ripanti to the stretcher, he was so limp. "The doctor's right in there," I shouted as we started for the medical bunker. Halfway there George ran up with a doctor. We stopped to check the ashen-faced lieutenant.

"It's all right," I reassured the badly wounded man, patting his shoulder.

The medical officer knelt, felt for a pulse, peeled open an eyelid, then stood. "He's dead," he pronounced. "Nothing more to do."

Dead? Ripanti couldn't be dead! I'd talked to him in the club last week. I looked again, really looked, and had to admit he'd been dead when I first saw him in the Huey. Ben and George respectfully draped a poncho over his body. Behind us, the Huey crew chief emptied a five-gallon water can to rinse off the chopper floor, then they lifted away to refuel and rejoin the other helicopters over Laos.

It was three more hours, 7:00 P.M., by the time the Bright Light team and the RT New Hampshire survivors landed at Dak To. Miraculously, Monty's bold move had caught the NVA off guard, and they broke through the encirclement without additional casualties. While the choppers refueled, RT Maine's men hurriedly gathered all their gear; in minutes they were loaded up, happy to return to Kontum and a week of stand-down. Ben, George, and I watched the procession of choppers climb away, leaving behind an eerie quiet at Dak To. Now we were the Bright Light team.

The following morning RT Kentucky arrived aboard the helicopters, to be inserted as our sixth team on the ground. Led by One-Zero Dave Kirschbaum, with One-One Ron Gravett, their target was near Highway 110, the most heavily defended supply road in southern Laos. Gravett was an old friend and communications training classmate at Fort Bragg.

Arriving with them was Bob Howard, who came to Dak To just to get away from Kontum for a day and to be closer to the field. As always, this great soldier's every word was noteworthy and I paid heed when he came over to talk to me. Lighting his trademark Lucky Strike, Howard asked how I was handling it. I knew what he meant, that the ghosts lingered here at Dak To where seven weeks earlier I'd parted with my RT New Mexico teammates. I was just fine, I said, then asked, "With all your combat—how do *you* handle it?"

He studied me for a second. "It's the close friends," he said, "that's the worst—losing close friends." He drew deep on his cigarette. "I don't make too many close friends."

We spoke for a moment about combat, that I had yet to actually be in a firefight. Did he have any advice? Howard recalled his worst situation, when his whole team was shot up and he'd been knocked unconscious by an explosion. When he awoke, everyone was gone, he didn't even have a weapon, just a signal mirror. But he made it through. "Instead of panicking, John, you've got to force yourself to ask, 'What do I do now?'"

By now the RT Kentucky men were camouflaging their faces, any moment expecting Covey's call for a launch. Howard walked over to talk to Kirschbaum and Gravett.

The chase medic, Joe Parnar, sat with George Bacon and me, watching Howard. Obviously, Howard would have liked nothing more than to grab a rucksack and weapon and go with the team, but that was no longer possible. Word had just arrived at Kontum that the U.S. command in Saigon had forwarded to Washington the recommendation for Howard's Congressional Medal of Honor. In a few weeks he'd be presented an interim Distinguished Service Cross, but it was only a matter of time before he would be in the White House to have the president drape that pale blue ribbon around his neck. As a Medal of Honor nominee, he could no longer go on combat operations.

Just four weeks earlier, former RT Maine One-Zero Sergeant First Class

Fred Zabitosky had stood in a White House ceremony to receive the Medal of Honor from President Richard M. Nixon for rescuing two pilots from a burning Huey after it was shot down. "Before that," George reported, "another recon company guy got a posthumous Medal of Honor. Lieutenant George K. Sisler."

"With Howard," I said, awed, "that's three Medals of Honor for recon company."

"No," Parnar corrected me. "That's the fourth." He paused, recollecting. "There was another guy last year, from New York—Specialist Five John Kedenburg. A posthumous award. I was flying chase medic that day." He saw that we wanted to know the story, so he continued.

Kedenburg's RT Nevada had spent most of that day outrunning a 500-man NVA battalion that was right on their heels, catching up with them each time they paused. Finally, Kedenburg sent his One-One, Specialist Five Steve Roche, ahead with their Yards while he fought a rear-guard delaying action. When the twenty-three-year-old One-Zero rejoined the team, he learned one Yard had become separated. Then they found a break in the treetops where a Huey could drop them ropes for a string extraction. The Covey Rider, Gerald Denison, said, "Let's go for it." The first chopper made it out with four Yards, braving sporadic fire but not suffering any hits.

Then Parnar's Huey arrived to extract the second half of the team. Hovering seventy-five feet above RT Nevada, the crew chief and another medic, Sergeant Tony Dorff, lay on the floor to lower the ropes while Parnar covered them from the left door. A heavy 12.7mm machine gun opened fire on a facing hillside, arcing tracers past their chopper. Then Parnar spotted a man waving a panel only about seventy-five yards away, apparently the missing Montagnard. The Yard dashed below to where Kedenburg was snapping in the last of his men.

"It seemed like an eternity," Parnar said, "but the pilot just kept hovering in that fire." Finally the pilot had to pull out to keep from being shot down, inadvertently dragging the recon men through the trees. "We beelined it to Ben Het," Parnar recalled, "where we touched down to evaluate the injuries." John Kedenburg was not there. At the last minute he'd given up his extraction harness to the returning Montagnard, remaining on the ground to face certain death from mass-assaulting NVA. An air strike went in where Kedenburg had fallen. RT Nevada's One-One Roche and the others survived.

The next day a Bright Light team inserted to recover Kedenburg's body. It was led by Sergeant First Class Sherman Batman, with One-One Specialist Five Jim Tramel, and One-Two Specialist Five Tom Cunningham. A medic,

Sergeant Bryon Louks, volunteered to accompany them. They extracted the young Green Beret's body by strings without incident, then marched a half-mile to a bomb crater they could expand into an LZ by chopping bamboo. Batman put Cunningham and two Yards on high ground to cover them while the others chopped.

Unknown to them, however, two NVA platoons—about seventy-five men—had been shadowing them all morning and had quietly surrounded them. One-Zero Batman spotted an NVA creeping toward them, quick-fired an M-79 grenade launcher. One-One Tramel shouted a warning and opened fire. Then enemy fire engulfed the whole team from three sides. An exploding grenade wounded Tramel and an RPG blast wounded Cunningham, cutting off him and two Yards, but Cunningham's CAR-15 bursts killed five NVA and threw back a human wave that had almost overrun his high-ground position. Louks, too, had been wounded by incoming RPGs but managed to kill three NVA and send a squad fleeing. Despite his wounds, Tramel fired at six NVA, advancing to kill three and repulse the others. Then a barrage of grenades killed both Yards fighting alongside Cunningham, leaving him alone to hold the up-hill flank. Then One-Zero Batman single-handedly assaulted into a swarm of NVA, killed several, and ran back into the perimeter. When he saw that the wounded Jim Tramel had been cut off, Batman joined with Louks to fight their way to him and drag him back to safety. With Covey overhead, they somehow managed to fight off repeated assaults until, supported by A-1 Skyraiders and Cobra gunships, they pushed the enemy back and were extracted.

The cost to recover John Kedenburg's body had been considerable—two Montagnards killed, plus four Americans and two Yards wounded.

That evening, Kedenburg's body arrived at the FOB-2 dispensary. Because he was the newest medic, it was Joe Parnar's chore to handle the body. "Cleaning John's body, preparing him for shipment back home," he told us, "was the greatest honor I've ever had."

I was humbled into speechlessness.

Seeing RT Kentucky donning their rucksacks and trekking toward the cranking Hueys, Parnar grabbed his medical aid bag, waved, and left to ride as chase medic. While the Huey rotors cranked, Howard walked with the RT Kentucky men to their bird and helped their Yards climb aboard. All of us in the launch site gave them a thumbs-up, and Kirschbaum and Gravett returned the gesture. Momentarily they lifted away, their mass of birds heading toward Laos.

They landed safely, with no sign of the enemy. It was quiet the rest of the day.

The next morning all the teams gave Covey a "Team OK." But, hardly an hour later, after the choppers had landed at Dak To, RT Kentucky had made contact, exchanged fire with the NVA, and begun running for their lives. The Cobras launched to find them, in hopes they could shake off their pursuers.

The Hueys stayed at Dak To, but all the crewmen had donned their helmets and body armor and stood beside their aircraft, ready to go. To keep my mind busy I went into the hooch to recheck my gear and machine gun. Then, just in case, Ben got us into Swiss seats, ready to rappel, and we joined the chopper crews standing beside their aircraft.

On the ground, One-Zero Dave Kirschbaum was calling Cobra rockets and miniguns danger-close. Within fifteen minutes the Cobras had expended their ordnance but then RT Kentucky again clashed with the NVA, with Gravett suffering a shrapnel wound to his head. That was it. Covey declared a Prairie Fire Emergency, diverting a pair of A-1 fighter-bombers to them while the Cobras returned to Dak To to rearm, refuel, and return with the Hueys to extract the team.

Now came another Bright Light task—rearming the gunships. Ben, George, myself, and our Vietnamese organized like a racing pit crew to help the aviation armorer turn the Cobras around fast. Discarding our Swiss seats, we tore open crates of warheads and 2.75-inch rocket bodies, screwed them together, then stacked them where the four Cobras would land. Beside us the armorer readied cans of minigun ammo and long belts of 40mm grenades.

By the time the Cobras settled in before us, the Hueys were at full RPMs, ready for takeoff. Hefting the six-foot rockets, we quickly slid and locked each in a launcher tube while the armorer reloaded the more complicated miniguns and grenade launchers. Working in front of all those armed weapons was a gross safety violation, but we didn't give a damn—men's lives were on the line. In less than two minutes the Cobras were ready to go, the whole armada lifting up, fifteen helicopters flying into Laos to pull out one six-man recon team.

We stood glued outside the radio shack, catching bits of radio messages. A Huey was taking fire, now the Cobras were returning fire, then more ground fire. We could hear Covey, but not the team on the ground. Pressed too hard to reach a normal LZ, the team would have to come out by McGuire rigs— "strings"—with the Hueys dropping ropes through the treetops. Then came word: RT Kentucky was out, riding strings back to Dak To. Twenty minutes later, peering to the northwest, an RT Illinois Vietnamese announced, "They come." In the distance I could barely make out specks dangling on threads below two Hueys.

In five minutes they'd grown to human shapes, then the choppers had to

slow as they gradually descended the final 300 feet. Swinging above us, pendulum-like, the RT Kentucky men had lost circulation in their legs, so we caught
each one as he landed, laid him on the airfield, and unsnapped his extraction
rig. The injured American, Sergeant Ron Gravett, had suffered a frag wound in
his forehead, which the chase medic patched up. He'd be fine. Though they'd
just fought their way through a life-and-death encounter, Dave Kirschbaum
shrugged it off, no big thing at all. Just another mission. Tonight he and Gravett
would have cold beer, a steak, a shower, and clean sheets. That's what occupied
their thoughts.

That night I was sound asleep when a thunderstorm woke me—then I remembered Vietnam didn't have thunderclaps, just soundless heat lightning.
This thunder pounded steadily, a distinct rumble that must have lasted twenty
seconds. Then it stopped. I sat up. In his cot, Ben Thompson didn't even open
an eye. "B-52 strike," he explained. "Up by Ben Het. Nothing to get worked up
about." I went back to sleep.

The next morning we should have had another team arrive for insertion because there were only five teams on the ground. But no team came up with the
choppers.

However, an infantry battalion from the U.S. 4th Division landed on C-130
transports, then a mass of perhaps twenty-five Hueys arrived to carry them
into the hills around Dak To. Hundreds of young American soldiers sat in small
clusters along the runway, waiting for their chopper ride. They were loaded
down like animals, with whole cases of C rations and mortar ammo lashed
atop their already stuffed rucksacks. These GIs were so overburdened that they
couldn't employ stealth, and without stealth there was little chance of surprising the enemy. George and I wondered how they could fight like that—wait
until they're attacked, then call air and artillery around them? Everything that
was wrong with the war was right there—field soldiers attempting to succeed
but burdened with rules and requirements dictated by higher-ups who never
wore a rucksack.

In less than an hour they were all gone. It was quiet the rest of the day.

That night at Ben Het, nine miles away, the siege hit a new high. Thousands
of NVA infantry supported by artillery and mortars had been unable to crush
the isolated camp, so the enemy raised the ante, launching its second armor attack of the war. Under the cover of darkness, a force similar to the one that
overran Lang Vei Special Forces Camp a year earlier—ten PT-76 tanks and a
battalion of infantry—broke from a western wood line, having just arrived
from Laos. Unlike Lang Vei, however, SOG intelligence had prepared the well-
armed defenders, and they made quick work of the NVA. Not one vehicle got

closer than 800 yards, with half the tanks smashed by bombs, artillery, and recoilless rifles. The survivors had to run for their lives.

It seemed almost a one-two punch the next morning when a 100-man Hatchet Force company flew into the launch site, then inserted deep behind the NVA attackers, on a hilltop overlooking Laotian Highway 110. Now the NVA's most critical supply line was cut off from the survivors' rear. Led by Captain Barre McClelland, the SOG company dug like mad and toppled trees with chainsaws to construct a roadblock. So long as they held that hilltop, not another NVA convoy could pass.

That evening, more 122mm rockets slammed into Dak To. For all their sound and fury, they damaged nothing of consequence.

Early the following afternoon, another team declared a Prairie Fire Emergency—"Get us out quick or we'll be overrun"—and this time there was no doubt: it was RT Hawaii, my buddy Glenn's team. We needed few details to grasp the danger, for they were in Target Juliet-Nine, a place always crawling with NVA. Under Bill Delima's leadership, they'd shot their way clear of an enemy platoon and were running for an LZ, pausing and shooting on the way, even as our helicopters flew westward to extract them. It was a hell of a nail-biter, listening to Covey describing their hectic advance. It reminded me of the way another One-Zero had put it, jumping through doors before they slammed shut. Delima's timing proved perfect. They reached the LZ just as the choppers got there, and came out without a single casualty.

A half-hour later their chopper settled in front of the launch site, their faces shining with the familiar euphoria of men who'd just escaped death. For Glenn and Lieutenant Glashauser, this was their first gunfight. I shook Glenn's hand and helped him carry his gear into the launch site. "How was it?" I asked.

He shook his head. "Close as shit. Lots of NVA."

Agitated like he had ants in his pants, one RT Hawaii Yard tore off his shirt, exposing a vicious fifteen-inch welt where an AK slug had grazed his back but hadn't broken the skin. In my book, too, that was close as shit. For his coolness in directing air strikes that day, Glenn would receive a Bronze Star for Valor.

The following day was our last of Bright Light duty. Riding in with the choppers that morning was our replacement, RT South Carolina, led by Lieutenant Tom Waskovich. With only four teams on the ground, and no additional insertions so long as the 100-man Hatchet Force was fielded, it was a slow day. Our helicopters flew resupply missions to the roadblock while we spent the day playing gin rummy and reading.

That night we flew back to Kontum with no fanfare.

Our replacement Bright Light team saw action, at least their One-Zero did.

After an NVA mortar barrage wounded the only Hatchet Force American qualified on the 90mm recoilless rifle, Lieutenant Waskovich volunteered to take his place. A Huey whisked Waskovich out to the roadblock, where he spent the next five nights killing NVA trucks on Highway 110, braving heavy machine gun fire and incoming mortars to keep blasting. Not one truck got past him. For three weeks the Hatchet Force held that hilltop, rotating companies twice, until holding it became untenable. At one point so many NVA were in the open that Covey Rider Luke Dove was shooting at them from the open window of an O-2 forward air control plane flown by Captain Al Rose.

The night we got back from Dak To, I went to the club with Glenn and Bill Delima. When Delima learned no one had yet sung "Hey, Blue" for Lieutenant Ripanti, he waved over Captain Lesesne and they led everyone through that sad song. Ripanti's closest friends and teammates bore the worst of it, choking up until tears fell during the final verses.

Singing along, I recalled what Howard had said at Dak To. I hardly knew Lieutenant Ripanti, except that he was a good man. I felt no gut wrenching, no weeping, just sadness and sympathy for Jim's family, as I'm sure he'd have felt for my family if things had been reversed. He wasn't Glenn or George or Ben. I lifted my voice in respect and thanked God that this time we weren't singing for a close friend.

That luxury would last but three more days.

Chapter Five

After actress Martha Raye left Kontum, her one-woman USO tour shifted to our CCN sister compound in Da Nang. Never star-conscious and hardly rank-conscious, Raye avoided the officers club's formality, settling into, instead, the relaxed atmosphere of CCN's unofficial recon club, a bamboo-lined former team room called the Bamboo Lounge. There she continued her role as the Florence Nightingale of Green Beret morale.

Her funny stories, show business memories, and tableside crooning had a way of reaching into each man and making him feel special, assuaging whatever transitory ills were affecting him, ministering to him as surely as any nurse. Among the recon men, Raye took an instant liking to the RT Copperhead One-Zero Ricardo Davis—my Fort Bragg friend who'd first told me about SOG. Maggie just loved Ricardo Davis. Outgoing and witty with a Latin warmth, Ricardo could befriend anyone—as could Maggie—so it was natural that they hit it off instantly. That night Raye entertained the men with Broadway show tunes and old medleys but Davis kept insisting, "You have to sing something with me!"

At midnight, the CCN commander, Lieutenant Colonel Jack Warren, sent his sergeant major to close the Bamboo Lounge. Maggie announced to a cheering audience, "We'll see about that!" She phoned Warren, declared, "My date-of-rank puts me senior to you," referring to her honorary lieutenant colonelcy. *"And we're staying open!"*

And they did.

Late that night Ricardo told her the story of SOG's memorial ballad, "Hey, Blue," and explained what it meant to recon men. That story so moved her that Raye ended the night with an arm wrapped around Ricardo, dolefully singing a duet of that sad ballad, her smooth jazz voice adding to it a polish and feeling the men hadn't heard before.

Ricardo's assistant team leader, Jim Lamotte, joined their choruses of lost men's names, but he noticed something had changed in his old One-Zero. Maybe it was singing that song with Maggie, or just the premonition a recon man sometimes got thinking about how many times he'd beaten the odds. A few days later Davis wrote a letter and gave it to Lamotte, instructing, "If I don't come back, send this to the address on the envelope." He'd never done that before. The effervescent optimist turned fatalist?

To the tough, Detroit-born Lamotte, that just didn't seem like his One-Zero. "Ricardo was the first man that ever put his arm around me without me thinking I might have to break it," which Lamotte could have done handily as a karate black belt. But he loved Ricardo like a brother.

A few days later their RT Copperhead flew on a C-130 Blackbird across Laos to SOG's most secret launch site, at Nakhon Phanom (NKP) Air Force Base in northeast Thailand. Hidden away in an unmarked building, SOG teams had been staging from NKP for more than a year, allowing insertions from the westerly back door of Laos when monsoon storms precluded launches across its easterly South Vietnamese border. SOG teams could not remain overnight at NKP due to Thai political sensitivities. Either a team inserted that day, or it flew back to Vietnam on a Blackbird and returned to NKP the next morning.

After several days' commuting, RT Copperhead's two Americans and four Nungs climbed into a USAF 21st Special Operations Squadron HH-3 "Jolly Green Giant" helicopter and flew east into the Laotian morning sky. Their chopper flight was long, requiring a refueling stop at a CIA-supported outpost. Then they saw it below, the bright clay of the NVA-controlled Highway 165, which carried enemy convoys to the South Vietnamese border due west of Chu Lai. Two Jolly Greens descended, zigzagging low-level to mislead enemy LZ watchers. As they neared their true LZ, through the trees, Davis and Lamotte caught flashing glimpses of trails and hooches and trenches, confirming the heavy enemy presence they'd been warned to expect. Several other teams recently had been forced out by large formations of NVA.

Finally RT Copperhead's bird hovered, the Air Force crew chief kicked out ladders, and Davis, Lamotte, and the four Nungs descended, then dropped and slid down a hill. They were on the ground, safe and, as far as they could tell, unobserved. Their mission was area recon with the expectation of finding a phone line worthy of the wiretap gear Ricardo carried.

For several hours they moved uneventfully, crossing old trails and hearing an occasional gunshot in the distance, but they encountered no NVA. In mid-afternoon, Davis had them pause for Lamotte to attempt radio contact, but no one responded.

Knowing they couldn't call for air support if they made contact, Davis steered them away from likely enemy locations, keeping them in thick jungle. They moved slowly and quietly, varying their direction so the enemy—if they'd drawn trackers—could not anticipate where they were going and ambush them. They moved until almost dark, then burrowed into head-high elephant grass for the night. At last light, Covey should have overflown RT Copperhead for their end-of-day situation report, but they never heard his engines and, again, no one responded to their radio calls. Growing more concerned, Davis and Lamotte sat up most of the night.

When dawn brought no Covey and no radio contact their tension grew palpable. *What the hell was going on?* Had there been some cataclysmic attack—a repeat of Tet '68—and they were on their own until the battle had subsided? Could they have been forgotten?

In full daylight, Davis could see that their overnight position wasn't defensible—they had to move. But hardly had they left than signal shots rang out, just 200 yards behind them. Now they had to keep going to shake off their trackers. For the next two hours they moved evasively, but every time they seemed to lose the trackers, more signal shots rang out. Then they heard movement on a flank and had to steer away from it.

Before long, inexorably, Davis and Lamotte realized they were being steered toward a low ridge. They hurried there and found large fallen trees that offered good cover from rifle fire, but beyond the crest the jungle opened into expansive grassland and old slash-and-burn fields. They couldn't go back the way they'd come and now forward movement was all but impossible. Their only option, Davis decided, was to hide among the downed trees.

At noon Lamotte again failed to make radio contact. Then, at the limits of his vision, he caught glimpses of NVA. Anxiety built among their Chinese Nungs. Davis shifted two of them outward as early warning. Lamotte activated his emergency radio beeper, which could be received on any passing aircraft. No one responded.

Then Davis and Lamotte sat against a log to weigh alternatives; their best, they reaffirmed, was to stay hidden until night, then slip away in the dark. Lamotte had never been in a heavy firefight so Davis joked that this was all part of his "master plan," to get Jim the proper experience he needed to take over the team. Davis whispered, "You know, if someone doesn't take a shot at you soon, I'm gonna take a shot at you just so you know what it feels like." Lamotte chuckled.

Then their tail gunner, On, scurried toward them on all-fours, anxiety etched on his face, and Lok, a grenadier, held his hand to his throat to signal, "Enemy in sight." Before Lamotte could turn—*gunfire, gunfire everywhere!* Something hit Lamotte hard in his back, throwing him facedown into the dirt. Beside him, he heard Ricardo Davis call, "Jim!"

On two sides, NVA stormed toward them firing AKs. Lamotte fired one magazine, ejected the empty magazine, reloaded, let the bolt fly forward and nothing happened. Correcting the jam seemed to take forever. He glanced at Davis and knew his friend was dead, killed instantly by a round to the head though several bullets had struck him. Multiple bullets should have killed Lamotte, too, but all four rounds had hit his pack and its radio, rendering it useless. Their tail gunner, On, had been hit in the initial burst, while Lok, too, was hit, but not so badly.

Now Lamotte was really afraid. If the enemy's first bursts had been placed so well, and they were clever enough to have inched their way hundreds of yards without detection, then these had to be special counter-recon troops. What chance did Lamotte stand, with no radio and half the team wounded or dead?

Firing tapered off, then stopped. Then Lamotte thought he was hearing things: In perfect American English, an NVA shouted, "Hey, you don't have a chance! Why don't you just surrender?" Lamotte's pent-up anger, frustration, and fear overcame good sense—he jumped to his feet, screamed, "Fuck you, bastards!" and fired his CAR-15. The NVA returned fire and Lok and Sang crawled to Lamotte. The NVA voice screamed for a cease-fire, things quieted down. Then the voice called to the Nungs, in Vietnamese, "Surrender the Americans! You can go free!" Lamotte looked to his Nungs, who scowled defiantly and shook their heads.

With the team radio destroyed, Lamotte checked his survival radio only to find its antenna had been shot off. But that made little difference since there was no one to communicate with anyhow. He left it lying there. The wounded On moaned. Lamotte crawled to him and saw that the Nung had been paralyzed by a spinal wound; bleeding from the mouth, he would not live much longer. That recognition made Lamotte shake so badly that it was difficult holding steady the morphine syrette to inject his teammate so he could die in peace.

Then Lamotte and the Nungs talked and agreed they were all going to die, and for a moment they huddled together and wept for Davis and On. Then the NVA started shooting and an enemy squad began inching closer. Lok was hit again, in his forearm—he couldn't fire his M-79 anymore. Lamotte saw they had to move or the NVA would have them completely encircled. The only remaining cover before the immense clearing was another cluster of logs. He looked to Ricardo Davis's body and felt overpowering guilt about leaving him behind—but it was go or die.

Rolling and firing, then crawling on hands and knees, Lamotte and the

Nungs hurried the fifty feet to the last logs. They caught their wind in a moment of silence. Then an NVA machine gun burst spurred both Lamotte and Lok to leap behind an inch-wide twig, and they bumped heads. They looked at each other and that tiny twig and had to laugh despite the enemy fire. All of them laughed and that momentary euphoria wiped away their fear.

They were ready to die.

Lamotte positioned the Nungs, counted his remaining magazines and grenades to decide how best to expend them—then he heard a tiny, tinny voice—"Roger, Mayday! Roger, Mayday!" Miraculously, Sang had brought along the discarded survival radio and got it transmitting by pinching the snapped antenna together. The radio urged, "Beeper, beeper, come up voice!" Lamotte knew he should switch the radio to voice mode, but he couldn't—*he'd already made up his mind to fight and die and join Ricardo.*

But survival instinct compelled him to snatch it up, whispering, "Prairie Fire! We have a Prairie Fire Emergency." Momentarily he heard the FAC's engines, joined almost immediately by the roar of F-4 Phantoms. For the first time that day they stood a chance.

Lamotte wedged his men between the logs and brought in the F-4s right across their position, the 20mm Vulcan cannons groaning and churning up the ground everywhere and knocking branches off trees. Repeated strafing runs convinced the NVA to pull back slightly, even as more fighters began stacking up overhead.

For four hours, fighter-bombers strafed, rocketed, and bombed the North Vietnamese encircling RT Copperhead. Then the Jolly Greens arrived. The first extraction attempt failed—NVA fire so badly damaged the HH-3 that it had to turn back immediately for Nakhon Phanom. Under the cover of more bombing, Lamotte tried to fight his way back to Ricardo's body but the NVA would yield no ground. Guilt overrode him, knowing Ricardo's body would not be coming out.

At least he could make sure that Lok, who'd been wounded twice saving Lamotte's life, would make it. As another Jolly Green neared the LZ, Lamotte carried Lok piggyback beneath the protective tracer fire of the helicopter door gunners. His two other Nungs hustled aboard, then lifted Lok off Lamotte's shoulders. But Lamotte couldn't climb aboard; he had to go back for Ricardo or die fighting in the attempt.

A door gunner jumped out and wrestled him onto the helicopter. Then they flew away.

During the long flight back, he agonized about how he'd done all that he could, but Ricardo was gone forever. Had it not been for "The Conversation," he could not have lived with himself. Not long after he'd joined RT Copperhead, Davis had hollered, "You dumb fuck, if you ever get killed trying to recover my body, I'll come back and haunt you!" They joked about it, but they agreed. And they meant it.

Not long after that mission, Martha Raye revisited CCN and came to the Bamboo Lounge in search of her singing partner, Ricardo Davis. She saw Jim Lamotte and asked about his teammate; he told her Ricardo had been killed and his body left behind. This time Maggie didn't join those singing "Hey, Blue." She just excused herself from the table and left.

Lamotte found her outside, alone, weeping for Ricardo as she'd undoubtedly wept privately for other lost men. Ever the stage professional, Raye stayed out there with Lamotte until, composure restored, she could return with him to grin and sing and laugh, and bring the men the psychological boost they needed. "She was a very compassionate lady," Lamotte said.

Across SOG and across Special Forces, word of Ricardo's loss stunned and saddened his friends. At Kontum, we lifted glasses to his fine memory, and those who knew him best sang "Hey, Blue." SOG headquarters never offered a satisfactory explanation of why RT Copperhead had been left on its own, with no communications and no Covey flyovers. Somewhere between NKP, Da Nang, and Saigon, there had been a failure to coordinate, or confusion about who was to monitor RT Copperhead. In a continuing war with more men dying weekly and more missions to run, there was simply too much happening to dwell long on what had passed and could not be changed, however tragic.

And then, at SOG's never slowing pace, only four days after Ricardo's death, my team was assigned another mission, which put me in the back seat of an O-1 Bird Dog spotter plane on a brilliant March afternoon over the Laotian-Cambodian border. Chugging along a quarter-mile behind an identical O-1 carrying my One-Zero, Ben Thompson, my plane buffeted in low-level thermals as I got the lay of the land on a visual reconnaissance, or VR, of our new target area.

I sat on a simple canvas seat, the O-1's back windows hooked overhead so I could look upon the passing countryside or, as many recon men were wont to do, fire my weapon or toss grenades if we spotted enemy soldiers. My pilot, an Army captain belonging to the 219th Aviation Company, chewed on a sandwich as we flew, completely at ease in these unfriendly skies. The 219th pilots were nicknamed "SPAFs" because these initials (meaning, "Sneaky Pete Air Force") were stenciled on the stolen jeeps we gave them. Flying exclusively for SOG, they relayed team radio messages, transported SOG photographers, or, as today, flew recon men on VRs. Typically they flew in pairs so that should one be shot down, his wingman could summon helicopters to rescue him.

Beneath us the scenery ran from monotonous to spectacular—bamboo forests, wild rivers, waterfalls, lush buttes towering above fog-shrouded valleys. I felt hostile eyes though we drew no fire. My pilot explained, "They won't shoot unless we get too close to something—good fire discipline." He doubted we'd see any NVA traveling the road. "They wear lots of leaves, like walking bushes. If we catch 'em in the open they squat and freeze so they'll look like a tree stump. Look for a man, you'll never see one; look for clumps of bushes or movement."

I saw no NVA but lots of bomb craters, everywhere. Most were fresh, reflecting the Air Force's latest interdiction campaign. President Johnson's bombing halt on North Vietnam a few months earlier had given enemy convoys a bomb-free run from the Haiphong dockyards to the Laotian frontier. With bombing suspended in the North, thousands of air strikes had shifted to the Laotian Ho Chi Minh Trail. Of course, the North Vietnamese adjusted, too, transferring thousands of antiaircraft guns into Laos, making the Trail corridor the most heavily defended terrain on earth.

Yet, once enemy trucks reached the Cambodian border, where we flew, as surely as an umpire waving his hands above a runner sliding into home, they were safe in "neutral" territory, immune from air attacks. What made sense to diplomats in Washington seemed preposterous in that O-1. Out one side of the aircraft—bomb craters stretched to the horizon. Out the other side—southward—the road disappeared into lushly forested Cambodia, not a bomb crater in sight.

In five days, we would go beneath those trees, and if we ran into trouble, not one U.S. fighter plane could come to our aid. Those were the rules.

Somewhere below, within sound of our engine, the NVA had hidden a battalion of artillery with which they continued to bomb Ben Het Special Forces Camp, some ten miles east. Well apprised of U.S. policy, the North Vietnamese knew their guns would not be bombed by U.S. planes in "neutral" Cambodia. That was our mission: to find those guns. Yet flying low over this heavy jungle I could scarcely keep track on my map. Every hill looked the same, every narrow valley a repeat of the last; I may as well have been looking over the side of a boat, trying to see beneath the waves. Our O-1s turned back to South Vietnam.

Ten minutes later we passed the bright clay hills of Ben Het Special Forces Camp, where four long-barreled 175mm guns, belonging to the U.S. Army's 6th Battalion, 14th Field Artillery, pointed westward. Ben Thompson already had met the artillerymen face-to-face. Neither the camp's Special Forces team nor the artillery unit had been briefed on SOG's top secret cross-border missions; all they knew was that if our team called for artillery, they were to fire, even into Cambodia, a retaliatory measure inexplicably approved in Washington. Ben Het's 175mm guns could reach twenty-one miles, the longest-range artillery in the U.S. inventory, but they also were the least accurate. This weapon's circular error probable (CEP) of 110 yards—considering its 100-yard bursting radius—meant that by the time you called it within 100 yards of yourself, it was as likely to hit you as your target. But 175s were better than nothing.

Our counter-artillery mission actually had begun three weeks earlier, when RT Texas killed one NVA and captured another near Highway 110 on the Cambodian-Laotian border. One-Zero David Gilmer, One-One Richard Nowak, and One-Two Clarence Long got their man out alive, and soon he was telling Saigon interrogators that he belonged to an artillery-carrying party. The prisoner and several dozen comrades were manhandling the guns bombarding Ben Het, hand-dragging them or dismantling and carrying them between carefully camouflaged firing positions.

Based upon the prisoner's information, RT California—with One-Zero Joe Walker and One-One Richard Gross—infiltrated northeast Cambodia to look for the hidden guns. After a fruitless first day, they were walking a heavily jungled ridgeline when the ground shook and they heard a heavy gun's roar. Soon they came upon a trench filled with expended 85mm artillery brass. The gun couldn't be much farther, Walker knew, so he radioed Covey.

He was instructed to pull back into an adjacent valley and secure an LZ. The next morning, RT Wyoming, with One-Zero Squirrel Sprouse and One-One John Peterson and six Montagnards, landed, giving Walker enough men to raid the artillery position.

For two days they listened to the distant gun firing, gradually slipping past other NVA and climbing uphill to get above the cannon. Then, before dawn, they came sneaking down, steadily, quietly, toward where they'd last heard it fire. That morning the gun never fired, and at first, when they reached a one-lane dirt road and still hadn't found the artillery piece, Walker wondered if they'd become disoriented.

Then Gross took a closer look at the slope beside the road—to his astonishment, not twenty feet away were two immense doors, fashioned from bamboo and plastered over with mud, so perfectly camouflaged that they'd walked right past them. "It was fantastic," Gross said. "The thing was so well camouflaged that we stumbled on it purely by accident."

By human tracks and scrapes, Walker could see where the NVA had taken away the gun by hand, a monumental task that he estimated required about forty-five men. Like slaves building the Pyramids, they'd lashed ropes to the gun and pushed and tugged it from the tunnel and, evidenced by the scrapes, taken it to another position or to a road where a truck could haul it.

Swinging open the twenty-foot-high bamboo doors, they saw how the artillerymen had dragged the gun out, fired, then pushed it back into the hand-hewn tunnel to hide and protect it from counter-battery fire from Ben Het. Gross crawled into a narrow hallway and found a room where the NVA had planned their fire on a map and calculated the gun's adjustments. Beyond that was another chamber with sleeping platforms where Gross found helmets, cooking pots, gas masks, and jackets, even a guitar. Walker estimated that the NVA had left the previous day, depriving him of RT California's sweetest booty—its own artillery piece, which, he insisted, he somehow could have brought back. Instead, he had to be satisfied with some 85mm shells, twelve of which he carried out as proof positive for any doubtful debriefer.

Later that day when helicopters arrived to extract Teams California and Wyoming, another team, led by Sergeant First Class Asa Ballard, landed on the same choppers to continue the hunt. Unfortunately, all the activity had attracted the NVA and within hours Ballard's men were fighting for their lives, narrowly escaping in an emergency extraction that afternoon.

Then our team, RT Illinois, was alerted to go in and find the hidden gun positions, this time with an eye toward calling U.S. 175mm artillery on them from Ben Het.

At our operations briefing, I listened keenly to the intelligence officer describe enemy forces in and near our target area. The NVA 66th Regiment had been one of those besieging Ben Het, but now it was plotted back in northeast Cambodia, presumably to refit and receive replacements. The 66th took pride in fighting Americans and would become famous as the 1st Air Cavalry Division's opposing force in the book and movie *We Were Soldiers*. Numbering approximately 2,500 infantrymen, their exact Cambodian location was unknown; all we knew with certainty was that this sizable force was somewhere in our general area.

In the S-2 intelligence office, which collects and distributes intelligence, I learned that the shells RT California brought back belonged to a D-48 Soviet 85mm gun, which could hurl its thirty-four-pound projectile ten miles. Weighing almost three tons, it was the lightest Soviet artillery piece, intended to be truck-towed. During the French Indochina War, the 85mm was a Communist favorite because, as Joe Walker had discovered, it could be manhandled into position.

George Bacon and I scoured our target folder, then studied target folders for adjacent areas to see what else we could find. Less than five miles north of our target, my first recon team, RT New Mexico, had been overrun. Other target folders disclosed more accounts, from the loss of my classmate Bill Copley to the missing Lieutenant Jim Birchim. Two thirds of teams recently going into northeast Cambodia had been forced out after contact, or "shot out," as it was called.

In January, RT Colorado had landed there, led by One-Zero Ralph Rodd, whose reddish hair, freckles, and friendly face seemed more fitting behind a drugstore counter than a CAR-15. Accompanied by Joe Parner, Craig Davis, Ken Worthley, and Dan Harvey, along with three Nungs, Rodd superbly out-witted trackers and pursuers who seemed determined to corner and kill his team. At one point, the audacious—and more numerous—NVA shouted, "Americans! We know where you are! Come down and fight us! We're ready!" Rodd was half tempted to take the challenge. That night NVA soldiers clacked bamboo around RT Colorado, like beaters trying to flush birds, but the recon men stayed quiet and avoided discovery.

The next day the game continued. In the stillness of noon, as they sat back to back eating rice, they heard an NVA tracker creeping in on them through tinder-dry bamboo sheaves, *crunch-crunch-crunch-crunch-crunch,* sounding like he was crushing potato chips. It was silent for a half-minute, then, *click*—he snapped off his AK's safety—instantly, all eight recon men snapped their safeties—*click-click-click-click-click-click-click-click.*

There followed a moment of deathly silence. And reconsideration.

Then the NVA tracker's muted *click*—followed by his ponderous *crunch-crunch-crunch-crunch* until he was gone. After chuckling at the momentary humor, Rodd's men beat feet before the tracker returned with his friends. The next day they made contact with a dog-led tracker team, killing the two han-dlers. Later, they were extracted under light ground fire.

John St. Martin's RT New York, too, had been pursued aggressively near there by NVA trackers using a dog. St. Martin knew the wet ground precluded using tear gas powder to throw off the dog so he had to improvise. Leading his men to a stream, he recalled how, in *The Last of the Mohicans,* Hawkeye had res-cued two girls from a Huron camp and escaped pursuing braves and dogs by dangling a piece of a pettitcoat on a broken branch upstream, then going the other way. St. Martin didn't have a pettitcoat so he conspicuously broke a branch and scuffed the bank as if his team had climbed from the stream, then had his men wade downstream and exit where they wouldn't leave a trace. This threw off his trackers and their dog.

George and I could see that our mission would be a hunt—RT Illinois hunting for the guns, and the NVA hunting for us.

Rearming the team with AKs dominated our pre-mission training, since State Department deniability rules precluded us from carrying American weapons into Cambodia. My Swedish-made submachine gun was just fine. At the range we practice-fired our weapons and, gaining confidence, progressed to immediate action drills, peeling off smoothly after firing against simulated NVA, then fleeing in a new direction.

On our last afternoon at Kontum, we inspected our Vietnamese soldiers to ensure their weapons were clean, all gear was packed, and magazines and canteens full. Everything looked fine, then I picked up Loi's claymore mine, which uses a C-4 charge to propel a pattern of deadly steel balls, very much like a shotgun. Oddly, his claymore felt unbalanced—then I noticed pry marks on its seam so I pulled it apart. Half the C-4 was gone. Sabotage? I wanted to choke Loi, but Ben calmly noticed Loi's half-grin and waved a finger at him. "He burned the C-4 to heat rations," Ben explained, then demonstrated how a marble-size C-4 ball emitted enough flame to boil a cup of water. Solomon-like, instead of disciplining Loi, Ben gave each man a block of C-4 so no one would disable his claymore—and we'd have extra explosives along on the mission.

The morning of our insertion, we donned sterile jungle fatigues and disposed of all our ID in the unit safe. My burdensome rucksack slumped me forward like an old man as we walked to the helipad, where, one by one, we test-fired our weapons into a sand-filled 55-gallon drum, taped the muzzle to protect the barrel, then boarded our Hueys.

Early that afternoon at Dak To, our helicopters lifted away with Ben, George, Suu, Hai, and Binh in the first aircraft, and myself, Loi, and Lam in the second, followed by four empty Hueys and four Cobras. In five minutes we could see Ben Het Special Forces Camp and, 1,000 yards to the west, two knocked-out enemy tanks from the failed NVA attack three weeks earlier. Here we banked left, toward Cambodia. As we flew up the Dak Klong River Valley, we passed patterns of fresh B-52 craters, then, at the valley's western edge, we overflew Hill 875, where hundreds of Americans had died in intense fighting in 1967. Beyond that ridge, not five miles away, the bomb craters stopped and there loomed the low hills of Cambodia.

Momentarily our formation went into a wide left orbit; then, two of the Hueys—Ben's bird and my own—began a spiral descent. Sitting in the open doorway, I experienced a sickening, sinking feeling—butterflies spiraled downward into my gut, the anxiety rising as our altitude declined until, feeling the jungle's humidity, I knew we were within range of hidden men wielding AKs, listening for the sound of our approach.

Now below the hilltops, along with the door gunners I aimed my weapon slightly ahead, as each spot that might conceal a gunman came into view, tracked on it as we rushed past, then picked up the next suspicious spot, watching for a muzzle flash, movement, any sign of hostility. Like the earlier O-1 flight, at such low altitude I couldn't tell where we were—I saw only indistinct trees and ridges. Somewhere ahead, I knew Ben and George's Huey was landing; my helicopter would find its way there.

Then our pilot banked hard—were it not for centrifugal force Lam and I would have slid out—and I realized we were turning in. This was the final run-in, the LZ lay just ahead. Suddenly a Cobra gunship appeared ahead of us, escorting us the last half-mile.

My eyes stayed on the Swedish K's sights until the rotor's downwash pushed aside the LZ grass, then I glanced down and jumped out, my Vietnamese teammates jumping with me. We trotted toward the closest wood line in the direction of the Huey's nose, as Ben had trained us; the grinding, whining aircraft lifted away, swirling the foliage around us, but we didn't even look up, hurrying toward cover, shadows, and safety. Slightly off to one side, George waved and we formed a defensive semicircle around Ben and the radio.

A moment ago, high in the air, it was a busy world of unlimited horizons. Now, it was just our silent team, the buzzing insects almost washing away the sound of Covey's engines, the horizon shrunk to a green curtain a few yards away. Like the previous mission, we hid beside the LZ for about ten minutes, then Ben radioed Covey a "Team OK," releasing the choppers—and off we went.

As assistant team leader I was tail gunner, the last American in our column, responsible, among other things, to erase evidence of our passage. The damp soil beside our LZ made that all but impossible, though soon we were on firmer ground and, thankfully, my spine was accustomed to my heavy load so I could walk erect again. For an hour, Ben kept us at a steady, moderate pace to get away from the LZ, then slowed to a deliberate gait for better stealth.

As tail gunner my attention focused on our backtrail and possible trackers. With the help of Loi and Lam, I reinterwove foliage where it had been pushed aside, smoothed over scrapes, and, every five steps or so, looked back for any sign of movement.

That afternoon we heard a distant shot but George shook his head unconcernedly, meaning it wasn't a tracker's signal shot—probably an NVA hunting monkeys or wild pigs. Relaying George's expression to Lam—who understood instantly—I began to see I did not need one audible word to warn of danger, or to indicate directions, to express hunger or thirst, to signify a number, to tell someone to run or stop or freeze. We would go like this for days, growing so accustomed to not speaking that a normal voice startled as much as a gunshot.

Our first night proved uneventful. We heard no artillery and no indicator of the enemy except a few faraway shots probably having nothing to do with us. Inspecting our sleeping site the next morning, I found crushed plants and leaves where our men had lain; I did my best to erase our sign.

A couple of hours later we were halted on a hillside for an hourly break when—KA-POW!—a signal shot cracked behind us, perhaps 200 yards. I signed to Ben, recommending that I booby-trap our unwanted shadowers, to which Ben nodded his assent. With George covering, I fell back to hide a claymore mine, then rigged it with flashlight batteries, a clothespin, and trip wire, leaving a crushed cigarette pack to lure the trackers across the dull green wire.

Forty-five minutes later, we were climbing the next hill when, "W-O-O-O-O-M!" My claymore. While Ben put the team in a defensive perimeter, George and I crept back with great hopes of capturing a wounded tracker. Our boldness evaporated 100 yards later when voices called to one another from two directions—at least several squads, probably thirty men. Silently we backed off, then rejoined the team, careful to leave no tracks. Thanks to Ben's expert evasive movement, we saw and heard no more trackers. And like the first day, we heard no artillery firing.

Late that afternoon, Ben took special care selecting our overnight position, putting us on a steep eastern hillside facing Ben Het, about twelve miles away, so we had communication directly with the artillery battery there. The 50 degree slope offered thick undergrowth in all directions, making it difficult for the enemy to sweep toward us, and, situated some 200 yards below the crest, we were beyond the range of grenades thrown from the top. Huddled together on the downhill side of a six-foot-wide tree, we could squeeze seven men—*but we had eight men.* Since I was tail gunner, Ben decided, I would sleep, alone, on the uphill side of the tree. I put out my claymore facing uphill while the others put their claymores to our flanks and downhill. Ben radioed our end-of-day situation report to Covey.

Just before dark, I unrolled my ground cloth and sleeping bag against the tree, then munched a rice ration, my Swedish K submachine gun resting on my lap. A light rain began to fall.

About 8:00 P.M., an hour after sunset, I was almost asleep when I thought I heard something uphill. I couldn't say it was a bump or a cough or a footstep—it was *something.* I sat up quietly, turned my head toward the sound, and cradled my Swedish K. What was it? I held my eyes shut, reopened them and saw no difference in such complete pitch-blackness.

There was another sound, about the same distance uphill, but more off to one side, indistinct, like leaves rustling. This wasn't the random falling of a leaf but a pattern, however vague, a subtlety that reminded me of a Minnesota deer trying to slip past me—tenuous, testing, halting, listening, smelling. Or in the undertone of light rain, *was it nothing?*

Again, a rustle—a branch bending, compressed, sliding against something, maybe thirty yards uphill. This was not my imagination. Delicately, I slid sideways, leaned my head around the tree, and slowly whispered to Ben, "Movement—up here."

"Yeah," he whispered back. "I'm getting on the radio." I heard his poncho rustle as he pulled it over his head to muffle his voice; pressed low against the tree, he whispered into the radio. We stood little chance of slipping away without detection. It was better to lie tight and, Ben decided, to call artillery.

Another noise—the crunch of a dried branch, only fifteen yards away. Any second I expected the *bang-whoosh-bang* of incoming RPG fire. Was this how my teammates on RT New Mexico had died? I imagined an RPG gunner there, rocket loaded, ready to fire, pointing it at me. I could not muffle my pounding heart.

From behind the tree, I heard Ben's voice—then George's low, "Sh-h-h!"

I'd had time to think—fear set in. My hands trembled. That impenetrable blackness reminded me of a hiding game we played as children in my parents' basement. We'd squeeze behind an old sofa or under the laundry tub, and another child, growling like a monster, would come hunt us in the dark. As then, I felt alone and trapped in the blackness, on the uphill side of that immense tree, unable now even to whisper. My heart raced. Should I fire my Swedish K? Detonate my claymore?

I speculated on what had happened. Somewhere uphill a tracker had crossed our backtrail, they'd calculated we couldn't go much farther before dark, then they'd formed up along the ridge and swept downward. They planned to drive us downhill, then fire at us from the high ground. If we ran noisily right or left, their entire line would fire into us. They knew exactly what they were doing.

Then, high overhead—*wo-wo-wo-wo-woosh*—*B-O-O-O-O-M!* At last, the first 175mm shell impacted, but it was hundreds of yards west of us, completely over the top of the ridge. Ben would have to adjust by sound, an inexact, slow process—complicated by the gun's inaccuracy and our enemy's proximity.

Could I shoot and run? No, I was too close to too many NVA; probably ten men now crouched within a dozen yards, and their first AK bursts would focus on my muzzle flash. That realization made my knees shake, and the more I thought about it, the more my whole body shook. What had Howard told me? *No matter how bad a situation, you have to ask yourself, "What do I do now?"* That's how I regained control, asking myself what next to do. I gave up trying to make out the approaching NVA, and shut my eyes so I could listen better.

Wo-wo-wo-woosh—BOOM! Another shell hit perhaps 500 yards beyond the NVA.

If I had to fight alone, I told myself, that would draw the enemy from my teammates, and in the confusion, after blowing their claymores, most of them might escape. But I would not escape.

The NVA's low Vietnamese voices were discernible now, quick whispers and labored breathing. Within twenty feet, I guessed, there must be four, maybe six of them. Overall, probably a platoon of forty or fifty. They listened for an endless minute, then edged two steps closer with more leaf rustling as they adjusted. Will they find my claymore? That was irrelevant now—they were closer than my claymore.

Another 175mm round crashed above us, maybe 200 yards away.

It was time to ready a grenade, better yet, two grenades. Quietly, ever so slowly, I straightened two grenade pins, then held one upside down so I could pull both pins simultaneously. In the two minutes it took to do this, the NVA had stepped still closer, not a dozen feet away—so close that my grenades were useless. With excruciating patience, I laid aside the grenades, the nearest NVA now so close I could almost touch him. I considered pulling my razor-sharp Gerber Mk II stiletto; I'd extend my left hand to touch him, then stab him hard and deep in a kidney so the pain paralyzed him. No—his comrades would hear his falling body or dying groan and they'd be on me. The knife offered no advantage.

No matter what I did, I finally accepted, I had only minutes to live. My mind swam with regrets, the bad things I'd done to people, good things I'd never gotten around to doing, and the people I'd never see again. Finally, remorsefully, I accepted my imminent death and with that my fear evaporated. A calmness settled over me, I could think clearer than before.

Another 175mm shell sailed past supersonically, then, *WHOOM!*—I felt the ground shake and heard fragments tear through trees above us. Dirt clods fell like hailstones. With this shell hitting less than 150 yards away, even with no adjustment the next 175mm round was as liable to hit us as the NVA, but that didn't bother me.

I resolved to fire my Swedish K, shooting as many as I could. Even with the silencer, the sound of my bolt recoiling—*clack-clack-clack-clack*—would draw their RPGs and I'd be killed. Maybe I'd last long enough to blow my claymore. Well, fuck it, that's all right. I just hoped it wouldn't hurt too much.

By now Ben couldn't chance whispering on the radio anymore—the entire team was flanked on two sides by alert NVA, listening for our slightest sound. Somewhere below me, I knew, George held his claymore firing device and a grenade. I sat there, my Swedish K leveled at the nearest NVA, my finger on the trigger, waiting.

Another 175mm round crashed into the hillside, spewing fragments everywhere. Then the rain became a steady downpour.

The nearest NVA crept three more paces—and I realized he was past me. The whole line of NVA, extending fifty yards right and left of us, likewise crept forward, then they were past our entire team. In this heavy rain, complicated by darkness and falling artillery, the NVA had completely missed us. And now, abandoning any pretense of stealth, they gave up, they quit, they just plain walked the rest of the way downhill, coughing and talking.

Inside of two minutes I couldn't even hear them anymore. Ben halted the 175mm fire. The rest of the night we slept little but heard not one suspicious sound.

With dawn's light I noticed that tape still covered my muzzle to protect the bore from mud and water. I'd never been so close to death, yet I'd fired not one shot. Those eternal five minutes, listening to the whispered voices of men bent on finding and killing me, etched onto my psyche. Never again would I sleep securely on a mission; the slightest sound would flash me instantly from sleep to heart-pounding-in-my-throat total consciousness, a fear that served me well. I thought about how that immense tree had acted like an obstacle against a flow of water, splitting the NVA and steering them slightly right and left of our team. That's what saved us; but for Ben's choice of that spot, they would have swept upon us and by sheer numbers overwhelmed us.

When we left the position we were alert for an ambush. But nothing happened. We stayed in the target another two days and heard no signal shots, drew no trackers, and never saw another NVA. Nor did the enemy guns fire at Ben Het. It was up to the intel analysts to make sense of it, but personally, I believed enemy artillery officers had found SOG's gun hunting too close to risk, and withdrew their 85s deep into Laos, beyond our reach.

Sitting with George on the chopper coming out, looking back at the jungle that had almost swallowed my life, I accepted that I would die running recon. I didn't resist, didn't deny it, just accepted death as the logical result of great hazard and let that wash away any hope of surviving, much as I'd learned that night to fight fear by embracing doom. Fatalism became realism, an attitude that gave recon men strength; accepting inevitable death made everything easier.

Equally, we realized that if captured we would be summarily executed or tortured to death and this inspired its own black humor. Staff Sergeant Craig Davis didn't worry about long captivity; his shirt bore the boldly embroidered name tape, "Fuck You Ho Chi Minh," knowing he'd be shot as quick as the NVA got their hands on him. Jim Storter's cigarette lighter was engraved, "If you find this while searching my dead body, Fuck You!" While on operations, some men left a wad of money in the unit safe to finance their own wake; Larry White locked up his gold Rolex with instructions that it be rewarded to the Bright Light team leader for recovering his body. It was funny, but he meant it. I took delight writing quips in my notebook for the enemy intelligence officer who'd have to translate it; he'd be busily translating the dead Yankee commando's description of an NVA base camp when, without warning, he'd read, "and Ho Chi Minh fucks little fat boys." Making light of it, accepting death, made it all easier, giving us clearer vision and unfettered decision making; this also minimized the chances of self-survival concerns conflicting with what was best for the team and the mission. Putting team and mission above yourself goes with camaraderie and leadership—succumbing to fear is, after all, a form of selfishness.

Ricardo Davis and Jim Lamotte were not the only recon men to have had "The Conversation"—all recon men got around to it, almost as a ritual. After a week of shared dangers behind enemy lines, some night on stand-down— usually after a few drinks—one man would declare, "When I'm dead, don't you die trying to get out my stinking, rotting body!" His teammates would agree, they'd toast to it—nothing teary about it—and that was that, as solemn a contract as anywhere in Special Forces. George and Ben and I had "The Conversation" during our stand-down, and all agreed that we'd fight to the death or even kill ourselves rather than be taken alive. That was no death wish; on the contrary, it gave us a fuller appreciation for life.

After that brush with death in Cambodia, simple bowls of Chinese noodle soup tasted better, hot showers flowed wetter, even humor seemed funnier. So typically for SOG, one day something terrible happened, the next day the zaniness returned, people were laughing again—there was always humor aplenty. While we were on stand-down, a One-Zero objected to Bob Howard about pulling details between missions. "Today's my birthday," he griped, "and I just made sergeant first class." He thought he should have the day off. Howard shook his head and sent the man's team to the supply room to help the logistics officer, a captain.

In two hours a C-130 Blackbird was due to land cargo at Kontum and the captain didn't have time to talk. He pointed to a three-quarter-ton truck and said—let's call the One-Zero "Sergeant Smith"—"Sergeant Smith, that truck is loaded with demo too old to issue. Take it to the range and blow it up."

Smith's hurt feelings evaporated, his eyes narrowed, but the captain didn't notice. "Let me get this straight, sir. You want me to drive this truck up to the range and blow it up?" Long afterward, the gullible captain would dispute his exact response, but, indeed, he did respond, "Yes, go blow it up."

"Yesssss, sir!" Smith exclaimed, saluted, and the rest was Special Forces legend.

Two hours later the nervous captain began pacing—Smith and the truck hadn't returned from a simple, one-hour task, and he needed the truck to haul supplies from Kontum airfield. The range was a ten-minute drive, allow another twenty minutes to offload the crates of dynamite, dried-out C-4, and old mortar shells, then ten minutes to prime it and wire it—why, Sergeant Smith should have been back thirty minutes ago.

Another hour passed.

The exasperated logistics officer was walking over to the recon company orderly room to have a word with Howard when he espied Sergeant Smith's team filing through the front gate. Then Smith himself appeared. "Where's my truck?" the irate officer demanded.

Sergeant Smith assumed an innocent countenance. "Why, sir—you told me to blow it up."

The captain's face looked like his bowels had moved. "What!" he shrieked.

Heaped beneath a half-ton of explosives, that old truck had gone up like the original Big Bang—*the finest birthday promotion fireworks any Special Forces sergeant first class ever had*. And Smith had done it with such finesse that no one said a word about it, just dispatched a team to steal another truck. Henceforth, the captain was especially careful in wording instructions to recon sergeants.

As RT Illinois's week-long stand-down finished, Glenn Uemura and I iced down six cases of beer outside his RT Hawaii team room for a small celebration—our sergeant stripes had arrived.

We'd both made E-5, and surprisingly fast; it never occurred to us that accelerated promotions were the handmaiden of high battlefield casualties. That night we sang and laughed and drank. Then, not long after sunset, something in the wind caused us to turn our heads southward, listening—small arms fire, lots of it. Our camp alert siren wailed and someone shut off the power, leaving us in darkness, everyone scurrying for weapons. Ben and George ran back from the shower room, towels around their waists. "They're hitting the Yard Camp," Ben hollered. "Get the team on the wall."

We manned our alert bunkers well into the morning though no NVA stormed our wire; but that wasn't the case at the Yard Camp. Our company-size satellite Yard Camp had been attacked by some 200 NVA. The next morning George and I drove with the recon company commander, Captain Lesesne, to visit the camp, about four miles away. The two-acre compound housed a 100-man Montagnard Hatchet Force company, commanded by Captain Ronald Goulet. Everywhere, we saw fresh bullet holes and shattered buildings that had been rocked by mortar rounds—but the SOG men had repelled the NVA decisively. Not a single NVA had made it through the wire.

A handful of Montagnards had been killed and my Hatchet Force friend Henry Kramps had been slightly wounded. First Lieutenant Greg Glashauser, who'd previously served with Glenn Uemura on RT Hawaii, had fired an egg-size 40mm grenade round into an attacking NVA's head, killing him even though it didn't detonate. Though he received no high medal, no one displayed more courage that night than Sergeant Allan Farrell, who was leading a seven-man night ambush patrol outside camp when he detected two NVA platoons approaching. Farrell's critical radio warnings enabled the defenders to ready themselves and stop the assault cold. Farrell and his American teammate—abandoned by their terrified indigenous soldiers—slipped past the NVA, dodged friendly fire, and made it safely back to camp, along the way shooting up an enemy platoon that was firing at helicopter gunships.

Inspecting the wire the next morning with George, I saw the enemy's bangalore torpedoes—five-foot bamboo tubes stuffed with explosives—with which they'd intended to blow aside the concertina wire and breach the defenses. Despite their considerable handiwork, though, not a single bangalore went off, due to faulty Russian-made detonators.

All the Americans gathered in the Yard Camp's tin shack bar to salute the defenders and Captain Lesesne, who, I learned, had built the camp a year earlier, his design having contributed to their success. When glasses were lifted, though, Captain Lesesne deflected sole credit. "Actually," he said, "this camp was built as much by Mo Worley as by me."

That name—*Worley*—seemed familiar? Then it came to me: *the badly wounded NCO who'd instructed us from a chair at Fort Bragg.* I asked Lesesne about Worley and his eyes lit up. "You had Mo Worley as an instructor? Why, he got his Distinguished Service Cross right here, with this Hatchet Force company."

Over another drink, Captain Lesesne told me Worley's incredible story.

With Worley's assistance, Lesesne had recruited and trained SOG's first Montagnard Hatchet Force company at Kontum, and built the Yard Camp to house them. After months of building and training, Worley was invited by his old friend RT Nevada One-Zero Jim Lively to act as his assistant team leader for a recon mission in Laos.

They landed on 14 January 1967 near Highway 110, where they scouted a length of the road while dodging trackers. Repeatedly they discovered enclaves of NVA and watched lines of supply-laden bicycles roll past. By the fifth day, Lively's Yards were worn down so he had them extracted and, on the same LZ, a thirty-three-man Chinese Nung Hatchet Force platoon landed, led by First Lieutenant George Dias and Sergeant First Class Bob Franke. Lively and Worley were to help the Nung platoon snatch an NVA prisoner.

The next morning Worley was walking with the platoon's lead squad when he noticed that the foliage didn't look right, the jungle didn't feel right, and monkeys weren't chattering—dead calm in the jungle in early morning? Worley smelled an ambush so he deployed his Nungs left and right, laid down a base of fire, assaulted, and just where he'd sensed them, NVA began popping from behind trees and logs and ran.

Worley pressed them aggressively. "Those Chinamen will follow you into the gates of hell if they respect you," Worley believed. "But if you lie behind a tree, poke your muzzle in the air, and make sound effects, they aren't going to follow you." Worley had expended all his magazines for his Swedish K and was about to find an M-16 when, just ahead, he spotted an NVA's hair protruding above a log; he pulled his Bowie knife, boldly ran ahead, reached over and grabbed the startled soldier by the hair, pulling him to his feet. He laid that big blade along the trembling NVA's neck and whispered, "You're comin' with me." They had their prisoner.

The NVA prisoner was extracted immediately but, so typical for SOG, the platoon was left on the ground to see what else it might achieve.

The next day Worley again volunteered to take the point squad and again he thwarted an NVA attempt to ambush them. And again, astonishingly, when Worley aggressively pushed back the enemy the platoon seized another prisoner.

But by now, having twice suffered casualties and had comrades taken prisoner, the NVA launched their own assault, with soldiers as aggressive as the SOG men. Enemy fire instantly killed the three Nungs nearest to Worley. Charging the enemy, Worley shot three NVA, then an NVA leaped out and fired three AK rounds into the Green Beret's right arm, nearly severing it. Another slug tore through his face, and grenade fragments penetrated his chest cavity and legs. Somehow Worley managed to pull the damaged arm into his webbing to protect it. Just five yards away, Bob Franke couldn't even lift his head, the NVA fire was so intense, but he kept Worley supplied with grenades and ammo, lobbing it to him. Enemy grenades rolled in but Worley couldn't see them—they exploded, shredding his legs and chest with shrapnel. Then he drew his Browning pistol with his left hand, and fighting off shock, shot and killed the NVA who'd shot him, and emptied the pistol into still more NVA. Then Worley grabbed a grenade with his left hand, pulled the pin with his teeth, and tossed it, finally silencing the enemy fire.

The NVA broke and ran. Worley, weakened by his wounds and loss of blood, could not stand. His SOG comrades got him on an improvised stretcher and dragged him to an LZ. Sergeant First Class Charlie White, an enormous African-American, jumped out of a hovering H-34, lifted Worley over his head, and managed to get him into the Kingbee helicopter, where Special Forces medic John McGirt worked on him as they rushed to Dak To. (Later, Sergeant First Class White became SOG's first MIA in Cambodia when he slipped from a McGuire rig. A Bright Light team led by Medal of Honor winner Fred Zabitosky searched fruitlessly for White and came back convinced he'd been captured. White's fate remains unknown.)

Captain Lesesne told me he met the Kingbee that brought out Worley at Dak To.

I opened another beer. "So, Worley was medevaced?"

Lesesne grinned. "Not right away." The same helicopter had to go back for the endangered Nung platoon. Knowing it would take forty minutes for a medevac chopper to get there from Pleiku, then another forty minutes to fly back, Lesesne doubted Mo Worley could last that long. Lesesne ran to a Huey already cranking, about to take off. "Can you take a man to Pleiku, to the hospital?" he hollered over the whining turbine. "He's badly wounded."

The pilot was sympathetic but shook his head. "Captain, we got a full load already—supplies for a unit in the field."

Lesesne announced, "You aren't quite as loaded as you think you are," and, holding his .45 automatic pistol on the pilot, waved over the men carrying Worley. At Pleiku doctors narrowly saved the SOG man's life. The hijacked pilot, who'd have done the same for a friend, filed no complaint against Lesesne.

It was still touch-and-go when Worley arrived in the Philippines, then another three months in a Japanese hospital to gain enough strength to fly home. He spent a year at Ireland Army Hospital in Fort Knox, Kentucky, far from his Special Forces friends, under constant pressure to amputate his hand, install a hand-shaped prosthetic device, and accept a medical discharge. "If you cut my hand off," the cantankerous NCO insisted, "I want a stainless steel hook on that son-of-a-bitch."

"Why?" a doctor asked.

Worley's face gleamed strangely. "Can't you see me, walking down Broadway in New York City, with my green beret on—*and a steel hook!*"

That twisted humor got him an appointment with a psychiatrist, who asked, "Why are you fighting this amputation so hard?"

"Well, doc," Worley offered insincerely, "my hand just fills out my sleeve so well."

Eventually the medical staff rebuilt his hand and arm, installing a steel rod and transplanting a tibia from his leg. It worked—or, at least for a man like Worley, he'd make it work. Stuck in Ireland Hospital with no release in sight, Worley phoned his best friend, Special Forces Sergeant Major Robert K. Miller. Could he get him reassigned to Fort Bragg? "Any job," Worley pleaded, "anywhere, as long as it's Special Forces." A few days later, that big, gruff sergeant major, in spit-shined paratrooper boots and a Class A uniform with a chestful of combat ribbons from World War II, Korea, and Vietnam, topped by a green beret, strutted into Ireland Army Hospital and announced to the young medical detachment commander, "Captain, *I'm* taking Worley."

"I cannot possibly allow that," the officer insisted. Miller snatched up the captain's phone and dialed Mrs. Billy Alexander, the Special Forces Assignment Supervisor at the Pentagon. He spoke a few words, then handed the phone to him. And that was that.

When Sergeant Major Miller rolled Worley's wheelchair outside, there was no waiting ambulance or taxi—Miller had driven his own car all the way from Fort Bragg. They drove overnight, back to the home of Special Forces, where Worley received the Distinguished Service Cross, the decoration second only to the Medal of Honor. Worley should have been convalescing in a hospital but he insisted upon full duty, and that was where I met him, heavily bandaged, propped up in a chair, instructing our class on methods of instruction. He was a hell of soldier.

With Lesesne's story finished, I looked around the little shanty barroom where men drank and listened to country-western tunes. I felt nothing but admiration for all of them, and honored to be in their company. What would unfold next? I had no clue.

But even as we drank and laughed, B-52 bomber crews on Guam were readying for a new, secret aerial offensive, whose existence would be denied for years. The debriefing from our Cambodia mission had been added to a tall stack of similar reports, documenting the heavy NVA occupation of "neutral" territory, and finally, the Nixon administration decided to act. In days the immunity would end, with whole waves of B-52s secretly bombing the sanctuaries.

To support the clandestine raids, SOG would dispatch recon teams to assess the strikes. In northeast Cambodia, the very first team to go in on a B-52 strike would be RT Illinois.

And this time I would not return with tape covering my weapon's muzzle.

Chapter Six

There was no doubt in Captain Randy Harrison's mind that thousands of North Vietnamese troops infested Cambodia's Fishhook, a heavily jungled twenty-mile wedge where the border jutted into South Vietnam. As SOG's assistant launch officer at the Quan Loi launch site, Harrison had watched team after team board helicopters to infiltrate the Fishhook sanctuary, some seventy-five miles northwest of Saigon, only to be forced out or overrun by aggressive enemy reaction forces. A former recon company commander at SOG's southernmost cross-border unit—Ban Me Thuot–based Command and Control South—Harrison was hardly your typical staff officer. While recon commander, he had accompanied several teams behind enemy lines to see how they performed, including one desperate mission for which the Huey pilot who extracted them, First Lieutenant Jim Fleming, received the Medal of Honor.

Nor was Captain Harrison exactly deskbound at the Quan Loi launch site. Often he followed the insertion helicopters aboard an Army O-1 Bird Dog, just to watch teams go in and to listen to them on the radio. Thus, he knew the area and he knew the mission.

So when a pair of inexperienced Saigon staff officers arrived at Quan Loi on 17 March to direct the insertion of a recon team into the Fishhook the next day, Harrison could barely conceal his disdain. "I was pissed because that's what I had been doing day in and day out for months," he explained. Just two weeks earlier, the North Vietnamese had chased, cornered, and overrun an entire team in the Fishhook, killing Sergeant William Evans, Specialist Five Michael May, and their indigenous soldiers. Their bodies had not been recovered.

And only the previous day Harrison had extracted another hotly pursued team—with First Lieutenant Bill Ortman III and Specialist Five Barry Murphy—barely managing to get them out under heavy ground fire. And now the Saigon newcomers were in such a rush to insert a team that they'd persuaded Ortman to go back into the Fishhook, allowing his team hardly twenty-four hours to rearm and prepare. But this time there was a difference: *Their landing would be preceded by the concentrated bombardment of four dozen B-52 bombers.* That meant nearly 5,000 500-pound bombs. This first-ever strike into Cambodia was very secret, very compartmented, and, Harrison thought, very asinine—Ortman's men would be landing among thousands of craters, yet, should they need air support, the old State Department rules still applied—they could receive no fighter support, only helicopter gunships.

Despite the hectic pace, the BDA mission (bomb damage assessment) could not have been entrusted to a more devoted One-Zero. Harrison knew Lieutenant Ortman as "very gutsy, very smart," and "a can-do guy." If anyone could do it, Ortman could.

It was the Saigon officers' impetuousness that bothered Harrison, who didn't realize their impatient demands had begun twenty-four hours earlier with a rush order directly from the White House. The previous morning, Secretary of State William Rogers, Secretary of Defense Melvin Laird, Joint Chiefs Chairman General Earle Wheeler, and National Security Advisor Henry Kissinger had joined President Nixon to review SOG's extensive documentation of enemy sanctuaries in Cambodia. The newly inaugurated President Nixon wanted a bold gesture to distinguish his policies from those of the Johnson administration, which had virtually ignored Hanoi's use of neutral Cambodian territory. And having just witnessed a month-long enemy offensive that had killed more than 1,000 Americans despite the ongoing peace talks in Paris, Nixon felt it high time to strike, both for combat effect and to send an unambiguous message to Hanoi. What more fitting target than the Fishhook, thought to contain two or more enemy divisions, at least 25,000 soldiers? For purposes of diplomacy, however, there would be no announcement in Washington or Saigon, no acknowledgment at all unless Cambodia's ruler, Prince Sihanouk, protested the attack—which was unlikely because no Cambodians lived in the sanctuary. Only the B-52 pilots and navigators would know where their bombs fell, cutting the chance of leaks to nearly zero.

President Nixon ordered the raid executed immediately, as quickly as B-52 crews on Guam and in Thailand could be briefed. As an afterthought, it was decided to task SOG with sending in a team to assess what certainly would be catastrophic destruction.

That team, led by Lieutenant Ortman, stood by their choppers the following morning at Quan Loi while four dozen B-52 bombers slightly overflew their official target on South Vietnam's border, then dumped nearly 1,300 tons of bombs into NVA base camps three miles inside the Fishhook. As they prepared to launch, Captain Harrison asked the Saigon officers, "Can I help? Is there anything you want me to do?" They all but ignored him.

Then Harrison noticed an O-1 pilot, a friend with whom he'd flown before, watching the 195th Assault Helicopter Company Hueys and their escort gunships lift away. The Bird Dog pilot offered, "Wanna go up and watch?"

"Hell, yes!" Harrison replied, and jumped in his plane to follow the choppers northwest. As the formation neared the border, they could see smoke rising ahead of them in the Fishhook. Aerial observers already had counted seventy-three secondary explosions, meaning the bombs had to have struck a major enemy concentration.

Faint smoke rose everywhere as the insertion chopper descended into the landing zone, one indistinguishable crater amid a sea of fresh craters. Sitting in the Bird Dog's back seat, Captain Harrison watched Ortman, Murphy, and their four Montagnards jump off the helicopter. It lifted away.

Then all hell broke loose.

Intense fire erupted from several directions, splitting the team, forcing Ortman and the Yards to go one way and Murphy the other, leaping into bomb craters to fight for their lives. As the gunships rolled in to help, an AK slug burst a white phosphorus grenade on Ortman's rucksack, setting fire to everything within five yards, including the young officer. Severely burned, he'd probably have died there but for his loyal Montagnards, who fought the enemy and prepared their team leader for extraction. Fighting from his own crater, Murphy was able to direct the gunships but he couldn't move. A courageous Huey pilot whisked through heavy fire to extract Ortman and the Yards.

Harrison heard Murphy's voice on the radio, still shooting, pinned in a bomb crater. Then a terrible groan—Murphy was hit. And hit again. And again. The young Green Beret shouted once into the radio, then it went dead. Intense ground fire drove away the helicopters. (SOG records indicate that another CCS man was killed the same day, Sergeant First Class Margarito Fernandez, Jr., who may have accompanied Ortman's mission into the Fishhook.)

Murphy's body was not recovered. His One-Zero, Bill Ortman, was evacuated to the States, where he required extensive surgery. The B-52 strike was an eye-opener for Harrison. "My father was an Air force pilot and I was under the distinct impression that nothing could survive a B-52 strike," he said. "Sometimes they're effective," he concluded, "and sometimes they aren't."

This strike was effective, the Air Force believed, since the team had encountered troops directly where the bombs had impacted. Not considered, however, was the possibility that the enemy had somehow obtained advance warning and put its troops safely underground, only to reemerge to attack Ortman's team.

Afterward, Prince Sihanouk voiced no protest. Nor did Hanoi say a word—and how could it? The North Vietnamese had always insisted they had no troops in Cambodia. That the outside world learned nothing of the massive Cambodian strike was unsurprising, but most of us in SOG heard nothing, too, verifying how compartmented the information about the bombing had been.

Though word did not reach us of that strike, one month later we did hear about the second B-52 raid. All of Special Forces heard about it.

With no progress in the deadlocked Paris talks, President Nixon had approved a second B-52 raid, this time against a Cambodian target proposed by General Creighton Abrams, the commander of U.S. forces, and Ambassador Ellsworth Bunker: COSVN, the Central Office for South Vietnam, the Vietcong's political and military headquarters. This time the number of attacking bombers would be doubled—ninety-eight B-52s—and instead of sending in a six-man recon team, a CCS Hatchet Force company would perform the bombing assessment.

At CCS, the BDA mission fell upon its most accomplished man, that living legend known to all of Special Forces—Sergeant First Class Jerry "Mad Dog" Shriver. *Mad Dog!* At Fort Bragg no one mentioned SOG but everyone had heard of Jerry Shriver, dubbed a "mad dog" by Radio Hanoi. Now into his third year in SOG, Mad Dog Shriver had practically gone native, preferring the company of his Montagnards and his German shepherd, Klaus, to that of most Americans. He cared not one whit about medals, though he'd been awarded a Silver Star, five Bronze Stars, and the Soldier's Medal. And he was phenomenally adept in the jungle. "He was like having a dog you could talk to," Captain Bill O'Rourke, the Hatchet Force commander, explained. "He could hear and sense things; he was more alive in the woods than any other human being I've ever met."

Among the dozen Americans accompanying Shriver on the COSVN mission was an old Boy Scout friend from Minneapolis, Lieutenant Greg Harrigan, whom I'd not yet found a chance to visit at CCS.

On the morning of 24 April 1969, a half-hour after the last of the ninety-eight high-flying B-52s dumped their loads on COSVN, the Hatchet Force company launched from Quan Loi. Twenty minutes later, descending into incredible devastation, the choppers dropped off the seventy men and climbed away.

Again, an instant killing zone.

From everywhere, automatic weapons and RPGs pounded the SOG men, pinning them in craters right on the LZ. Sergeant Ernest Jamison dashed out to retrieve a wounded man; heavy fire cut him down, killing him on the spot. On the far side of the LZ, Jerry Shriver radioed that a machine gun bunker had his men pinned and asked if anyone could fire at it.

No one could. It was up to Mad Dog. Shriver and several Yards rushed into the jungle, and Mad Dog was never seen or heard from again. He vanished.

Forty-five minutes later, while calling gunship fire around his position, Greg Harrigan was shot to death.

Trapped on that LZ most of the day, a majority of the men were wounded. Finally, someone in authority looked the other way and allowed fighters to bomb the encircling enemy, which enabled choppers to extract the survivors. In addition to Shriver, a number of Yards were missing.

In Saigon, the reaction was shock. "That really shook them up at MACV [Military Assistance Command, Vietnam, the U.S. headquarters], to realize anybody survived that strike," Chief SOG Colonel Steve Cavanaugh reported. Had the enemy learned about the strike beforehand? Cavanaugh wondered. It was an unsettling possibility that caused him to reconsider security inside SOG, where already there had been rumors of an enemy mole in the Saigon headquarters.

At Kontum, a small huddle of Shriver's friends drank that night and shared memories, many refusing to believe he actually was dead. The loss of the legendary Mad Dog caused even the most confident men to remark, "If they could get Mad Dog, they can get me." Word of Greg Harrigan's loss circulated slower; it bothered me deeply that he had been so near, an hour's flight away, and now I would never see him again.

Then, a week later, Ben, George, and I had finished our stand-down when we were called into the Tactical Operations Center for a mission briefing from a bald-headed officer filling in for the absent Major Jaks. Though the operations officer disclosed nothing about the origins of our mission, he announced that we would conduct a bomb damage assessment and pointed to a map where a grease-penciled rectangle signified where the bombs would fall.

The rectangle lay across northeast Cambodia.

We had no idea this was President Nixon's third secret strike; all our cross-border missions were dangerous and highly classified, so it seemed just another mission. Then the officer continued, "In six days, the Strategic Air Command will saturate this target with waves of bombers. Over a five-hour period, 102 B-52s will drop more than 10,000 bombs," one of the biggest B-52 strikes of the war. I could not visualize such an immense bomber formation. The target was the NVA 27th Infantry Regiment and units supporting the NVA forces besieging Ben Het Special Forces Camp. Ground Zero was only two miles from where we'd run our last mission, where the NVA had swept past us so menacingly in the dark. I dreaded the idea of going back there, even after a B-52 strike, and I sensed Ben and George shared my feeling.

The officer began rambling about where he thought we should land, but Ben cut him off. "Sir," he snapped, "you can't brief me on *how* to run this mission—you've never been on the ground."

The major asserted, eyes flashing, "*I* am the operations officer."

"That don't make no difference," Ben countered. "When I'm on the ground *I'm* the operations officer, *and* the commander. And when I call, everybody jumps." I was astonished to see Ben, a sergeant first class, dressing down a field grade officer. But the fuming major could say nothing, for Ben had couched his rebuttal with military courtesy—and he was right. The major had no business telling Ben or any other One-Zero how to run a mission. Despite Ben's authority, though, we were offered not one word of warning about the fate that had befallen Lieutenant Ortman and Barry Murphy during the first Cambodian BDA, nor the fact that Mad Dog Shriver and Greg Harrigan had been lost on the second BDA. Somewhere on high it was decided we just didn't need to know that.

Afterward, walking from the Tactical Operations Center, I asked Ben, "Why RT Illinois?"

The answer was obvious to him. "Look around. How many teams we got combat ready, right now?" Since January 1 our little sixty-man recon company had suffered six Americans killed, and another twenty-two Green Berets wounded—meaning, in three months almost half our U.S. personnel had become casualties. As a result, the eight or so green teams—those teams up and ready—carried a disproportionate mission load, going out again and again, even though our manning board listed about twenty teams. But why put us back in the same target?

"Military logic," George offered. "The staffers ask themselves, 'Who knows the area best?' And the answer is, 'The guys that just came out of there.'"

Recon men didn't appreciate that logic. "Bein' run to death" is what RT Wyoming One-Zero Squirrel Sprouse called it, being inserted over and over into the same area, using every tactic and trick you could devise until, eventually, you defied the odds once too often and paid a terrible price. And the better the One-Zero, the better the team, the more likely you'd be run to death.

Having had no time to train since our last mission, for the next five days we trained especially hard, focusing on live fire immediate action drills, and procedures for crossing danger areas like trails and streams. We practiced a hasty prisoner snatch built around my suppressed Swedish K submachine gun. Ben didn't bother flying a visual recon over the target because, after 2,500 tons of bombs impacted, the terrain itself would change. State Department rules still forbade U.S. fighter support but the requirement for foreign weapons was relaxed permanently; apparently the NVA had captured so many U.S. weapons by May 1969 that American arms were no longer convincing evidence of U.S. operations inside Cambodia.

Still, I kept my Swedish K, cradling it in my arm as our chopper climbed out of Dak To, en route to northeast Cambodia. For this mission we'd be inserted by Vietnamese-flown Kingbee H-34 helicopters, obsolete birds that these master pilots handled like spirited ponies. Unlike the turbine-driven Huey, the piston-powered Kingbee had only one door—the right—and employed rubber wheeled landing gear rather than skids. Ben and George and three of our Vietnamese flew in the lead Kingbee; I rode the second bird with Binh, Loi, Huynh, and Quang. Riding that Kingbee's door, I watched the now familiar terrain slip past—bubbling rivers, the dirt road to Ben Het Special Forces Camp, then the orange hills of that besieged base and the long trails of bomb craters along its valley floor. Instead of Cobras, flying escort today were older Huey gunships—Charlie models—with huge red and yellow Cougar patches on their noses and miniguns and rocket pods hanging at their sides. A USAF A-1 Skyraider probably carried ten times the payload of these gunships; we were about to land in an area that intelligence declared swarming with NVA, it already had been hit by thousands of bombs, yet the rules of engagement denied us fighter support. Why, I could not fathom.

Security and deniability, these were the overriding watchwords for the secret bombing. The previous night at Pleiku's "Peacock" radar center—which guided B-52s over the Central Highlands—a SAC representative sent away all but those with a need to know. Then he had technicians electronically redirect the incoming B-52s from their cover target inside South Vietnam to the real impact point in northeast Cambodia. The first wave struck at about 3:00 A.M. Then more waves hit the same target, over and over, saturating the area with bombs.

Early that morning, just before dawn, USAF Captain Don Fulton was flying his O-2 forward air control plane back to Pleiku Air Force Base from southern Laos. He knew he wasn't supposed to overfly Cambodia without clearance but the shortcut seemed harmless. "Suddenly, the world blew up underneath me," he recounted. His plane shook in the concussion of rippling explosions. He flew safely away, delighted to see so worthy a target bombed, but angered that he'd almost been killed for the sake of compartmenting information.

Then, just before 8:00 A.M., the final dozen B-52s dumped the last of 10,000 bombs.

As we turned west from Ben Het we saw the distant smoke and rising dust, which settled enough that fifteen minutes later, overflying ground zero, we witnessed the awesome effect. It looked as if both an earthquake and a tornado had ravaged the ground, uprooting and snapping trees, churning down much of the jungle, sliding entire hillsides into streams to block or divert their flow. In some places craters overlapped craters and not one tree stood.

As our helicopter armada went into orbit, I swung my legs in the Kingbee door as if I were riding a porch swing, confident, relaxed. But the opposite was true. Fear and dread welled in my belly. I couldn't wait to get away from the noisy helicopter into the cover of the jungle.

Overflying our LZ, the Cougar gunships had not taken any fire so our Kingbees spiraled down to join them; as on our last mission, my stomach sank with the altitude, like riding a falling elevator. Then we were less than 100 feet, flying an evasive pattern while I shouldered my Swedish K, ready to return any ground fire. Among the fallen trees I glimpsed bunkers and trenches on several ridgelines, while here and there human tracks crossed the fresh gray powder of pulverized earth. It all flashed past, then at last our chopper hovered and we jumped out onto a refrigerator-size clod of freshly churned earth.

Thank God, we were on the ground! Like a dusting of dirty snow, a layer of powdered soil covered every leaf and twig and much of the ground where we lay in a tight circle, listening for the enemy. About ten minutes later, Ben radioed a "Team OK" to our Covey Rider flying with the Air Force forward air controller. Then thumbs-up all around and we were on our way, walking a gentle rise through the jungle. I swished a leafy branch to scatter dust across our tracks.

I'd trod heavily forested northern Minnesota after a tornado but could not imagine this kind of destruction. Ben routed us around bomb craters and fallen trees but at times we had to climb over tree trunks, slowing our movement almost to nil, with lots of stop-and-go relayed by hand signals from Binh and Loi, the only men visible ahead of me.

We'd gone twenty minutes when Loi raised his left palm—*halt*—then swept his hand slowly back and forth—*trail*. Momentarily we advanced and angled onto a footpath that roughly paralleled our route, littered by leaves and fallen branches. It was not in current use. Since the trail led approximately in our direction of movement and bypassed a cluster of downed trees, Ben decided to follow it and put some fast distance between us and our insert LZ.

We'd not gone another fifty yards and again Loi raised his hand. We paused.

I turned, motioned for Quang and Huynh to face backward, and together we covered our backtrail, kneeling to make ourselves smaller targets.

Another relayed signal—left hand to Loi's ear: *someone thought he heard something.* A false alarm? Then our file resumed moving. I clicked my tongue to get Huynh's and Quang's attention and we were up again but at a slower, more deliberate pace.

We paused again—I turned to watch the backtail.

Clack-clack-clack! AKs! Up front. *Clack-clack-clack-clack!* Then an M-16, *brrrt-brrrt-brrrt-brrrt! Clack-clack-clack! Brrrt-brrrt! Clack-clack-clack-clack!*

This was no immediate action drill, no one was peeling off. Someone was pinned down or hit. More gunfire. Just like treeing a squirrel back home, I scrambled left to rush the enemy's flank but before I'd gone five paces here came Ben, half dragging our point man, blood spurting from Hai's left arm.

Ten yards ahead, two of our Vietnamese opened fire as Ben lowered Hai to the ground and tore off his rucksack, and George shoved a pressure bandage against the wound. I attempted to open fire but couldn't shoot around our two Vietnamese, so I threw a tear gas grenade over them. Ben turned to me, almost out of breath from carrying Hai. "Buy time," he ordered. "See you at the LZ." Then Ben was up again, hefting Hai, waving the team back toward our LZ and radioing, "Covey, Covey! Prairie Fire! Prairie Fire!"

I opened fire toward a shouting NVA's voice thirty yards away—and noticed George still there, beside me. "Get out of here!" I barked. He just smiled and fired his M-16. I insisted, "George, get out of here! I'm the One-One, this is my job." George fired another burst. I snapped, "Who do you think you are, John Wayne?"

Return fire cracked over our heads as he raised an eyebrow. "Nope, just George Bacon. Now let's shoot some of these guys." I chuckled, calm again.

Enemy fire had tapered off. Just beyond our visibility, about fifty yards away, the NVA were reloading, handling their wounded if they had any, and planning their next move. That couldn't last long. I threw another tear gas grenade down the trail; in the heavy humidity its cloud hung in the air like rising steam. Rather than stay where the enemy knew we were, George and I pulled back another twenty-five yards, kneeling behind trees on opposite sides of the trail.

Then a shout, and here they came, running and spraying their AKs, their bullets sounding like a ruler slapping the edge of a desk, *Crack-crack! Crack-crack-crack!* George fired—*brrt-brrt-brrt-brrt-brrt!*—I let loose my suppressed Swedish K—*pft-pft-pft-pft-pft.* We shot as fast as we could change magazines, not waiting for clarified targets like you get on a rifle range. As quickly as anything appeared I let loose a well-aimed burst. I shot at glimpses of movement, muzzle blasts, breaking brush, a flash of reflected sunlight, a voice, any indicator of the enemy. Our goal was to keep the NVA at arm's length, to throw their plan off balance, disrupt their aim, delay them, confuse them, and to make them pay in blood for each step they came closer. Their fire was becoming too concentrated—twigs fell off trees, bark flew, dirt kicked up, and ricochets twanged past us. By now there were about twenty NVA shouting and shooting at us.

Then brush broke thirty yards to my left—an NVA squad trying to flank us. I fired into the brush, burst after burst, then heaved a fragmentation grenade to buy time to change magazines. Just as the NVA got so close that they might surround us, George and I nodded to each other, tossed another grenade, then fell back, spraying the trail and bushes as we ran.

Ten seconds later we were at the next clump of trees, ready to do it all over again. We shot from there for three or four minutes, until we heard another NVA squad trying to flank us; George threw a white phosphorus grenade, which spewed white-hot sparks and a billowing mushroom cloud. Cloaked by its smoke we ran down the trail to the sound of burned men's screams, then halted again.

This, my first gunfight, was not how I'd imagined it. The foliage absorbed so much noise that gunfire didn't sound half as loud as on a range. Unlike the movies there was no exciting theme music, just the sound of my own heavy breathing, the weight of my rucksack, and the sting of sweat in my eyes. I'd begun with a dose of adrenaline but ten minutes later it was gone, and what kept me going was physical conditioning and mental determination. My parched throat begged for water but I didn't think about grabbing my canteen. I kept shooting.

Enemy soldiers shouted to one another from several directions, and again attempted to flank us, and again they met our grenades, arced so they'd detonate in the air. Grenades alone must have killed several.

Then, *Ka-Boom!*—*flash!*—an ear-splitting explosion. RPG! The rocket's detonation shook the ground behind us, narrowly missing George. I tossed my last tear gas grenade and George heaved our last white phosphorus. We ran like hell as AK bursts tore into the dirt, slapped trees, and ricocheted around us. We reached a low rise, paused, turned, and fired at the sound of enemy shouts and breaking brush, heaved another fragmentation grenade or two—then heard the most beautiful sound of my life—Covey! God bless him, it was Covey's engines!

Then, brush broke again, loud, to our left flank—George fired toward it, I heaved a grenade for all I could, then we got up and ran, sprinting fifty yards, and jumped behind trees on either side of the trail. No enemy in sight, so we cut through the jungle toward our LZ, hustling as fast as we could. The NVA were still behind us, but not as close as before.

At last we reached the LZ but Ben and the team were nowhere to be seen. Across the opening, seventy-five yards away, a hand waved—Ben! George and I raced across the open ground, then leaped into the bushes among them. Looking back across the opening, I was struck by Ben's tactical genius; instead of halting as soon as they reached the LZ, Ben had the men run across it, meaning enemy pursuers would have to cross the open area to get to us, or sweep slower through the bordering jungle. Ben's quick thinking gave us an excellent field of fire and bought us time for the gunships to get there.

While George tended to Hai's wound and Ben radioed Covey, I arranged our Vietnamese to fight off the assault that was certain to come. Hardly had I finished when, across the LZ, several NVA soldiers emerged, only to be cut down immediately by our fire. Then the NVA laid down a base of fire and sent troops skirting the LZ to envelop us on our left.

At last the Cougar gunships arrived and Ben unfurled a neon orange panel to direct their fire. As quick as they confirmed our location, Ben put their growling miniguns on the NVA—*Gggrrrrrrppppp! Gggrrrrrrppppp!* Enemy fire ceased while the NVA scrambled to evade these firehoses of tracers—*Gggrrrrrrppp! Gggrrrrrrppp!* Then came 2.75-inch rockets—*Ka-pow!*—a white javelin flashed into the trees—*Boom!* Then *whop-whop-whop-whop*, a Cougar banked hard to come around again. Instantly his wingman hit the same spot— *Ka-pow!* then *Boom!—Ka-pow—Boom!—Ka-pow—Boom! Gggrrrrrrppp!* Spent minigun brass fell around us like golden rain.

Lying beside me, Loi emptied his rifle into the dirt ten yards away, his eyes scared shut. I hollered at him, then knelt above him. AK slugs smacked the dirt beside me. I dropped, rolled on my side, and spotting an NVA just twenty-five yards away, shot him hard with a five-round burst, knocking him down. It was the first clear shot I'd had. I knew I got him.

For the first time I checked ammo—amazingly, I had just one more loaded magazine. What about grenades? I'd thrown all my fucking grenades. I was down to just that last magazine, thirty-six rounds. Jesus Christ! Ben hollered, "Get ready! Cover while they load Hai!"

A Cougar made another gun run along the LZ's left flank, a second gunship let loose a barrage of miniguns and rockets, then behind him came a third bird, a Huey that settled into the LZ while still another gunship flashed past, also firing.

As quickly as the Huey landed, I was up, gun ready, advancing on the LZ to cover while George and two Vietnamese helped our point man into the Huey. Carefully I covered the spot where I'd dropped an NVA moments earlier—he was gone. I fired toward where he must have crawled, a door gunner added fire from his M-60 machine gun, then the Huey lifted away with George and three of our Vietnamese. I ran back to where Ben was radioing Covey.

The gunships passed again, strafing and rocketing, and here came our second Huey. We all ran for it, firing all the way, both door gunners shooting their M-60s. We jumped aboard; the bird rose and pivoted as I fired into the wood line.

Then we were above the trees and I was totally out of ammunition. That terrible place blended back into the jungle, just another grassy spot in a valley full of grassy spots. Quang turned toward me and smiled. *SMACK-thunk!* He collapsed into a groaning ball, blood everywhere. Ben tore off his web gear while I pulled open his shirt; an AK slug had penetrated his buttocks and exited the center of his stomach, spilling his intestines through a gaping wound. It took two pressure bandages to cover the wound, but, worst of all, we could do nothing about the internal bleeding, since George, our talented medic, was aboard the other ship treating Hai. We tried to divert Quang's agony during the ride to Dak To, lighting a cigarette for him and pouring water on his intestines to keep them moist.

At Dak To a Vietnamese Kingbee pilot waved us to his cranking bird to fly our wounded men to the 71st Evacuation Hospital in Pleiku. George went along to treat them on the way, and to make sure our wounded "Vietnamese" soldiers were not forgotten in an emergency room corner. As we watched the Kingbee lift away, a Cougar gunship pilot told Ben he'd spotted 100 NVA running down a trail toward our LZ—a few minutes more and we'd have been trapped.

Later, a second Kingbee flew the rest of us to Pleiku, where we learned Hai would fully recover. Quang would have died had it not been for the quick work of American surgeons and nurses. Hai would remain hospitalized for days; Quang for weeks.

It was almost dark by the time the Kingbees carried us back to Kontum. No one knew we were landing so the helipad was empty; we walked silently back to our team room. Only there did I notice the tape had been shot off my muzzle. I'd been in my first gunfight. It had all happened too fast to feel fear, and now I'd never felt such exhaustion.

It was not until I looked at my dirt-smeared face in a latrine mirror that I noticed Quang's blood sprayed across my jungle fatigues. I thought about our men's wounds. An AK slug had torn away a lemon-size chunk of Hai's thin biceps, leaving the skin hanging hideously. Quang's wound was worse. Those visions burned into my mind the deadliness of our calling as no logical explanation could. We'd dodged hundreds, maybe thousands, of AK rounds, and all it took was one bullet to almost kill Quang and to disable Hai for life. I thanked God it hadn't been me. I threw water on my face, then noticed a man standing there, watching me.

"Hi," he said. "I'm Fred Abt."

I turned and saw that he was a lieutenant colonel. He shook my hand and asked, "How'd it go out there, tiger?" He was short, gray-haired with blue-gray eyes that conveyed an almost grandfatherly sincerity. Until that moment, I had no idea our commander, Lieutenant Colonel Bahr, had rotated home and that Abt was our new commander.

"Kinda bad, sir. But we got out of it." He waited for more. I looked in the mirror, critiquing myself. "I ran out of ammo. Never again! *Fuck carrying a handgun!* I need harness space for more magazines and grenades."

"That's important," he agreed. "Anything I can do?"

"They didn't hear my Swedish K, sir—the silencer. Unless I actually shot someone, they didn't even know I was shooting, but when I did shoot this guy, he didn't stay dead. Nine-millimeter *sucks*. I need a weapon that when I shoot somebody, they go down, they stay down. Sir, I need a CAR-15."

Abt patted my back. "I'll see what I can do," he said, and left.

During the next morning's debriefing, I couldn't help but stare at the intel shop's wall-size maps, which pinpointed enemy sanctuaries and base camps on the Cambodian and Laotian borders. I recalled the stock reporter's phrase— "the elusive enemy"—which raised the specter of guerrillas slipping away unseen into the jungle. That was crap. American units wasted weeks, even months, fruitlessly sweeping for this "elusive enemy" inside South Vietnam while our SOG teams found NVA almost every single day across the border, and always in great numbers.

Our debrief was short and sweet. Beyond the details of our running firefight, all we could say was that these hard-core NVA were right there where the bombs had hit, which apparently pleased the Air Force and the Nixon administration. As a result, the secret bombing would be expanded, so that by year's end nearly 1,000 B-52 sorties would have dropped almost 27,000 tons of bombs in northeast Cambodia alone. SOG recon teams would perform BDAs on most of those strikes.

After our debrief I was called over to the supply room, where Dave Higgins handed me a CAR-15. Lieutenant Colonel Abt had come through. It bore serial number 905442, a number I'll remember forever, for that weapon served me with perfect loyalty. Dave offered no explanation but I came away suspecting Abt had found it decorating some staff officer's wall; I cared only that, after five months in recon, I finally had my own CAR-15, a weapon whose bullet generated four times the ballistic lethality of a Swedish K's 9mm. Handing Higgins my suppressed Swedish K, I swore that I'd never again be seduced by a weapon's sex appeal. Firearms are tools, I'd come to see, and the more exotic the tool, the more limited its usefulness.

Around this time our unit at Kontum was renamed CCC for Command and Control Central, reflecting a new status equal to our former higher headquarters at Da Nang, Command and Control North, and to Command and Control South in Ban Me Thuot. Our area of operations did not change—northern Cambodia and southern Laos—only our chain of command, so that we now answered directly to SOG headquarters in Saigon. Overnight, everything from jeep bumpers to the sign over our mess hall switched from CCN FOB-2 to CCC. As innocuous a name as the Studies and Observations Group, Command and Control Central intentionally inspired yawns and kept the curious at bay.

Despite spending only one hour on the ground on our bomb damage assessment, we got a full week off and spent it relaxing and blowing off steam. One evening, talking about our last mission over a beer, I asked Ben where he'd learned his brilliant tactic of running across an LZ. He thought about it for a second, then replied, "Well, no place. Just made sense. I could see it was the right thing to do."

What! Like the first time your eyes finally see a 3D poster's hidden image, Ben's answer let me see what I'd been looking at all along without realizing it. I thought about it for hours.

I'd been absorbing everyone's lessons but not thinking deeper; now, Ben had shown me that memorizing and repeating other recon men's trials and errors wasn't enough. I had to think and see in a new way. On a mission, I now realized, everything I encountered offered tactical possibilities—opportunities or dangers—but it was up to me to be conscious enough to notice them—*situational awareness.* And then I had to be shrewd enough to assess and exploit them, a skill I later dubbed *tactical sense.* I saw that terrain, like weather, was neutral, and it was up to me to figure out how to use it to my team's benefit. Just as an animal might see its surroundings as both predator and prey, from here on I would constantly scan and evaluate everything about me, from shadows and light to smells and sounds and colors. *See that downed tree? It's an obstacle if we have to run that way, but it's also cover from small arms fire if we duck behind it.* With practice, I'd learn to assess everything in view at a glance. That's how Joe Walker saw his surroundings, I knew without even asking him. *A great One-*

Zero thought constantly. On top of this new clarity, I began adopting small habits like gliding from tree to tree instead of just walking in the jungle, so I was always near cover if the enemy ambushed us. By noticing and exploiting many little things a bit better than the NVA, cumulatively we'd be decisively superior. Along with paying heed to other men's lessons learned, my newfound consciousness and tactical sense would evolve with time and experience into near-instinct, just as Ben had displayed at our LZ, and would save my life and my teammates' lives many times.

While I digested this revelation, our war continued. Just two days after our Cambodian gunfight, a SOG O-1 overflew our B-52 target for an aerial BDA only to be knocked down by enemy antiaircraft fire. While the pilot and back-seater hid in a bomb crater, their wingman, Captain Pete Johnson, buzzed approaching NVA and Covey Rider Luke Dove fired an M-16 from the back seat, buying time for our choppers to safely extract them.

A week later, on 13 May, Sergeant First Class Mike Scott was riding back seat in First Lieutenant Bruce Bessor's O-1, overflying a recon team in Laos forty miles northwest of the Dak To launch site. Suddenly, 37mm antiaircraft fire enveloped their small plane, bringing it down. For five solid days, monsoon clouds precluded an aerial search, after which all signs of the plane's crash had disappeared. The recon team later told debriefers, "When it was shot down we heard the enemy yell and cheer."

Scotty and Bessor, alive or dead, were never found.

Our own losses never abated, and how could you expect otherwise? Constantly outnumbered, deep behind enemy lines, no communications at night, and only aircraft for fire support and extraction—hazardous conditions meant high losses. But that only tells half the story. As it was said in the club, "Some days you eat the bear, and some days the bear eats you." Yes, the bears were after us, but we were devouring a lot of bears, too, and making life in their rear areas as dangerous as possible.

Although our gunfights constantly inflicted greater losses than we suffered, our ambushes took a phenomenal toll, too, and our teams proved adept destroyers of trucks. One night, Joe Walker ambushed a whole convoy, then backed away and called air strikes on it. Bob Howard ran alongside a truck at night and tossed a claymore mine among the NVA solders crammed in back, blowing them sky-high. He escaped without a scratch.

Truck mining disrupted traffic, too. One-Zero Luthor "Luke" Dove, One-One David Gilmer and One-Two John Miller knocked out an enemy truck on Laotian Highway 110 with an antitruck mine. Then, applying what he'd learned on that mission, later, as a One-Zero himself, Gilmer repeated the trick with RT Texas. Along with Lieutenant Greg Glashauser and Specialist Four Richard Nowak, he cleverly placed a mine underwater at a river ford. For good measure, Gilmer laid detonation cord from the mine to two concealed claymore mines and two white phosphorous grenades.

At midnight they heard a truck far off, coming closer and closer. Gilmer began to think it had missed the mine, then, *KAAAAAA-BOOOM!* And more explosions, secondary detonations of explosive cargo aboard the truck, which continued for a quarter-hour. Colonel Abt hailed Gilmer's feat, as we all did. He couldn't buy a drink when he got back.

Another successful truck killer was One-Zero Oliver Hartwig, RT Ohio, who, along with One-One Tim Lynch and One-Two Mike Kuropas, blew up a truck on Highway 110 about ten miles east of Gilmer's mining. The NVA didn't even try to find Hartwig's team, apparently believing that the truck had been hit by a bomb, not a mine.

Another devious mine-planter, One-Zero Gerry Denison, called his dastardly hobby "the one thing I love to do." His specialty was antipersonnel mines, whose presence he disguised by having a Yard defecate in the middle of a trail. "Here's the little private on his way to South Vietnam, AK over his shoulder," Denison explained, "coming down a trail and all of a sudden there's a pile of shit in the trail. Charlie don't want to step in shit! So he walks around it, BOOM! Steps on my mine!" His shit trick worked more than once.

Great though it was to kill a truck and mine roads, the greatest coup and most dangerous feat was to snatch an enemy prisoner. Snatching meant a likely gunfight along busy roads and trails and near base camps, and usually against forces that outnumbered your team. After you grabbed him, the prisoner slowed your pace while other NVA flocked after you, knowing you held one of their buddies. But bringing back a prisoner—and through him, fresh, firsthand intelligence—assured the team and its One-Zero the highest respect and accolades, plus a free R&R to Taiwan for the Americans, and a new Seiko watch and bonus to each native team member.

Only the finest One-Zeros brought back prisoners, with the best technique a subject of unending NCO club debate. Some One-Zeros believed a snatch should be a deliberate ambush, employing a carefully placed gunshot or explosive charge to disable one NVA while gunning down his companions. They advocated everything from exotic Astrolite liquid explosive to suppressed .22 pistols. Other One-Zeros thought it better to pounce upon a lone NVA, if one could be found, and knock him into submission to avoid the chance of accidentally killing him. One team leader, considering police-style chemical mace, went so far as to spray unsuspecting Vietnamese passersby near our compound, then ask via an interpreter how the victim felt, pay the gagging man 500 piastres ($5), and send him on his way. His tests convinced him not to employ mace against an armed NVA.

Everything imaginable was tested or attempted but, despite sophisticated tactics, courageous men, and plenty of incentives, SOG teams snatched fewer than fifty prisoners from Laos and Cambodia during the entire war. It was just plain hard to do.

Some of the best snatches were improvisations, exploiting an opportunity, as had happened when David Gilmer's RT Texas captured an enemy soldier on Highway 110 who was playing possum after a firefight.

Another team attempted a snatch, with five men pouncing upon an NVA who walked past them. After losing his AK, that lone soldier fought like a cornered rat and punched, kicked, and bit his way through the entire team, then ran down the road. "The One-Zero had so much respect for the son-of-a-bitch," Bob Howard recounted, "that he wanted to see him get away. But before [the One-Zero] could shove down the muzzle, one of the Yards shot the guy."

RT Florida One-Zero Master Sergeant Norm Doney disabled a lone NVA with a suppressed .22 pistol, and had him down, ready to be hog-tied, when a large NVA unit happened on the scene. An exploding RPG peppered Doney with shrapnel, and his would-be prisoner leaped for his AK but Doney groggily managed to shoot first, popping him several times with the suppressed pistol and killing him. With the NVA unit almost upon him, Doney rejoined One-One Joe Morris and ran to an LZ, where they found the rest of their team.

Someday, I hoped, I'd destroy a truck, or snatch a prisoner. With that in mind, I began my own experiments, making frequent use of our compound's demo bunker, a cornucopia of mayhem—plastic explosives, dynamite, blasting caps, det cord, time delay detonators, exotic mines—anything I wanted, as much as I wanted, just blow it up, then come back for more. I thickened gasoline for a napalm claymore that hurled its jellied fuel like a quart wad of snot but wouldn't ignite. Then I tested a time fuse firefight simulator, whose exploding blasting caps, I hoped, would fool the enemy into thinking they were being shot at. It worked marginally. My one real success was a technique to ignite smoke and tear gas grenades with a time fuse so they'd go off seconds, minutes, or even tens of minutes later, which isn't found in any pyrotechnics book, though it would be a year before that trick came in handy. My explosives experiments never ended.

Innovative as my experiments were, though, they were child's play compared to a demolition man on a sister team—let's just call him Sergeant Jones. Rather than use Army-issue mines or booby trap devices, Jones developed his own, which no one else wanted anything to do with. Apparently they worked, the very strangeness of his infernal devices ensuring some curious NVA toyed with them. Jones wasn't especially tough, but everyone knew—*don't mess with this guy!*

His reputation, though, did not carry into our Vietnamese community, to whom he was unknown. Therefore, regarding him as just another target for thievery, one night a Vietnamese slit the window screen over his bed and snatched his brand-new cassette player, purchased that very day at the PX. When he discovered the loss, he didn't report it and insist on a search of the indigenous barracks. No, true to his spirit, he simply went to the PX and purchased another radio-cassette player, identical to the first.

Returning to his room, he disassembled it, setting aside the guts but retaining the switches and dials. Then, through clever rewiring, he made another of his infernal devices, replacing the electronic guts with a half-pound of C-4 plastic explosive. This radio was his gift to whoever had stolen the first. Should someone else steal the radio, that was fair enough, too. In genteel society, his teammates might have stopped him, or run off and reported him, but in SOG's fatalistic world it seemed a case of frontier justice.

And now there was only one final detail—soldering an electric blasting cap to the batteries and radio switch. In a minute it was done. He had only to slip the blasting cap into the explosive and reseal the radio's plastic chassis. He stared long and hard at the radio, then it occurred to him, "How do I know it will work?" Incredible as it sounds—this is the absolute, honest-to-God truth—he *had* to know—he grabbed that radio dial—*and turned it!*

It worked perfectly.

Fortunately he had not inserted the cap into the C-4, otherwise he'd have disappeared. Still, the exploding cap's aluminum casing peppered him with fragments from forehead to waist and he was heard screaming all the way to the dispensary. He was quickly medevaced and that was the last we heard of him. The compound was a bit safer, especially for his immediate neighbors, who'd long feared they might all go up in smoke.

Whatever our antics, Lieutenant Colonel Abt proved remarkably tolerant, and as we got to know him better, he showed himself as down-to-earth and decent as my first impression of him suggested. Some nights he sat with us in the club, telling us about his combat experiences as a young infantryman in World War II; he vividly described ducking beneath olive trees in Italy, hugging the earth for his very life while German planes bombed his unit. He was always ready for a round of horseshoes, open to all comers. And like a good leader, Abt did anything he expected us to do, and then some.

One afternoon he showed up at the Dak To launch site just as RT Hawaii was preparing to insert. Sporting sterile fatigues, without rank, and carrying an M-16 with web gear, he looked no different than any other team member.

A nosy 4th Infantry Division lieutenant, apparently upset that no one saluted as he passed, stormed to the launch site gate and demanded to know who had authorized our men to wear unmarked uniforms. "Our commander," Abt replied. The snooty lieutenant noticed Abt wasn't wearing dog tags, then learned no one had ID cards, either. Enough of that! The young officer pulled out pen and notebook to take down everyone's names, beginning with Abt.

"Abt," our commander replied cheerfully, "that's, A-B-T, Frederick."

"OK," the lieutenant continued, "let's have your rank, buddy."

In perfect monotone, as unimpressively as possible, Abt replied, "Lieutenant colonel." The lieutenant blinked, looked up, then folded his notebook shut. He said not one word, just saluted, about-faced, and left. "Have a nice day, Lieutenant," Abt called after him.

Momentarily, when RT Hawaii boarded choppers, Colonel Abt climbed in with them, going along for the ride. To One-Zero Bill Delima's astonishment, though, when they jumped out onto an LZ deep in Laos, Abt jumped out, too.

It was a fast, three-hour B-52 bomb damage assessment mission, which Abt thought the perfect opportunity to see how a team operated in the field. He acted like just another Montagnard and kept quiet except when he asked Glenn Uemura what Glenn wanted him to do next.

Afterward, when Chief SOG in Saigon learned Abt had gone into Laos, he soundly chewed his backside, but there wasn't a recon man who wouldn't do their all for Abt.

"I had the greatest respect for him," Uemura later said.

My team, RT Illinois, ran a couple more missions into Laos and Cambodia, Ben always managing to outmaneuver the NVA who hunted us. On one mission, accompanied by Sergeant First Class Mike O'Conner, we found a recently abandoned base camp on a river, and brought back a soil sample in a plastic bag, which long afterward I learned was for Project Popeye, a CIA program to air-drop emulsifiers to clog the enemy's highways with "super-mud."

Then George Bacon, who'd taught me so much, rotated home. Not long afterward, Ben was walking back from showering in the latrine when I pointed out to him that he'd forgotten to rinse the soap off. He looked at me as in a trance, then looked at the suds in shock. Ben knew it was time to hang up his rucksack.

Ben wanted to fly Covey but was not selected, so he finished his tour instructing at SOG's recon school at Camp Long Thanh, near Saigon. That left me as the sole American on RT Illinois, my fate to be decided by Bob Howard, the acting recon first sergeant, and our new recon company first sergeant, Norm Doney, who'd been One-Zero of RT Florida. Two years earlier, Doney had made the cover of *Saga* magazine for an extraordinary mission he'd led while running recon inside South Vietnam with Project Delta, in which he'd called a devastating air strike on an enemy battalion standing morning formation at the Cambodian border.

Doney and Howard weren't sure I was ready, even though I had seven missions under my belt.

Among my peers, the first to make One-Zero was John St. Martin, who led RT New York with One-One Ed Wolcoff and One-Two John Blaauw. Their previous One-Zero had been shaky, the final straw being his refusal to board choppers at Dak To for a late afternoon insert, insisting there wasn't enough daylight left. Abt relieved him and got St. Martin on the launch site radio.

"Hey, tiger," Colonel Abt asked the RT New York One-One, "do you think you can take it?"

"Yes, sir!" St. Martin replied.

"OK," Abt said, "go get 'em." St. Martin led a successful mission, uncovering a major communication wire and an apparent ammo dump. A close-run thing, at one point he narrowly bypassed an NVA patrol and stayed a full seven days on the ground. His former One-Zero became a gate guard, derisively nicknamed "Ninety-Ten," because he was 90 percent "show" and 10 percent "go."

My best friend, Uemura, was being groomed as heir apparent to Bill Delima on RT Hawaii. He'd acquitted himself well and in weeks, we knew, he would be One-Zero.

It was Bob Howard who broke the news to me, explaining, "John, when you're ready, you can lead any team on this compound, even RT California." He shook his head. "But not yet."

That wasn't all bad since, like half the men in recon, I wasn't sure I wanted to be a One-Zero. Actually, the best job was One-One: Unburdened by the weight of a One-Two's radio or a One-Zero's responsibilities, a One-One's sole job was fighting. Being a gunfighter, a One-One, was cool, the ideal, all the opportunities to fight and to play demo dastardliness. On the other hand, why be a One-Zero? He had to deal with the staff and the commander, to be concerned about the team and the plan, could never be his own man. With that prestigious title went a lot of unwanted responsibility: I didn't want other men's lives in my hands. It was fine to risk my own life, I just didn't like the idea that someone else's life would depend on my judgment. I resolved to be the world's greatest One-One, to keep the backtrail sterile, watch for trackers, and fight a delay to let the team escape. The ambusher supreme, that would be me.

"We've got a new man coming in," Howard continued, "John Allen. He's your One-Zero." I could not have asked for a more experienced man, Howard explained. During a previous tour at CCN, Allen had led RT Alabama, and in February 1968, he'd gone into Camp Lang Vei after it had been overrun, and with a dozen other men rescued the survivors. Then, in May 1968, trapped in a bomb crater in Laos, surrounded by hundreds of NVA, John's team fought off the enemy for two days while he called in more than 100 fighter sorties. Horrifically, John's eight teammates died one by one, until, finally, John was the last man. Down to two magazines, he called one final air strike on his own position, then ran for his life, right through the encircling NVA. His desperate tactic worked. Many men thought John deserved the Medal of Honor. He was awarded a Silver Star.

Yes, I'd gladly follow a man such as John Allen.

The next day he arrived, his intense, thin eyes assessing me when we shook hands. A solidly built man with big shoulders and a South Boston accent, he accepted me as readily as I did him. With John at the helm, I expected a long career as a One-One. Maybe someday I'd be a One-Zero.

That day would arrive far sooner than I expected.

Chapter Seven

As our helicopters neared Ben Het Special Forces Camp, the door gunners test-fired their guns and my right thumb found my CAR-15 safety. In Vietnam's sweltering humidity the safety could rust tight overnight, leaving you helpless in a gunfight. Mine rotated crisply.

Shimmering in noontime haze, the border lay ten miles west, yet already the Huey in front of us began its downward spiral, following a pair of Cobra gunships. My Huey joined in behind them. The rest of our birds, some eight Hueys and Vietnamese Kingbees, stayed high above.

Today's target was right here, within sight of Ben Het's defenders; it was unsettling to know that as many enemy as friendly eyes watched us fly toward a facing ridge about four miles east of the camp. Along that ridge the NVA had tightened their noose another notch, emplacing an antiaircraft regiment with truck-towed 23mm and 37mm guns and .50 caliber machine guns. Now, when C-130 crews made the run in to parachute supplies to Ben Het's besieged soldiers, they ran a gauntlet of intersecting tracers and exploding flak.

Those guns were a threat to us, too, as we raced across the treetops, and they were the focus of our mission: RT Illinois was to infiltrate this ring of fire, find a high vista from which to pinpoint the guns when they shot at cargo planes, then call air strikes on them. Problem was, two NVA infantry regiments—perhaps 5,000 soldiers—manned the siege, making for some interesting statistics compared to our eight-man recon team.

Aboard our first bird, dodging between treetops, rode One-Zero John Allen with our new One-Two, Sergeant Geoffrey Garcia, and three Vietnamese teammates. Though new to recon, Geoff had spent almost a year in our compound's communications bunker; he'd volunteered to run recon his last months before rotating home. Smart and unassuming, Garcia absorbed our every piece of advice.

Aboard the second Huey, I stepped out on the skid, my CAR-15 ready, as we slowed to land. After the gunfight in which I'd fired all my ammo, I'd discarded my pistol holster to make room for more pouches. I now packed thirty magazines—600 rounds—a heavier load, but I didn't care. Ask anyone who's ever run out of ammo.

Our LZ materialized on a steep slope, the grass still compressed where the first Huey had hovered; then our Huey held steady, its right skid near the slope, and we all piled out and ran to the rest of the team, just inside the jungle. There we lay in a tight circle.

Before John was ready to radio a "Team OK," Garcia shook his head and whispered, "We've got Vietnamese on the radio." John nodded to our interpreter, Suu, who leaned over and listened to Geoff's radio handset. Suu's eyes widened. "VC," he whispered. "Know we here. Talk 'bout team. *They come here!*"

John's eyes flared—*It's starting again,* his eyes said, and I realized he was reliving that RT Alabama mission a year earlier, the two-day ordeal that only he'd survived. He'd not been on a mission since that day. John looked around for cover, for places we could evade or maneuver or run. Downhill, the jungle gradually thinned out to the heavily cratered valley floor, offering slow movement and poor concealment. The ridge, about 500 yards above us, offered thicker cover but, intelligence said, that's where the antiaircraft guns were. We weren't so much trapped as sandwiched, with a fair chance of getting away if we hurried—or, since the choppers were still in the air, we could extract and later reland on a better LZ. John decided upon the latter.

It took a few minutes for the S-3 (operations) officer at Kontum to decide, but he approved John's request. We were extracted and flew back to Dak To.

Due to weather, that afternoon we could not reland. Nor the next day. And the next.

Then our mission was scrubbed because, finally, the B-52 strikes, artillery bombardment, SOG's forays behind enemy lines, and ground attacks by Special Forces, Mike Forces, and South Vietnamese Rangers had broken the siege. The North Vietnamese were pulling back into Laos; Ben Het was peaceful for the first time in six months.

Because we'd been on the ground we got a one-week stand-down, though it didn't seem that we'd earned it. Potentially it had been dangerous as hell, yet it hadn't escalated beyond potential. During the stand-down and subsequent weeks of training, I got to know John Allen better.

He'd grown up in the tough streets of South Boston, staying out of trouble through Golden Gloves boxing, at which he excelled. In addition to a full previous tour at CNN, John also had spent a year in combat with the 101st Airborne Division. Unsentimental yet sometimes humorous, he'd walk into the club and holler to the bartender, "I want to buy everybody a drink!"—then point to some object of his ire and add—"Except him!" That was good for a laugh.

Or, when we sat in the club and an unwanted presence plopped down at our table, John would give me "the look," and we'd launch an idiotic, disjointed conversation—John recalling the worst haircut his kid ever got, me describing a Minnesota canoe trip. It was confounding, leaving no gap for the puzzled third party to wedge into our conversation. It was lots of fun.

When we were alone, though, John's eyes sometimes glazed over and I could see his mind drift away into a torment I did not trespass. He never spoke about the loss of his RT Alabama teammates, nor did he ask about my lost mates from RT New Mexico. Maybe that's why Bob Howard put us together, because of those similar, quiet memories.

Equally, we both appreciated tactics, on which John tested me one night, asking in his South Boston accent, "NVA's sneakin' up on yuh at night, yuh gotta open up—whadda yuh do first?"

"Throw grenades," I replied, "so they can't tell where you are." He grinned and shook my hand, realizing his tutelage could start at an advanced level. John taught me and our Vietnamese to eliminate the *twang* when tossing a grenade by pulling the safety pin and holding the grenade to our ears, then delicately lifting the spoon until we heard the soft *click* of the striker. It was so quiet, it didn't seem the five-second fuse had activated—but God help you if you didn't heave it fast. And when it came to throwing grenades, he showed us how to arc them so they air-burst above the enemy. He made me a believer in grenades.

Under Ben Thompson I'd learned the fundamentals of immediate action drills, in which our team unleashed a concentration of fire, then peeled away to break contact and escape a numerically superior NVA force. John refined our IA drill and had us practice it live-fire, over and over, until each man really clicked; we performed his IA drill several times a week.

When we weren't training, John and I hung around the team room or the NCO club. He had no particular musical preference, while mine was varied, everything from jazz and Top 40 to Broadway show tunes—anything except hard, acid rock. Older Green Berets pretty universally were country-western fans, though some, particularly younger men, appreciated different sounds. One-Zero Barry Keefer relished Country Joe and the Fish's "I-Feel-Like-I'm-Fixin-to-Die Rag"—he liked the sound of machine gun fire at the end. Though Joe Walker was hardly a rock 'n' roll fan, he turned his stereo up full for Steppenwolf's "The Pusher," because he liked the idea of shooting drug pushers, perfectly willing to take on the job himself. There was a degree of cultural tolerance, especially when ironic, but that had limits. One afternoon I heard a commotion in a neighboring barracks, where a stereo played Joan Baez's rendition of the antiwar song "With God on Our Side." The song halted abruptly amid grunts and a bunch of mumbled "motherfuckers." Looking down the hallway, there was Squirrel Sprouse followed by a non–Special Forces signalman waving his arms, with Squirrel holding the signalman's reel-to-reel tape deck over his head, wide-eyed, like Moses about to heave down the Ten Commandments. When the thrown tape deck did not shatter, Squirrel stomped back into his team room only to reappear with his CAR-15, and—*brrt, brrt, brrt, brrt, brrt*—emptied a twenty-round magazine into it, doing a frenzied dance while the other man stood petrified.

I'd missed the first part of the conversation but caught the last. Nostrils flaring, physically spent, Squirrel shouted, "Sure, you can play *any* fucking song you want! *Sure!*"

As soon as we finished stand-down, RT Illinois was alerted for another mission, this time into a target potentially hotter than even the Ben Het mission. Designated Alpha-One, it was a remote valley some forty-five miles northwest of the Dak To launch site; I didn't appreciate the target's dangers until I flew an aerial recon with John Allen.

Wedged into the back seat of a Vietnamese-flown U-19 spotter plane, we crossed ridge after ridge of verdant nothingness, then it opened before us, a deep, wide valley along which ran Laotian Highway 165, a major east–west road with so many turnoffs I could not begin to estimate its truck traffic. Heavily used trails and roads snaked up the facing ridges, and here and there, squarish holes stood out prominently—abandoned antiaircraft gun positions, at least 37mm, maybe larger. Where are those guns now? I wondered. On the valley floor, despite numerous bomb craters, Highway 165 appeared in perfect repair, and I noticed fresh truck tracks glistening from the morning's rain. Combine the antiaircraft crews, road engineers, truck drivers, and logisticians—plus security forces—and there had to be thousands of enemy down there. Terrain did not favor us, either, with too much head-high elephant grass and open fields in which we'd be easily channelized or cornered.

Target Alpha-One was only a few miles south of where Ricardo Davis had been trapped and killed, this area encompassing CCN's southernmost and CCC's northernmost targets, making it out of the way for all our recon teams. The remoteness had become worse in the past year, with the loss of Kham Duc Special Forces Camp and its SOG launch site, which had been overrun back in May 1968. Combined with the Marine withdrawal from Khe Sanh, this left not one friendly base on the South Vietnamese frontier from the Demilitarized Zone south for 100 miles. All these borderlands, thousands and thousands of square miles, now belonged to the North Vietnamese.

On our way back we landed at the Dak To launch site to refuel. While the Vietnamese pilots serviced the plane, John and I walked toward the launch site across the strip. Suddenly all the SOG chopper pilots grabbed their flight vests and ran for their birds—the Bright Light team appeared, fully armed, ready to go.

As we neared the radio shack, a Bright Light man hollered that a team was in trouble—RT Hawaii, Uemura's team. Then on the radio we heard the Covey Rider report, "I confirm, one Straw Hat is Kilo-India-Alpha." One Straw Hat—*one American*—was dead, KIA. Was it Glenn? No one could say.

RT Hawaii had inserted late the previous afternoon into Juliet-Nine, an area of limestone canyons honeycombed with roads, always swarming with NVA, the final resting place of many a recon man. Glenn had felt really up about this mission, his first ever as a One-Zero. Bill Delima, Glenn's longtime team leader, was scheduled to rotate home, so he'd gone along to advise and help. Also along was Joe Morris, a commo classmate from Fort Bragg; Joe had served earlier on Norm Doney's team, RT Florida. A fourth man had volunteered to go to carry the radio, Dennis Bingham, from RT New Hampshire.

Intermittent showers and heavy overcast had delayed their insert until late afternoon, not leaving much daylight to get away from the LZ. By dark, RT Hawaii was hiding in a bamboo thicket, only about 700 yards from where they'd landed. They hadn't seen or heard any NVA.

Then, about eleven o'clock, Glenn heard *wo-wo-wo-wo-wo-wo*—incoming artillery—*boom!* At first he thought it was the mighty 175mm guns at Ben Het; then he realized he was far beyond their maximum range. *Wo-wo-wo-wo-wo-wo—boom!* The team hadn't dug in, only the thin bamboo offered cover and that was splintering and sizzling over their heads. Shell after shell hit all around them.

Then it stopped. They heard and saw nothing more all night.

By dawn they were up and alert but no enemy materialized. Then Covey overflew them for the morning radio check. Afterward, they moved out, slowly and cautiously. Covey had just flown beyond radio range when the point man motioned with two fingers, *people walking*. It was a major trail but the point man hadn't spotted it until they were almost on it. Passing NVA were only yards away; they couldn't back off without being discovered. Glenn signaled to sit and stay quiet. Then an enemy soldier spun toward the team, jerking his AK off his shoulder. Glenn had to shoot, killing that man and another. The whole team fired, broke contact and ran, sustaining no casualties, but now the enemy was on to them.

Behind them, sporadic fire erupted and they could hear signal shots and shouts, leaving only one direction clear, which took them back toward their insert LZ. Hiding on that clearing's edge, Uemura radioed distress calls for an hour until, at last, he heard the Covey Rider's voice—and the news wasn't good.

"Go high and dry," Covey warned, meaning, *Don't move, avoid contact, hide.* RT Florida and RT Washington were in two separate contacts, the helicopters were otherwise occupied, no help was available. Returning to their insertion LZ had been a calculated risk that Glenn thought was worth taking if they got out fast—but now they were stuck there, for God knows how long. Uemura could feel danger growing with each passing minute.

After an eternity of four hours, at last Covey returned with the helicopters. The Covey Rider radioed, "I'm sending in the first bird. Get up, get into the clearing."

Point man leading, four men left the jungle—*and the whole world opened up.* The entire facing wood line crackled with AKs that instantly knocked down the point man; it was all Glenn could do to drag him back into the trees while the rest of RT Hawaii returned fire.

Then more NVA opened fire and closed on them, squeezing the team into a tiny perimeter. While Bill Delima directed the team's fire, Glenn checked the point man and found that a round had torn through both lungs. The Montagnard looked up at him, trying to talk, but there was nothing Uemura could do. The Yard bled to death internally.

Then an RPG blasted the tree beside Uemura, its fragments miraculously missing him but hitting Dennis Bingham, who was beside him. Glenn pulled a shrapnel chunk from Bingham's throat, reassuring him, "You're going to be all right, buddy." But when he lifted Bingham, he found more wounds, then, looking closer, he saw the life leave Bingham's eyes.

Meanwhile, Glenn's teammates were fighting for their lives, throwing grenades and shooting at NVA who'd come so close that the Cobra gunships couldn't hit the enemy without hitting the team. "Just put it on us," Uemura radioed, but Covey refused, insisting that Glenn mark his position. Glenn fired pin flares, then brought the Cobras' fire danger-close.

Finally, the combined fire of Cobras and USAF fighters enabled the first chopper to come in. Delima ran to the Huey for help to carry the two bodies but a sudden enemy volley panicked the door gunner; he jerked Delima aboard, causing three RT Hawaii Yards to panic and jump in, too. The pilot took off. That left just Glenn, Joe Morris, and two Yards to hold the perimeter and get both bodies to the next aircraft.

They took more fire, Glenn called in more air strikes. Then a second Huey came in. Uemura tried to lift Bingham but the husky farm boy's lifeless form proved impossible to carry and drag with one hand while firing a CAR-15 with the other. The door gunner jumped off, ran to Glenn, and together they got Bingham's body aboard, then the point man's body. They flew away, through heavy fire, escaping that deadly ground.

RT Hawaii was en route to Dak To when our Vietnamese pilots waved, signaling that our U-19 was ready to leave. That evening John and I joined the rest of recon company on the Kontum helipad when the Hueys brought back RT Hawaii. Delima's face conveyed fear, anger, and sadness; he'd gone a whole year without losing a man, but on this, his last mission, luck had run out. That mission was enough for Joe Morris; he transferred into the commo bunker.

In the club that night, Delima led us in "Hey, Blue," sung as emotionally as ever I'd heard it.

Though Glenn displayed little emotion, I saw that this mission had changed him. Never again was he quite so happy-go-lucky, and to anyone who asked why, he'd reply, "How would you like being a One-Zero for the first time and get two guys killed?" His actions that day had been genuinely heroic, yet the devotion that caused him to risk his life repeatedly to save his team and to bring back the bodies of Bingham and the Yard left him believing he could somehow have done more. Because of that, he no longer wanted to be a One-Zero; he never quit, but from then on, he chose to be a One-One or a volunteer on other teams, but never again a One-Zero. (By tragic coincidence, only three Binghams—unrelated—served in SOG recon, and all were lost. In addition to RT Hawaii's Dennis Bingham, killed on 17 July 1969, Staff Sergeant Klaus Bingham, CCN, went Missing in Action with all of RT Asp on 10 May 1971. Then Sergeant Oran Bingham, Jr., CCN, was killed on 7 August 1971 with RT Kansas.)

Dramatic as it was, RT Hawaii's fight was by no means SOG's only momentous action of 17 July 1969. At the very moment that Glenn's team was fighting for its life, 100 miles away, also in Laos, our Fort Bragg Commo School classmate Jim "Mule Skinner" Pruitt was fighting for his life, too, with his CCN team, RT Asp.

Along with Specialist Four Michael Buchanan, One-One, and five Montagnards, Pruitt's team had just landed in Laos when only fifty yards away they spotted a passing NVA platoon. Buchanan whispered to Pruitt, "They're right here, by the LZ. Let's assault, grab one guy, and extract." Mule Skinner thought it a splendid idea.

Sending Buchanan and four Yards to the right, Pruitt and another Yard assaulted square into the astonished NVA. During the attack, Buchanan killed two soldiers and helped Pruitt wrestle another to the ground when the platoon fell back—they had their prisoner. But that NVA platoon wasn't operating alone. In minutes, two more platoons arrived, and now an entire 100-man company swept toward RT Asp, firing AKs, rockets, and machine guns. Enemy fire raked their position, grinding away with such intensity that the prisoner was killed inadvertently by his own comrades. Then Covey arrived, and Pruitt called in fighters and helicopter gunships. Buchanan spotted another enemy soldier, somewhat isolated from his comrades. Pruitt momentarily halted the bombing. Then he and Buchanan rushed forward, and while Pruitt shot dead two NVA, his One-One grabbed the lone soldier—they ran back with another prisoner.

More determined than ever to destroy RT Asp and retrieve their comrade, the NVA mass-assaulted right through an air strike, killing one Yard and badly wounding another. Determined to get this prisoner out alive, Pruitt shielded the enemy soldier with his own body—but heavy AK fire killed the man and badly wounded Pruitt. He continued to direct fighters and gunships until so weakened by loss of blood, he had to yield command to Buchanan. Although painfully wounded himself, Buchanan managed to direct more strikes that pushed the enemy back, then guided in the helicopters to extract the team. Despite heavy ground fire, they somehow got out. It was a remarkable incident, even for SOG. In twenty minutes, Pruitt and Buchanan had twice assaulted enemy forces that outnumbered them six to one, then almost twenty to one, and captured two prisoners only to have them killed by intense enemy fire. In addition to Purple Hearts, both were awarded the Distinguished Service Cross, second only to the Medal of Honor. Jim Pruitt's serious wounds sent him back to the States and ended his military career.

But there was even more on that 17 July. The reason Covey could not respond immediately to RT Hawaii's call was that ten miles away RT Arkansas already had been hit, with two Americans seriously wounded. Led by Staff Sergeant Ralph Rodd, RT Arkansas had gone in that morning with One-One Sam Barras, One-Two Randy Rhea, and a volunteer, Captain Richard Moss, only to find themselves deluged by monsoon rains. With the skies closed over RT Arkansas, no helicopters or fighters could support the team, so One-Zero Rodd knew to avoid enemy contact.

But that afternoon, while they sat for a listening break, Rodd's Yard tail gunner signaled *I see somebody*, and sure enough, Rodd saw an NVA tiptoeing past, only fifteen yards away, alert, weapon at the ready. Another shape furtively passed, then another—Rodd estimated ten men.

The sky had cleared temporarily. "If something's going to happen," Rodd decided, "it's got to happen now so the helicopters can get us out." He raised to his knees, hurled a grenade, and just as it reached the desired spot, a flash—*RPG backblast!*

Rodd threw himself down, the rocket exploded before him and fragments tore into his forearm, then heavy gunfire erupted all around. Rodd fired, too, but he could use only his right arm, for shrapnel had sliced the tendons of his left, making it unusable. Then Sam Barras called, "I'm hit, I'm hit!" Rodd saw a hole between his eyes and told him it would be OK but couldn't believe Barras was still conscious, so much blood had flowed down his face.

They fell back, having so bested the enemy that all ten NVA were wounded or dead; no one pursued them. They crossed a stream, formed a perimeter around an opening large enough to extract by ropes, then called Covey. By now they'd heard more NVA, many voices, and they realized they were surrounded. Then came bad news—the sky had closed again and extraction was impossible. Covey warned Rodd, "Go high and dry"—*Don't move, avoid contact, hide*—then left them to go to RT Hawaii's aid.

The dry part proved difficult in the renewed deluge, but, amazingly, the NVA avoided contact, having lost a complete squad to RT Arkansas, and instead held a perimeter around them, waiting to shoot at the helicopters that were no longer coming. The rest of the day and into the night, the stalemate continued; Rodd considered slipping away in the dark, but that wasn't possible with Barras's serious wound. Huddled together, they waited out the enemy, hour after hour.

Back at Kontum, during the wake for Dennis Bingham, everyone in recon company feared the worst for Rodd and his men, both for their untreated wounds, and the likelihood of a mass enemy assault. But that terrible weather would not yield.

A second day, Rodd and his men lay motionless while rain poured upon them. The NVA made no move, but RT Arkansas heard them out there, talking and coughing. The rain never broke.

By the third day, USAF Covey pilot Captain Don Fulton decided it was time to get them out, despite the terrible weather. After studying a map, he flew his O-2 low-level down a long valley, beneath solid clouds that touched the ridgelines all around; what he was attempting was tricky, not taught in any flight school. Directly over the team, he found 1,000 feet of flying space. He pulled his nose up, climbing blindly through the cloud layer, and radioed a pair of A-1 Skyraiders above the clouds, telling them, "Watch where I break through; that's the center of the valley. Dive right where you see me climb out and you'll break through."

Momentarily, his gray and white Cessna Skymaster topped the clouds, and both A-1s dived; on the ground, it was an inspiring moment for Rodd's men when the sound of powerful reciprocating engines buzzed the treetops. Then, Covey pilot Fulton met the Kingbee helicopters and led them down a rabbit hole in the clouds and, one following the other, up the valley to RT Arkansas.

It amazed Rodd's men, but more important, it surprised the NVA, who'd pulled back, probably thinking no aircraft could fly in such conditions. RT Arkansas was pulled out without a shot fired. Ralph Rodd, one of our most accomplished recon men, and Sam Barras were medevaced to Japan, then flown Stateside for more surgery. The gutsy Covey pilot, Captain Fulton, was awarded a Distinguished Flying Cross.

Then it was time for our team, RT Illinois, to insert into Target Alpha-One. We sat around the launch site, waiting for a break in the weather. Covey found time only twice a day to fly that far north, some thirty miles beyond our other deployed teams. With the teams so spread out, his plane would seldom fly within radio range once we were on the ground.

It became a foreboding routine, flying to Dak To only to sit there all day and think about what we'd seen on our earlier aerial recon. As much as anything, I feared that a "sucker hole" might open in the monsoon clouds, through which we'd insert, then it would close behind us, cutting us off from air strikes or extraction. I began to wonder how many of our missing recon teams had vanished in such weather. I'd have rather gone into *any* target other than Alpha-One.

Anxiety grew with each trip to Dak To. One morning we boarded the Hueys and flew all the way to Alpha-One, but by the time we got there the weather had closed again. When danger is thrust suddenly upon you, there's no time for fear—but this! Our eyes had seen that valley, and now all day long, a whole week, we just sat beside the airstrip, apprehensions and premonitions growing. Bad weather had almost killed RT Arkansas; get stuck in similar weather along the perilously remote Highway 165, and we would all die. I grew weary and could feel the team's confidence eroding. The psychological pressure became so evident that the operations officer gave us a two-day break. Thank God.

Relaxing back at Kontum, we did not even speak of Alpha-One that whole first day. Then the second day I awoke feeling dizzy and feverish, with stomach cramps. I vomited and even water wouldn't stay down. By lunch I had no appetite and felt so weak I lay down; by then the cramps so overwhelmed me that I could not sit up. That afternoon I lost control of my bowels and had to stagger to the dispensary. Then my wobbly legs wouldn't work.

The medics started an IV as I lost consciousness. Later I learned that I had a life-threatening affliction, bacillary dysentery, that so ravaged my body that by the time I stabilized thirty-six hours later, I'd lost twenty-two pounds from dehydration. The source was who knows what—in the tropics, disease is everywhere.

When finally I awoke, I looked up to see Bob Howard. He wished me a quick recovery and told me he'd had a long talk with John Allen. After what John had been through with RT Alabama—a miracle he was still alive—it wasn't right for John to have felt obligated to come back to recon. He didn't need to prove he could still do it, though he had.

"John's going down to Long Thanh, to instruct at the Recon One-Zero School," Howard announced. "They can use a good man like him down there." And what about RT Illinois?

"RT Illinois is yours now," Howard said. "You're One-Zero, John. Take a couple of weeks and just train."

That news and plenty of tetracycline had me back on my feet two days later, just in time for the recon first sergeant, Norm Doney, to send Glenn Uemura and me to a promotion board. Combat attrition left an abundance of staff sergeant stripes, so Glenn and I came back newly promoted from E-5 to E-6. Back on RT Illinois, though, everything seemed in a state of flux. I had inherited Geoff Garcia as my One-One and picked up as One-Two another volunteer, who had been a gate guard. Both had promise, but they were short-timers; within a few weeks they began processing to rotate home, leaving me the only American on the team.

Then, hallelujah, it was like I had a first-round pick in the NFL draft. First Sergeant Doney gave me the just arrived Staff Sergeant Bill Spencer, a career Special Forces NCO with a previous Vietnam combat tour in Project Delta recon, plus a year in Thailand with the 46th Special Forces Company training indigenous soldiers. Bill was smart, strong, enthusiastic, and seasoned—I couldn't have picked a finer man. Though he was seven years my senior, he was utterly professional and loyal. Between us, we had bedrock for a team.

With Bill's help, I'd soon have RT Illinois green, ready for combat.

One afternoon in mid-August, Bill and I were in the recon company orderly room when First Sergeant Doney arrived from the Tactical Operations Center to announce, "RT New York is attempting a prisoner snatch." Along with several One-Zeros, we noticed the waning daylight—it was 5:00 P.M.—and wondered at the wisdom of starting a fight so late in the day.

RT New York's John St. Martin had taken in eight men, including One-One Ed Wolcoff, One-Two John Blaauw, and five Montagnards. His team had inserted two days earlier, less than two miles from where Dennis Bingham had been killed on RT Hawaii.

They heard no signal shots, saw no trackers, and came upon no fresh trails—no sign of the enemy whatsoever—until late that afternoon, their third day, when they emerged from a bamboo forest to discover heavy log buildings, well camouflaged beneath double-canopy jungle. Creeping forward, St. Martin watched three NVA walk about and tend a cooking fire. It was a large encampment, stretching beyond his vision, and he could see by the worn paths between the buildings that it had been there several years. The camp's inhabitants, St. Martin concluded, must be road engineers, away working on Highway 110.

He pulled RT New York back 100 yards to think. The camp was a great find, but wouldn't it be even greater if he snatched one or two of those NVA, and seized some documents from one of those buildings? On this, his sixth mission, he would achieve as great a coup as any One-Zero ever scored—but time was of the essence since it was late afternoon.

Radioing his discovery to the S-3 operations officer via Covey Rider Karate Davis, St. Martin said he intended to snatch a prisoner and asked that the helicopters at Dak To prepare for an emergency extraction. The Covey FAC flying Karate, Captain Don Fulton, thought it was a great idea. Immediately executed, St. Martin's plan may have succeeded. But the S-3 had to add his own touch, announcing, "OK on the prisoner snatch, but call in an air strike first."

That's stupid, St. Martin thought. Surprise will be gone when the first bomb hits. He resisted and radio messages went back and forth. Finally the S-3 radioed, "That's an order."

But now came more delay, more daylight lost waiting for fighters. When the A-1s arrived it was almost sunset and they were low on fuel, having already flown a mission to rescue a downed pilot. Worse, they could offer no cluster bombs or napalm, just 500-pound bombs, not the best ordnance for this situation. But bombs would have to do because there wasn't enough daylight to wait for another set of fighters.

St. Martin's men could not mark the target with smoke or flares without disclosing their presence, yet the blast danger from 500-pound bombs precluded being close enough to watch the bombs impact. So RT New York had to pull back, signal their location by mirror, then adjust by the sound of the explosions. Stuck with this inexact technique, St. Martin brought the bombs so close that the concussion bounced him in the air.

Then, overhead, Karate Davis radioed that the A-1s were dropping one last bomb.

St. Martin crawled to a log and peeked over to find that the bombs had totally missed the buildings. Then he saw three armed NVA trot to a bunker. St. Martin whispered to One-One Wolcoff and two Yards, "Take the right flank. I'm going to sneak up and initiate contact. While I have their attention, you sneak in and we'll see what we can get." Behind them followed a second line, led by the radio operator, Sergeant John Blaauw, and three Yards.

St. Martin pulled a grenade pin and stepped over the log.

"We're going in," One-Two Blaauw whispered into his radio.

St. Martin cocked his arm but NVA fire stitched him—*cack-cack-cack*—ankle, thigh, stomach—whirling him around. His ears rang and the world spun as he pivoted backward over the log and somehow dumped the grenade harmlessly. Pain nearly paralyzing him, he looked down to see his intestines had spilled out. He knew that few people survive so grave a wound and began to pray. AK fire cracked everywhere.

With supporting fire from his teammates, One-One Wolcoff ran to St. Martin and dragged him back. His One-Zero's wounds were worse than he'd expected: In addition to being painfully gun-shot, another slug had shattered his right thigh, and a third had almost severed his foot at the ankle. Wolcoff secured the stomach wound by tucking St. Martin's jungle shirt into his pants, then dragged him farther back.

Already Karate Davis had called Dak To for the Cobras but they wouldn't be there for another twenty-five minutes, and F-4 Phantoms were still at least ten minutes away. That left just Don Fulton's unarmed O-2 for air support, so he dove to the treetops and pummeled the jungle with white phosphorus marking rockets, and Karate cranked open the plane's right window and fired his CAR-15. For a dozen minutes, Fulton and Karate braved antiaircraft fire to fight off the NVA gathering around RT New York. A passing Covey FAC, First Lieutenant Rick Felker, arrived to rocket the enemy, too.

On the ground, delirious in pain, St. Martin barely noticed the explosions and gunfire. He chose to find relief in death. OK, God, he thought, I'm giving up. He closed his eyes and went limp—then opened his eyes. "Damn," he groaned, "it didn't work."

At last, F-4 Phantoms arrived and immediately began strafing with 20mm cannons, joined soon by Cobra gunships. In the waning light, they pushed back the NVA.

Meanwhile, One-One Wolcoff slid an extraction harness on St. Martin as the first Huey hovered on the treetops, dropping four ropes to the team. Under a low cloud ceiling, in light rain, almost dark, the Huey pilot had to turn on his landing lights, which drew enemy ground fire. While three others snapped on to the ropes, Wolcoff cinched St. Martin's pistol belt to hold his intestines, snapped in his harness, then waved off the bird.

Lifting away, pain wracked St. Martin's body. Even worse, flying in that black sky, one Montagnard banged into St. Martin's shattered right leg, over and over, each time spiking pain to his brain. Somehow he endured that one-hour ride, dangling 100 feet below a helicopter buffeted by rain at ninety-miles-per-hour airspeed, with no medical attention. The weather was so stormy that the pilots could not find Dak To airfield. They flew on for Pleiku. At one point, St. Martin told himself, "If I'm going to die, I might as well die now." Then the lights of Pleiku sparkled through the gloom and he added, "I take it all back, God. I don't want to die. Please, don't let me die."

In the emergency room, he slipped into unconsciousness, having lost six pints of blood. He hung there that night, on the verge of death. Two days later, when his teammates visited him, he was reinvigorated enough to give Wolcoff the finger. John St. Martin would survive, but his debilitating wounds ended his Army career.

His mission, though incomplete, was by no means a failure. Two weeks later, a Hatchet Force company raided the enemy encampment discovered by St. Martin and, supported by massed airpower, inflicted heavy losses on the enemy, putting them to flight and capturing much matériel, including an anti-aircraft gun. Intelligence analysts later estimated the hidden camp had contained a regimental or higher headquarters.

RT New York's One-One, Ed Wolcoff, had proven himself a courageous leader, so he was appointed the team's new One-Zero. He and One-Two Blaauw received Bronze Stars for Valor, while Karate Davis was awarded an Air Medal. USAF Captain Fulton, whose O-2 limped back to Pleiku with fresh bullet holes and no fuel on the gauges, got his second Distinguished Flying Cross in as many months.

RT New York needed a new One-Two, RT Illinois needed a third American, many teams had openings, so replacements flowed in from Fort Bragg. Awed by their first glimpse of SOG's secret, covert world, these rosy-cheeked, gullible newcomers offered an opportunity too attractive to resist—they were perfect foils for practical jokes.

First Sergeant Doney sent one such unfortunate soul—let us call him "Wendell"—to our team room, instructing Bill Spencer and me to get him oriented and answer all his questions. We had that day off, partying with a neighboring team on stand-down. While chugging beers, we explained to Wendell how to carry his gear, described the rations he'd have in the field, and demonstrated how to prepare them. Wendell lapped it all up.

After an hour, my eyes met Bill's and we agreed silently to have some fun with our new guy. Inspiration sprang from a bottle of multivitamins I noticed on a shelf. "We should warn Wendell about venereal diseases," I suggested, "what with a whorehouse just outside the front gate." In graphic detail, we took turns describing various VDs—from venereal warts to gonorrhea and worse—pausing here and there to shake our heads. When I described syphilis, Bill added, "Terrible, terrible. Goes to your brain."

"But, Wendell," I cautioned, "the one thing you gotta do your damnedest to avoid—it'll kill you, but only after destroying what miserable life you have left. That's the *Black Syph*." The rest of the guys just shuddered, one adding, "Also called mushroom dick."

There was no such thing but Wendell didn't know that.

I continued, "Wendell, they've kept it out of the papers to avoid upsetting families back home. You see, there's no wonder drug to knock this monster down. And since there's no cure, you can't go home. There's this island off the coast of Vietnam, that's where they keep 'em."

Wendell was momentarily lost. "Keep who?"

Bill was catching on, and answered, "Why, any GI who catches Black Syph."

"You can never go home," another guy lamented.

"With enough funding, maybe someday there'll be a cure," I hoped. "Then those poor GIs can go back to their families, clean and whole again."

I kept waiting, waiting, then, finally, Wendell asked the obvious question. "Gee, Sarge, how do you know if you've got Black Syph?" *Damn! We got him!*

"Your urine, Wendell. Turns bright orange—as orange as a glass of Tang." Wendell would know instantly if he contracted the dread disease. *By no small coincidence, that was a side effect of a drug I had on my shelf, right beside the bottle of multivitamins.* "As long as we're talking about health," I scooped up the bottle of multivitamins, "we take vitamins every day."

Bill agreed. "We live in the jungle, beyond sunlight. We need our vitamins."

Enthused, each grabbed a multivitamin, downed with beer, except, of course, I slipped Wendell a Pyridium. This brown pill, left over from a minor kidney infection, would cause him no harm, but as the medics had informed me—*it turns your urine as orange as Tang.*

We drank all afternoon, then afternoon turned into evening and somewhere along the way Wendell wandered off. I told the others what I'd done, we had a good chuckle, then continued drinking in the club. I completely forgot about Wendell, the Black Syph, and Pyridium.

Trudging to the mess hall for coffee the next morning, all I had on my mind was relieving a terrible hangover. As I passed the dispensary, the screen door flew open and a medic screamed, "You dirty bastard! Get in here!"

That didn't sound like the doc. I thought he was my friend. I walked in, looked past the doc, and there, shivering in the corner sat Wendell, convinced he was going to die on some island while his dick rotted away. After leaving us the previous afternoon, Wendell had discovered the house of ill repute, sampled its wares, and now found himself urinating Tang!

"Tell him it's bullshit!" the doc shouted.

"I-I-I made it up, Wendell." I almost laughed, looking at his trembling hands. "I'm sorry you took it so bad." Wendell flashed out the door, gone. The doc turned to me, angry, then he burst out laughing, and we both laughed until tears flowed.

The funniest experiences of my life happened in SOG, but each moment of hilarity seemed to be followed by a day of agony, one emotion making the other all that more pronounced. It was like that when we lost Ken Worthley a few days later.

Those of us not in the field were preoccupied with Bob Howard's departure, knowing he was going home to receive the Medal of Honor, the fourth one to a recon man from Kontum. While Howard packed his bags, Ken Worthley's RT Florida was roaming northeast Cambodia, with One-One Bob Garcia, One-Two Dale Hanson, and four indigenous soldiers.

Garcia spoke for all of us when he called Ken "one of the best persons you could ever meet—really clean-cut, wholesome, the All-American kid." Raised in a religious farming family in Minnesota, Ken's parents shipped him clothing for local Montagnard villages and Kontum's leprosy home. There wasn't a recon man who didn't like the courageous, compassionate, selfless, soft-spoken One-Zero.

In Cambodia, Ken's team ambushed a senior NVA intelligence officer and captured his satchel, containing top secret documents about enemy spies in South Vietnam. They fought their way clear, evaded many pursuing troops, and were being lifted out on ropes when a rifle shot hit Ken, killing him instantly. One Yard sustained a minor wound, while Hanson had a finger shot off and a bullet grazed his head.

True to tradition, we heartily sang "Hey, Blue" to Ken's departed spirit, as well as named a barracks for him, "Worthley Hall." Then Bob Howard took it another step, delaying his arrival home in Alabama by three days, so he could personally escort Ken's body to Sherburne, Minnesota. There could have been no finer gesture, nor done by a finer man than Bob Howard.

It had been a tough month for One-Zeros—John St. Martin, Ralph Rodd, and Jim Pruitt shot up and medevaced, Ken Worthley killed, and Glenn Uemura losing two men. And now it was my turn, my first mission as a One-Zero.

Along with One-One Bill Spencer and our new One-Two, Charles "Weird" Herald, I sat through our mission briefing. Our target was northeast Cambodia, not five miles from where Ken had been lost. RT Maine had been in this area, too, and its talented One-Zero, David Baker, had eluded an NVA counter-recon company for three days. Eventually Baker's men got boxed in, so he boldly ambushed the NVA, ran like hell, and got away. I'd listened to Baker describing it over a drink in the club, and I'd sat with other One-Zeros to hear a detailed debriefing put together by First Sergeant Norm Doney. I learned a lot in Doney's debrief sessions, one of his great innovations, in which a returning One-Zero shared his experiences with other One-Zeros.

Sitting in the intelligence briefing with Bill and Weird Herald, I learned that the 66th NVA Regiment, having withdrawn from Ben Het, was believed to be in our target area. Beyond this, intelligence was too vague to be of much benefit.

Bill Spencer and I flew the aerial recon, seeing lots of trails but no people or hooches.

Two days before insertion, I walked into our Vietnamese team room with great news, that Armed Forces Radio said North Vietnam's Communist leader, Ho Chi Minh, had died. My interpreter, Suu's, eyes widened and his normal glibness escaped him—he looked like his world had collapsed. Then he blinked, smiled, and offered, "This is good. Very good."

It wasn't enough to challenge his loyalty, but Suu's reaction troubled me. We had long suspected that enemy agents—moles—had penetrated SOG, most likely in Saigon. Many Vietnamese felt caught in the middle, between the nationalistic appeal of Ho Chi Minh and the corrupt but democratic government in Saigon. In Suu's case I could not tell where his loyalties lay.

The next evening I planned my LZs with Karate Davis, our Covey Rider. Then we got to bed early and didn't drink a single beer. I awoke fresh, my health restored, ready to lead my first mission as a One-Zero.

As our choppers crossed the border into Cambodia, I looked down into those now familiar hills, confident that we were ready, thanks to weeks of solid training with Bill Spencer. Inspired by John Allen, I had refined our immediate action drills, adding tear gas for the M-79 grenade launchers, then live-firing over and over until it unfolded perfectly. Like Ben Thompson, I carried the team radio, but only for insertion; afterward I would switch rucksacks with Weird Herald.

Riding our Huey's right door, I recognized a distinct hill and knew when to step out on the skid, waving my CAR-15 to return fire, but there was none. Then we were hovering, I jumped away, and we were on the ground, trotting to the jungle. Momentarily, our second Huey arrived with Bill Spencer and three Vietnamese.

Some One-Zeros preferred to bring six men, so they could fit in one helicopter, generating less visual and sound signature. I preferred eight men— three Americans and five indigenous—a lesson I'd learned when Hai was shot. Even though Hai was walking-wounded, it took two men to keep him going. Had he been unable to walk, that would have taken away a third gunfighter, diverting two thirds of a six-man team. I believed eight men was a fair balance between staying small enough to hide, but large enough to fight and carry your casualties along.

The morning of insert, the intelligence officer issued me a case of booby trapped 82mm Chinese mortar ammo, designed to explode when fired. We were to leave it conspicuously on our LZ so it would be discovered and taken to enemy officers who would suspect that any nearby ammo caches might be contaminated. Bill Spencer carried it in, only too happy to get rid of it as quick as we landed on the immense LZ, as big as ten football fields. That was Karate's idea, to land on a huge LZ, since the enemy expected us to use smaller ones.

It must have worked, because we didn't see or hear any NVA, and sent the aircraft away with a "Team OK." It wasn't until mid-afternoon that we heard distant rifle shots.

Recalling how the NVA had swept through our night position on the earlier mission, I sought the best cover and terrain to hide the team. I selected a thickly forested spot on a slope so steep that we had to sleep with trees between our legs to keep from sliding downhill. On such ground, no enemy counter-recon unit could stay on line in darkness.

That night we heard a dog on the ridge above us and my first thought was, How dare man's best friend work for the enemy! Though the dog never came close, we did not sleep soundly. Then sometime after midnight, I felt an earthquake and realized a B-52 strike had hit nearby, maybe five miles away.

That second day we saw no enemy at dawn, but all morning we knew they were nearby, and in considerable numbers. The NVA was actively hunting us, probably two or more platoons, and as the morning passed, our Vietnamese soldiers grew fearful. By noon, we had changed directions or backed away four times and twice enemy searchers swept past our front. Sooner or later, Bill agreed with me, we'd make contact or shake clean of the NVA and go our own way—but it was too early to tell which. I felt like a matador swinging his cape as a bull brushed past.

Then we heard NVA shout to one another, petrifying our indigenous soldiers. Suu said the voices were too garbled to understand. And then Covey, Karate Davis, flew over, warning us, "Go high and dry," and left. Remaining stationary during an aggressive search effort, I believed, would lead to discovery and an overwhelming blow by the NVA's numerical superiority. It was better to keep moving, though very carefully. Bill agreed.

I circled us back past our insertion LZ so our fresh tracks would overlay the ones we'd left the previous day, an American Indian trick for confusing cavalry scouts. As we passed that immense field, astonishingly, we saw an NVA platoon in the open at port arms—and they were carrying the case of 82mm mortar ammo! Saigon would be happy to hear that. We lay there for fifteen minutes, watching thirty-odd NVA searching our insert LZ. The Americans' fascination was not shared by our Vietnamese, their faces fearful at seeing the NVA well within hailing distance.

Then something changed.

I noticed our Vietnamese whisper among themselves and exchange furtive looks. Something was wrong—very wrong. I recalled Suu's reaction to Ho Chi Minh's death, and noticed his shifting eyes avoid mine, glancing at the enemy formation. He mumbled something low in Vietnamese to the point man. My mind flashed back to Floyd Ambrose's story of the NVA offering to let a team's native soldiers escape if they turned over the Americans. Suu knew of the offer, the Vietnamese all did—plus Suu had claimed the NVA shouts were too garbled to understand. Were they? I saw Suu's hand nervously flexing his CAR-15 grip, edging it toward me, so I swung my CAR-15 between his legs, two inches below his crotch. He looked up to me, and for an instant I could see his eyes calculating.

In one glance, I had to decide. I'd have to shoot Suu, first, then the point man—he was the best with a weapon—and any others who looked hostile. But could I drop enough of them before they shot me, or Bill or Weird Herald? There was no time to warn Bill or Herald. It would happen any second, any second.

Then Suu's hand relaxed, the moment passed. His muzzle shifted away— had it swung one centimeter closer, I'd have killed him. But we weren't out yet.

I signaled Hai, the point man, to move out. He hadn't gone twenty-five paces when he spun sideways and opened fire, *shooting at nothing*. As they'd been trained, the entire team went instantly into an immediate action drill, concentrating their fire where Hai had, *against nothing*. Bill and I went along with it, pretending we didn't realize no one was shooting back—there were real NVA, possibly hundreds of them, within a half-mile, so now was hardly a time to discuss it. I pointed in a new direction, and Hai led us that way while Weird Herald radioed a distress call to Covey. There was nothing fake about the grave danger of disclosing our exact location to every NVA within earshot. We had to flee, fast.

Distrustful of Hai, I took point myself and kept a steady trot. Momentarily we reached a trail across which I jumped, then waved the rest, not even pausing, one continuous flow. I counted my men to ensure no one had been left behind. When my count reached eight, I pivoted to follow—my eye caught a flicker of movement. Down the trail, not twenty yards away, two running NVA burst over a rise, the lead man carrying an RPG on his shoulder, his companion behind him with an AK. My CAR-15 was aimed squarely at the first man's chest—the RPG man knew he was going to die but he tried to fire anyway. My first burst knocked him down, the impacting bullets puffing dust off his dirty shirt, then my second burst killed his companion. I ran after my team; perhaps five seconds had passed. Now the enemy had our current location.

Our pace increased to a full run. There was heavy gunfire on our backtrail, where the NVA must have found their dead comrades. I slowed our movement and turned us hard right to confuse any pursuers. Then Weird Herald waved—he had Covey and it wasn't good news. Karate was busy extracting a Hatchet Force company and until that was done, at least a half-hour, we were on our own. A few minutes later we reached another immense LZ, across which we saw a formation of NVA sweeping at high port directly toward us. Taking the handset, I radioed Karate, "Expedite, expedite. We have enemy maneuvering on us, in the open."

"This is SPAF," another voice crackled on the radio, that of an O-1 Bird Dog pilot. He was nearby with a photographer, shooting pictures of the previous night's B-52 strike. "We can come and help," he offered. The NVA would be on top of us in minutes.

"We've got an estimated platoon in the open," I reported, then whispered to Bill, "What the hell can a Bird Dog do?" He couldn't get us fighter support in Cambodia, and Covey had the Pink Panther Cobras firing for the Hatchet Force. Bill shrugged, but at this point even an unarmed O-1 was better than nothing. "Roger that," I whispered. "Assistance appreciated."

Moments later, three dozen NVA were halfway across that immense field when the O-1 flashed past at treetop level—enemy soldiers dived for the ground, ran, or squatted, but not one fired at the plane, nor did the plane fire at them. When the O-1 came back around, the NVA had partially re-formed, many shouldering AKs to greet the little Bird Dog. But when it buzzed low across the field—*brrrrt, brrrrt, brrrrt!*—from its back window an M-16 fired quick bursts and the NVA broke ranks and fled from so startling a spectacle.

Not a single NVA appeared to be hit, but that strafing bought us a precious few moments.

Then across that wide LZ, at least 500 yards away, I watched three NVA on a hilltop rearrange freshly cut brush to camouflage a 12.7mm antiaircraft machine gun position. I leaned into a tree, aimed my CAR-15, but there was little chance of hitting them so far away—and it would have told the whole world where we were hiding. I wished I had a sniper rifle.

Momentarily Karate arrived with the last thing these NVA expected—or I expected—a pair of A-1 Skyraiders. *Why, that was unauthorized!* Karate radioed, "Now, just where are those bad guys?" After Bill signaled him with a mirror, I described the hilltop. One A-1 scattered cluster bombs perfectly across it, then his wingman hit it with two napalm canisters. Officially, of course, they had dumped their ordnance in Laos, for the Hatchet Force extraction.

We took only light ground fire coming out, and not one single round from that hilltop.

It was euphoric riding that swaying, climbing Huey, like a dream in which the hand of God lifts you away from terror. I looked around; it was quiet, a peaceful, sunny day, only the sound of rotors and rushing air. I slapped Bill's back. It was great to be alive.

Back at Kontum, I found Lieutenant Colonel Abt at his favorite pursuit, tossing horseshoes. I told him what had happened, how close I'd come to shooting my interpreter, and that the false contact almost got us killed. "Well, John," he responded, "it's your team. What do you want to do?"

I could never take them out again—nor could I stick another One-Zero with any of them. I recalled that calculating look in Suu's eyes and how his muzzle drifted toward my belly.

"I must fire the whole team, sir. And train a new team."

Abt nodded.

An hour later, I had all nine Vietnamese, our entire team, bring their weapons to me for an "inspection." Once their weapons were stacked, I announced they were fired. Bill and Weird Herald with holstered pistols escorted them to supply to turn in their gear and get paid.

They went out the front gate in their underwear.

That night, after our preliminary debrief and a T-bone dinner, Bill and I set out to find the gutsy photographer who'd fired from the Bird Dog. We found

him in the club, Staff Sergeant Pete Wilson, a SOG headquarters NCO up from
Saigon. Over a drink, Wilson confessed he'd become so target-focused that
he'd shot a hole through the plane's wing strut.

Disillusioned with his cushy job in air-conditioned, whore-infested Saigon,
he'd volunteered to fly the photo mission because he'd joined Special Forces to
see combat, not a desk. Bill and I poured so many compliments and drinks into
Pete that by morning, he insisted that he would leave his desk job and come
here, to run recon with RT Illinois.

Sure enough, one week later Pete Wilson was back, replacing Weird Herald, who'd gone on to another team. Now a genuine recon man, Pete needed a
code name. The good life in Saigon had added inches to his girth, so we pro-
claimed him "Fat Albert," after the Bill Cosby character.

And now, with Fat Albert aboard, we had to recruit and train an entirely
new team.

Chapter Eight

The more I got to know Fat Albert, the more I liked him—indeed, everyone liked thirty-year-old Peter J. Wilson. I'd have guessed him to be a professor at some small eastern college, not a Green Beret covert warrior. A product of upstate New York, Fat Albert exhibited wit and style with a flair for the pseudodramatic; one evening, for example, when we entered the club, he commanded, as if a Roman legionnaire, "Wine for my troops!" Afterward, whenever he entered a bar, he called, "Wine for my troops!"

Though he absorbed tactics and mastered weapons as well as the best, there was always a kind of fish-out-of-water quality about Pete, as if he were secretly an anthropologist studying the rest of us, fascinated by all he saw. Bill Spencer, my One-One, proved as different from Fat Albert as night from day. Lean and athletic, Bill abounded in hard-knocks cynicism and a devil-may-care fatalism. Yet their differences didn't matter—maybe they complemented—because we melded as one. What a team! Both Bill and Pete displayed the leadership qualities of potential One-Zeros; I knew I'd better make the most of them, for too soon they'd have their own teams.

But first we had to train a new RT Illinois. We began by hiring a Montagnard interpreter, Bui, from our compound's security detachment, then holding daily interviews over hot green tea at the outdoor Chinese soup restaurant. Bui generated sufficient word of mouth that two dozen Yards walked in from their villages, presenting carefully folded Parachute School diplomas and letters of commendation from U.S. Special Forces units. Had we been hiring ordinary laborers, an interpreter might have practiced nepotism or steered friends our way—especially considering SOG's relatively high pay, about $100 per month, as much as a South Vietnamese Army captain. But Bui knew his life, all our lives, depended on these men, so he pulled no chicanery.

Within three days, I'd hired a new, all-Montagnard RT Illinois: Bui, Phyit, Boui, Hlien, Lun, Wo, Pher, Pouih, Gim, and Yeo. Each hill tribesman had but one name, which took some getting used to; all were Rhade, the largest Yard tribe in the Central Highlands. Darker and stockier than Vietnamese, the Montagnards resemble Polynesians, to whom they are ethnically related. They are a proud people: Their shoeless children never begged, nor did their women prostitute themselves, while their men lived by their word. Yards displayed a cheerful outlook with childlike faith in their friends, and once accepted, they would die for you.

Many Montagnards professed Catholicism but they could not escape generations of animism, the belief in ghostly spirits inhabiting rocks and trees. Omens and spirits told them when to plant crops, when to wed, or when to build a new stilted house.

Our Yards loved American movies, especially westerns, which they watched on an outdoor plywood screen. One night a Yard sat beside Captain Jim Storter, absorbed by a western in which the cavalry shot hell out of a band of surrounded Indians. The perplexed Montagnard looked to Storter, entirely serious, and asked, "Why Indians no call Kingbees?"

"He just had no concept," Storter chuckled, "that back in 1877, there were no helicopters."

Training our Yards proved quite a challenge. Largely illiterate and unaccustomed to formal instruction, they relied heavily on repetition, with some tasks acquired solely by rote. Their mathematical skills—"One, two, three, many"—left much to desire, as well.

Initially I emphasized shooting, getting us to the range almost daily, where we allowed the Yards no uncontrolled spraying, just semiauto fire, aimed through the sights. We practiced rapid magazine changes, keeping the right hand on the weapon and feeding magazines with the left, never taking eyes off the target. I demonstrated how to track their muzzle: Wherever a man's eyes went, his muzzle followed, so that when his eyes snapped instinctively to a threat, his weapon would be aimed there, too. For amusement, I demonstrated how my right hand *always* gripped my CAR-15, doing everything with my left hand, even picking my nose. They nodded at that wisdom. Finally, we taught them to shoot full-auto, in accurate, five-round bursts.

Taking them to the next level—tactics—proved almost impossibly abstract. These concepts just weren't sinking in. Then one afternoon I watched two Yards sit cross-legged on the ground, playing Montagnard checkers on a rectangular grid drawn in the dirt, each with a dozen pebbles as pieces. When one player's pebble was caught between two of his opponent's, it was lost, until one man conquered the whole grid. Watching them gave me insight to their true intelligence and subtlety—without doubt, they could understand tactics. The problem was presentation.

I acquired some toy soldiers, twelve of which I named, so each Yard and

American could see his miniature counterpart. Then I arranged the figures in formations to represent our team and the NVA. In miniature, Bill, Pete, and I taught them everything from ambushes and perimeter defense to immediate action drills, which we'd afterward practice full-size, even live-fire. In a few days, the Yards understood all our formations and tactics, thanks to those toy soldiers.

Because they understood so well, I was able to refine my immediate action drill: Upon contact, each man jumped right or left, fired his first magazine full-auto (all tracer ammunition), then peeled off, switching to semiauto for any subsequent firing. Meanwhile, one man pulled out a claymore mine pre-rigged with a thirty-second fuse, which he ignited. Our two M-79 grenadiers fired one high-explosive round, then, peeling away, fired a second round—tear gas—over their shoulders. After firing, the interpreter and I tossed tear gas grenades, and my radio operator, Fat Albert, instantly radioed Covey to request air support. We practiced this drill over and over, dozens of times each day during our third, and final, week of training.

Then it was time for a dress rehearsal, in the form of a local mission.

That early fall of 1969, a sniper occasionally had fired at vehicles on Highway 14 and at our men when they jogged along the road. Whether he ever hit a vehicle I did not know, and he had yet to hit anyone from CCC. Still, the incidents had grown from once a week to several times, a frequency that generated serious concern; before he left, even Bob Howard had begun jogging with a weapon.

The S-2 gave us enough information to assemble a profile: He fired one shot just after dawn, always from the east side of Highway 14, about one kilometer south of our compound. That afternoon, while Bill drove a jeep, I eyed the terrain along the highway. Engineer plows had bulldozed the jungle for about 300 yards on either side of the road; along the stretch frequented by our sniper sat a solitary peasant hooch, the only local inhabitants. The sniper spent his days hiding somewhere up there in the jungle, I theorized, working his way to its edge just before daylight to take his shot and withdraw. That's the way I'd have done it.

Back in our team room, Bill, Pete, and I huddled around a map, thought it through, then came up with the best plan: In darkness, RT Illinois would infiltrate the jungled high ground, quietly spend the night, then break up into small groups to intercept the sniper at dawn, when he fired. Instead of trading shots at 300 yards with scoped rifles, we would kill him at twenty-five yards with CAR-15s.

Just after sunset we applied facial camouflage and let our eyes adjust to the darkness. Twenty minutes later we filed unseen through the north gate. We were moving stealthily, and the night march took twice as long as I'd estimated. By the time we'd crossed an intervening stream, bypassed the hooch, and curved eastward through the jungle to the trees above the road, it was almost midnight and so dark I could barely make out the highway 300 yards down the slope.

We gathered tightly in a perimeter and slept. The night passed without incident.

About thirty minutes before daylight, Bill, Pete, and I huddled for last-minute coordination, then split into three elements, each of us leading three Yards to an overwatch position, perhaps 150 yards apart, to wait for the sniper to show his face. As the center element, I crept noiselessly to the jungle's edge with our point man, Boui, interpreter Bui, and Phyit, an M79 grenadier. As daylight grew, I saw that a slight rise was blocking our observation—we had to move fifty yards to higher ground, quick.

We were halfway there when, *BANG!*—a shot—*but not in the jungle, somewhere below.* A South Vietnamese Army jeep sped away, apparently the target of this latest attack—then I spotted a flash of movement through bamboo 100 yards below, so quick it was gone by the time I raised my CAR-15.

He wasn't running up toward the jungle, but downhill, toward the road!

I ran like hell down the open hillside, the three Montagnards following, watching for the gunman to reappear on the other side of the bamboo; he did, trotting slower but his hands were empty. He'd dumped his rifle somewhere in the bamboo. Fleetingly, he appeared and reappeared, offering no clear shot. Then I saw where he was going.

Ahead of him, cooking smoke rose from the thatch-roofed hooch, where a peasant wife laid out a breakfast of rice and greens, and two children sat at its open doorway. Now the gunman walked at a normal pace, carrying some farm implement, acting as if nothing had happened—but I knew he had fired the shot. While he squatted down with the woman and two children to eat, we approached unseen to less than fifty yards, and knelt in thick foliage.

I sent Boui to get the rest of the team, then watched one child in the doorway eating from an aluminum rice bowl. What a stupid bastard! I thought. He doesn't have a pot to piss in, all he's got in the world is his family and he's endangering them. Was he a terrible shot or was he purposely aiming high? I could have apprehended him, but two months earlier John Allen and I had captured an armed Vietcong suspect while training in the jungle, about a mile from the CCC compound. Dutifully, we gave him to the Vietnamese provincial police. A day later I saw him on the back seat of a Honda—he gave me the finger. I wasn't going to make that mistake twice.

My sight centered on the man's chest but I hesitated to shoot, waiting for him to step away from his kids. I imagined the pitch he'd heard from those who'd recruited him—the same nice Vietcong who'd slaughtered a jeepload of Catholic orphans just up Highway 14 to let everyone know they could control the road at will. "Do this for the revolution, brother. Shoot at the puppets and Yankees, comrade." Right, or they'd disembowel him in front of his family.

Five minutes had passed since the shot was fired. Phyit asked, "Truong Si [sergeant], he die?"

I was tempted to shoot him and attribute it to the sniper who'd been plinking at our joggers—there's a touch of irony. I laid my sight on him as I flipped my CAR-15 off safety.

Then I noticed his kids, squatting down, shoveling rice into their hungry mouths.

I lowered my CAR-15 and swapped it with Phyit for his M-79 grenade launcher. I replaced his gold high-explosive grenade with a gray one—tear gas—held the sight on the hooch, raised it to compensate for distance, and— POONK!—off it lobbed, smashing through the shanty's wall to billow inside. The whole family leaped to their feet, spilling their bowls, children crying and grabbing their mother, the father trembling and coughing.

We walked off, leaving an indelible message: "We know who you are, where you are, and what you've done." Maybe he could convince the Vietcong that he'd lost his usefulness.

However it worked out, we never got another report of him taking a shot. And our mission was chalked up as a success—RT Illinois was deemed ready for a cross-border mission. But we weren't targeted immediately because the monsoon had slowed our frequency of operations. So we trained hard each day, and each night socialized in the club. One night we gathered around a just returned One-Zero who stood, held up his drink, and summarized his latest mission in one memorable line: "Christians seven, Lions nothing."

Everyone laughed, some roared until they cried. His metaphor became shorthand for inflicting losses and escaping clean, and the imagery wasn't off— inserting in Laos or Cambodia, it often felt like you were stepping into the Roman arena, a sacrifice for the amusement of others. We always, *always* fought outnumbered. Fat Albert especially loved that Roman metaphor and sometimes strolled into the club, adjusted his invisible toga, then heralded some team's latest triumph, like, "Recon Team Texas: Christians te-welve, Lions zee-row!"

But that lightheartedness disappeared when things went the other way—

never once did anyone allude to the Roman metaphor when "Christians" were lost. There was nothing to make light of, nor any need to post the result. Tragic news always traveled fast.

A company-size Hatchet Force mission, led by Captain Barre McClelland with 100 Yards and a dozen Americans, fought an especially aggressive NVA force in Laos that September. In a single fight a score of Yards were wounded, plus six Americans—Lieutenants Frank Longaker and Ken Snyder, and Sergeants Peter Tandy, Robert Wallace, Terry Minnihan, and Richard Joecken. Their only medic, Specialist Four Cecil Keyton, did his best, but heavy ground fire drove away their extraction helicopters. Keyton spent the whole night treating the wounded but he could work no miracles—young Joecken died before dawn. At least the rest got out alive.

A few weeks later another Hatchet Force mission came to grief. Led by Captain Ronald Goulet, a former recon company commander, the force landed under ground fire; the fearless Goulet rescued Staff Sergeant Mike Sheppard from a burning Kingbee, downed on their insert LZ. Then Goulet's men mounted an aggressive assault, forcing the NVA to retreat. That evening, Goulet and another captain who'd volunteered for the mission, Neil Coady, looked long and hard at each other; something was familiar. Finally they realized they'd been kindergarten classmates in Slatersville, Rhode Island.

For two days the Hatchet Force skirmished with NVA squads. Then they stumbled upon a major ammunition stockpile, capturing it after a short fight. Realizing the enemy would mount a counterattack, Goulet hastily redeployed his men, and almost as quickly an RPG crashed into the perimeter. Coady rushed over to find his kindergarten classmate badly wounded.

Captain Goulet died in a Huey, halfway back to Dak To. He was a fine, brave man.

More "Hey, Blue," more gut-wrenching in the club. At times it seemed so many were dying that you had to remind yourself that people were going home, too. Reinald Pope, wounded in Laos, was riding an extraction rig beneath a Huey when he realized his carabiner link had failed to snap shut; for twenty minutes he rode at 3,000 feet, looking up at the link's quarter-inch jaw teetering, about to slide off the rope, but it never quite did. He went home shaken, but in one piece. Bill Delima made it despite being wounded and a lot of hairy trips into Target Hotel-Nine. Bob Howard survived, with an incredible six Purple Hearts. Floyd Ambrose went home with one Purple Heart, as did RT Hawaii teammates Lonnie Pulliam and Greg Glashauser. Even RT California's Joe Walker, though wounded, survived it all, but Joe was a special case—he didn't exactly go home. Joe arranged a tour with the CIA in northern Laos, packed up a footlocker full of everything he'd need and took it with him. He told me he'd be back in a year.

Joe's RT California went to an old hand who'd already served one recon tour at CCN to return for another at CCC, Sergeant First Class Richard "Moose" Gross. He retained Walker's One-One, Bill Stubbs, and brought in Bob "Patches" Mohs as One-Two. Together, they ran several successful missions, particularly in our remote, northern area of operations. By October they'd been targeted there for the third time; it felt to Stubbs like they were being run to death, and he had a terrible premonition. When he turned in his personal effects to First Sergeant Doney for the third mission, Stubbs instructed, "If anything happens to me, put all my money on the bar."

RT California's target lay thirty miles northwest of Dak Pek Special Forces Camp, the most remote outpost left on the Laotian border. Enemy ground fire drove them from their first insertion attempt; they returned to Dak Pek. Late that afternoon they low-leveled past meadows and old slash-and-burns to land atop a tall hill overlooking a river. Gross thought the LZ could be seen for miles, but they took no fire so he decided to make the best of it.

Not 100 yards away they discovered an abandoned LZ watcher's hut, then a cloudburst so slicked the hillside that they left pronounced tracks in the mud. At dusk, Gross had them circle back to the empty hut. They slept there that night under an unceasing rain.

Early the next morning the rain abated. By mid-morning they reached a deep gorge and across it they spotted many hooches and trails not visible from the air. Gross heard chopping and voices 500 yards below them, down by a stream.

For another hour they descended toward the voices but when the jungle thinned out, Gross halted them. Arrayed on the steep hillside, one above the other, they sat along a rocky outcropping. The last man in the column, Bill Stubbs, sat two arm lengths beyond the rest. Mohs attempted a radio check with Covey and when that failed he took off his rucksack to attach the long antenna. Stubbs looked back—*three AK muzzles, right there.*

Ka-ka-ka-ka-ka-ka-ka-ka! The first burst riddled Stubbs and seriously wounded three Yards. An NVA officer shouted, *"Bhat sanh! Bhat sanh!"*—"Take prisoners! Take prisoners!" Stubbs was killed so quickly that Gross couldn't absorb it. He blurred through three magazines and lobbed a grenade so fast he didn't get the pin out. Mohs fired his CAR-15 over Stubbs's body, tried to grab his rucksack—only five feet away—but AK fire was too intense to touch it. He shot the radio and followed the others, sliding and rolling down the hill, shooting all the way.

Gross's men slid down to the stream, then hustled up the next hillside and sped across a network of trails leading toward the hooches they'd seen earlier. At last, safely behind an immense boulder, Gross paused to treat his wounded. An AK slug had passed cleanly through the point man's neck, hitting only muscle tissue. Another Yard, Prin, had lost half his left biceps. A third Yard had one finger shot off. Mohs was uninjured. But Gross realized RPG shrapnel had slashed his own neck.

Gross pulled his survival radio only to find that a bullet had shot off the antenna; pinching it together, he called fruitlessly for Covey. For two hours they evaded and hid until Covey arrived; then A-1 Skyraiders got there and, covered by continuous bombing and strafing, RT California extracted at last light, escaping in a dusk sparkling with muzzle flashes and tracers.

The next morning Gross went back with RT New York, under John Blaauw, to recover Bill Stubbs's body. Enemy gunners fired at their aircraft and spoke gibberish on Stubbs's survival radio, but the team did not make contact. Nor did they find Stubbs's body. Indeed, the enemy had so sterilized the gunfight site that they found only a half-dozen fired brass cartridges.

In the club that night, the wake began when First Sergeant Doney held up $200 and announced, "Sergeant Stubbs wanted this on the bar, in his name. Drink on Billy Stubbs. God bless him." That we did a lot, at 25 cents a shot, then everyone sang "Hey, Blue" and toasted our lost comrade.

Afterward I found Gross sitting alone. I sat beside him and patted his shoulder. "Dick," I said, "tough luck. Stubbs was a good man." He nodded but said nothing. "What can you tell me?" I continued. "I just got a warning order. My team's going into the same area."

Gross looked over and his eyes narrowed. "Be careful, John. Those weren't clerks and jerks. They got within three feet of Stubbs before anyone saw 'em. I mean they were right on us. Watch yourself. Just watch yourself."

The next morning Bill, Pete, and I sat in the briefing room. The wall-size map displayed a grease pencil square—our target—not two miles from where Stubbs had been lost. It lay way north, nearly fifty miles above the Dak To launch site, farther even than my nemesis of July, Target Alpha-One. Our mission, the S-3 operations briefer announced, was to look for a new road reportedly hidden along a deep north–south valley. We would refuel as RT California had done, at Dak Pek Special Forces Camp, the final border outpost all the way north to the Demilitarized Zone.

Next came the S-2 intelligence briefer. I kept waiting to hear him repeat Gross's warning and point to the location of Stubbs's death, but he just babbled a superficial repetition of vague intelligence that described anywhere in southern Laos, e.g., "The vines are so thick, hills are so tall, enemy occupation forces here and there, high antiaircraft threat along major roads," etc. In the past, we'd been briefed by Roy Lamphier, a great intel man who'd gone out of his way to connect the dots by scouring adjacent target folders. Roy had even accompanied a Hatchet Force roadblock. But this guy, a sergeant first class desk jockey, looked more familiar with whiskey labels than target folders. My blood boiled but I kept quiet until the briefing finished.

Finally, the S-3 officer retook the podium and asked, "Are there any questions?"

I looked to the intel briefer. "Bill Stubbs," I asked. "Where did he die?" He looked dumbstruck. "And there was a CCN team hit up there, lost a guy—just where was that?" Afraid to speak and afraid to say nothing, he only blinked and shifted on his feet.

"Sergeant Plaster," the S-3 officer intervened, "is that in your area of operations?"

I stepped to the map and jammed a finger to where Bill had died, so angry I could hardly speak. "Three kilometers west, sir. Are we supposed to risk our fucking lives with this kind of shit for intel?" The major ushered us from the room. By the end of the day, the intel sergeant was reassigned to our camp security detachment; had he not been, all our One-Zeros and First Sergeant Doney would have raised holy hell. With Lieutenant Colonel Abt as commander, that was not necessary.

A day later, Bill and I rode a pair of O-1 Bird Dogs past Dak Pek, then turned northwest into Laos. Soon we passed a major landmark, a perfectly round lake, probably a meteor impact crater, the only lake for hundreds of miles. Now came steep ridges of 5,000 to 6,000 feet, the highest I'd seen in Laos, so high that their grassy tops sprouted scraggly Asian pine trees rather than jungle. Then an especially deep valley opened before us, almost a Shangri-la—bright, green bottomland, limestone bluffs, a cascading river, and caves big enough to hold trucks. This mountainous hideaway lay between two major highway networks, a sanctuary far from any pounding B-52 strikes. We caught glimpses of enemy activity—trails, row crops, and palm-covered roofs. Intelligence was right; something was happening there.

Landing anywhere in that valley was begging for trouble. Instead our spotter plane flew east, to the next valley, where I found just what we needed—an innocuous-looking one-ship LZ nestled in an out-of-the-way depression. I recorded its location, then photographed it.

Three days later we were at Dak To, ready to go, but we went nowhere. In Laos, a Hatchet Force platoon was in deep trouble: They'd been in a bloody fight the previous afternoon, then mortars had pummeled them all night. That morning, air strike after air strike went in around them, and it still wasn't certain they would get out. Our helicopters stood by to extract them and, if needed, RT Illinois would reinforce the Bright Light team to go after them.

I had two good friends with the platoon, Frank Belletire and Ron Bozikis. An accomplished recon man, Belletire had run with Floyd Ambrose, then gone to the Hatchet Force seven weeks earlier. "It's a better feeling," Frank had explained. "You have more men with you."

My other friend, Ron Bozikis, was smart, strong, athletic, and gregarious, the outgoing sort who letters in multiple sports in high school. A month earlier, Bozikis and his best friend, Hatchet Force squad leader Wayne Anderson, had teamed up to rescue the badly wounded Carlos Parker, who'd stepped on a mine. Anderson rushed through enemy fire to Parker's side, injected morphine, applied a tourniquet, then, while the stout Bozikis lifted Parker, Anderson held off the enemy. A formidable team, they got Parker to safety inside their platoon perimeter.

The day before RT Illinois arrived at Dak To, Belletire and Bozikis had gone into Laos with a forty-five-man platoon led by Captain Joseph Whelan. With them were Lieutenants Clint Davis and William Hatchett, plus Sergeants Dave Brock, Dennis Digiovanni, and Floyd Taylor. The plan was for a week-long reconnaissance-in-force, but they began taking fire even as their four choppers landed.

From their LZ, Captain Whelan spotted a few NVA run across a facing hillside, only 400 yards away—he ordered a quick assault to seize that high ground. The platoon rushed into an intervening depression only to be hit from all sides—*ambush!*

Outnumbered at least three to one, several Americans and Yards went down, including Captain Whelan. Seeing their leader twice thrown to the ground by exploding grenades, Belletire rushed his squad toward him; then an RPG detonated virtually atop Whelan, killing him instantly and shattering Belletire's skull. Lying there, dazed, Belletire's fingers felt for the wound, touched his exposed brain, and induced a convulsion. He blacked out.

"It was terrible," Covey Rider Karate Davis said of the ambush.

Another squad leader, Sergeant David Brock, rushed up, saw Belletire's grave condition, but was too busy fighting to stop and help. Lieutenant Davis took command and—realizing that to stay pinned there meant annihilation— ordered an immediate breakout, leading his men on toward the hill. The magnificent Ron Bozikis boldly rushed upward, firing his weapon on the run, his Yards following. His squad burst through rank after rank of NVA, opening the way for the whole platoon. Then, only yards from the top, his squad was caught in a horrific crossfire and young Bozikis collapsed, mortally wounded. Emboldened by his action, his Yards continued the fight and routed the North Vietnamese from the hilltop.

Meanwhile, Jim Brock's squad fought upward on the right, broke through trees into tall elephant grass, then Jim looked around to find himself all alone. He saw the grass shift fifteen yards away, squatted, fired his M-16 and at the same time an NVA fired his AK. Brock killed the enemy soldier, but one AK round slammed through Brock's thigh and exited his back. And his rifle jammed. Another NVA popped up and shot Brock again, this time hitting his left arm and exiting his back. Brock heaved a grenade and as it exploded he ran a few yards, collapsed, and rolled down the hill. When Brock halted, he was beside the still form of Captain Whelan. Brock crawled to the platoon medic, already busy working on Belletire. Temporarily blinded, Belletire somehow got to his feet and made it with the others to the top of the hill.

On that small hilltop Lieutenant Davis rallied his troops. With so many casualties, the platoon lacked the mobility and firepower to push the enemy back; meanwhile, air strikes had limited effect because the NVA stayed virtually alongside his platoon. One bomb detonated so close it shattered Brock's M-16 butt stock. Helicopters twice attempted to extract them but both times heavy ground fire drove them back. "Dig in," Davis ordered, and they hurried to get belowground before the barrage that was sure to come.

By dark, they'd scraped out shallow holes just as the first mortar shells impacted. Then a USAF AC-119 Shadow gunship arrived to add 20mm Vulcan cannons to the fray. All night, NVA mortars pounded the platoon and Shadow gunships fired. It never let up.

Gunship tracers tore a red luminescent wall only twenty-five yards around the SOG men, and exploding claymore mines deterred ground probes. But relentless mortar fire took a steady toll; one by one, bursting shells blasted Montagnards and Americans in their shallow holes. In one lightning-like flash, Belletire made out human limbs on the ground, torn off some poor Yard who'd been blown to bits in his foxhole. Dead bodies were dragged in front of fighting positions to improve protection. After each bombardment, the SOG men hollered to report wounded and dead so Lieutenant Davis, the platoon leader, could shift or tighten the perimeter.

As dawn approached the NVA added shoulder-fired RPGs to the bombardment. An enemy ground assault would have overrun them but the NVA must not have realized how badly the platoon had been depleted. Then, at daylight, fighters filled the sky, dumping bombs and strafing the entire area until, finally,

A-1 Skyraiders blanketed the valley with bomblets spewing concentrated tear gas, and in came the Hueys. It was difficult flying the helicopters while wearing gas masks, but the pilots performed superbly, weaving between streams of tracers to reach the LZ. The Hatchet Force men, too, wore gas masks, except those with severe head wounds, like Belletire. Intense enemy fire searched the sky but—their aim degraded by coughing and water-filled eyes—the NVA gunners failed to down a single aircraft.

Back at Dak To, I stood beside the airstrip with Bill and Fat Albert and made out the specks of returning Hueys. When their first bird landed, several of us helped Belletire out and sat him on a sandbag wall to treat his wounds. Belletire's eyes had rolled upward and his teeth chattered uncontrollably; he didn't recognize anyone, didn't understand where he was, just shook and groaned and tried to talk but couldn't. Three inches of his skull were missing, and inside his wound I saw the shiny gray of his brain. We didn't touch his wound for fear of further injuring him. "You'll be fine," I lied, but I thought Frank was going to die any minute. Several of us lifted him to his feet and helped him to a cranking Huey, which momentarily carried him, Brock, and some other severely wounded men to the Pleiku evacuation hospital.

We had not inserted that day, so that night in the club, Bill and Fat Albert and I joined everyone to sing "Hey, Blue" to Captain Whelan and Ron Bozikis. Afterward, Bozikis's best friend, Wayne Anderson, expressed the lament of many a soldier who's been elsewhere when his closest comrade died: "If only I'd been there," Anderson grieved, "it would never have happened." We felt for him, but no one knew what to say.

After losing a teammate, some men needed time to think, grieve, and adjust, the way civilians handle a relative's death. Other men wanted back to the field and combat so they couldn't dwell upon inconsolable loss. Still others raged against this unfair fate, grasping for some way to balance, to do something. If he had been helpless to save Ron Bozikis's life, Anderson decided, at least he would avenge his death. Anderson thrust his drink in the air, shouted, "Bozikis!," then downed it with one long, hard pull, threw away the glass, and cried, "I'll kill ten NVA for Ron Bozikis!" He shouted it over and over, and he meant it.

At the hospital in Pleiku, Frank Belletire barely hung on. Emergency surgery relieved his brain swelling and removed damaged tissue. For days he couldn't talk, then, finally, he recognized several comrades in his ward and his mind began to work again. In Japan he would almost die from a brain infection, but eventually he'd make it home.

The morning after his extraction, though, we were back at Dak To, climbing into a Huey under clear skies, bound for our far-north target. As our Huey cranked, Fat Albert assumed his Roman persona, adjusted his invisible toga, and hollered, "Let the games begin!" During that long forty-minute flight, I felt like a Christian descending into a pit of lions, watching all semblance of civilization and friendly outposts slip far, far behind us. I was confident in my recon abilities and tactical judgment; it was things beyond my influence that concerned me, particularly the weather, which, as we neared the target, became cloudy and overcast.

As on the last mission in Cambodia, I'd swapped rucksacks with the radio operator—now Fat Albert—to carry the team radio during insertion. We'd switch back after our "Team OK." Coming over the treetops, slowing, I shifted my CAR-15 from shadow to shadow, then stepped out on the skid, still scanning for any movement, any faces, any fire. Our Huey flared above the depression I'd photographed earlier and went into a steady hover five feet above the foliage. I jumped—everyone jumped—and that's when our trouble began.

What had looked like knee-high bushes was a tangle of Asian briars seven feet high, so thick we couldn't fall through to the ground, but not substantial enough to crawl across. Like an upended turtle, I could not move. Then the second Huey drifted over so close I could touch its skid, the tail rotor dipping toward my face, spinning like a buzz saw. As it swung and dipped I had to turn my face sideways to keep from being slashed. Then the Huey lifted away, and it was as if there never had been any danger. In a few minutes, we'd crawled from the briars and with no sign of the enemy I radioed a "Team OK."

Led by our point man, Boui—disguised as an NVA, complete with AK and chest web gear—we spent a long, hard day walking uphill, at times having to pull ourselves up. Late that morning, I had hardly touched a tree when fifty fire ants leaped upon me, racing to bite my neck and arm. Sweeping them off I turned to warn the Yard behind me, Yeo, but already he'd plucked one ant-covered leaf, folded it over and begun gingerly munching his "sandwich." He grinned up at me, ants falling from his lips.

By late afternoon we were two thirds of the way to the mountaintop. We spent that first night on a steep slope where the NVA would have a hell of a time sweeping against us. When Ben was One-Zero, I noticed everyone slept too securely knowing someone else was awake on guard. What if that man on watch fell asleep? I did away with that—no one would be on watch so no one would rest comfortably. At the slightest sound you'd jerk up, fully awake, panicked heart in your throat, a paroxysmal fear preceding knowledge of why you'd awakened. That was much better. No one slept securely on my missions.

The next morning we continued our long, hard climb. Finally by early afternoon we reached the ridge, where visibility opened to fifty yards. We searched among Asian dwarf pines and ferns but found no trail. Evidently the enemy didn't frequent the mountaintop. Momentarily we reached an opening where we could see into the target valley, 3,000 feet below. I could not believe my eyes. Camouflaged far below, beneath the trees, lay fifteen or twenty hooches, with people walking among them. Hurriedly I dug out binoculars from my rucksack for a better look—yes, armed men in khaki uniforms, but also women and children. It was a Communist Pathet Lao village, allowed to remain at the pleasure of the NVA.

Turning the glasses northward, I made out traces of a brown line in the trees—the suspected road. It was the right grid coordinate, but this path was too narrow to accommodate trucks. Equally, it was too wide and well maintained to be a village walkway; it was a major NVA trail.

I passed the binoculars to Bill, then Fat Albert. And then we backed away into thick foliage to discuss our options. We'd already accomplished our primary mission, but I saw a bolder option: Those Pathet Lao looked completely at ease. The valley where we'd landed was so deep that they'd probably never heard our helicopters. North Vietnamese troops didn't seem to be among them, and we'd spotted no heavy weapons like mortars or machine guns, not even fighting positions or trenches. "Looks perfect for a raid," I observed. Bill and Pete grinned.

It was well known that the Pathet Lao lacked combat prowess. Only a couple of weeks earlier, RT Colorado had fought a short engagement with a Pathet Lao squad in which One-Zero Willie McLeod, One-One Charles Erickson, and One-Two Frank Greko captured two men—who later died from wounds—and seized several weapons in such poor shape that they had jammed during the firefight. They were not pushovers, but RT Illinois could take that village, with a bit of help.

Along with that evening's "Team OK," I requested that our former teammate Charles "Weird" Herald and three other Yards reinforce us, with an M-60 machine gun, a 60mm mortar, and extra grenades; we'd meet them in the valley where we'd arrived. With four Americans and nine Montagnards, we'd seize the village, search it for documents, and bring out its adult males as POWs. As quickly as my message was decrypted back at Kontum, the S-3 officer replied, "Approved. Good luck." This would be an operation worthy of Joe Walker.

What would the morning bring? It was exciting thinking about it as I drifted off to sleep.

A hand grabbed my mouth. My eyes shot open in total darkness. I forgot where

I was until Bill Spencer whispered, "Sh-h-h-h. Listen." I sat up and laid my CAR-15 across my lap.

At first it seemed only the rustling pines. Then a wind gusted up from the valley. I whispered to Bill, "Singing. Lots of people." I grabbed my binoculars.

Along with Pete Wilson, we crept to a break in the trees where we could see into the valley. The village was silent, but on the trail a long line of lights bobbed from the north. These weren't vehicle headlights but kerosene lanterns on poles, lighting the way for hundreds of North Vietnamese. Their echoing voices, our interpreter said, sang of Ho Chi Minh and the coming liberation. They were NVA replacements, it seemed, marching to South Vietnam. That's why the trail was there—to let dismounted troops bypass the highways and B-52 strikes. I recorded the observation in my notebook, then went back to sleep.

Covey's engines sounded higher the next morning, well above the overcast that blanketed our ridgeline. A drizzle that had begun during the night had become a steady, soaking rain and Karate advised that no helicopters or fighters could come to our aid if we got in trouble. The reinforcement and raid would have to wait for better weather. We could not see down into the valley, and had no idea what the enemy was doing below. It rained and rained.

By the end of that miserable day, our clothing was saturated—our underwear was soaked, the socks inside our boots were soaked, everything was dripping wet no less than if we'd been swimming. There was no way to get dry and nothing dry to put on; we could only tell ourselves not to let it affect us. Late that afternoon, I repositioned the team 500 yards to thicker jungle and a more defensible position.

That night the rain never let up, drenching us as it had for the past twenty-four hours.

It rained the entire next day, too. Before this I'd imagined monsoon rain as a gentle afternoon shower that cut the edge from the sultry, tropical heat, like a shampoo commercial, in which a lovely girl lathers her hair, then a gentle, warm rain rinses it away. In truth, this rain was bitter cold despite the ambient temperature, and against our clammy skin it was bone-chilling. Though we could feel it draining our bodies of warmth, we could do nothing about it.

By the third day of rain, it began to get to us. Recon teams always went in heavy on ammo and light on chow, and now, our fifth day on the ground, no one had any food left, not even a stick of gum. Between the wet and cold and hunger, it would have been easy to gripe on the radio, but our predicament wasn't anyone's fault. We were all miserable, but I would never show it.

On the mission's sixth day, that monotonous, lulling sound of rain hitting leaves continued unabated. I'd learned at Fort Bragg not to talk about food, so I kept us whispering about movies, women, our favorite cars, guns, anything but blueberry pie. Here in Laos we suffered not just hunger, but from that cold, constant deluge and the grinding down and exhaustion that came with it. Then Fat Albert had to replace the PRC-25 radio battery only to find that the spare was bad. Each American carried a survival radio; first we'd use Fat Albert's, and to conserve its battery, we would not turn it on until we heard Covey's engines.

Now into seven days on the ground—five days under continuous rain—the inability to sleep restfully and lack of food began to take its toll. Misery begot misery. We shivered constantly and even huddling shoulder to shoulder we had difficulty staying warm. I had the men take turns doing jumping jacks or stationary runs to keep their circulation flowing. Imagine sitting in your shower for days on end, wearing all your clothes while cold water sprays you—hour after hour after hour. That's what it was like, unrelenting, day and night, soaked by that continuous downpour, no relief, no warmth. At least Fat Albert's unending banter kept us reasonably sane. And we may have had no cards, but Bill spent hours describing his winning blackjack strategy.

Days began to lose their distinctness, with one shivering, water-soaked day melding into the next. I had to remind myself that the real threat was the enemy. We felt like trapped miners waiting for our rescuers to drill down to us. By the mission's tenth day, we'd been without food for six days, rained upon for eight days—and for three days we had shivered uncontrollably as hypothermia slowly drained our body core temperature. None of us could feel anything in our feet, and I had difficulty holding a pencil steady enough to write. I could not sleep, could not rest, could not stop shaking, just constantly shaking. I was exhausted from shaking. When Fat Albert's radio battery expired, we switched to Bill's radio.

I recalled the fire ants Yeo had eaten and they weren't so unappetizing anymore—but wait! My One-Zero medical kit contained antacids! To raise morale, I made a ceremony of divvying them up. Pulling out my pocketknife, I carefully cut the tablets into eight equal shares, then passed them out as if they were rations. Damn, but the men savored those little chalky wafers, even sucking the powdery residue from their fingers. What a meal! That afternoon, at Fat Albert's urging, we tried eating pine nuts, extracted from pine cones, as taught in survival training. Bitterly acidic, they puckered our lips and gave us bellyaches.

Until now we dared not move, for to encounter the enemy with no possibility of extraction or air support, especially in our weakened physical condition, was the height of foolishness. Yet it was time for the trapped miners to start tunneling out, while they still had any strength. The evening of that tenth day, I radioed Kontum that if they could not pull us tomorrow, we would dump anything nonessential, then begin a forced march eastward. I didn't know how fast we could move, but we'd keep heading east until we walked into sunshine.

Looking down that eleventh morning, the Covey Rider, Lieutenant Jim "King Arthur" Young, saw only the highest mountaintops jutting from a sea of white, and understood fully what it was like to be beneath those monsoon clouds. As One-Zero of RT Arizona, three months earlier he'd been rained in with Sergeants Kyle Dean and Mike Wilson. Similarly deluged, he'd had half his men remove their boots to dry their feet only to see their feet swell so large they could hardly squeeze them back in. Their laces no longer fit. When finally he got out, aboard his extraction Huey, Young's body began to shut down. Medics had to lift him out of the helicopter and lay him on a stretcher. Then he heard a female voice. "You all right, son? You all right, son?" Incredibly, it was Martha Raye. Young could only smile and assure her, "Yes, ma'am. Yes, I am."

And that, Young realized, was after five days—RT Illinois had been rained upon for nine days.

Young's pilot, USAF Captain Bob Manz, having heard our predicament for more than a week, agreed—it was time to get the team out. After we confirmed that we heard their engines, Manz spotted a rabbit hole in the clouds and spiraled downward until they broke through, danger-low, only 200 feet off the deck—almost directly above us.

I stood in a break in the trees, waving an orange panel while Bill Spencer radioed, "Look right, nine o'clock, nine o'clock!" I looked up and saw those O-2 wings wiggle and had to keep from jumping and shouting.

"Get your people ready," King Arthur radioed. "We'll be back."

Captain Manz banked hard, then turned southward and, while Young navigated off a map he held in his lap, dodged hilltops and ground fog through several valleys until it opened into bright, clear skies. There Manz flew a wide orbit until the helicopters joined them, then turned around to lead the whole procession, low-level all the way back to our valley.

Young's voice crackled on the survival radio, "We're going to have just once chance. There isn't space to orbit beneath this stuff, so we're coming straight in. Get a smoke ready. When you hear my engines, pop smoke." I rogered, knowing, too, that the battery was almost shot on this, our last working survival radio.

We heard engines to the south—wait . . . louder . . . wait—*now!* I nodded. Bill threw a white phosphorus grenade. Any bad guy in the neighborhood would see our smoke, but it was go-for-broke time. I dodged particles of burning phosphorus, looked up, and Young's plane flashed over, waving his wings. They saw us!

Though the Bright Light rescue team rode chase birds ready to carry us if necessary, we were able to walk and climb aboard ourselves, though too weak to show the euphoria we felt. When we landed at Dak To, Lieutenant Young and Captain Manz were already there. I couldn't help myself—fuck the pain— I ran, leaped in the air, and smothered Young in a bear hug, sticking my tongue in his ear. He couldn't stop laughing, nor could the rest of us.

Along with Bill and Pete, I fought the urge that evening in our mess hall to grab my steak with my bare hands, but still wolfed it down half chewed. In a moment we were at the door, our shrunken stomachs giving up this sudden bounty. For months afterward, anxiety overwhelmed me at meals; I forced myself to cut each forkful deliberately, then chewed it twenty-two times. Recalling that famous scene in *Gone With the Wind,* I swore I'd never let myself be hungry like that again.

As expected, our feet ballooned to almost twice their normal size; the medics issued us crutches. "Just take it easy," Recon First Sergeant Doney told us. "No duty for the next two weeks." What he *thought* he meant was, Stay in your team room, take it easy, hobble over to the mess hall and club. That wasn't the way we interpreted it. Despite the impediment of shower shoes and crutches, an hour later Bill, Pete, and I swung our throbbing feet over an open tailgate, onto a C-130 Blackbird, en route to Saigon.

For the next fourteen days it was like spring break. We partied night and day, swinging our crutch-supported bodies up and down Tu Do Street, guided by our Saigon old hand, Fat Albert. At the You & I Bar, a Special Forces hangout, I found the bullet holes behind the counter where a drunken One-Zero had won a shooting contest by hitting the most whiskey bottles. Pete introduced us to the owner, Mama Bich, a plain, middle-aged woman who'd loved a South Vietnamese Ranger killed years earlier, and had since adopted the crazy Green Berets. Pete told us of a martial arts contest held there in which a drunken recon man smashed a table with one slice of his karate-hardened hand, "K-i-i-i, A-h-h!" Not to be outdone, his companion similarly shattered a table, which brought Mama Bich running from her office, honking like an angry goose. But they atoned, laying money in front of her until she smiled. In Pete's version of the story, they kept it up until they ran out of money, in another, it was said, until Mama Bich ran out of furniture, but in both she followed them, negotiating the price for each item before they smashed it—"How much for this chair?" "And that table?" She was accommodating to Special Forces.

We also toured SOG headquarters, escorted by Fat Albert's old buddy Gary

Bittle, then feasted on lobster at the Peacock restaurant and drank late into the night at SOG's safe house, where we were staying, Number 10 Nguyen-Minh Chieu, known as House Ten.

Two days later, we hopped another SOG Blackbird and kept the party going in Nha Trang, the seaside resort town where the 5th Special Forces Group was headquartered. As we swung into the Streamer Bar, Fat Albert of course commanded, "Wine for my troops!" Not to be outdone, Bill announced he would eat a highball glass, a trick he'd learned in Thailand. "You grind the pieces in your teeth," he explained, then cut hell out of his lip. That ended his demonstration.

Later, sitting in a booth in the Nha Trang Hotel tea room, Fat Albert entertained us with ribald stories; he so resembled Orson Welles that he made the tawdriest tale seem somehow intellectual.

Then, out of the blue, he condemned my code name, saying, "You're no, no—'Hiawatha!'" Pete shook his head. "Negative, *nyet*. You're . . ."—he thought a second, then smiled—"you're *'Plasticman'!*" That sounded just enough like a superhero to have some appeal.

"Nope," I drunkenly insisted. "Either I'm *the* Plasticman, or I want nothing to do with it."

We compromised, shook, and I had a new code name: *The Plasticman*.

Our craziness and drinking continued all week—with Fat Albert even leading us in a crutch-swinging conga line. Then, our money exhausted, we flew back to Kontum.

As our convalescence ended, a CCN team fought an inspiring engagement. RT Crusader, led by Captain Nick Manning, with Staff Sergeant Jimmy Riffe, One-One, and Sergeant Larry Zaika, One-Two, and five Yards, were in their overnight position, waiting for Covey's first morning radio check, when an NVA platoon assaulted them. Fighting their way free, they evaded, then occupied a nearby hilltop.

By the time Covey and the Hueys arrived, Zaika had crept from the perimeter to emplace two claymore mines and just in time—six NVA assaulted, three shot dead by Zaika, then he detonated his claymores to kill the other three. A Huey attempted to land but concentrated fire riddled it so completely that it dived, nose-down, into the treetops and burned furiously. Manning radioed Covey, offering to go after survivors, but the destruction appeared so complete that Covey didn't think it was worth the risk.

Undaunted, Manning's men shot their way through encircling NVA to reach the wreckage, with Zaika taking frag wounds across his back and head. Amazingly, they found the seriously injured pilot alive, and the other three crewmen relatively unhurt. Deteriorating weather left enough time to extract only the aircrew and the wounded Zaika. Manning and Riffe remained overnight, then spent most of the next day in running firefights until, late that afternoon, they were extracted. The three Green Berets were awarded well-deserved Silver Stars.

Back at Kontum just a few days, our feet again normal, we were assigned Bright Light duty, to stand by at Dak Pek Special Forces Camp, where our launch site had temporarily shifted, to support the teams operating in our far northern Laos target area.

Issued plenty of extra ammo and medical supplies, and drawing a 60mm mortar and M-60 machine gun, RT Illinois flew past mile after mile of demolished bridges and overgrown traces of Highway 14 until we reached the remote Dak Poko River Valley. The most isolated outpost left on the Laotian border, situated on seven hilltops, Dak Pek was built around a short runway—its sole lifeline to the world—where our six Hueys and five Kingbees settled beneath the tropical morning sun. The Cobras were about five minutes behind us.

As quickly as we touched down, carrying all our gear, Bill, Fat Albert, the Yards, and I trudged up an adjacent hill to the tent where we would live for the next week. We had just dumped our rucksacks when—*BOOM! BOOM! BOOM-BOOM-BOOM!*

"Mortars!" someone shouted and everyone ran for cover. They were 82mm shells, very lethal, but focused down along the runway, where pilots rushed to get their vulnerable birds back in the air. Between the gray-blast of impacting shells, I saw the birds crank, then scramble like a covey of quail, flying anywhere to get away. Almost as quickly, here came our Cobras. Their rockets pounded a spot on a facing hillside, where the Cobra pilots had spotted the mortars and now made life hell for them. Then the fire ceased. It had lasted not even two minutes.

All the Hueys and Kingbees were coming back to reland. Along the runway, everyone got up, dusted off, and looked around. On the tarmac, though, one man still lay there. Two men rushed to him, turned him over, saw no wound, but he was dead. Our chase medic finally found a pinpoint in his chest where a tiny splinter had penetrated his heart. The dead man was Randy Rhea, a former recon man who, a few months earlier, had been so spooked on a mission that he went to work at the launch site for a while. When the shells began falling, instead of running for cover, he'd run into the open to help a pilot and now death had stalked him as determinedly as it had in Laos, behind enemy lines. A good man, he deserved a better break. Some SOG men asked, "Who was killed? Was it Randy Rhea of CCC or CCN recon man Ron Ray?" Friends of Ron Ray could take relief, but only for one day. By cruel coincidence, twenty-four hours later, Ron Ray of CCN's RT Rattler and his teammate Randy Suber were lost, Missing in Action.

That week passed quickly at Dak Pek because instead of just standing by, we flew several missions each day to insert cases of sabotaged Communist Chinese ammunition into enemy-held areas along the Laotian border. For each insert, Covey spotted a major trail with a nearby sit-down LZ, so each time we landed, hustled to the trail, dumped several cases as conspicuously as possible, then double-timed back to the LZ and extracted. We spent no more than fifteen minutes on the ground each time, and pulled it off without a single contact.

Toward the end of the week, an Army OV-1 Mohawk observation aircraft was downed about ten miles north of Dak Pek. We climbed into our rappelling gear but a 100-man company of indigenous troops happened to be nearby and got to the crash site first. They reported that the pilots were dead, their bodies intact. We were told to relax, that the body recovery was underway.

That afternoon, a Chinook helicopter arrived with two Army majors who stood near the airfield arguing while their bird refueled. Within our earshot, they compared dates of rank to determine which of them would be first man off the aircraft at the crash site. That made no sense until one muttered, "Listen, this could be a DSC"—a Distinguished Service Cross—"so I'm first one off. You got it?" We looked to each other, gagging—two pilots were out there dead, and these officers were arguing about who would get the higher medal for some exaggerated account of how their bodies were recovered.

A few minutes later, they flew away, and God knows what resulted.

During our stand-down, another Hatchet Force mission went into Laos, and at last Wayne Anderson had an opportunity to avenge Ron Bozikis's death. Anderson's platoon was hit by a full NVA company. Like Bozikis, he rallied his Yard squad and courageously assaulted the enemy position that most threatened his platoon, and he, too, repelled the enemy, ran through a hail of fire, and he, too, was mortally wounded, dying at his moment of triumph.

And like his best friend, Wayne Anderson received a posthumous Silver Star. When next we sang "Hey, Blue," Wayne's name immediately followed that of his combat soul mate, Ron Bozikis. They were both fine young men. Wayne's platoon leader, First Lieutenant Harry A. Anderson, also was awarded a Silver Star, with Bronze Stars to platoon members Sergeant First Class Adolph Straussfogel and Sergeant Bob Seper.

And now, my tour almost over, Glenn Uemura and I sat in the club talking.

The men we most admired had multiple combat tours—what SF soldier wanted to say he had only *one* year in combat? Looking back, the year didn't seem so bad. We were ready for more—not a full year, just six additional months. Besides, the Army would give us a free thirty-day leave anywhere in the world. So we extended for an additional six months.

Bill Spencer would be acting One-Zero and RT Illinois would continue training while I was gone, maybe running local security patrols. Even Bill was feeling up—he'd just exchanged letters with his wife, and it sounded like their marriage might work out. He talked about meeting her on R&R in Hawaii and seeing his toddler son.

Ten days later, I was in Hawaii with Glenn, then it was back to snow-swept Minnesota. I partied with high school buddies, frustrated at first that I could not tell them anything of my SOG tour. Then, like most combat veterans learn, I realized civilians wouldn't have understood anyway. It was easy to remain silent.

For a few days it was great being home—then, strangely, I found I missed my SOG comrades, the satisfaction of doing something important, and that tingle of outwitting the enemy in his own backyard. Squirrel Sprouse had warned, "Recon gets in your blood." I felt that allure of secret operations, of being on the inside of things that were news on the front page of the *New York Times*. I loved hearing our SOG activities denied by the president. In northeast Minneapolis I was just another twenty-year-old lying about his age for a beer at my local bar. But in SOG's covert world, like other One-Zeros, I was a god. I knew where I preferred to be.

It was Christmas, then New Year's Eve, then time to fly back to Fort Lewis and on to Vietnam. Recrossing the Pacific my mood was optimistic. Finally I'd gotten it just right. I was a One-Zero with two great teammates, Bill Spencer and Fat Albert, and nine loyal Montagnards we'd trained from scratch. We'd soon be running great missions together. It was a great feeling.

But that wouldn't happen.

For Bill and several of our Yards were dead.

Chapter Nine

"What happened?" I asked.

Pete Wilson looked to me, then to Bill Spencer's empty bunk. Appearing exhausted, the normally loquacious Fat Albert searched for words. He wasn't sure where to start.

"You know, Plasticman," Pete began, "how Bill could be impatient?" I nodded. "Well, he got anxious. Didn't like waiting a month for you to get back from extension leave."

"So they let him take out the team?" I couldn't believe Norm Doney would allow that to happen.

The answer was more complicated. The irrepressible Spencer, Pete went on, could not stand still for thirty days and didn't like the idea of waiting months to be a One-Zero. Hardly ten days after I left, Bill bumped into an old Special Forces friend, who over a drink talked him into joining his III Corps Mike Force company. In an ordinary American unit—say, the 101st Airborne Division—you couldn't possibly reassign yourself, but as a Special Forces NCO, Bill simply packed his bags, caught a plane to Bien Hoa, and joined the Mike Force.

Only a few days after Bill got there, the Mike Force deployed to Bu Dop, on the Cambodian border, where an encircled Special Forces camp was fighting for survival. Riding aboard one of the first Hueys going into the LZ, Bill raced for the jungle under enemy fire, then noticed two wounded Yards. He was running to help them when an RPG detonated virtually upon him, killing him instantly. *Dead, only minutes into his first operation.*

Bill had no death wish, we knew. He'd pretty well patched things up with his wife and had talked proudly about his young son. And now he was gone. *Damn. Damn.*

"But what about the Yards?" I added. "I heard several of our Yards were killed."

Fat Albert explained while we walked to the Montagnard team room. As the last RT Illinois American present for duty, Pete had been transferred to another team to make it combat-ready. Then more missions came rolling in and, with a shortage of teams to run them, a new One-Zero was assigned to RT Illinois, Staff Sergeant Ronald Weems.

In the RT Illinois Montagnard team room I saw three empty bunks, mattresses rolled up. Our RT Illinois interpreter, Bui, who had left a safe rear echelon job to join the team, was dead. My new point man, Boui, who'd performed so well in training, was dead, too. And Lun, our grenadier, had been badly shot up, still hospitalized in Pleiku.

Ten days before I got back, Pete continued, One-Zero Weems had been given a mission to monitor truck traffic on Laotian Highway 110. Weems took along two American volunteers, Staff Sergeant Wendell Glass, a seasoned medic, and Captain Willie Merkerson, our new recon company commander, who'd been awarded a Distinguished Service Cross during a previous Special Forces tour.

Their first afternoon near the highway, they fought a short engagement when trackers walked up on them. They broke contact and successfully evaded, but after dark they heard NVA sweeping the jungle for them. The next morning Weems managed to lead them through the encirclement, but just before noon enemy trackers again caught up, compelling Weems to initiate contact and kill two NVA. Up to this point, with no friendly casualties, perhaps it seemed they could continue outfoxing the enemy—but Weems's luck had run out.

Though the team outran their latest pursuers, nearing Highway 110 they had to halt to let several approaching trucks pass. But instead of rolling on, the trucks jerked to a stop and forty NVA leaped out and rushed Weems's men, firing AKs and RPGs. All the Americans were hit—Weems took shrapnel in the arms and legs, Captain Merkerson was hit by RPG fragments in his head and hands, and Glass, too, was wounded by an RPG. Then AK slugs hit the interpreter, Bui, and point man, Boui. Glass rushed to them and frantically applied first aid but it was no use. Then another RPG exploded, knocking Glass to the ground; despite his wounds, he covered the withdrawal of his wounded comrades.

There was no option but to leave behind Bui's and Boui's bodies. Calling in air strikes, Weems managed to break contact, led the men to an LZ, and got out.

Fat Albert and I spoke a few minutes with the surviving Yards, then walked to the club and saw Ron Weems. Despite his words to the contrary, I could see by Ron's face that he blamed himself. I told him it wasn't his fault, that he hadn't fucked up, that it was a miracle anyone got out. It was a misfortune of war, the occasional but inevitable result of running dangerous missions; you can do everything right and people still die. That's what defines hazardous missions.

In the club I learned there'd been more losses. A new Covey Rider, Sergeant First Class James "Sam" Zumbrun, had been killed along with his USAF FAC pilot, Captain John Lehacka, on 10 January. An old hand, Sam had been a medic at CCN in 1966, then served another six-month tour in 1969 to run recon with us at Kontum, and only weeks earlier had come back to fly Covey. Though I'd never been on the ground with him, I knew Sam to be a courageous and resourceful recon man, one of the best.

Sam and Lehacka were supporting a Hatchet Force operation in Laos when heavy ground fire hit their O-2 aircraft. Lehacka was killed and Sam did not know how to fly. Unable to control the plane, he rode it into the ground. A Bright Light rescue team brought back their bodies.

Still another man, First Lieutenant David Lechner of RT Arizona, had been killed in December. He had arrived at Kontum, joined a team, and died in a matter of weeks. I never knew him.

Fat Albert and I sat there, drinking, commiserating over Bill and Sam and our lost Yards. I thought about avenging Bill's death, then realized I was almost in the same spot where a couple months ago Wayne Anderson had vowed to kill ten NVA for Ron Bozikis. Getting myself killed would do nothing—the NVA who killed Bill were only soldiers doing their duty, just like us. There'd be no special revenge, but damn, I missed Bill.

My dreary mood contrasted markedly to that of a group of recon men across the barroom, whose eyes danced with fire as they toasted each other. With them stood our commander, Colonel Abt, and our operations officer, Major Jaks. Now what was that all about?

"They ambushed a convoy last night," explained Willie McLeod, RT Colorado's One-Zero, who'd sat down with us. "Killed a bunch of NVA and destroyed a couple of trucks. But it was called a mission failure."

"What?" I snapped. "How the hell could that be a *failure?*"

McLeod's eyes gleamed. "'Cause they were trying to snatch a truck driver, but he got killed."

What a classic Special Forces SOG mission—infiltrate a heavily defended highway twenty-five miles behind enemy lines, boldly ambush a night truck convoy, make off with their lead truck driver, and escape the hundreds of enemy certain to pursue you. Killing trucks *and* snatching a prisoner—the two greatest recon achievements rolled into a single operation.

That got my blood percolating. We walked over and joined the group, where one ambusher, John Grant, told me about the mission. It had come straight from the commander of U.S. forces in Vietnam, General Creighton Abrams, who wanted to know where a sudden upsurge of night convoys was going so the Air Force could hit the stockpiled supplies with B-52s. Chief SOG Colonel Steve Cavanaugh had decided the best way to find out was to assemble a special, all-American recon team, led by Major Jaks, to ambush a convoy and kidnap the lead truck driver.

Jaks had selected the eight recon men in the club: Bill Spurgeon, Oliver Hartwig, Daniel Ster, Ray Harris, John Blaauw, Tim Lynch, Forrest Todd, and John Grant. For their mission, code-named Operation Ashtray, they trained a week at SOG's Naval Advisory Detachment base in Da Nang, to master vehicle ambush techniques far from any prying eyes. Then they flew by C-130 Blackbird to Dak To, inserted by chopper into Laos, and the night before my return ambushed a seventeen-vehicle convoy. Unfortunately, Jaks's men hit the trucks so fast and so hard that though they suffered no friendly casualties, every NVA was shot dead.

"We came so close," Jaks lamented aloud, "so damned close. We'll go again," he promised, "and this time, we go for broke. We take wounded, we hide them, we press on—nothing, nothing will stop us." Jaks could be dogmatic with his unswerving focus on mission, yet I could not help but respect him. He was the only field grade officer I met in SOG who personally led a ground mission, and a truly dangerous one at that. Hearing his vow, several One-Zeros, including myself and McLeod, volunteered to go along.

Later, Fat Albert and I wandered away with Bill Spurgeon, the RT Texas One-Zero. Sitting under the stars with a case of beer, we talked about Bill Spencer, who'd been one of Spurgeon's best friends. It became our private wake, swapping stories and laughing and regretting. Then Spurgeon observed that no one had sung "Hey, Blue," for Bill.

We agreed that it wasn't right to sing "Hey, Blue," since Bill had died as a Mike Force man, not on a SOG recon mission. But it wasn't right not to sing anything.

Then Spurgeon recalled that Bill's favorite song that fall had been the Hank Williams classic "I'm So Lonesome I Could Cry." Sitting on a sandbag bunker, we sang that poignant ballad in salute to Bill, with its fitting final line: "And as I wonder where you are, I'm so lonesome I could cry."

And that's the way we felt. We wiped our eyes and toasted Bill many times until we had nothing left to drink.

The next morning found me in the same status as a year earlier—a man without a team, due to combat losses. But now I was a One-Zero with twelve missions on the Ho Chi Minh Trail, so there was no hiatus. First Sergeant Doney immediately reassigned me to Floyd Ambrose's old team, RT Washington, which had two Americans but lacked a team leader.

By early 1970, RT Washington's One-One was Sergeant Joe Quiroz, with about five months' recon under his belt, and a new radio operator, Jerry Guzzetta, who had yet to run his first mission. I knew several of the Yards, especially the constantly grinning point man, Knot, whose good nature was known throughout recon company.

Glenn Uemura had also returned from leave and could have been a One-Zero, but he'd resolved to be a One-One. Well respected, Glenn had his pick of teams and chose to go to RT Vermont, then led by One-Zero Franklin "Doug" Miller. Though Glenn no longer wanted a leader's slot, he was hardly shirking dangerous action. Running recon with Miller, he was certain to find it.

Miller had half the SOG recon experience that Glenn did, but already had established himself as a dynamic combat leader. A New Mexico native, Miller was Special Forces–qualified yet had been diverted to the 1st Air Cavalry Division in 1966, where he spent two and a half years. Bold almost to the brink of recklessness, Miller soon was compared to the legendary Mad Dog Shriver, and in some ways he even resembled Shriver—tall and lean—but without the antisocial attitude. That hardly made him a conformist: Miller sounded and acted more like a California surfer than an Army NCO, and preferred an old French paratrooper jacket over an American one. A hard-charger, his furious audacity sometimes precipitated gunfights.

Two weeks before I got back, on 5 January, all of Miller's qualities had come to the fore in a remarkable engagement in northeast Cambodia. Late that morning, RT Vermont landed about two miles from a hilltop where a Hatchet Force company had been attacked the night before; about a dozen men had been wounded, including Sergeant First Class Adolph Straussfogel, Staff Sergeants Bernie Mims and Rheuben Morgan, and their commander, Captain Richard Todd.

With the mission of scouting for the company, Miller led his men halfway to the hill when they came upon a fresh enemy trail. Miller's One-One, Sergeant Robert Brown, had one previous mission, while their One-Two radio operator, Specialist Five Edward Blythe, was on his first mission. Their four Yards were Prep, the indigenous team leader, Hyuk, point man, Gai, the interpreter, and Yube, tail gunner. Advancing on the path, one Yard noticed a thin cord and, not thinking the enemy would booby-trap his own trail, he yanked it—a tremendous roar and Prep fell, badly hit, Yube took hundreds of frags, while Brown, Blythe, and Gai all suffered multiple wounds. Only Miller and the point man went unscathed.

The explosion echoed a half-mile through the jungle to the closest Hatchet Force position, where Sergeant First Class Andrew Brown, a medic, felt the reverberations and realized Miller's team had been hit. That explosion also alerted dozens of nearby NVA, who formed up into squads and platoons and rushed toward the incapacitated team.

Miller helped bandage the wounded, then ordered his men to abandon their rucksacks as he led them across a stream and 150 yards uphill to a bomb crater. They'd hardly gotten to cover when Miller and Hyuk saw a North Vietnamese officer examine the rucksacks, then wave over more NVA and signal for a sweep toward where the SOG men were hiding.

Miller shifted his team farther uphill, then, with only Hyuk to help him, crept forward to confront the estimated forty NVA. Miller's opening burst killed two soldiers, Hyuk added more fire, and the NVA fell back. Then NVA reinforcements arrived and fanned out right and left to rush the hill, advancing despite the recon men's well-aimed CAR-15 bursts.

Meanwhile, Blythe got Covey Rider Karate Davis on the radio, only to learn it would take at least twenty minutes to get fighters and helicopter gunships. While Karate orbited over the threatened team, Sergeant First Class Andy Brown left the Hatchet Force perimeter, leading four Montagnard volunteers toward the beleaguered RT Vermont. Then, ahead of them, Brown heard the eruption of heavy AK fire, answered by only two CAR-15s.

The second NVA assault had begun, with such fire concentrated on Miller's position that his point man, Hyuk, collapsed, shot dead, and Miller took one slug through his forearm, and a second bullet through his chest. Though shot through a lung, Miller continued firing and maneuvering, all alone, buying time for his men to limp away. On Miller's emergency radio, Karate heard heavy gunfire as Miller twice fought the NVA to a standstill, hitting them so ferociously that the NVA fell back. At last, weakened by loss of blood and difficulty breathing, Miller rejoined his team.

Then Andy Brown's Hatchet Force men hit the NVA, shooting their way through to reach Miller's position. Their fight was short but deadly; all four of Brown's Yards were shot and killed, with only the American medic making it through. Still, there was no time to spare; Brown found Miller almost unconscious from loss of blood, and managed to patch him up just as helicopters arrived overhead.

When the first Huey hovered on the trees, heavy enemy fire drove it away. Karate Davis brought in gunships to push the NVA back and, at last, RT Vermont's men snapped into extraction harnesses and lifted away. Living up to the One-Zero ethic, despite his wounds Miller would not allow himself to be pulled out until all his men were in rigs and ready to go.

It was an astonishing engagement. RT Vermont's interpreter, Gia, later wrote, "Sgt. Miller saved our lives on many occasions that day, and by doing so he greatly risked his own." One-One Bob Brown added, if not for Miller, "the enemy would have overrun and killed us." Karate Davis, the Covey Rider, called Miller's action "the greatest feat of gallantry I have ever witnessed."

Miller was submitted for a Silver Star. But as the recommendation filtered through higher echelons it was upgraded to a Distinguished Service Cross, then later, at U.S. Army, Vietnam, level, further upgraded to the Medal of Honor and forwarded to Washington for approval. Had he been submitted originally for the Medal of Honor, Miller would have been pulled from further combat operations. But because it had begun as a Silver Star, he continued to run recon, which was just fine with him. He assumed no airs—he was as funny and tough and cynical as ever. Miller didn't give it much thought, just continued performing missions. Eventually, Miller's would be the fifth Medal of Honor for our tiny, undermanned recon company, making this sixty-man outfit the most highly decorated unit of the Vietnam War.

And now, three weeks after that mission, Glenn Uemura volunteered to run recon with Miller, just as his new One-Zero's wounds healed and he returned to duty.

If it was surprising that Miller quickly recovered from his wounds, it was absolutely astonishing that Robert Masterjoseph, One-One on CCN's RT Moccasin, even survived another gunfight. The night before a mission in Laos, the New York native stood drinking in the CCN club and loudly offered, "I'd give my left nut for a prisoner!" He chugged down his drink, shook his head, and insisted to his recon buddies, "I mean it. I'd give my left nut!"

Early the next morning Masterjoseph's throbbing head reminded him it was a mistake to drink before a mission; during his team's Blackbird flight to Thailand he napped and drank plenty of water. An Italian-American who grew up in Yonkers, Masterjoseph's father had sent his young son upstate each summer, where he learned to shoot and track and hunt.

When Masterjoseph arrived at CCN, one of the few officers running recon, First Lieutenant Mike Duggan, took him onto RT Moccasin, but considered the New Yorker too cocky for his own good. Masterjoseph found his One-Zero a stickler for detailed planning and repetitious training, "as serious as a heart attack" and "a real pain in the ass." But Duggan's discipline had its effect, and they soon respected each other as Special Forces recon professionals.

Duggan's leadership proved almost magical: RT Moccasin stayed in dangerous targets three to five days where other teams couldn't stay overnight. They ran six missions together and despite lots of ground fire and NVA looking high and low for them, they'd never had a major firefight.

Recovering from his hangover, late that morning Masterjoseph, Duggan, and six Montagnards lifted away from a Thai airbase aboard a USAF Jolly Green helicopter for insertion along Highway 9, twenty miles west of the old Khe Sanh Marine base. Intelligence believed a cave deep in the hills overlooking Tchepone, Laos, contained a major storage site or headquarters. Large enough to accommodate trucks, the cavern and its approach road were invisible from the air.

Their Jolly Green attempted to land on a ridge above the suspected cave, but Duggan spotted trails and hooches nearby, so he waved them to the alternate LZ, down in a valley across the ridge from Highway 9. They landed below a cliff and in the distance saw a corrugated metal roof, which Duggan thought worth investigating.

After the aircraft departed, they advanced in a wide arc toward the metal roof, along the way discovering a cluster of camouflaged hooches. The buildings were deserted, but they found abundant evidence that enemy soldiers had recently been there.

By then it was midday. Duggan had Masterjoseph and five Yards hide in the jungle while he and the point man crept forward fifty yards to where he could watch the metal-roofed building through binoculars. To cover one another, Masterjoseph positioned his men to face inward, then leaned into his rucksack and propped the radio handset against his ear. In the midday heat, he closed his eyes, listening to the low buzz of radio static. There wasn't a sound in the jungle.

One Montagnard reached in a rucksack to pull out a bag of rice—and blurted, "VC!" As Masterjoseph jerked forward, an AK burst cracked around him. He lifted his CAR-15 but nothing happened—a slug had cut through his right forearm, leaving his hand useless. Another burst and he collapsed, hit again, and more AKs fired, and still more rounds smashed his body as he rolled over, grappling for his CAR-15.

He'd already been hit nine times and a dozen NVA stood just ten yards away, shooting at him—so close he could see the expressions on their faces. On his back, feeling like he was about to die, incredibly, he saw *fear* on *their* faces and that realization gave him strength. *The NVA were afraid!* They'd shot him over and over, yet he wasn't dead. When enemy soldiers paused to change magazines, he saw their fumbling, shaky hands. Then Masterjoseph remembered—he'd laid a claymore mine directly before them. He threw his bloody body onto the firing device and squeezed—*KA-BOOM!* When the smoke dissipated not one NVA was standing. He'd killed or seriously wounded every one of them. Using his left hand, Masterjoseph switched on his emergency radio and relayed word to Covey, who was soon on the way.

The Montagnards, who'd run to Lieutenant Duggan, now returned with him to find a cluster of enemy bodies and Masterjoseph bleeding from his face to his knees. Hastily wrapping his shattered arm, Duggan told him, "Drop everything but your weapon and some ammo." The One-Zero looked inside Masterjoseph's blood-soaked pants and knew he didn't need to see more. Duggan rigged an improvised bandage over his One-One's crotch but couldn't inject morphine because Masterjoseph was allergic to it. He'd just have to grunt it through.

With one Yard helping him walk, they trudged forward and saw that a hidden trail was only ten yards away—that's how the NVA got so close with no one hearing them. And, looking at the bodies, they realized the claymore's effect had been awesome. Then one body moved. Though missing an arm and paralyzed below the waist, one NVA still lived—and a major, no less. Bringing along the heavily bandaged enemy officer, Duggan got them to a nearby LZ just as Covey arrived. The Covey Rider, Sergeant First Class Richard "Dirty Dick" Dalley, brought his plane down to the treetops and fired marking rockets to keep the NVA from reaching the team.

While awaiting the helicopters, Masterjoseph finally could count his wounds. Incredibly, three AK bullets had hit his right arm, plus another burst of three had hit his groin. A bullet had grazed the inside of a leg, one more had creased his thigh, and another had skidded across his chest. Nine gunshot wounds! And he was still alive!

The Jolly Greens arrived, lowered a jungle penetrator, then winched RT Moccasin and their prisoner aboard while fighters kept the enemy occupied. The first chopper whisked Masterjoseph to the 95th Evacuation Hospital in Quang Tri, where he lay for two weeks to stabilize for a flight back to the States.

Compared to life at CCN, it was VIP treatment—Masterjoseph had his own ward with a personal bodyguard, to preclude patients and visitors from learning he'd been on a secret mission. After a few days, he felt well enough to hobble into a maximum security ward to see the NVA officer his team had captured. Speaking through an interpreter, Masterjoseph offered, "The war is over for us."

Paralyzed and missing one arm, the enemy officer nodded resentfully and complained, "My injuries are worse."

"Whaddayah mean!" Masterjoseph snapped back, grinning. "I lost my dick and balls!" The NVA officer couldn't help but crack a smile. They shook hands and parted with no hard feelings. Later, Masterjoseph learned, the major cooperated with debriefers and provided a gold mine of detailed information.

Another afternoon, three recon buddies arrived, telling the ward nurse that Masterjoseph needed a top secret debriefing in a secure setting. It was difficult to get him into a wheelchair with his right arm suspended in a cast, his left arm trailing an IV bottle, and a urinary catheter draining to a bag. Then they carefully wheeled him to an empty ward and, when the nurse left, hustled him into a jeep and drove him to the CCN club. Jovial but hurting, Masterjoseph recalled ironically, "I got my prisoner and, dammit, it cost me my left nut."

Five hours later his buddies rolled him back, so drunk he couldn't remember his name, a six-pack and a bottle of scotch in his lap. An irate nurse chased the three Green Berets from the hospital. It was Masterjoseph's happiest day of what would become twelve months in military hospitals and a lifetime in VA centers.

While Masterjoseph stabilized in the 95th Evac Hospital, I was training RT Washington for our first mission. Hardly had I got the team ready when we received our warning order: We would conduct a bomb damage assessment in northeast Cambodia, about twenty miles southwest of Ben Het—almost the same spot where I'd had my first firefight a year earlier, also on a BDA mission. These raids were still top secret, known only to bomber crews and SOG teams and, of course, to the NVA forces pounded by these cataclysms. As earlier, should we get in trouble, no fighters—only helicopters—could enter Cambodia to help us.

RT Washington with Joe Quiroz, the One-One, and Jerry Guzzetta, One-Two, along with five Yards, would launch from Dak To just as forty-eight heavy bombers unloaded along Cambodian Highway 613, a scant five miles from the Laotian frontier and its connecting Highway 110. It was the haunt of the NVA 66th Infantry Regiment. We expected a hornet's nest.

As we stood at Dak To beside our cranking helicopters and smeared camouflage stick on our faces, we got word from Covey that the bombers had struck. A half-hour later, we were at 3,000 feet, circling the long trails of smoldering bomb craters, churned earth, and downed trees, and it struck me that this was becoming a way of life, almost routine. Though I still felt twinges of dread as our Huey descended toward the treetops, and still tracked the tree-lines with my CAR-15, I felt less personal concern and almost total focus on my team and our mission. Gone was being awestruck by destruction, replaced by a learned eye that watched for any tactical advantage in terrain or cover. Like most One-Zeros, I was becoming too busy being a team leader to think much about anything else.

We landed uneventfully, dashed into the collapsed Cambodian greenery, then lay low until our aircraft engines faded. Then, as on my previous BDA mission, we began exhausting hours of climbing, crawling, and squeezing through unending heaps of tree trunks and branches, only to remove our rucksacks and drag them after us, then slide in and out of bomb craters. In the sweltering heat and humidity, and pungent stench of explosive residue, Guzzetta, carrying our team radio, especially found the going difficult. Sweat streamed off his face. In the rear, Quiroz had a tough time erasing our tracks because the bombs had generated a thick layer of gray, pulverized soil on every leaf and branch and bit of exposed earth. Crawling through the dust, soon we were the same gray color, head to toe. Despite continuous, grueling movement, in three hours we'd not gone 500 yards. Then we got lucky—I looked across a downed tree and noticed a stream, five yards wide, headed in the same northerly direction I wanted to go. Perfect.

Silently we slipped into the cool water, then gently skimmed our boots below the surface rather than lift them, to preclude any sound of splashing. The bombing had so muddied the water that our tracks could not be seen along the streambed, while the chest-high bank kept the many uprooted, overhanging trees above us, creating a sort of watery tunnel that allowed us relatively fast, unfettered movement. All afternoon we carefully trod that knee-deep water, careful not to lift our feet, putting nearly a mile between us and our insert LZ. We heard birds, insects, the wind, but not one human sound and found no sign of the enemy. Perhaps the bombs had been wasted.

Late that afternoon, we left the stream and I followed Joe Walker's advice about walking roads or trails: "You can walk it, but do it once, then get away from it and don't go back." Putting an hour of tough crawling and climbing between us and the stream, I never even cut back toward it. Then we found a good defensible spot and settled down for the night.

That night we heard no sound of enemy, not even signal shots, and I wondered again, had the B-52s wasted their bomb loads?

An hour after daylight, we heard the welcome hum of Covey's engines and Guzzetta radioed our morning situation report. Then it was time to pull in claymores and continue our assessment.

Hardly had we hefted our rucksacks and—*whoo-whoo-whoo-whoo-whoo—BOOM!* Artillery! And again—*whoo-whoo-whoo-whoo-whoo—BOOM!* I guessed they were 85mm shells, impacting about 400 yards away. Guzzetta tried to reach Covey but he was beyond radio range.

Then it stopped. No adjustment to bring the shells closer, not one more shell. I realized what was happening. Coming so quickly after our morning radio contact, the enemy must have found us by radio direction finding—the electronic triangulation of our transmitter. Yet their fix wasn't all that exact (or they had poor-quality maps) because that 85mm gun could have dropped a shell much closer if whoever was firing knew precisely where we were. Therefore, it wasn't much worse than hearing a signal shot 400 yards away; close enough for concern, but you just press on.

Leaving our overnight position, we were alert to any sign of the enemy and Joe Quiroz stayed keen to the presence of trackers, but we heard and saw nothing special. Then, at last, we came upon our first bomb fatality: our point man, Knot, found a roosterlike jungle fowl, killed by concussion. I posed Knot for a picture, grinning, holding it up.

The bomb craters thinned somewhat, but still our going was slow and tedious until we intersected a trail around 10:00 A.M. Like the stream a day earlier, it was going our way—and it was long disused with overhanging branches and fallen leaves—so I signaled Knot to follow it. We made quick time compared to the jungle, heading generally north.

Just before lunch, we slipped about 100 yards into the jungle to set up a perimeter. There we stayed, eating and listening, for more than an hour. Again, no noise, no sign of the enemy. Then it was 1:00 P.M. and time to continue.

We hadn't gone another 100 yards when we reached a massive earth slide, where a string of bombs had cleared a whole hillside, leaving an open area the size of a golf fairway. To our right, uphill, the clearing extended perhaps 300 yards; downhill, on our left, another 200 yards; and straight across, about seventy-five yards. Stairlike bomb craters climbed the hill about every fifty yards.

How should we cross this? I wondered. In such thick jungle, complicated by craters, it would take all day to circle to the right; downhill, I saw a stream and mud and a lot of open ground. There was only one choice, I decided, to dash across, right here, seventy-five yards, one at a time.

I explained to Knot that I'd cover him as he crossed, then handed my Pen EE camera to Guzzetta and whispered, "As you come across, snap a few photos of the bomb damage." He nodded, slung his CAR-15, and raised the camera to his eye.

Knot trotted low, along the edge of a crater, and made it safely to the other side. Momentarily he tipped his head, signaling all-clear. Next, I shuffled along the crater, made it halfway to the wood line when, ten yards above me, on the next crater, a figure in dusty gray stepped completely in the open. I thought, "What the hell's with Guzzetta, wandering so far uphill to snap photos!"

But this figure was carrying an AK!

Instinctively I slid to my knees, raised my CAR-15, flipped to full-auto—in my peripheral vision stood Guzzetta, his back to me, snapping pictures—while another, second gray figure—*clearly, an NVA soldier*—walked out where the first enemy had been. Neither NVA looked down at me, just walked right across the uphill crater lip, their AKs slung on their shoulders, oblivious to my CAR-15 muzzle tracking their every step. Hardly a dozen yards away, I was completely in the open. It seemed impossible that they did not see me.

And here came two more.

Every instinct screamed, "Shoot! Shoot!" But I didn't. Unable even to shift my eyes, I hissed, "JERR-Y! JERR-Y!" Joe Quiroz and the point man, Knot, I hoped, by now had seen the NVA and were covering me. I hoped but dare not look.

Another two NVA walked past, then came four more, the first of whom glanced down and pointed a finger directly at me. Their faces showed neither fear nor hatred. They looked tired, burdened by bulging rucksacks. Most of their group noticed me, but they walked past as uninterestedly as the first group, not even unslinging their weapons. By now there were too many to shoot with four or five full-auto bursts—my magazine capacity. My thumb flipped my CAR-15 to semiauto so I could fire longer. Any second, one of these guys would go for his weapon, I'd have to shoot, and all hell would break loose. Any second, it had to happen. My eyes darted back and forth, back and forth— if one man grabbed for his AK or pivoted a barrel toward me, that's it, I'd fire. One startled look, one flash in their eyes. I squeezed the slack out of my trigger. But the soldiers only walked past as if so many zombies and disappeared into the next wood line, following their comrades.

Then came six more NVA. I could take out three, maybe four—Joe Quiroz would drop a couple, and my point man, Knot, might get one or two—but there'd still be enough NVA to shoot me dead, here in the open, while I was changing magazines. Miraculously, though every one of these NVA looked down, saw me holding my CAR-15 squarely on him, not one went for his weapon.

And still more NVA walked into view—sixteen, seventeen, eighteen, nineteen.

Groups of three and four NVA continued to pass for five minutes, by the end of which I had counted twenty-eight, probably the surviving remnant of a forty-man platoon hit by our B-52s. As quickly as they were gone, I hustled the team across the mountain slide, formed a defensive perimeter, and radioed Covey, declaring a tactical emergency. Outnumbering us more than three to one, any second that NVA platoon could dump their rucksacks, return, and assault us. It would have been the height of naïveté to think this was some kind of "live and let live"—maybe they didn't want to die today, but in minutes they'd reach an NVA 66th Infantry Regiment base camp, report us, and hundreds of soldiers would flock our way.

To slow that reaction, I called in a pair of Cobra gunships to pound the jungle north and east of us. With that bombardment as a sound diversion, we swung downhill and west, hurrying about 500 yards to a stream—*but we couldn't cross it!* A string of 750-pound bombs had hit squarely in the water, their craters leaving unfordable holes and quicksand-like mud. And worse, the mud along the creek contained dozens of fresh human tracks, heading in the same direction as the NVA who'd passed us. I took stock: Uphill, many NVA who knew we were here. To our left, the unfordable stream. To our front, a bamboo forest too open to conceal us. And behind us, on soft ground our tracks stood out so boldly Joe could not obliterate them.

Between the restricted terrain and enemy presence we'd had it. It was time to come out. I requested an extraction. A half-hour later, following several hot passes by Cobra gunships, we came out under light ground fire. None of the helicopters was hit.

Back at Kontum, we told the debriefer our amazing story of enemy soldiers covered in gray dust that momentarily looked just like us, but even once they knew the score, they hesitated to fire, and we held our fire, too. Our self-control had saved lives—probably including my own—while there could be no doubt that the B-52s had hit enemy troop locations. Afterward, in the hallway I encountered the S-3 operations officer who'd led Operation Ashtray, Major Jaks. He'd already heard about our astonishing Mexican standoff.

"They had to have been bombed pretty bad, not to open fire," he said. I agreed, the B-52 strike had left them dazed and demoralized. "Very tough," he said, "to override your instinct to shoot."

I chuckled and agreed. "Awful damned hard, sir." Jaks nodded, studied me for a moment, then walked off. I wasn't sure what he was thinking, but didn't give it much thought. I should have.

As it was, what followed was a typical week of stand-down, spent mostly in the club drinking and swapping stories with other teams resting between missions. About the only thing different was that I teamed up with another One-Zero, Will Curry, to try my hand at songwriting. Going hand in hand with our abounding fatalism, it was black humor that kept us sane—an irreverence reflected in sick jokes, impertinent attitudes, and in the case of Curry and me, by rewriting Broadway musicals. Thus, in addition to singing such standard club fare as a terrible rendition of "Jingle Bells" or a wickedly funny song about a Western Union clerk singing a telegram to a dead GI's mother, Will and I penned our own lyrics, such as this one, sung to the tune of "High Hopes"

Once there was a lone VC
Hidin' in the bushes,
Shootin' at me.
Everyone knows,
That you can't
Shoot somethin' you can't see.

But we've got tac air!
We've got tac air!
Just look to the sky
As they fly by,
We've got tac air!

So anytime you're surrounded,
Don't be astounded,
When the sky goes black with tac air,
And,
Whoosh, *there goes another NVA,*
Whoosh, *there goes another NVA,*
Whoosh, *there goes another NVA,*
SPLAT!

As our stand-down ended, I learned the B-52 BDA would be my only mission with Quiroz and Guzzetta. The recon first sergeant announced he had another team in mind for me, and gave RT Washington to Sergeant First Class Eulis "Camel" Presley. In Eulis, the team had a fine leader.

Presley had run recon at CCN in 1968, rotated home and come back to fight with our Hatchet Force. But his latest Hatchet Force mission—a 100-man, company-size roadblock on Highway 110—had been a bloody debacle, souring him on his commander and convincing him that he preferred the autonomy of being a One-Zero. Attempting to repeat 1969's successful roadblock, his Hatchet Force company had occupied the very same hill, but this time the enemy rerouted traffic to hidden bypasses, and aggressively massed troops against the SOG men.

The Hatchet Force called in fighters all day and USAF AC-130 gunships all night, while heavy 175mm guns at Ben Het fired around the clock. Quicker to react than the previous year, the NVA soon were pounding Presley's hilltop with mortars and RPGs and recoilless rifles, and ringing the area with antiaircraft guns. By the third day, resupply choppers could not land, instead racing past at low level to kick out cases of badly needed ammunition. Then the NVA began digging trenches up the hill. "I don't think we got any sleep," recalled Presley's good friend Sergeant First Class Rich Ryan.

On the fourth night, U.S. intelligence intercepted an enemy radio message: The entire NVA 27th Infantry Regiment—1,500 strong—was massing to overwhelm the surrounded SOG company. The next morning it got so bad that Presley laid out his magazines and grenades and wondered how much time they had left and where he'd be shot first. A Kingbee helicopter carrying medic William Boyle attempted to come in for the worst wounded but heavy fire riddled the H-34. Ryan watched it turn nose-down and crash in flames that engulfed everyone aboard. Boyle's body and the bodies of the pilots were not recovered.

There was little else to do but get out: Sergeant First Class Lloyd "O.D." O'Daniels, their Covey Rider, brought in A-1 Skyraiders with tear gas bomblets to disrupt the enemy and F-4 Phantoms with heavy 500-pound bombs to pound the half-mile route to an extraction LZ. Cobra gunships fired smoke rockets to mask their march, which bogged down several times.

At the LZ, to expedite their extraction, they abandoned everything but radios and weapons. Despite sporadic ground fire, the exfil came off smoothly, until the final chopper load. When that last Huey came in, the only men left were Presley, his company commander, and a badly wounded Yard. The captain jumped aboard—breaching the SOG ethic that a leader comes out last— while Presley struggled to load the Montagnard and had to lay his CAR-15 and radio in the Huey. Then ground fire forced off the helicopter, but the captain stayed aboard, flying away with Presley's CAR-15, leaving him alone and unarmed with the unconscious Yard. Another chopper eventually got Presley and the Yard, but that was it for Presley. He transferred to recon company, taking over RT Washington.

Presley, who could display zany, crude humor in the club, equally possessed great depth of character. The 5th Special Forces Group commander, Colonel Francis Kelly, once brought along several South Vietnamese officers to a Mike Force club and called upon Presley to propose a toast, "To our Vietnamese allies, our combat comrades." Eulis clinked glasses with three young Vietnamese officers he knew had guts and had never run from a fight. Then he turned to the others, majors and colonels Presley knew as corrupt cowards, and added, "And to the rest of you chickenshit, stay-behind motherfuckers—*fuck you.*" Presley stormed away.

Colonel Kelly followed, angrily reproaching him, "You know, Sergeant, you put me on the spot."

"No, sir," Presley replied, "you put *me* on the spot." Kelly didn't know what to say.

Though I laughed at Presley's antics, it was his poignant, deeper side that I most admired. Not long after taking RT Washington, he and his new One-One, Staff Sergeant Tommy Batchelor, and four Yards found themselves cornered in a Laotian box canyon. Hiding in a bomb crater, Presley snapped Batchelor and two Yards into extraction harnesses, then watched a Huey lift them safely away. A second Huey hovered overhead and dropped ropes, but only two lines made it to the ground, so, living by the One-Zero ethic, Presley snapped in Meou and Nigon, the last two Yards, and radioed that he'd wait for a third aircraft.

As the chopper rose, the new pilot—flying his first SOG mission—heard his door gunner fire, got excited, and flew away before the Yards cleared the tree-tops. Dragged through the trees, Nigon broke his neck before the crew chief desperately cut the ropes to keep the chopper from being pulled down.

An hour later, One-Zero Steve "Jade" Keever, commanding a Bright Light team, rappelled down where the Yards had fallen, and found Meou, shaken but alive, and Nigon, dead. Steve's team, the newly reorganized RT Illinois, brought them out.

That night, Eulis Presley sat outside the dispensary, at the morgue refrigerator containing Nigon's body, and spoke to the Yard's spirit. "You should have lived, Nigon," he said, "you were a good man. If this country prospers, like we hope it will, I wanted you here for that. They'll need men like you. I am sorry you won't be here, Nigon. But I will remember you. I hope you understand."

Things had been moving quickly. I'd turned over RT Washington to Eulis Presley, Jerry Guzzetta had gone to RT Arizona, then one morning in late February I was called to the recon company orderly room. First Sergeant Doney pointed to the manning board, where I saw my name grease-penciled, *One-Zero, RT California.* I'll be damned, I realized. I've got Joe Walker's old team.

In my mind, there was no finer team than RT California, whose Montagnards had been drilled by that superb, exacting taskmaster. After Walker left for CIA duty in northern Laos, California had had two One-Zeros—Dick Gross and Lloyd O'Daniels—but they knew they were only caretakers, keeping the team trained and ready for when Joe returned. Those three would be tough acts to follow, but after fourteen months in recon and twice being a One-Zero, I felt ready for the challenge.

Moving into the RT California team room, I met my new teammates. Senior among them was Sergeant First Class Rex Jaco, a cheery Tennessean with country wit and style, who'd come over from the Hatchet Force. Although Rex, my One-One, outranked me and was about ten years older, his loyalty and support knew no bounds. Now on his second Vietnam combat tour, he'd previously served with the Special Forces airboat unit in the Mekong Delta, racing along at forty knots to riddle VC sampans with machine guns. By the time he got to RT California, he'd been on the Hatchet Force's Company A for five months, and had fought in several major engagements.

Along with Rex, I inherited Staff Sergeant John Yancey, an old comrade of Rex's who'd served with him on the airboats. Entirely reliable but with a nonconformist edge, John never carried a wallet, keeping everything from snapshots to ID cards and money balled up in one of his pockets. He refused to wear socks, perhaps a habit from having had his feet wet in the Mekong Delta.

For the first time, I had a team with a fourth American, Richard Woody, who'd already been in-country six months. Slim with a faint mustache, Woody earlier had fought with the Special Forces Mike Force battalion that assaulted Nui Coto Mountain, an old Vietcong sanctuary northwest of Saigon. The junior man, he'd been at Kontum about three months.

All three were reliable, courageous, and, most importantly, ready to fight as a team. With these Americans and Joe Walker's RT California Yards, I knew, we could achieve great things.

And what Yards we had. The interpreter, Weet, spoke passable English, but unlike many interpreters, he was also a fine recon man and a natural leader. Our point man, Angao, had such keen instincts and jungle experience that it was like having a hunting hound on point. Hmoi, the indigenous team leader, bore a terrible scar where an AK round had transited his neck—suffered when Bill Stubbs was lost, four months earlier—yet he'd fought as if he hadn't even been hit. Prin, too, had been badly wounded, yet fought like a tiger. And the M-79 grenadiers, Wo and Wo—renamed by Joe Walker "Wo-One" and "Wo-Two"—were the finest grenadiers I'd ever encountered. All our Yards were bright, dedicated, and as skilled as most Americans.

Still, though, we needed ten days to train as a team and learn to function together. I began by reviewing fundamentals: Their muzzles tracked their eyes automatically, so they could react in a split second to a surprise. They all knew how to reload rapidly, but I drilled it, live-fire, until all could reload their CAR-15s smoothly in under four seconds. My RT California M-79 grenadiers could pump out ten rounds per minute, aimed fire, and fifteen rounds per minute, fired instinctively, an astonishing rate that would overwhelm our foes.

In the nearby jungle, we practiced walking tree to tree, so each man was close to cover if fire suddenly erupted. Soon our team movement acquired a sinuous, natural gait, like a serpent slithering through the jungle, tree to tree. Our jungle movement also exploited shadows, staying hidden in shade and by-passing even tiny sunbeams, which could illuminate you like a spotlight. We moved in total silence, relying upon hand and arm signals, which all soon understood.

On the shooting range, most of our time was spent in live fire immediate action drills, the orchestrated ways a team reacts to enemy contact. Upon contact, I taught them to drop to one knee, reducing their size as targets while retaining good shooting support. Compared to sitting or lying prone, kneeling made it physically—and especially, psychologically—easier to get up and go when it was time to move through fire. Such little things would keep my men alive.

Soon we had the basic drills down pat, allowing me to elevate the men to a higher level of sophistication. A great believer in tear gas, I had the two grenadiers fire gas rounds after their initial barrage of four explosive rounds, while, my interpreter, Weet, would throw a gas grenade whenever he saw me throw one. Also, I had claymore mine bags sewn on the point man's and tail gunner's rucksacks, so whether we were hit from front or rear, the last man to withdraw would ignite a half-minute, time-delay claymore, to further confuse and disrupt enemy pursuers. We drilled for being hit from the front, the back, the right flank, the left flank, carrying along wounded men, assaulting through an enemy ambush, withdrawing from an enemy ambush, employing a 60mm mortar, even hasty ambushes for snatching prisoners. And all of it was live-fire, shooting our weapons over, beside, and between each other, danger-close.

By the end of ten hard training days, our coordinated shooting reminded me of the smooth-firing pistons in a Ferrari—perfectly tuned, in unison, and exactly how I wanted it. Now RT California was really up and ready, more combat ready than any team I'd been on before. What would be our first mission? First Sergeant Doney told me to report to the operations officer, Major Jaks.

This was unusual. Normally, a One-Zero simply went into the Operations Office and received a warning order from a captain, then a couple of days later a full-fledged mission briefing. I wondered what Jaks wanted.

I found him in the Tactical Operations Center, at his desk, talking to a new, young captain. Jaks waved me to a chair. As always, he was direct, to-the-point.

"This is Captain Krupa. I think you know him." Though I'd hardly ever talked to Fred Krupa, I had noticed the blond-haired, Pennsylvania native, and knew he was RT New Hampshire's relatively new One-Zero. By the 1st Air Cavalry patch on his right shoulder, I knew he'd already served one Vietnam combat tour.

I nodded. "Yes, I do, sir."

Jaks continued, "Saigon has approved another Ashtray mission. Chief SOG wants another convoy ambush and the snatch of a truck driver on Highway 110. Operation Ashtray Two."

I began to repeat my offer from the club a month earlier. "I'll go if you—"

Jaks interrupted, "I cannot lead Ashtray Two. Saigon says I cannot go." Security concerns overrode again risking the capture of a well-briefed SOG staff officer.

Jaks paused, looked at me long, the way he had ten days earlier, in the hall.

"The U.S. ambassador to Laos has authorized us to send eight Americans on this operation. But this time we cannot close down half our teams to pull volunteers. No, this mission will involve just two teams, you and Krupa and all your Americans. Plaster, you have more experience, you are in charge of Operation Ashtray Two."

I was almost overwhelmed.

Jaks extended his hand. We shook, then I shook Krupa's hand. All I could think to say was, "I'll do my best, sir."

Chapter Ten

Operation Ashtray Two would assemble a twelve-man team of eight Americans and four indigenous soldiers. From my RT California that meant Sergeant First Class Rex Jaco and Staff Sergeants John Yancey and Richard Woody, along with my two superb M-79 grenadiers, Wo-One and Wo-Two. Captain Fred Krupa's RT New Hampshire contributed Sergeants Paul Kennicott and A. Michael Grace, along with a medic, Specialist Five Jim Galasso. Krupa also brought his Nung point and tail men, Phung and Pheng, who would carry AKs and wear NVA uniforms.

We began our Ashtray Two preparation in the intelligence office, scouring every file, debrief, and report we could find concerning enemy trucks, NVA convoy procedures, and Laotian Highway 110. Krupa and I spent hours studying photographs of Soviet-built trucks.

Like American vehicles, Russian trucks put the driver on the left where, conveniently, there was a running board beside the door. Unless it was raining, the driver's-side window usually was rolled down, we learned. The truck's shifting and steering would occupy the driver, so even if he had a weapon he couldn't grab it quickly. If guards were riding in back, the cargo compartment's wooden slat sides would force them to stand and raise their heads to fire down on us, silhouetting them for our return fire. Since these trucks were diesel-powered, fuel was unlikely to ignite easily, giving us latitude to employ gunfire and explosives.

An NVA driver, we discovered, stayed with his assigned truck, every night traveling the same stretch of road so he could master it despite darkness or rain. He spent his days in carefully hidden truck parks, resting and maintaining his vehicle and refreshing its camouflage. Drivers were usually draftees with little combat training and unlikely to offer much resistance. Still, with Ashtray One's recent ambush, the NVA may have added an armed assistant driver, or increased firearms training for drivers. One agent report said that drivers sometimes were chained to their steering wheels, so they couldn't abandon their trucks during an air strike.

Enemy convoys of up to 100 trucks were the norm early in the war, but night prowling by FACs and USAF AC-119 and AC-130 gunships had reduced each convoy to ten or so well-dispersed vehicles to make them more difficult to detect. On east–west Highway 110, these convoys followed a simple pattern: Eastward-rolling convoys carried cargo toward the border with South Vietnam, while westward-rolling trucks mostly were empty. Using no lights or only tiny blackout lights, they finished their runs before daylight and rolled into truck parks containing about a dozen vehicles, wisely dispersed to limit damage from B-52 strikes. Of no small concern to us, convoys sometimes were escorted by armored cars and even light tanks.

Dismounted security concerned me the most. For five years, American-led SOG teams had been making life difficult for NVA forces along the Laotian highway system, and following each successful blow, the NVA had responded by layering more security. By 1970, with tens of thousands of soldiers defending the Ho Chi Minh Trail, the North Vietnamese had posted stationary night guards on all major routes and aggressively patrolled the jungle beside highways—all in addition to the trackers and counter-recon forces that usually hunted us. Were we lucky enough to reach the road undetected, and fortunate enough to stop a truck and snatch the driver, there'd be hell to pay afterward, with NVA units chasing us all night long. With that realization, Krupa and I studied maps, focusing on a stretch of Highway 110 east of where Eulis Presley's Hatchet Force company had blocked the road for five days in February. From several target folders, we gleaned suspected enemy locations—such as supply dumps and bivouac sites—so we wouldn't wander inadvertently into them. When finally we'd selected our best ambush spot, one intelligence report placed an estimated battalion base camp just 500 yards away. It would be essential that we grab that driver and get away fast.

Importantly, we also studied failed snatch attempts in which a prisoner was unintentionally killed and concluded that merely grabbing him didn't assure success: we had to exploit our momentary surprise and seize him so quickly that, like a deer dazzled by headlights, he had no option but to submit. One second, he'd be at his steering wheel, the next he would be handcuffed and hustled away.

After digesting all this, Krupa and I and our teammates brainstormed over drinks in the club. "What about Phung's NVA uniform?" Krupa suggested, referring to his point man. "He could just wave down a truck." That was simple and direct, but Phung's disguise might not match NVA uniform markings, such as a distinctive armband. Even the gesture to halt was unknown to us since no SOG team had ever observed an enemy soldier stop a truck. Further, Phung might lack the confidence to pull off the masquerade and, despite hefty incentives to take prisoners, indigenous soldiers were too quick to shoot NVA.

No matter what, I emphasized, we had to physically halt that truck, which is no small thing. *How do you stop instantly two tons of moving mass, traveling twenty miles per hour?* Already, Jaks had warned me, "There's nothing in our manuals, nothing anywhere." By the end of our first brainstorming session, already, I concluded, the solution would involve explosives, which inspired a series of demolition experiments.

Each day, we spent half our time studying intelligence and planning and testing explosives, and the rest of it training together to integrate our twelve men into a single team. Initially, we practiced formations and hand-and-arm signals, progressed to immediate action drills, then live fire exercises at the range. By the third day, we were live-firing everything we did, but we still hadn't settled upon the means for halting the truck.

Understand, it's an easy thing to blow up a truck—any demo man can calculate a suitable charge of C-4 explosive to do the job. But how do you employ explosives to halt a vehicle instantly, *without* blowing its driver sky-high? Plus, the technique or device had to be selective so we could allow an armored car or truckload of troops to roll past, yet hit the truck we wanted. Burying an explosive device beneath Highway 110 was out of the question because its hard clay surface would betray signs of spadework. The U.S. Army Ranger manual suggested a slick trick from World War II: Lay a cord across a road, then pull a mine into the path of the vehicle you select. But pulling that mine to exactly the right spot to catch a wheel—in the dark—seemed too risky.

"Drop a tree in front of it," Yancey suggested, and that was our first test.

I prepared two charges, linked by detonation cord: At the base of a tree, we taped a cutting charge and a second, smaller charge about ten feet above the ground—what demo men call a "kicker"—to push the snapped tree across the road. We knocked down several trees before I concluded we'd need too much explosive and too big a tree to block a two-ton truck.

Eventually we came full circle and agreed with Ashtray One's demo man, John Grant, who'd tested a variety of explosive charges and settled upon a semicircle of three claymores to focus their blast and collapse the truck's front wheel. Several times we tested Grant's rig against truck tires, achieving an acceptable likelihood of success.

Now that we'd settled upon the means of halting the truck, working outward, we had to develop a complete ambush around it. Who would detonate the claymores? I would because that detonation would signal the start of our ambush; a leader doesn't relay such a signal, nor does he convey the signal by whistle or the wave of a hand, lest surprise be lost. Further, since this was a selective engagement—allowing armored cars and trucks loaded with troops to pass—my own hand on the firing device assured me the means of an instantaneous response.

Who would grab the driver? As our largest man, John Yancey could best subdue and control the prisoner. Yancey also had a good bit of combat experience in the Mike Force, giving me confidence that he would not hesitate at the critical moment.

Of necessity, Yancey's hands would have to be free to grab the driver, so he'd need at least two men to cover him—Captain Krupa beside Yancey, while I'd run around the hood, jerk open the passenger door, and cover from that side. I would eliminate any assistant driver, and help John remove the driver, if necessary.

The fourth man in our assault or snatch element—Richard Woody—would cover the cargo compartment, ready to eliminate any security troops and armed passengers before they could fire. To minimize the danger of hitting each other, we rehearsed that, after the first shot, every assault team member would drop to one knee and fire upward into the truck.

Beyond the ambush site, 100 yards up and down the road, two flank security teams—containing three men each—would block the road and prevent any NVA from interfering with the snatch, as well as delay reaction forces long enough for the assault team to withdraw with the prisoner. Each security team—led by Jaco on our west, and Kennicott to the east—included a Yard M-79 grenadier and a Nung with a CAR-15, plus two claymore mines. They'd also have LAW antitank rocket launchers in case they had to engage approaching vehicles.

Upon hearing my verbal shout "Withdraw!"—repeated by Woody as a whistle blast—each flank security team would ignite three-minute time delays on their claymores, while their grenadier fired two tear gas cartridges down the road. All elements would meet at the rally point, some 100 yards back in the jungle, where we'd have left our radio operator, Grace, and medic, Galasso, and all our rucksacks.

The plan seemed complete.

"What about destroying the truck?" Krupa asked. No sweat. While Yancey and Krupa were handcuffing the prisoner, I'd toss a satchel charge in the cab, place a 2,000 degree thermite grenade above the engine block, and activate a time-delay white phosphorus grenade to set it afire. Then, with the truck a flaming beacon, we'd bring in an AC-130 Spectre gunship, whose 20mm and 40mm guns would pulverize Highway 110 while we fled through the jungle. Perfect!

Recon Team New Hampshire silently crosses a stream behind enemy lines in Laos. *(Photo by Will Curry)*

One-Zero Ron Knight *(rear, center)* disguised his RT West Virginia team in North Vietnamese uniforms, complete with Chinese weapons. In front is One-One Larry Kramer. *(Photo courtesy of Ron Knight)*

A supply-laden North Vietnamese truck bounces along a Laotian highway on the Ho Chi Minh Trail. *(North Vietnamese Army Photo)*

Large enough to house one hundred enemy soldiers, this heavily camou-flaged bivouac site was just across the border in Laos. *(Photo by the author)*

Caught by the camera, this passing enemy patrol was unknowingly photographed by a SOG recon team. *(Photo by Terry Soresby)*

A North Vietnamese armored car patrols a Laotian highway, alert for any possible SOG ambushers. *(Department of Defense Photo)*

A CCN team rides ladders after an emergency extraction from Laos. This Huey is from Company B, 158th Assault Helicopter Battalion. *(Photo by Gary Whitty)*

Lieutenant Colonel Frederick T. Abt, CCC commander 1969–70. A three-war veteran, he was much admired by his recon soldiers. *(Photo by Mike Buckland)*

Captain Charles Pfeifer, a CCN Hatchet Force commander, killed more than a dozen enemy commandos during the 1968 attack on SOG's Da Nang base. *(Photo courtesy of Chuck Pfeifer)*

RT Illinois One-Zero Ben Thompson took me on my first missions into Laos and Cambodia. *(Photo by the author)*

Sergeant First Class Joe Walker, RT California, the epitome of a SOG One-Zero, displayed both courage and innovation. *(Photo by Billy Greenwood)*

RT New York One-Zero John St. Martin *(left)* and One-One Ed Wolcoff at Dak To launch site, ready to launch into Laos. St. Martin was severely wounded but brought out alive thanks to Wolcoff's courageous actions. *(Photo courtesy of Ed Wolcoff)*

One-One Bill Spencer, my assistant team leader, at SOG's Dak Pek launch site, November 1969. He was killed thirty days later. *(Photo by the author)*

Tape shot off my muzzle, an empty ammo pouch on my hip, like any recon man, I'm glad to be back at CCC after another firefight. *(Photo by Terrance Spoon)*

Captain Fred Krupa, just before convoy ambush, hams it up for the camera. *(Photo by the author)*

A self-portrait, shot just before convoy ambush in case I were killed and the camera captured. *(Photo by the author)*

North Vietnamese truck ambushed by my team in southern Laos. Note thermite grenade I placed on hood. *(Photo by Fred Krupa)*

Calling in air. Glenn Uemura *(right)* and I help adjust an air strike on an enemy antiaircraft gun that's preventing RT Vermont's extraction. *(Photo courtesy of the author)*

Two hours after a heavy fight in Laos, RT Vermont is safe at Dak To. *Back row, left to right:* unidentified pointman, Medal of Honor recipient Franklin Miller, One-One Glenn Uemura, and me. *Front row:* One-Two Chuck Hein and two unidentified Yards. Two weeks later, Hein was killed. *(Photo courtesy of the author)*

Sergeant First Class David "Baby Huey" Hayes left a comfortable communications job to run recon. Fatally wounded by an RPG rocket, he bled to death. *(Photo by the author)*

Fresh bulldozer tracks through this heavily bombed pass almost launched my team on a major ambush mission. *(Photo by Ted Wicorek)*

"Hey—Hey, Fat Albert!" The irrepressible Pete Wilson *(center)*, the life of any recon gathering. Band-Aid on cheek of Charles Bless *(right)*, covers the spot where an AK slug hit his face to no great effect. Also shown, Recon First Sergeant Forrest Todd. *(Photo by Ed Wolcoff)*

After Pete "Fat Albert" Wilson went missing in action, this Recon club was renamed to memorialize him. *(Photo by Will Curry)*

Sergeant First Class Larry White, RT Hawaii One-Zero and Covey Rider, recruited me to fly Covey. *(Photo courtesy of Larry White)*

The "backseater" or Covey Rider's view aboard an OV-10 Bronco Forward Air Control aircraft. *(U.S. Air Force Photo)*

On the treetops. A Covey OV-10 passes low-level above the Laotian jungle. *(Photo by Frank Greko)*

U.S. Air Force Captain James "Mike" Cryer beside his OV-10. I flew many missions with Cryer, including the one during which we lost David Mixter, SOG's final recon man MIA in Laos. *(Photo courtesy of Mike Cryer)*

Covey Rider Ken "Shoebox" Carpenter attired to "greet" General Creighton Abrams, U.S. Commander in Vietnam—oversize boxer shorts and a Crown Royal bottle around his neck. *(Photo by Mike Cryer)*

Badly wounded, One-Zero Jim "Fred" Morse rides an extraction rig into Dak To. Note the vine dangling from his waist, from being dragged through the trees. *(Photo courtesy of Jim "Fred" Morse)*

Taking fire. With an extracted team on board, a Huey dodges machine gun tracer fire (vertical streak to the right), while an exploding rocket from Cobra escort hits the treetops, just ahead. *(Photo by the author)*

Recon man's best friend: A-1 Skyrider heavily loaded with cluster bombs, napalm, and 20mm cannons orbits above a SOG team. *(Photo by the author)*

Scratch one tank. USAF F-4 Phantom bombs a stalled PT-76 tank on Laotian Highway 110. *(Photo by the author)*

Staff Sergeant Eldon Bargewell with RT Michigan Yards, Contua and Lang. My plane fortuitously overflew a badly wounded Bargewell fighting off numerous NVA, and brought in two airstrikes to help him escape. Today Bargewell is a two-star general. *(Photo courtesy of Eldon Bargewell)*

My last day. With Covey Rider Lowell Wesley Stevens, awaiting departure at Kontum Airfield after three years of continuous combat. *(Photo courtesy of the author)*

One day after I rotated home, a 122mm rocket crashed into my old room, detonating on my empty bunk. My roommates, Sergeant First Class Gerry Denison and Staff Sergeant Ken McMullin, were seriously wounded and medevaced. *(Photo by Les Dover)*

Lieutenant Colonel Bob Howard *(right),* at the 1982 Vietnam Veterans Memorial Wall dedication, his Medal of Honor around his neck. Today he is America's most highly decorated serviceman. *(Department of Defense Photo)*

Krupa and I met with Covey Rider Charlie "Putter" Septer, to select an LZ about two days' march south of the highway, then arranged with the S-3 to get an AC-130 Spectre to loiter just over the horizon, waiting for our radio call. Our plan was complete.

We celebrated over drinks in the club, but I wondered, was that AC-130 really locked in? What if there's bad weather? Or heavy antiaircraft fire? The more I thought about it, the more I recalled Joe Walker once advising me: "Never start a fight that you can't win with everything you have right now." When our three claymores exploded, the whole countryside would be alerted, and like some gigantic posse every NVA within earshot would descend upon us.

I told Krupa, "We won't count on Spectre alone."

Therefore, to assure our escape, I gave each American except the medic and radio operator a small canvas bag containing five time-delay grenades to ignite and scatter during our withdrawal, leaving behind a virtual minefield of fragmentation, white phosphorus, and tear gas grenades that would cook off at odd intervals for forty-five minutes. Every time an NVA dared to advance in the dark, another device would explode, spewing fragments or burning phosphorus and a cloud of choking tear gas.

The second week we spent rehearsing and refining our ambush. After tracing the outline of a truck with my heel, I conducted a lengthy walk-through in which each man learned his role, phase by phase. Whether on the assault team, flank security, or the rally point, each man had a list of specific duties to memorize. Talking them through, in the open, each man could hear and see what the others were doing, achieving quick synchronization. By noon, we were ready for a more realistic walk-through, this time in nearby jungle that duplicated the Highway 110 ambush setting. Then it was dry runs, beginning with dumping our rucksacks at the rally point, dividing into assault and flank security elements, and advancing stealthily to our respective positions.

Thanks to these rehearsals, we learned we needed radios to communicate between our positions, which we did by replacing our survival radios with new PRC-90s, which had a separate FM band. Also, to expedite our escape, when I shouted "Withdraw!" instead of the flank security teams stumbling through the jungle to the rally point, they would run right down the road to the truck and depart with the assault team. And, though he didn't like it, Yancey learned he'd have to carry bolt cutters slung over his back in case the driver was chained to the steering wheel.

Once this fine-tuning was finished, we rehearsed the ambush over and over, growing in speed and confidence with each repetition. To be ready for any option, we practiced assaulting a truck traveling east or west. For our last daylight simulations, we ambushed a real truck with my RT California interpreter, Weet, playing the driver. Over and over, Yancey jerked Weet out the door so fast that the diminutive Montagnard virtually flew through the air.

After that, it was nighttime rehearsals, initially as dry-fire walk-throughs, then finally, for the last dress rehearsal, live-fire at night, including exploding claymore mines. By that point, we could halt a truck with exploding claymores, clear it, and seize a driver in less than ten seconds, a well-orchestrated action as polished as the best NFL special team.

At last, two weeks after receiving the order, I reported to Major Jaks that we were ready. The next day Krupa and I briefed our entire plan to Jaks and our commander, Lieutenant Colonel Abt, who approved it on the spot. Normally that would have been it, but Ashtray Two had been conceived personally by Chief SOG Colonel Steve Cavanaugh, who wanted his own briefing in Saigon.

Two days later, Krupa and I briefed the plan to Colonel Cavanaugh. I noticed his eyes drawn to the symbol for that estimated battalion base camp just 500 yards from our ambush site. When we finished, Cavanaugh sat back in his chair, thoughtfully silent for thirty seconds. "Your planning and preparations are thorough," he announced. "But that zone south of the road where you'll withdraw, that's what concerns me."

Cavanaugh tapped the map. "The North Vietnamese have camps hidden all along the road network. In the dark, you could wander right into one." He required that we run a short, two-day recon of that area to ensure we didn't stumble into a hidden enemy camp.

While the rest of us hustled to ready all our gear and explosives, Krupa and Yancey and four Yards ran this quick mission, inserting on 23 March about five miles northwest of a team already operating in northeast Cambodia, RT Pennsylvania. For Krupa and Yancey, everything was running smoothly, but that wasn't the case with RT Pennsylvania. The second morning, Krupa had his men halt when Yancey heard on the radio that the other team had been in contact.

Three ridgelines away, One-Zero John Boronski, One-One Jerry Pool, and One-Two Gary Harned were about out of luck. For several days they'd been bobbing and weaving with NVA pursuers who had been hunting them relentlessly, day and night.

Early that morning, a Covey Rider, Lieutenant Jim "King Arthur" Young, overflew RT Pennsylvania and heard Pool whisper, "We hear voices all around us." Even worse, the NVA had brought in dogs. Yet Boronski didn't request an extraction. This was Pool's first mission and, though a lieutenant, he was subordinate to Boronski, a staff sergeant, who had more experience. Had it been up to Pool, they'd have been extracted immediately.

At midday, Young's replacement Covey Rider, Lloyd "O.D." O'Daniels, arrived and overflew RT Pennsylvania. He learned they'd just been in contact, two men had minor wounds, and they were barely outrunning the enemy. The NVA had even set the jungle afire to push them toward an ambush, which they'd narrowly escaped. Yet Boronski wasn't ready to call for an extraction. O'Daniels understood. "Some team leaders didn't want to be the one that asked to come out," he explained. "So you as the Covey Rider had to interpret, and you had to know who this guy was because some of them would never come out. They'd never admit it was too hot."

All morning O.D. reported the team's worsening situation, recommending to the S-3 Operations Office that he extract them, but always with a negative response. Then suddenly, there was a decision to pull RT Pennsylvania.

When the flight of 170th Assault Helicopter Company Hueys arrived, the team was not yet at an LZ so the aircraft had to orbit high overhead, waiting. Then Lieutenant Pool radioed that NVA pursuers were right behind them, and he brought in Cobra gunships to strafe and rocket their backtrail. Evading the enemy and reaching the LZ was taking forever. After forty-five minutes, their fuel running low, the Huey flight lead, Warrant Officer Jim Lake, led his birds back to Dak To to refuel, leaving behind one chopper, commanded by Captain Mike O'Donnell, in case a Cobra gunship went down. Flying with O'Donnell were Warrant Officer John Hosken and Specialists Four Rudy Becerra and Berman Gande.

The refueled Hueys were returning when One-Zero Boronski radioed that his men were at the LZ and had to be extracted immediately or they'd never make it out. Knowing it might be now or never and the team already had two wounded men, Captain O'Donnell descended into the small clearing. It took four minutes to get the men aboard, all while the Cobras made gun runs around them. Then Covey Rider O'Daniels watched the Huey rise to the treetops—*a tremendous explosion rocked it*—"RPG, dammit!" he cursed. Somehow the pilot, O'Donnell, kept it in the air. The bird wobbled a quarter-mile, then a second explosion tore it to pieces, showering flaming debris through the treetops.

A Cobra, call sign Panther 13, made several passes through the sooty smoke. Halfway back to Pleiku Air Force Base, Covey Rider Jim Young heard the Cobra pilot's voice: "There's nothing left. I was following the slick [Huey] when it exploded and there's nothing left."

Warrant Officer Lake trolled the treetops and saw "a big secondary [explo-

sion] under the canopy accompanied by a lot of black smoke, which I took to
be his fuel cells going off." Heavy ground fire drove Lake off. Covey Rider
O'Daniels detected no emergency radio beacon, no signal smoke or panel, just
enemy ground fire that challenged any aircraft that passed within range. "They
blew the chopper out of the sky, with the whole damn recon team," O.D. reported.

Five miles away in Laos, John Yancey heard O'Daniels's radio message and
knew the terrible fate of RT Pennsylvania. But Krupa's team encountered no
NVA along our Ashtray Two withdrawal route. A couple of hours later, the
same helicopters extracted Krupa and Yancey and the four Yards.

Rejoined in the club that night, all eight of the Ashtray Two Americans
lifted our glasses and our voices with fellow recon and Hatchet Force men to
sing "Hey, Blue," adding Boronski, Pool, and Harned to that sad, growing litany. RT Pennsylvania was the first complete CCC team lost since my old RT
New Mexico had been overrun a year earlier.

Afterward, Fat Albert—Pete Wilson—sat down with me to wish me good
luck on Ashtray Two, and I could tell he wished he was going along. Fat Albert
had just learned he was about to make One-Zero and get his own team. I congratulated him. Glenn Uemura wished me good luck, too.

The following day, we finished packing our gear, after which Krupa and I inspected everything to make sure we were ready. That night everyone got a
good night's sleep.

By 9:30 the next morning, I was sitting in a Huey doorway, watching Ben
Het Special Forces Camp drift past. If we could get to the road, I was convinced
we would succeed. Though we practically overflew the spot where RT Pennsylvania had been lost forty-eight hours earlier, I forced that tragedy from my
mind and concentrated on our own mission. We were primed, ready, confident—we would succeed.

As requested, Covey Rider Charlie Septer, flying with USAF Captain Gary
Green, landed us two ridgelines south of Highway 110. There was no ground
fire. In ten minutes I gave a "Team OK" and we moved out, heading north toward the road.

All that day we advanced steadily and deliberately. Except for hearing a few
distant signal shots and discovering an abandoned bunker area, we passed that
day uneventfully. The first night we heard nothing, but the second night, about
10:00 P.M., I awoke and sat up, straining my ears—*engines*. Trucks, maybe a mile
away—six of them, perhaps ten. In the shadows around me, everyone else was
sitting, too, listening, saying nothing. We all knew, tomorrow was our day, provided we made it undetected to Highway 110.

By the spring of 1970, reaching any Laotian highway had become a major achievement. NVA security forces discovered most SOG teams while crossing a heavily patrolled security zone, roughly a half-mile beside any road. Thus it was that we infiltrated the final 500 yards as stealthily as a pride of lions stalking antelope on the Serengeti plain—*step, listen, look, pause*—*step, listen, look, pause.* Then, at last, just before noon, the jungle thinned and there, before us, lay Highway 110. Krupa and I slipped forward the last forty yards and found fresh truck tracks on its hard-packed surface. Looking around, I realized this was a terrible ambush site: a thin bamboo grove downhill from the road, offering minimal cover or concealment—but so unlikely an ambush spot, I thought, that we wouldn't draw enemy guards and night patrols.

While the rest of the team passed away the afternoon in the rally point, Krupa and I lay in sight of the highway. As we lay there, waiting for darkness, I turned around my Pen EE camera to my face and, grinning smugly, snapped a self-portrait.

Krupa whispered, "What're you doing?"

"If they kill me tonight and capture this camera," I whispered, "I want 'em to see my smiling kisser on the film."

He loved the idea and asked, "Then get this shot, too." Fred lifted up and posed on his knees, like an alerted scout peering at the enemy. I snapped it.

We saw and heard no enemy all afternoon. About 5:00 P.M., I radioed a code word to Leghorn, SOG's mountaintop radio relay station, requesting the AC-130 Spectre gunship to orbit just over the horizon, ready to cover our escape. Then I gave each American a Green Hornet—a SOG-issue amphetamine—to ensure everyone had the stamina to run all night.

It was still daylight when I entered in my notebook, "1920 [7:20 P.M.]—One vehicle passed headed east to west. Contained some troops and large wooden boxes." Beneath mounds of foliage, Jaco saw flat armored sides, undoubtedly a Soviet-made armored car carrying security troops checking the road before the convoys began running.

Then I penned, "1925—Second truck passed headed east to west. Believe it was empty." I actually saw the driver's smiling face as he down-shifted. He may have been singing.

With daylight about gone, I signaled our flank security teams—Jaco on our left and Kennicott on the right—to advance to their blocking positions. Next, our assault team crept forward—Krupa, Woody, Yancey, and myself. With barely enough light to see, on the road's edge I laid out three claymores in a crescent, aimed at a prominent tree across the road. In the dark I'd watch for the truck's front tire to align with that tree and blow the mines.

Then we lay facedown beside the highway and waited for what seemed forever. Had the enemy detected us and canceled his convoys? Just before 9:30 P.M., we all heard the far-off sound of an approaching truck, growing gradually louder, until it seemed to roar toward us. As it rounded the nearest curve, a low-powered blackout light flashed. Seconds later a tire rolled directly before me and—*KA-BOOM!*—I blew the mines and shouted, *"Assault!"*

Instantly, Yancey, Krupa, Woody, and I rushed the Soviet-made GAZ-63 truck, which had jerked to a halt in front of us. I dashed around the hood to take out the assistant driver—there was none—then covered as Yancey dragged the driver out the opposite door, threw him to the ground, and pinned him while Krupa slid handcuffs on the stunned man's wrists.

Then Krupa pulled out his Kodak Instamatic and, standing in the middle of the notorious Highway 110, flashed away as I tossed a satchel charge in the truck, stuffed a time-delay white phosphorus grenade atop the fuel tank, and placed a thermite grenade on its hood. I shouted, *"Withdraw! Withdraw!"* Woody blew two whistle blasts, exactly as rehearsed.

Amazing! We had our man and were withdrawing in hardly more than one minute!

Then, from nowhere, a hidden enemy soldier shot Woody through both arms.

While Krupa and Yancey dragged away the prisoner, Jaco and I rolled Woody's bleeding arms into a makeshift sling, then Jaco led him toward the rally point.

That left only me at the truck to deal with the approaching enemy and buy time for the rest to get a head start. I began exchanging fire with enemy soldiers approaching down the road, shooting at their muzzle flashes. Meanwhile our men on the flank security teams were emptying their "goody bags," lacing the adjacent jungle with thirty assorted grenades that would cook off for forty-five minutes.

How long could I hold off the NVA? I knew the time delay grenades would start exploding in two minutes. If I wasn't gone by then, those infernal devices would get me.

At the rally point, Galasso, our medic, bandaged Woody as best he could. Despite his agony—both forearms had been shattered by AK slugs—Woody refused morphine for fear he would slow us down. He was magnificent.

Back at the truck, I realized it was time to get out when a Chinese grenade blast originating from I didn't know where threw me to the ground. Had it been a U.S. grenade, I'd have been dead. As it was, I stood, shook my head until I didn't see stars, then headed off to rejoin the others. As I backed away, I fired a few rounds and could hear NVA shouting and shooting from the road, converging around the ambushed truck. I'd not even reached the rally point when the five-pound satchel charge detonated, demolishing the truck and silencing the lot of them.

As I rejoined the team, Krupa radioed our mountaintop radio relay site only to learn *Spectre was not on station*. With more NVA shouting to each other at the road and signal shots in the distance, we had no time to argue about why the gunship wasn't there.

While we were running for our lives, back in Kontum, nothing was happening. Lieutenant Colonel Abt had rotated home that very morning, leaving in charge a questionably competent officer, lacking any sense of urgency. "Bullshit!" snapped Covey Rider O.D. O'Daniels, the loss of RT Pennsylvania fresh in his mind. "Let's get a helicopter to take me to Pleiku and go out there tonight."

O'Daniels, flying with USAF Captain Bob Mann, crossed the border at midnight but they had no trouble finding us—they saw burning trucks ten miles away. While we ran through that pitch-black jungle, O.D. used those flames to direct set after set of fighters, bombing the ambush site, the road, and our back-trail. All night we hustled through the jungle, pausing only twice to treat Woody and to check the prisoner's restraints.

It was still dark when the helicopters launched to arrive overhead at the very crack of dawn, Hueys from the 170th Assault Helicopter Company, escorted by Cobra gunships from the 361st Pink Panthers attack helicopter company. Then a pair of A-1 Skyraiders made a final pass with cluster bombs and O'Daniels saw the bomblets stream squarely across us. Though cluster bombs indeed exploded all around us, miraculously, not a man was hit. Warrant Officer Jim Lake, flying the lead Huey, brought his ship into the smoke and ground fog, spotted our pen flares, and landed. And we were gone—we'd made it, convoy lead driver intact, Woody seriously wounded, and myself with only minor shrapnel wounds. The success tasted all the sweeter, for this was the same Huey unit that had lost RT Pennsylvania and its wingman—Captain O'Donnell's Huey—just four days earlier.

Our flight back to Kontum became an aerial procession, all the choppers in formation. As we landed, the entire compound swarmed onto the helipad. During that tumultuous welcome, many hands shook ours and patted our backs and passed us cold beers, Americans and Yards alike. Our truck driver, still blindfolded and handcuffed, was led away by an intelligence officer. I was in the mood for a stiff drink when the recon first sergeant announced a SOG C-130 Blackbird would arrive in ten minutes to transport the prisoner and me to Saigon.

In as many minutes, I was beside the runway in Kontum, where a compassionate intel officer removed the prisoner's blindfold. The NVA driver took one look around, noticed my filthy fatigues and camouflage-smeared face, and realized I'd been on the team that snatched him. *"Di-dau,"* he asked, meaning he had to urinate. He held up his cuffed hands, gesturing that we should unlock him. The intel officer wasn't sure what to do.

I wasn't about to take those cuffs off. Lee Burkins, a recon man sent along as a guard, was mildly surprised but our commander, Lee noticed, "almost shit a brick" when I opened the prisoner's fly, pulled out his penis and held it while he whizzed, even shaking it before stuffing it back in. After that, the NVA knew he'd have absolutely no opportunity to escape.

Hardly an hour later we landed at Saigon's Tan Son Nhut Airport, where I delivered, handcuffed and blindfolded, the NVA convoy lead driver, exactly as requested. An unmarked commercial van whisked us to SOG headquarters, where the welcome was almost as jubilant as on our helipad three hours earlier. Chief SOG Cavanaugh was in the Philippines, so his deputy, USAF Colonel Louis Franklin, congratulated me and announced that we would be briefing the mission to General Creighton Abrams, the commander of U.S. Forces in Vietnam. After a quick shower and haircut, I donned a fresh uniform, then accompanied Colonel Franklin to MACV headquarters, where we waited our turn at a security checkpoint.

After the 101st Airborne Division's commanding general finished his presentation, an MP escorted us into General Abrams's inner sanctum. That small amphitheater contained a wide horseshoe table, around which sat seven two-, three-, and four-star generals, while in the center, chewing a cigar from his high-backed leather chair, sat General Abrams himself. For ten minutes I recounted Operation Ashtray Two, step by step. When I told them how the cluster of NVA shooting from the truck were silenced when it blew up, there was a chuckle around the room. Though known publicly for being rabidly anti–Special Forces, Abrams put aside his personal sentiments to shake my hand. "And tell your teammates," he said, "they did a fine and brave job."

That evening—exactly twenty-four hours after we ambushed the truck—I was in an air-conditioned nightclub with friends from SOG headquarters, trading toasts; my only regret was not celebrating that memorable night with my Ashtray Two comrades.

Later, Chief SOG Cavanaugh called Ashtray Two "undoubtedly our most successful operation where we had visualized doing something, planned it, then had it done." And though he had voiced optimism to his subordinates before the mission, Cavanaugh confessed, "In my wildest imagination I never thought that we would succeed."

Our prisoner proved cooperative. He told SOG interrogators his transportation unit was assigned to an artillery regiment, and that they'd recently been running many convoys to support an imminent major attack. American B-52s soon were pounding the truck parks and ammunition stockpiles he disclosed, but, as it turned out, it wasn't appreciated just how imminent that major attack would be.

The following night, while I slept in SOG's Saigon safe house, the North Vietnamese 28th Infantry Regiment launched a surprise attack on Dak Seang Special Forces Camp, about a dozen miles north of Ben Het. Though they were repelled, the 2,000-strong North Vietnamese force laid siege and continued fighting at Dak Seang for several weeks. Then another NVA regiment hit Dak Pek Special Forces Camp, seventeen miles north of Dak Seang, where our northernmost launch site was located. This, too, led to several weeks' intense fighting. Sergeant First Class Walter "Jerry" Hetzler, a Mike Force man who'd just finished a tour running recon at CCC, was awarded a Distinguished Service Cross for the courage he displayed at Dak Pek.

Those two attacks were bad enough, but the same night the enemy hit Dak Seang—April Fool's Day—a dozen NVA sappers crept through a waste-filled latrine ditch and penetrated our CCC compound at Kontum. Emplacing demolition charges, they blew up our Tactical Operations Center and set afire the field grade officers' quarters, then escaped without losing a man. Only one American was injured, the duty officer, Captain Neil "Wild Bill" Coady, who was in the operations center when a satchel charge exploded, bringing the ceiling down on him.

Covey Rider O'Daniels and Captain Krupa arrived at the fire only to have a senior officer order them to rescue his personal belongings from the flames. "So we went inside," O'Daniels recalled, "got his refrigerator that was full of beer, carried it out the back, sat down, and drank his beer and watched the place burn down." Medal of Honor nominee Doug Miller offered to smother the flames with a dynamite blast, which he knew would suck away the oxygen. The arrogant officer would hear none of that, so Miller didn't much give a damn, either.

That morning I returned to find a smoldering hole where the operations center had been. But the attack had little effect on CCC operations—fresh teams were at Dak To, ready to insert that afternoon. Interestingly, most of our men admired the NVA commandos for their ingenuity and dedication to wade through waist-deep lime and human feces to accomplish their mission.

Though we had professional respect for the sappers, we found troubling evidence that they'd had inside assistance. Several perimeter lights had been purposely shifted to cast shadows on the ditch through which the sappers had crawled. These collaborators may simply have been Vietnamese maids who hung laundry near the lights, but it reminded us of deeper, more alarming incidents of apparent treachery. That SOG teams were being compromised was no longer an issue of debate; too often the enemy seemed to be waiting for our teams for it to be mere coincidence. The question was where the compromises were originating. At the field level—at CCN, CCC, and CCS—most men suspected we had a mole in SOG headquarters, but the Saigon staff was in denial.

Convinced that our problem was communications security, Chief SOG Cavanaugh ordered our teams to carry the KY-38 radio scrambler, a cumbersome, heavy device that overburdened our already overloaded radio operators. But the enemy could triangulate the KY-38's transmissions, unlike later frequency-skipping devices, so there was little benefit for its thirty-pound weight. Most One-Zeros thought our manual encryption codes were effective and we didn't need to scramble them. Thus, many KY-38s "mysteriously" broke down at Dak To and were left behind by deploying teams. The larger issue of compromise, however, would continue to be a contentious subject.

Just before Operation Ashtray Two, I'd noticed an ad in *Guns & Ammo* magazine, offering thirty-round, M-16 magazines at $7.50 each; not only was this cheap, but despite SOG's much vaunted priority, our supply system hadn't been able to get us thirty-round mags. All we had were standard U.S. Army twenty-rounders, and even those were loaded with just nineteen rounds to avoid weakening the magazine spring. Air Force gate guards in Saigon had thirty-rounders, but we couldn't find them. Enough was enough. In the club I collected nearly $800 from a dozen One-Zeros, so each of their men could have one thirty-rounder, and sent it off to Sherwood Distributors in Beverly Hills, California. They turned the order around instantly, so that I could pass out the thirty-round magazines hardly a week later. I had no idea how decisively my new thirty-rounder would figure in my next operation. Indeed, I hardly realized how soon I'd be running my next operation.

Only a couple of days into my stand-down from Ashtray Two, I sat in the club with Glenn Uemura and his RT Vermont teammates One-Zero Franklin "Doug" Miller and One-Two Chuck Hein. They were preparing to go into a particularly hot Laotian target, and, over drinks, described their innovative infiltration technique.

"We're gonna bypass all their LZ watchers," Miller announced. "We're gonna rappel in." That was how they'd gone on a recent Bright Light mission to recover the body of an F-4 pilot, and it struck Miller that no one used rappelling to infiltrate on ordinary recon missions. "If there's no LZ, there's no LZ watchers," Miller reasoned.

"That's a great idea!" I agreed. To my knowledge it would be the first time anyone had rappelled into a recon target. It was dangerous, too, since you cannot rappel back into an aircraft, and, by intent, you would be landing far away from large, sit-down LZs. We discussed it a bit over drinks. Miller could be a persuasive man.

Three drinks later I volunteered to go along.

It was a bit crazy, using stand-down time to run yet another mission, and a dangerous one at that, but I'd always had reservations about Glenn's running with Miller, and I might be able to make sure he got out alive. Here, too, was my chance to see Miller, an admittedly audacious One-Zero, in action. And besides, it would be great to be just another gunfighter for a change.

Miller's radio operator, Chuck Hein, glowed with confidence. A handsome man with a solid physique and boyish smile, around his neck Chuck wore a small gold Buddha, given him, he explained, by a monk in Thailand. The South Dakota native embraced Buddhist mysticism, even undergoing a ritualistic blessing after which the monk assured him, "No bullet ever hurt you." Chuck believed this, absolutely convinced he would not be killed in combat.

A mere two days after our discussion in the club, we were at Dak To loading aboard two Hueys, just four men per bird—two per side—for a rapid rappel. The lead bird carried Miller, Uemura, one Yard, and myself, while Chuck Hein and three more Yards followed in the second aircraft. We wore Swiss seat rappelling rigs with a metal link to snap on the rope and heavy leather gloves to prevent rope burns.

Forty minutes later we were on the treetops, deep in Laos, about a mile south of Highway 110, and ten miles west of the Ashtray Two ambush site. Our chopper banked evasively between jungled hills, then a tight turn—*whop-whop-whop-whop*—another turn—*whop-whop-whop-whop*—then the crew chief nodded, and we stepped out on the skids beneath the whirring blades, a Yard and myself on one side, Miller and Glenn on the other. I felt naked, my CAR-15 slung over my shoulder, unable to shoot back if we took fire. Then our Huey began a fifty-foot hover, we tossed out four weighted rucksacks containing ropes, and looked down to confirm they'd unrolled. There it was. A small opening where an exploding bomb had swept away the trees and left a single crater. I reminded myself not to let my heavy rucksack turn me upside down, then, "Go!"—kicked off—one straight *zzzzzzzzzzzzzz*—I was on the ground. Three seconds and I was off the line, tossing aside my gloves and pivoting my CAR-15 off my shoulder. Great!

Beside me, Miller was free, too, already speaking into the radio. Glenn's fatigue shirt had become twisted in the rappelling D ring, so instantly he pulled a knife, slashed the rope, and freed himself. That left only the Yard.

Miller and I looked up to the hovering Huey and the Yard, his arms wrapped around the chopper's landing skid, hugging it for all he was worth. He'd lost his confidence and wouldn't let go, making Miller angrier by the second. It was almost comical—

KA-KA-KA!—KA-KA-KA-KA! AK fire! Just up the ridgeline!

"Oh, shit," I groaned. The door gunners opened fire as we pounced into the bomb crater. The AK fire was too high to be directed at us, we realized—the bad guys were shooting at the Huey, giving the pilot only one option: He flew away with the Yard still dangling from the rope. In the distance we heard more gunfire tracking the departing Huey.

We were in a hell of a fix. The Cobra gunships were still down on the treetops, so Miller had them strafe and rocket the hillsides to our north and west, which drew more ground fire from still more directions.

The best we could hope was that the Cobras could suppress the enemy, and a Huey could come in, drop ropes to us, and extract us riding on our Swiss seats. After about ten minutes of rocketing and strafing, Miller lifted the handset from his ear and announced, "We've got a Huey, inbound."

We heard his blades beating the air a couple of hundreds yards south—then came heavy gunfire from several hills, and he turned away before we ever saw him.

The Hueys would have to go back and refuel, Covey advised. For the time being, the three of us were stuck, trapped in that lonely hole. Miller ordered, "Let's get a defense going."

Glenn warned, "We gotta keep 'em from sneaking up, keep 'em off balance." He heaved a grenade far downhill, into the jungle. *KA-BOOM!* No enemy response—they knew where we were but hadn't closed around us—at least not yet.

Our situation reminded me of John Allen's when his RT Alabama was surrounded in a bomb crater. I remembered John telling me about how critical it was to get claymores out quick. That's it! I peeked over the crater lip and saw a spot where the jungle closed to within fifteen yards; any NVA there could hurl a grenade in our crater and kill all three of us.

I called, "Glenn, cover me!"

Unable to crawl with both my CAR-15 and a cradled claymore, I left my weapon behind, rolled out and propelled my body along the ground as Cobra gunships rocketed the nearby jungle and more enemy gunfire sprayed the sky.

As Glenn aimed over me, I prayed to God no NVA were there already because I'd be a dead man. At the jungle's edge, I erected the claymore as fast as possible; these were the nakedest moments of my whole life. Then I crawled back, grabbed my CAR-15, and felt secure again.

We could tell the NVA were reinforcing, but they didn't seem to be massing close by. They wanted to leave us there, pinned, dangling, to draw the helicopters that eventually must come.

Glenn heaved another grenade into a cluster of thick jungle. *KA-BOOM!* Nothing.

I tossed a grenade the opposite way. *KA-BOOM!* No enemy reaction.

I took quick stock, What have I got on me, what have I got with me. From a canteen cover I pulled five more grenades and stacked them for quick work. Yes, I had a full load of twenty-one CAR-15 magazines, including my brand-new thirty-rounder. Then the Cobras ran out of station time and headed back to Dak To. All the helicopters were gone.

Covey had been holding a pair of A-1 Skyraiders in orbit to the north, and now we saw them approaching—and *boom-boom-boom-boom!*—puffs of heavy 37mm flak guns air-burst just behind them. *Boom-boom-boom-boom!* The bursting gray smudges tried to catch up but the A-1s dived and began firing and bombing around us, too low for the flak guns to see them.

As we watched the flak gun air bursts high above us, and .50 caliber tracers flashing over the treetops, I felt as though a dome were sliding shut to keep our aircraft away. I had a twisting, sinking feeling in my stomach. You stupid son-of-a-bitch, I cursed myself. You're going to get killed. You didn't have to be here. You're on stand-down!

What followed was a half-day duel between antiaircraft guns and our fighters and gunships, virtually hours of air strikes with jet fighters screaming past with afterburners and A-1s seeding the hillsides with cluster bombs. Twice the helicopters came back to extract us, and twice they were driven away by heavy fire.

Finally, late that afternoon it reached the point where either we were going to get out or make a run for it. As the choppers came back for that third extraction attempt, we knew this was our last chance. Maybe it was too late already. Covey radioed that the U.S. command in Saigon had approved using CBU-19 tear gas cluster bombs to assist our extraction, but the helicopter crews didn't have gas masks with them. Rather than wait another hour for their masks to be flown from Pleiku, the lead pilot volunteered to fly beneath the enemy fire, wedge his Huey between the overhanging tree branches, and drop us ladders. With just three men to retrieve, it could be done quickly.

Miller turned from his radio and warned, "Get down low. Covey's bringing in Phantoms with heavy bombs." We slid to the crater bottom and covered our heads. For thirty seconds the earth shook from exploding 500-pound bombs impacting on suspected gun positions, then it stopped—and we heard the welcome sound of approaching chopper blades. Two Cobras flashed over, low-level, then, coming from the south, here came our Huey. As the bird neared, Glenn and Doug threw grenades and I detonated my claymore. That pilot flew splendidly, pivoting his Huey between tree branches to get low enough to drop twenty-foot aluminum ladders. Quick as they fell, we snapped our rucksacks on the bottom rungs, slung CAR-15s over our backs, and hustled up, all while the door gunners chugged away—*Bang-bang-bang-bang-bang—bang-bang-bang!*

As I reached the skid, the door gunner suddenly let go of his gun and threw himself back in the aircraft. Was he hit? I pulled myself onto the floor as the Huey lifted away, trailing the ladders, AKs popping beneath us, and fought the pulling Gs to swing my legs inside. Then we were clear. Across the compartment I saw Glenn and Doug. Out of breath, we just looked at each other, panting, euphoric grins all around. "Made it again!" I shouted and slapped Glenn hard on his back. We celebrated, passing around a canteen of water.

We'd been stuck in that hole directing air strikes nonstop for six hours.

As we unloaded at Dak To, I asked the door gunner, "Why'd you jump like that?"

His eyes got wide. "You didn't see?"

"See what?"

"The B-40." A B-40 RPG, he explained, had arced hardly two feet behind me, narrowly missing me and the spinning main rotor, then had fallen harmlessly to earth. By so slight a margin had we survived and, two weeks earlier, had perished RT Pennsylvania and an entire Huey crew.

That night as we walked into the club at Kontum, a recon buddy, Al Walker, shook our hands and reported, "We thought you guys were dead. This is dangerous shit, just powerful, dangerous, dangerous shit." Nobody disputed him.

That half-day stuck in a crater, shooting, watching ack-ack bursts, crawling, directing air strikes, almost being blown off the ladder by an RPG—that was all the excitement I needed for a while. But the area recon mission still had to be run, Saigon decided, and Miller's team was going back in.

I didn't have to go, but I couldn't let them go without me, not now. Thus two days after our bomb crater fight, there we were, back at Dak To, climbing into another Huey to go right back to that target. I had a bad feeling about it.

You stupid son-of-a-bitch! I shouted silently at myself, sitting in the Huey doorway, swinging my feet and waving to the guys at the launch site as we lifted away. I gave a thumbs-up to Glenn, sitting beside me, who also projected confidence, but I doubt his feelings were much different. We said almost nothing during the flight, lost in our own thoughts.

This time we didn't rappel but landed conventionally in a field of elephant grass, about two miles southeast of the bomb crater. We encountered no enemy and soon were on our way, heading north, toward the road.

All day, we came upon no fresh sign, though we discovered an abandoned base camp and crossed several old, disused trails. At last light I was sitting beside Glenn in our overnight position, eating rice with a plastic spoon, waiting for darkness. With no warning, an AK ripped the air—*ka-ka-ka-ka-ka-ka-ka-ka!* Not twenty-five yards away, illuminated beneath its three-foot flame, an NVA held his muzzle skyward, turning his head around, watching for our slightest reaction. The spoon still in my mouth, my right finger squeezed all but the last ounce from my CAR-15 trigger, aimed squarely at his head; but none of us fired, knowing that hidden nearby were dozens of counter-recon troops, ready to pounce. We refused to rise to their bait.

Within moments he faded into complete darkness. Thus began an uncertain night in which we sensed enemy soldiers around us and hardly dared to breathe. We lay there for hours, claymore firing devices in our hands, alert, listening. His voice muffled under a poncho, Miller radioed SOG's mountaintop radio relay site, and by 9:00 P.M., an AC-119 Shadow gunship orbited overhead, its welcome drone threatening to pour fire upon anyone who attacked us. The threat, though, was nearly empty: To direct Shadow's fire, we'd have to signal visually, which meant flashing a strobe light that would bounce on the bushy limbs overhead, pinpointing our location to the enemy. By midnight we still hadn't been attacked, telling us the enemy would wait until dawn—or had simply wandered away. We slept insecurely.

About 4:30 A.M., the gunship departed.

Covey launched early that morning, bringing his welcome engines within earshot just as it became light enough to see. Hearing Covey, Miller signaled to retrieve our claymores. I motioned to Glenn to cover me, then crept toward my claymore, some twenty-five feet away.

My eyes shifted to a large mahogany log—*something moved!* A foot—*brrrt!*—I shot the foot—*brrrt!*—shot it again—*brrrt!*—NVA coming over the log!—*brrt!*—nineteen rounds, I paused to reload, *another* NVA jumped up—but it's a thirty-round mag—*ten more rounds!*—before his AK muzzle found me, another burst—*brrrt!*—square in his chest. I didn't pause to reload but spun—Glenn fired, covering me—*brrrt!*—I ran three steps—*brrrt!*—vaulted my body forward—*brrrt! brrrt!*—my outstretched hand caught the claymore firing device, squeezed it—*KA-BOOM!* An RPG crashed into a tree overhead—*WHOOOM!*—shrapnel tore the foliage but missed us—Miller opened fire—*brrrt! brrrt! brrrt!*—the Yards blew all their claymores—*KA-BOOM!—KA-KA-KA-BOOM!* All of us were up, running in the direction opposite the NVA as Hein called loudly into his radio handset, "COVEY! COVEY! CONTACT! CONTACT!"

We dashed all out, distancing ourselves from the bloodied NVA, who had quit firing when our claymores detonated. As we ran, Covey rolled in, firing marking rockets to cover our escape.

In five minutes Miller signaled to slow down and, out of breath, we formed a hasty perimeter. No one was missing, he confirmed and, surprisingly, no one had been wounded. "We gotta keep going, but faster," Miller announced. "Everybody but Chuck, dump your rucks." In ten seconds our rucksacks were off and we were ready to go again, pausing only long enough for Glenn to flash a mirror at Covey so he could direct a pair of A-1s on our backtrail.

Several times we heard NVA pursuers but they never quite caught up. In an hour of fast movement we reached an extraction LZ and lay hiding in a bamboo grove until the choppers circled high overhead. Then Covey sent in the Cobras to check the LZ.

A .50 caliber antiaircraft machine gun opened fire from a ridge only 100 yards across the LZ. The Cobras dodged his tracers, but no Huey could possibly come in. Unlike the guns that kept us pinned in the bomb crater, however, this gun was close enough to adjust air on it. Miller had Covey bring in the A-1s, then, relaying word from Glenn and myself as we watched the ordnance impact, adjusted cluster bombs and napalm until the gun was silenced.

After that it was smooth sailing, just a few AKs that popped a begrudging farewell as our Huey escaped across the treetops. None of our aircraft was hit.

Back at Dak To we ate C rations and recounted our close call. All of us had been lucky, probably me the luckiest of all. Reassembling the images in my mind, I realized the first NVA I shot was aiming at me when I shot him. "Had I waited a split second, just one split second," I said, "he would have got me." And the second NVA had come over the log when I'd paused at nineteen rounds, to shoot me while I reloaded. My thirty-round magazine had saved me. The greatest irony, though, I confessed to Glenn, was that I thought my presence would help protect him, but as it turned out, his covering fire saved my life.

Glenn was easygoing about it. "You're lucky I was there."

"Yeah," Miller agreed, "worked out pretty cool!" It was a strange way to put it, but Franklin D. Miller was one of those rare men who showed no fear and I don't think it was braggadocio. Bob Howard, another of our Medal of Honor recipients, just plain refused to be afraid. I thought his valor a kind of emotional tenacity born of his great pride and patriotism. And Doug Miller? His intrepidity was more an aloofness, an unwillingness to let anything rattle him. I could immerse myself in my duties, my mission, my team and repress fear, but that was artificial compared to the natural valor of heroes like Howard and Miller.

In his first major contact, Chuck Hein had displayed some anxiety, but at Dak To he showed me his Buddha and reminded me that a Thai monk had promised him no bullet would kill him. He took it all in stride.

Along with the Yards, we posed for a photograph at Dak To, then flew back to Kontum.

Thank God, SOG headquarters decided twice was enough. We would not again risk our lives in that target, a decision even Miller welcomed. Despite that reprieve, though, in two short weeks, one of us would be dead.

Chapter Eleven

Three days after the dawn shootout with Miller's team, I was in the Cellar Bar in Bangkok, drinking Tiger beer with my Ashtray Two teammates. Our trip was courtesy of SOG—along with $100 apiece (a week's pay in 1970)—for capturing the enemy truck driver.

The Cellar Bar owner, Bill Book, a retired SEAL master chief, sat with us as we stirred our glasses with a toad someone had found on the street. When the wriggling creature reached Captain Krupa, he swallowed it whole, gagged a few times—looking as bug-eyed as the unfortunate toad—but somehow kept it down.

A man of sordid humor, Book decorated the bar jukebox with a photo of a dancing elephant slinging a four-foot-long erection. John Yancey shook his head at the image and dropped a few coins in the machine. Then he winked, leaned to me, and whispered, "Let's have some fun with Krupa." I didn't know what he had in mind but I was game.

Momentarily the jukebox blared John Lennon's hit, "Give Peace a Chance." At Yancey's instigation, we sang along to its refrain, "All we are saying, is give *war* a chance." Having been jolted by a few too many explosions, Krupa's ears couldn't distinguish between our voices and Lennon's lyric, which, of course, was "peace" not "war."

Everyone else in the bar heard "peace," but poor Fred thought he was hearing "war." His eyes lit up. "Damn!" he exclaimed. "I always thought Lennon opposed the war."

"Oh, no," Yancey lied beautifully. "He marched at the Pentagon, demanded more bombing."

"Wow!" Krupa cried. "That's great! I can't believe it!" He joined us enthusiastically as we sang, "All we are saying, is give war a chance." And I don't think he ever learned better.

In Bangkok we roomed at the Opera Hotel, an old Special Forces hangout because its management tolerated drunkenness, debauchery, and deviltry. By those standards our behavior fell short, little more than late night BLT sandwiches, cold beer, and pretty Thai girls. Our wildest day there, Krupa somersaulted from his third-floor hotel window, missed the pool, and crashed through a veranda roof. We thought he was dead, but he stood, dusted himself off, eyed the gaping hole as if the roof was somehow at fault, tipped his head back, and twisted his face in laughter.

But that wasn't our funniest episode. Our Thai driver, Vitoon, was transporting Krupa, Yancey, Jaco, and myself through a traffic circle when a chauffeured black, official-looking car rolled alongside. Vitoon announced, "That's fucking Russian ambassador!" We had no idea Thailand shared diplomatic relations with Moscow, but there he sat, a fleshy-faced Russian, looking more like a Mafia don than a diplomat, scowling at the short-haired Americans he took to be GIs. Unlearned in the ways of diplomacy, Yancey and I responded suitably: While Vitoon honked and hedged the ambassador's car against the traffic circle, we dropped our pants and pressed our jungle-paled asses against the car windows as Jaco and Krupa gave him the finger. When His Excellency's driver almost rammed us, Vitoon finally let him escape.

We laughed for hours.

While we partied that week in Bangkok, the fighting our prisoner had predicted raged around Dak Seang Special Forces Camp.

On Bright Light rescue duty at Dak To, RT Montana One-Zero Mike Sheppard was called to the radio shack to learn that a Huey had been shot down near the besieged camp, and four aircrewmen were running for their lives. Sheppard alerted One-One Joe Sample and One-Two Dennis Neal and they and their Yards boarded two helicopters to go after the imperiled aviators.

As RT Montana launched, Covey radioed RT Hawaii, about twenty miles away in Cambodia, to "go high and dry." Knowing the SOG choppers would be preoccupied for at least an hour, RT Hawaii's One-Zero, newly promoted Captain Greg Glashauser, halted his men—One-One Mike Kuropas, One-Two Ray Goodwin, and seven Yards—and set up a defensive perimeter.

Near Dak Seang, Covey spotted the downed aviators and brought in RT Montana's two rescue Hueys. As the first bird settled near the pilots, gunfire sprayed the ship, wounding Sample, Neal, and two Yards, plus three of their four Huey crewmen. Above them in the second bird, Sheppard and three Yards provided supporting fire as their wounded comrades grabbed two downed airmen and flew off. The first Huey had been badly damaged and now had to make an emergency landing at Dak Seang—but the camp was under attack. Both Hueys took more hits as they came in. One-Zero Sheppard dashed through heavy fire to help a wounded pilot from the first bird to safety, then returned to lift his teammate, Sergeant Neal, and lay him on the ground. Neal opened his eyes, spoke once, and died. Then Sheppard carried Joe Sample to cover. Despite enemy fire, Sheppard loaded the wounded men on two more Hueys and, at last, they flew away for Dak To. Of the other two downed crewmen, Art Barthelme died and Roger Miller was captured. He was released with other POWs in 1973.

While this was happening, RT Hawaii had been high and dry in Cambodia. About an hour into their break, one Yard held a hand to his ear, signaling he'd heard something—the others turned just as forty NVA opened fire with RPGs and bursts of automatic fire. One-One Kuropas raised his CAR-15—an AK round caught him, center-chest, critically wounding him. Returning the heavy fire, One-Zero Glashauser snatched up his wounded teammate, organized a withdrawal, and carried Kuropas, pausing once to treat his sucking chest wound. Meanwhile Goodwin had raised Covey, and a pair of Cobras arrived to tie down the enemy.

In less than an hour, RT Hawaii reached a small opening on a hillside large enough for a string extraction. Huey pilot Jim Lake hovered overhead and held his ship steady while Glashauser attached the badly wounded Kuropas to the extraction rig.

Realizing there wasn't time to snap anyone else in, Glashauser waved away the chopper, then led RT Hawaii as they shot their way through the enemy, ran a few more minutes, and reached a better string extraction point. This time all the men were lifted out, but as they reached the treetops, Glashauser saw that Goodwin's rig was loose; he bear-hugged his radio operator the entire flight. At Dak To they learned that Kuropas had succumbed to his wounds.

News of Neal's and Kuropas's deaths hit our jovial return from Bangkok like a hard slap across the face. Both were fine recon men and well liked.

Their loss was bad enough, but the following day a new senior officer compounded things by presumptuously sticking his nose where it didn't belong. He brought in a chaplain for a memorial service and ordered everyone to attend. Handling the deaths of our friends was hard enough, but compelling us to sit there and listen to the soothing words of a well-meaning chaplain who'd never even met them? It was too much. We preferred a wake in the club, singing "Hey, Blue," toasting them, then grieving privately, as we'd always done.

Oblivious in his contrived grief, the senior officer hadn't a clue how deeply we resented his farce, especially the mockery of his eulogy, looking to notes to recall their names. Dennis and Mike were our friends, we were the ones who had to live with their loss, had to go out tomorrow into the same damnable places where they had died and assure ourselves the same would not happen to us. After the memorial service we had little tolerance for the senior officer. Despite his rank, he was never taken seriously again.

Within a few days, my RT California was back in the grind of training, awaiting our next mission. I knew we'd have at least a week before another assignment because we hadn't yet received a new radio operator to replace the medevaced Richard Woody. Thus, because my team wasn't pressed, the recon company first sergeant called me into his office and asked, "How'd you like to go to Qui Nhon?" He was referring to a coastal town about 150 miles away, the Central Highlands's largest logistics base and seaport. "Captain Coady is taking some trucks to pick up steel I beams for the new Tactical Operations Center. He's got five Yards from the motor pool, but he needs somebody from recon company, another gun, to go with him." It would be a quick, two-day trip.

"Sure," I said. "I'll go."

I'd always liked Captain Neil "Wild Bill" Coady, one of those unconventional characters who could thrive only in Special Forces. Actually, I first met him one night when I came upon him hot-wiring a jeep with a pocketknife. Coady, I learned, was one of the greatest scroungers and thieves in Special Forces; everywhere he went he carried a canvas bag containing burglary tools, bolt cutters, license plates, stencils, and paint. In five minutes, he could steal a jeep or truck, hustle it to a nearby alley, and replace its unit markings with "CCC—5th SFGA." Glad to have the extra vehicles, our commanders kept themselves willfully ignorant of his larcenies.

When our administrative offices needed air conditioners, Coady dutifully traveled to Saigon disguised as a USAF captain and visited an Air Force office building to "inspect" its ventilation system. "Defective," he announced and had several enlisted men load ten air conditioners in his falsely marked truck. Presto!—we had air conditioners.

On his next Saigon caper, though, Coady reached too far: He swiped a seventeen-ton air conditioner, so big it had to be craned onto a flatbed truck. He concealed it in a top secret SOG compound, but industrious U.S. Army criminal investigators scaled a wall and spotted it. Coady was allowed to return it, no questions asked, to avoid a court-martial.

Coady still had his share of combat. The previous fall, he'd been with his childhood friend Captain Ron Goulet when Goulet had been killed on a Hatchet Force mission in Laos. And, ironically, Coady had been the only man wounded when sappers demolished our Tactical Operations Center, the rebuilding of which was the reason for our trip to Qui Nhon.

Grabbing my CAR-15 and all my gear, I rode shotgun with Coady in his jeep as we led the two-truck convoy, driving an hour south on Highway 14 to Pleiku, then heading east on Highway 19 toward the Vietnam coast. Here it became interesting.

About a dozen miles east of Pleiku we reached the S curves of Mang Yang Pass, a narrow, hilly defile so threatening that it raised the hair on most men's necks. If that "enemy-can-look-down-your-throat" topography didn't get to you, the history certainly did: High on a facing hillside, I saw the neatly mowed cemetery containing hundreds of French graves, legionnaires of Groupe Mobile 100, slaughtered here in a Vietminh ambush some sixteen years earlier. In ten minutes we were through the pass and back on straight highway.

Two hours later the Highlands fell away and just ahead we saw the South China Sea and the city of Qui Nhon. Then, nearing the town, we passed a hillside dotted by enormous petroleum tanks, looking like metal mushrooms sprouted from a spring rain.

At an American supply depot, Captain Coady presented our requisition—probably the first legitimate one he'd ever used—and eventually both flatbeds were loaded with steel. The Yards had brought their own C rations and would sleep in their trucks.

I expected a quiet night in some transient barracks, especially since the entire city was off-limits to American personnel. "That won't stop us," Wild Bill announced. Sure enough, he got us smuggled downtown by a friend from Company N, 75th Rangers, and it wasn't bad—a small hotel with a decent bar and brothel conveniently next door. Before leaving, Coady's Ranger buddy advised, "Stay inside and nobody will bother you."

For a few hours we followed his advice, until, invigorated by alcohol, Coady suggested, "Let's see the town." Outside the hotel he waved down two passing Honda scooters, offering the drivers money to show us around. Hardly had we driven off than an MP jeep jerked before us, blocking our path. Wild Bill ran one way and I the other, kicking heels for all I was worth, scaling fences and sprinting through backyards and alleys, losing my MP pursuers.

Coady wasn't so fast or so fortunate. Hauled away to the local hoosegow, he was asked by an irate MP major, "Captain, what were you doing in an off-limits area?"

Coady wisecracked, "Pal, after twenty-four months of Vietnam, I deserve a little fun."

The major went ballistic, declared him a disgrace to the officer corps, and threatened to see him court-martialed. Wild Bill had to suppress a chuckle.

Then—*the ground shook—and a tremendous, distant roar!* Everyone at the MP station raced to the door, where they saw flames raging against the night sky.

"God damn!" a young MP swore, awed by the glowing sky. "They've hit the tank farm!" The half-dozen MPs grabbed M-16s and rushed past Coady.

"I might be of assistance," Wild Bill told the MP major, who was shrewd enough to see they might just need this cocky bastard. "Go!" he hollered.

The MP vehicles—two jeeps and a two-and-a-half-ton truck—sped through the darkness toward the burning fuel depot, the sound of gunfire and explosions in the distance. As they cautiously slowed at the main gate, Coady could see flames leaping sixty feet from a demolished petrol tank and dead Americans lying around a destroyed guard tower. Only twenty-five yards to the right of the tower, a two-story barracks had been blown up and now burned fiercely.

A young MP checked the front gate and shouted, "It's locked!"

At a glance, Coady understood what had happened: NVA sappers had rocketed the tower, killing the guards, then their assault teams had scaled the fence with wooden ladders and poles.

"What should we do?" the young MP called.

Coady realized this was probably the first real combat any of these men had ever seen. He shouted, "I'll show you what to do," and jumped aboard the two-and-a-half-ton truck, grabbed the steering wheel, and floored it, smashing through the gate. Most of the MPs hung back. Only the two MPs who had arrested him went inside with Coady.

Now armed with an M-16, Coady trotted to the two bodies, confirmed they were beyond first aid, then ran to the burning barracks. Looking into the flames, he saw several charred bodies—*one figure moved*. Tossing his M-16 to an MP, Wild Bill dashed into the inferno, grabbed the man, and dragged him to safety.

The soldier, a middle-aged master sergeant, was alive but in terrible condition. One leg was missing and the other hung by a thread. He'd been seriously burned.

Coady turned to one of the MPs who'd arrested him an hour earlier. "I need your jeep. Gotta get him to a hospital right away."

The MP, mildly shocked by the situation, replied, "You're not an MP. You can't have an MP jeep." Already Wild Bill was loading the badly wounded sergeant. Coady waved over the MP, and ordered, "Just show me the way to the hospital."

Coady raced hell-bent through Qui Nhon, never slowing or stopping until he screeched to a halt at the U.S. Army's 95th Field Hospital. Then he carried the wounded man into the emergency room, and rushed straight back to the burning tank farm.

By then the action had largely subsided and, for the first time, in the twinkling light of parachute flares, Coady looked across the mile-wide rice paddy the sappers must have crossed to reach the front gate. He voiced his thought, "I don't understand how anyone could have come that far without detection."

"Oh, they *were* seen, sir." The voice was a specialist four, based on the compound.

"What?"

"The two men in the guard tower were on a field phone, trying to find the duty officer."

An angry sergeant explained, "We can't fire unless we get permission from the duty officer. And he couldn't be found." The dead men in the barracks, he added, didn't even have weapons. They were kept locked in an arms room.

Captain Coady roared, "Who the fuck is stupid enough to say you can't have weapons?"

From the flaming light emerged a Transportation Corps major who looked Coady up and down, thinking the gold leaf on his collar would intimidate this Green Beret captain.

Coady barked, "You're in a goddamn combat zone and these people can't have weapons! I wouldn't go anywhere without a weapon."

The major snapped, "Well, this is the Transportation Corps and we don't do things that way."

Ignoring the asinine officer, Coady looked to the sergeants and privates. "If the sappers came in this way, they ran straight through and probably went out the other way. I'm going after them. Anybody want to go with me?"

The two MPs who'd arrested him said they'd go.

Sure enough, on the far side of the base, several GIs had seen the sappers escape. Not knowing what to do, they had just watched the sappers run away. Coady led the MPs about 500 yards beyond the compound, to the edge of a village, where they could make out figures trotting along a distant paddy dike. Coady shot at them, then the MPs fired, too, but in the darkness they could not determine whether they hit any of them.

Later, back at the MP station, the two young MPs wanted to write up Coady for an award, but their major said, "He's lucky he's not in jail." They drove him back to the hotel, where Coady told me the story over a stiff drink.

The next morning we drove over to the 95th Field Hospital to see how the wounded master sergeant was doing. We found him in the emergency room where a nurse was running a tube into his lungs to extract blood and mucus. One leg was gone, I could see, and they were trying to save the other. He tried to talk but mostly gasped and coughed. He held Coady's hand and managed to wheeze, "Thank you." He began to weep. "For my family, thank you."

In the hallway a doctor told us he would have died had Coady not rushed him there.

We rendezvoused with the Yards and led their trucks out of Qui Nhon, necessarily passing the fuel depot on our way out. Coady had us park there beside the road. Together we walked through the gate he'd rammed the previous night. Before us lay one of the immense steel fuel tanks, blackened and collapsed. To our right the rubble of the two-story barracks yet smoldered. As we paused there, I looked down upon a row of eleven ponchos, covering the remains of as many young soldiers, their boots protruding into the morning sun.

It was a disturbing sight, all these dead young men. Coady pointed to where an RPG had hit the guard tower, killing the two men who had held their fire while trying to phone the duty officer. They had perfect fields of fire.

Coady turned and there stood the insolent Transportation Corps major. Wild Bill pointed a finger at the bodies and barked, "How could this happen? Who the fuck is responsible for this?"

Astonishingly, the major boasted, "I am."

The veins stood out on Coady's neck. He shouted, "How can you be in a war zone with the weapons locked up and they have to call and nobody answers the phone?"

The major, hands on his hips, snapped back, "You hot-shot guys think you know everything. But we live by rules here. This is my compound."

For a second I fantasized shooting that bastard myself. Then I had to leap in front of Coady, who'd already cocked one arm to smack him. As I shoved Coady back to our jeep, he shouted past me, "Your own dead men don't matter to you!"

Coady was too upset to drive so I took the wheel. All the way back to Kontum, Coady seethed. "You don't mind dying for a reason, but to die in your sleep because of a fucking idiotic asshole really bothers me. That major was a perfect bureaucrat. Their lives didn't mean a thing to him. Fuck him."

"Fuck him," I agreed.

By the time we got back to our compound my new team member had arrived, Staff Sergeant Galen Musselman. It was just in time, for all our teams were about to be overworked. In Cambodia, a coup had overthrown Prince Sihanouk, bringing to power an anti-Communist government led by Lon Nol, who let it be known he would welcome an American invasion of the border sanctuaries. For years, American policymakers knew enemy forces were using Cambodia's neutral soil but hesitated to act for fear of international reaction. In 1966, Lieutenant General Stanley Larsen, commander of U.S. forces in the Central Highlands, told reporters that NVA forces were operating from Cambodian sanctuaries, causing Secretary of Defense Robert McNamara to declare the evidence insufficient. Reporters went back to General Larsen, but all he could do was smile and announce, "I stand corrected." This American policy of downplaying, even denying, enemy violations of neutral Cambodia was simply without precedent. It was as if in World War II, ten Nazi divisions had attacked Patton's Third Army from Switzerland, then fled back across the border and the U.S. said nothing for fear of offending the Swiss.

For those of us in SOG who'd risked our lives to document a truth so at odds with media reporting and public understanding, this turnabout seemed a godsend. But President Nixon's announcement that U.S. forces were invading Cambodia ignited a firestorm of condemnation. Witnessing this avalanche of criticism, I wrote to my father, urging him to write the president and support him in this unpopular decision. I'd never known my father to write any politician, but my mother wrote back, saying he had written the president, just as I'd asked.

The invasion, launched on 1 May, featured massive American helicopter assaults and armored sweeps into Cambodia's Fishhook and Parrot's Beak regions, far to our south. SOG teams from Ban Me Thuot's Command and Control South heavily supported these units. But up in northeast Cambodia, in our area of operations, not a single GI crossed the border, and for good reason: Mountainous terrain and dense jungle favored the defense, promising politically unacceptable heavy casualties. The gradual withdrawal of American combat units, which had begun the previous summer, had been accompanied by a slackening of heavy combat and lower casualties. U.S. policymakers would not repeat Hamburger Hill, the terrible bloodletting of 1969 when 101st Airborne paratroopers stormed an enemy mountain stronghold in the Ashau Valley.

But what was happening in northeast Cambodia? U.S. intelligence wanted to know: Were the NVA fleeing westward and abandoning their hidden base camps and supply roads, as were their comrades down south? A handful of CCC recon teams, including my RT California, were assigned the task of answering that question.

Two days after the U.S. launched its incursion, my RT California was aboard two choppers descending into an LZ in northeast Cambodia. Toting the team radio was Staff Sergeant Galen Mussleman, otherwise it was our regular crew—Rex Jaco, John Yancey, myself, and five Yards. Everything was pretty standard except on this mission I carried, taped to my web gear harness, a freon-powered air horn. This was my latest trick, intended to enhance our immediate action drill in a way so off-the-wall that the NVA wouldn't know how to respond.

It had occurred to me that a bugle sounding a cavalry charge might confuse the NVA during a firefight, but I could not find a bugle, nor anyone to pucker reliably while under fire. Then I remembered freon-powered air horns from high school football games. Accustomed to fulfilling my odd requests, my father mailed me an air horn, which I painted black and taped to my web gear.

As we landed that morning, swarms of mosquitoes covered us, the worst I'd ever seen, biting our lips and eyelids, any flesh not smeared with repellent. When we climbed uphill they lessened, and by noon we were atop a long ridge-line running generally north, the direction I wanted to proceed.

After lunch, I signaled Angao, my point man, to walk the ridgeline north-ward, where the jungle thinned, almost forming a natural trail. We made good time. About mid-afternoon, we heard a sudden crashing of brush, sounding like a man running for all he was worth. I asked Angao if he thought it was an NVA. "Monkey," he whispered, jutting out his lower jaw like a baboon. A half-hour later, the jungle thinned enough for us to see about fifty yards and the ridge dipped slightly, forming a bowl ahead of us.

We advanced down into the depression and—*ka-ka-ka-ka-ka-ka-ka*—tracers flashed at us across the bowl and from our right. At least twenty NVA—AKs, machine guns, RPGs.

Instantly we opened fire and squatted down, below the tracers. But we couldn't fall back because that meant heading up the bowl, into the enemy's fire. *KA-BOOM!* an RPG exploded. My first magazine expended, I reached for a grenade but my hand found the air horn—I depressed the plunger a full fifteen seconds—*Aaaaaaahhhhhhhhhhhhhhhhhhhhhh!* When I lifted my finger you could hear a pin drop. The North Vietnamese had run away, abandoning their superior position, terrified of this Yankee mystery weapon!

I led the team to our left, downhill, then doubled back and ran a full ten minutes. Evading our pursuers, we made it to an LZ and an hour later we were extracted under light ground fire.

We could tell debriefers that the NVA had not abandoned northeast Cambodia.

I was relaxing on stand-down after our air horn firefight when one morning a Cobra pilot, Warrant Officer Ed Paulaskis, offered, "Wanna go for a ride?" He didn't have to ask twice. Minutes later I was climbing into that warbird's forward copilot-gunner seat. The Cobra was sleek, only three feet wide with a canopy coming down to my waist; I was awed as Ed lifted us to a low hover. I tried my hand at the stick but didn't have the educated touch it takes to hold it steady.

On the other hand once we were at altitude I had no trouble controlling that marvelous machine, racing along at 100 knots, climbing and diving and banking—*whop-whop-whop-whop*. It was a fantastic flight, the greatest helicopter flight of my life.

Afterward it turned out that about the same time as our flight, an unidentified Cobra gunship flew into northeast Cambodia without authorization and blasted former Prince Sihanouk's summer palace, near Virachey. By this time, the ever-scheming ex-monarch had openly announced his support for Hanoi in the war. Whoever rocketed his digs expertly blew out all the windows and ripped open the playboy prince's roof, leaving the ultra-modern building uninhabitable. Some recon men and even a few Cobra crews speculated that Ed and I were the culprits, though we denied it repeatedly. I'm not saying it wasn't worthwhile for someone to wreck it, just that we weren't the ones. No gunship crew ever stepped forward to confess.

For days after that Cobra flight I was riding a bit on air, that freeing sensation of low-level flying, dreamlike floating above the realities of war and combat. It was a great feeling. It must have been two days later that one morning I left my team room and heard, *Boom!* I looked up to see an angry white cloud blossoming above the next barracks.

White phosphorus.

I dashed forward, rounded the side of the barracks—everything was afire, several Yards ran past me, screaming, smoke boiling from phosphorus fragments burning into their bodies. A man lay there, an American, but I couldn't tell who he was. The front of his body had taken the full burst of exploding phosphorus. I knelt beside him, unable to touch him due to the raging phosphorus. "Who are you?" I called.

"It's me," the unidentifiable figure said, "Chuck Hein"—the radio operator from Miller's team, a man I knew well, a good friend. I had to smother that phosphorus, cut off the oxygen. I needed a blanket, I could wet it in the latrine, fifty yards away. "You'll be fine," I lied, jumped up, ran to the nearest team room, kicked in its locked door, tore a blanket off a bed, and dashed for the latrine. I was back in thirty seconds, but already John Yancey had arrived and lifted Chuck to his feet and, still afire, got him walking toward the dispensary.

But there was still the fire. Along with several men, I ran among the flames and smoke to kick burning phosphorus fragments off piles of high-explosive grenades and whole cases of 60mm mortar ammunition. Chuck had been issuing ammunition to his Yards for their next mission when the white phosphorus exploded. Any second all that ordnance could have gone off and killed everyone within a hundred yards. But we extinguished it in time.

Afterward, Jaco, Yancey, and I walked to the club; it was 10:00 A.M., hours before opening, the club manager, master sergeant Richard Smith, pointed out.

But when we told Dick what had happened, he poured us all double shots of straight whiskey. "God bless him," I said, and Yancey and Jaco added, "To Chuck," and, "Chuck." We poured it down. The toast was to Chuck, but the whiskey was for ourselves. Every man who ran into that burning phosphorus deserved the Soldier's Medal for risking his life trying to save another's. But what was that compared to what Chuck had been through? It never occurred to any of us to submit anyone for an award, and we never did.

Mercifully, Chuck died the following day at the Evacuation Hospital in Pleiku. The Buddhist priest had been correct; no bullet ever touched him.

Alone that afternoon I drove the recon company jeep to the range. No one was there. I looked at my web gear, where hung my own white phosphorus grenade, identical to the one Chuck Hein had grasped.

There's a long tradition in American paratroop units that a fatal parachuting accident must be followed immediately by another jump. The entire unit is issued fresh parachutes, climbs aboard planes, then leaps upon the very same drop zone so there's little time for doubts to arise concerning the reliability of parachutes, the effectiveness of training, or the soundness of jump procedures. Or the willingness of paratroopers to jump from airplanes.

The vision of Chuck's injuries still overwhelmed my mind as I looked at the phosphorus grenade in my hand. The cast iron felt cool to the touch. Chuck had dropped his grenade on a concrete step, cracking the grenade's iron casing. When he lifted it, he'd have felt its growing heat—as air reached the phosphorus—then curiously held it before his face. That's where Chuck's grenade was when it detonated, eighteen inches from his handsome face.

I wished I could not recall what I had seen.

I pulled the pin, cocked my arm, let the spoon fly, and threw it as far as I could. I watched the flash, the white mushroom cloud, and the cascade of twinkling, burning fragments. Carrying a WP grenade on my own web gear meant that a ricocheted bullet, a grenade fragment, or an RPG blast might crack it with an identical result. But I'd always carry one on my web gear. It had to be that way. There was no better means for quickly, effectively directing an air strike.

As the white cloud dissipated I drove back to the club to sing "Hey Blue" for Chuck Hein, and to drink myself to unconsciousness.

Unexpectedly, a few days later, Jaco, Yancey, Musselman, and myself and five of our Yards sat in the webbed seats of a C-130 Blackbird, en route to Ban Me Thuot. Due to the invasion, recon teams at CCS had been running back-to-back missions and had become so over-committed that SOG had to bring in teams from CCN and CCC to help out, including RT California.

That night we sat in the club where the most famous recon man of them all, Jerry "Mad Dog" Shriver, had pulled his between-mission antics. In a glass case Shriver's memorabilia was displayed, almost a shrine to the missing One-Zero, by then MIA for some thirteen months.

Shriver may have been gone, but I did see Jack Damoth, a good friend and communications classmate from my Fort Bragg training days. Word had spread about our success on Ashtray Two, so Jack had to know the blow-by-blow details. In return, Jack told me about his most recent snatch attempt, with RT Level, launched just five days after our convoy ambush.

His One-Zero, Sergeant Dave Crofton, had positioned their eight-man team beside a trail in Cambodia. Almost immediately a large enemy force walked past. A few minutes later, two more NVA appeared, and Crofton thought they seemed ripe for snatching. He jumped forward, CAR-15 to his shoulder, and the two NVA froze. In another second he'd have had them disarmed and restrained, but another enemy force arrived, spotted Crofton, and opened fire. The two would-be prisoners went for their guns—Crofton had to shoot them—then the whole team exchanged fire with the more numerous NVA. As the NVA attempted to sweep right and left to flank RT Level, Jack left the safety of cover and jumped in the open to better engage the enemy so his teammates could escape. His audacity helped them shoot their way clear.

That, alone, was a bad situation, but one of Jack's new teammates, Staff Sergeant Bill Deacy, had narrowly survived an even tougher ordeal a couple of weeks before that. RT Level, then led by Staff Sergeant Bob Malone, with Staff Sergeant Ernie Masci, One-One, and Deacy, One-Two, had been on their second day of a mission south of Cambodia's Fishhook.

As they and four Yards crossed a ridge, they spotted heavily camouflaged bunkers and NVA guards only a short distance downhill. They attempted to slip around the enemy installation, but a guard detected them, sounded the alarm, and dozens of NVA came after them. Following a quick exchange of fire, Malone got his men clear and eventually reached a clearing large enough for extraction. After another exchange of gunfire, Malone directed Cobra gunships on the NVA, suppressing them while their Huey extraction bird came in.

The hillside was too steep for a landing, so the chopper, from the 155th Assault Helicopter Company, dropped ladders. While the door gunners blasted away, the RT Level men scooted up, with Deacy last. To escape enemy fire, the Huey lifted away with Deacy still climbing.

He felt a shudder, heard a tremendous explosion, then the helicopter spun out of control, falling toward the ground. "I have to get out from under,"

Deacy told himself, trying to push away. Centrifugal force, however, held him in its unwanted embrace.

Everything faded to blackness.

Deacy's next sensation was intense heat, stinging him back to consciousness. He heard a voice say, "We've got to shoot him." The chopper, he came to realize, was on its side, and he was entangled in the ladder. He couldn't move. The Huey was burning, flames licking at his legs and left side. The crash had fractured his skull, compressed his spine, knocked out several teeth, and left a serious gash in his head. Deacy was dazed, unable to speak.

The surviving crew and teammates had tried to extricate him but were forced back by growing flames. The pilot warned that the Huey's fuel cells would explode any second. Out of mercy, a voice repeated, "We'd better just shoot him."

Another voice said, "Let's give it one last try." At that desperate moment, Terry O'Kelly, the Huey crew chief, lifted and heaved against the hot fuselage while One-One Masci grabbed Deacy's legs. Oblivious to the fire searing his flesh, O'Kelly found superhuman strength long enough for Masci to twist Deacy's body and unravel the ladder. "Crawl!" Masci urged and somehow Deacy pulled himself clear. But it was hardly over.

Still engaging the enemy, Deacy's teammates and Cobra gunships defended the LZ while another Huey arrived and dropped extraction rigs. But there weren't enough rigs to go around. O'Kelly snapped into one, then Deacy's teammates helped him climb onto O'Kelly's lap where he sat facing the crew chief. Deacy wrapped his arms around O'Kelly's neck as the chopper lifted them up and away. As they flew beneath the Huey, 3,000 feet above the ground, blood poured from Deacy's head wound and strength drained from his body. He felt cold, very cold. Then he couldn't hold on anymore. He slipped from O'Kelly's lap—down and down and down—until his head was at O'Kelly's waist and his arms were straight up. The only thing holding him were O'Kelly's powerful hands, gripping him under his armpits. Hardly conscious, Deacy looked down at the jungle, far below. "Please," he mumbled, "don't let me fall."

Miraculously, O'Kelly was able to hold on long enough for the chopper to descend to an airstrip where he delivered Deacy right into the hands of SOG medic Sergeant Ken Mertz. Another miracle—in only three weeks, Deacy was back at CCS, buying O'Kelly drinks in the club and ready for another mission with Jack Damoth.

The Cambodian situation proved fluid; RT California was targeted for one location, but advancing American forces got there so fast that our mission was canceled. U.S. armor and infantry drove the NVA from the town of Snuol, in Cambodia's Fishhook, then discovered a massive enemy base nearby in the jungle. The next day, 1st Air Cavalry Division soldiers, flying at treetop level, found "the City," a complex of 400 buildings and bunkers, complete with a swimming pool and street signs. Fleeing enemy soldiers had left behind 202 mortars and machine guns, 1,282 individual weapons, nearly two million AK rounds, plus 319,000 rounds for .50 caliber antiaircraft machine guns, 2,000 grenades, twenty-nine tons of explosives, twenty-two cases of mines, and thirty-four tons of food.

But where had all the City inhabitants gone? U.S. intelligence estimated that the base had housed at least 10,000 soldiers. Several SOG teams were targeted to sweep the jungle north and west of the City, well beyond conventional U.S. units, to intercept fleeing NVA columns.

After an intelligence briefing, we flew to the CCS launch site at Quan Loi—also a major staging base for the 1st Air Cavalry Division—and the next morning we inserted northwest of Snuol, on the western edge of the notorious Fishhook. With local elevation almost 1,000 feet lower than Laos, the jungle there was truly steaming. Both temperature and humidity hovered in the mid-90s. But the terrain was fairly flat and dry, so we made good time.

The first day we found nothing, but on our second day we made a startling discovery: At the edge of a rubber plantation, we found a fresh, five-yard-wide, cross-country trail of more bootprints than we could count, heading northwest toward Kratie. (In his book, *A Vietcong Memoir,* former senior VC leader Truong Nhu Tang identifies his escape route from the Fishhook, suggesting that, indeed, RT California had discovered that very trail. Truong also describes several B-52 strikes, including one that almost killed him.) There were so many tracks that it looked like a cattle drive. We also found where apparently the NVA had camped the previous night, with small dugouts for cooking fires every ten yards—across an area 500 yards wide and almost twice that distance long. I radioed that we'd found sign of at least a regiment—up to 2,000 troops—and began the pursuit.

The eight of us advanced as quickly as we dared, knowing that such an enormous force had a rear guard of several platoons at least. For hours we followed the beaten tracks, through rubber groves and bamboo forests, across streams and over low hills.

Late that afternoon, a USAF O-2 overflew us and its pilot radioed, "Get to an LZ immediately."

A half-hour later we were aboard choppers, flying back to the Quan Loi launch site. Our discovery got an "attaboy," and we learned we'd been extracted because B-52 bombers were on the way to hit the suspected enemy column. What resulted from that strike, I never learned.

At this heightened operational pace, there simply wasn't time for stand-down.

Two days later we went back into Cambodia, this time a bit deeper, west of Memot, where we were to screen forward of the 1st Air Cavalry Division. By then, the 1st Air Cav and ARVN 9th Regiment had seized a second major enemy complex, one they called "Rock Island East." Inside it they found more than 300 tons of munitions.

As in our mission near Snuol, the enemy appeared to be fleeing, not standing to fight, and, unlike Laos, I didn't think any NVA were trying to hunt us down. Therefore I kept us moving as fast as possible, to search as much territory as we could.

During our second morning, my point man, Angao, suddenly froze, then carefully tiptoed back to me. I signaled, "What?" When Angao couldn't find words to explain himself, I eased forward and beheld the swaying head of an enormous king cobra, its angry eyes five feet off the ground, glaring at me. Its inflated hood looked the size of a dinner plate. *I didn't know they got that damned big!* Agreeing with Angao, we prudently backed off and gave that serpent wide berth.

Aside from the occasional reptile, we were encountering nothing interesting. In that severe heat, my greatest concern was a lack of water; by day three, we had come upon no streams and our canteens were empty. We'd continued a whole day without water when one of our grenadiers, Wo-Two, grinned and tapped my shoulder.

Weet, my interpreter, whispered, "Him say, he smell water."

With my approval, Wo-Two dug his banana knife into a low spot, quietly hacking into the dark soil. Inside of three minutes, he looked up, eyes twinkling, and sure enough, a small pool of murky fluid was filling the hole. After widening it, he gradually filled all our canteens. It wasn't sweet, it didn't smell great, but it was wet. Like everyone else, I chugged it down gratefully.

The next day during our lunch break, what began as a minor stomach cramp quickly escalated to paralyzing pain. Suddenly feverish, sapped of strength, I could barely lift my legs. Nothing in my medical kit offered the slightest relief and, no longer able to carry my rucksack, I was compelled to request my own evacuation. As the chopper arrived to extract me, I turned the team over to Jaco, confident that he'd do a fine job.

Back at the launch site, I had to wait hours for a medevac chopper, bent double in spasms of pain, the worst I'd ever experienced. After sunset a medevac chopper arrived and, lost in fever, I stumbled aboard. In the darkness I found a place to sit among sacks of rice. Feverish, I groggily watched the lights of Tay Ninh Province drift past.

Then a sack moved—it wasn't a rice bag but a badly wounded ARVN soldier. I helped ease him aside and realized there were no sacks, these were all ARVN soldiers. And most of them weren't moving, including the one I'd been sitting upon.

Landing at Saigon's Third Army Field Hospital, I forced myself to walk from the chopper, but that sapped the last of my strength. Since the doctors initially suspected appendicitis, I was bedded in the surgery ward among two dozen wounded 1st Air Cav soldiers medevaced from Cambodia. All of us were too ill and too immobile for socializing.

The next morning a Protestant chaplain toured our ward, going bed to bed, encouraging the men. When he reached me, he asked, "And where are you from, my son?"

"Kontum," I mumbled.

He gave me a confounded look. "I mean, in the States! Your hometown!" The chaplain thought I'd been in Vietnam too long. I thought it was funny.

By the next day my affliction had been diagnosed as blackwater fever, a variety of dysentery, undoubtedly from that murky Cambodian water. For three days I consumed only antibiotics, clear broth, and Jell-O. By then I could walk again.

The doctor offered me early release if I promised to continue my semiliquid diet. I swore I would. An hour later I was on Tu Do Street at the Peacock restaurant, chowing down steak and broiled lobster. Life was good again.

Returning to Kontum, I learned Rex Jaco had run a good mission, and RT California was at Ban Me Thuot, ready to run another. Still recovering, I was too weak for field duty and had to wonder whether it was time to let someone else be One-Zero. Both Jaco and Yancey were ready and capable. For at least another week I wasn't going anywhere.

Knowing that, the recon company commander, Captain Joe Dilger, asked if I'd train three Americans who'd just taken over RT Ohio. Sergeants First Class Rich Ryan and Charlie Bless and Staff Sergeant Bernie Mims each had at least six months on the compound, but all were new to recon. Ryan and Mims had fought on the Hatchet Force, and Bless had served in the Commo Section—indeed, he was one of the most brilliant commo men I'd ever known.

Always short of teams, SOG had a horrible record of hurriedly assembling such inexperienced men and inserting them in dangerous targets with disastrous results, as had happened with my first team, RT New Mexico. If he could keep RT Ohio from being targeted for ten days, Dilger asked, could I give Ryan, Bless, and Mims enough training so they'd have a decent edge until they gained more experience?

Absolutely, I vowed.

We spent those few days in intense training—tactics, formations, immediate action drills, ambushes, rapid reloading, signaling techniques, rappelling. Each day, all day long, I helped RT Ohio drill and train and practice. Then, as best I could prepare them, they were ready to go.

A few days later Ryan, Bless, and Mims and five Yards inserted into Laos, and indeed, it was a dangerous target, just north of Highway 110. I monitored their situation reports, relayed through our Tactical Operations Center. The first day went well. Then, on their second day, they came upon a large body of NVA—at least fifty men—bathing in a stream, and attempted to call an air strike on them. But the planes didn't arrive until past sunset, too dark to direct a strike. One-Zero Ryan knew the NVA had noticed the orbiting planes and may have concluded a team was nearby. Believing it too dangerous to stumble around in the dark, Ryan backed off fifty yards, put out claymores, and planned to move out at first light.

The following morning a man rushed from the Tactical Operations Center to recon company. "They've been hit," he reported. "Ryan and Mims have been wounded, and Bless is missing."

It was a long, tense day, waiting for word on RT Ohio.

About noon, the Covey Rider, Lloyd "O.D." O'Daniels, reported he'd pulled Ryan and Mims—Ryan with a gunshot wound. Then, thank God, he radioed that Bless had been found and extracted, also with a gunshot wound. Gunshot wounds almost always were serious, many times fatal. They'd probably be medevaced. That all had survived seemed amazing—actually it was more amazing than any of us knew.

Late that afternoon, along with the rest of recon company, I stood beside the helipad to greet the returning RT Ohio. When their Huey touched down, we couldn't believe our eyes—all eight men walked from the aircraft, showing hardly any sign of injury! I shook their hands while First Sergeant Todd passed them cold beers and everyone cheered.

But hadn't they been shot, hit by AK fire? Must have been graze wounds.

No, Ryan and Bless later told me in their team room, each had been shot squarely in a vital spot. They should have been dead. Opening a beer, Ryan recalled how, that morning at first light, a large NVA force had hit them. RT Ohio blew claymores and fired desperately. Mims shot two NVA at close range. RPG shrapnel wounded all three Americans and three Yards. Realizing they had to run or be overrun, Ryan hurled several grenades, then led his men away. After falling back about 100 yards, Ryan paused for a quick head count. Charlie Bless was missing.

Ryan wanted to go back but they were outnumbered at least five to one, most of his men already were bleeding, and dozens of NVA were closing upon them. They had to keep going. At that critical moment Covey arrived overhead, with "O.D." O'Daniels. Small world, Ryan observed—O'Daniels had been best man at his wedding.

Less than an hour later, RT Ohio reached a suitable LZ, and Ryan crawled into the open to flash a signal panel to O'Daniels. As Ryan spoke into his radio, O.D. looked down and saw him spin around—he'd been shot. Ryan and his men scrambled into a streambed for cover. Pain throbbed from Ryan's side, where the bullet had hit him. But it wasn't bleeding too bad.

Soon the choppers arrived and, under the covering fire of Cobras, a Huey snatched away Ryan and Mims and the Yards. Though ground fire peppered their aircraft, they made it out.

As their Huey got clear, Charlie Bless whispered into his emergency radio, telling O'Daniels he'd been hiding under a log with NVA looking high and low for him. He'd become separated because he'd remained behind to delay the enemy while his teammates escaped. Minutes later an extraction rig was lifting Bless through the trees when a slug slammed into the side of his face.

In their team room, Bless showed me where the bullet had cut through his cheek and merely broken a tooth, not even exiting his mouth. He'd spit out the slug and saved it, holding it before me in his hand. Even more astonishing, Ryan lifted his jungle shirt to show me a fresh wound on his left side. The bullet had barely penetrated; a medic popped it out with his finger!

"Bad ammo," Ryan concluded.

"If it hadn't been defective ammo," Bless agreed, "it would have gone right through my head." They had to be the luckiest damned men ever to run recon.

With RT Ohio out and safe, I was ready to rejoin RT California, which was still down at CCS. Arriving in Ban Me Thuot, I learned Rex Jaco had come down with malaria and been medevaced. Therefore, the following day it was myself, John Yancey, Galen Musselman, and five Yards that rode USAF Hueys from the 20th Special Operations Squadron to the CCS northern launch site at Duc Co Special Forces Camp, due west of Pleiku.

We sat beside the airfield for about an hour, then rode the 20th SOS Green Hornet Hueys into the famous Ia Drang Valley, where the 1st Air Cavalry had fought America's first major engagement of the war in 1965. We landed exactly on the border and walked into Cambodia.

The Ia Drang may have been teeming with NVA five years earlier, but we searched it high and low for five days and found not a single living human being, nor any fresh sign. Sometimes it's important to know where the enemy isn't, and I guess that was our achievement. Afterward, we flew back to Kontum for our first real stand-down since the air horn firefight six weeks earlier.

During stand-down, I went by the mailroom one afternoon. The clerk held out a letter, did a double take, and raised his eyes. "How the fuck do you rate?" he asked. Grabbing the envelope I had no idea what he meant. Then I noticed the letter's return address and wondered, What kind of joke is this? Tearing it open I found a simple note:

> *Your own service in Vietnam and your understanding of the situation there lend special meaning to your encouragement for our country's goals in Southeast Asia. I was pleased to receive the message your father so thoughtfully forwarded to me, and I want you to know that your expression of confidence means a great deal to all your colleagues in uniform as well as to your Commander-in-Chief.*

It was hand-signed *Richard Nixon*. On White House stationery.

"I'll be damned," I swore and showed it to RT Hawaii One-Zero Larry White, who reacted similarly. Then we reread it and had to laugh. That phrase, "your understanding of the situation there," appeared to be an "I-know-you-know" thing. In recent months the president must have consumed reams of intelligence about the Cambodian sanctuaries, collected solely by our SOG teams. Virtually the entire invasion had been based upon our reports. The president could hardly write, "Thanks for gathering intelligence covertly in Cambodia," but seeing my unit address, and knowing we had gathered it, the president had written the note as subtle recognition to all of us. That phrase made the whole thing satisfying, a perfect pat on the back for the entire unit. I shared President Nixon's letter with everyone in recon.

Richard Nixon may later have acquired a reputation for deceit, but his declaration that all U.S. forces would be out of Cambodia by 30 June was completely truthful. Indeed, we thought he was too honest, for that limitation included SOG's covert forces. With little notice, CCC ceased recon operations there—shifting our effort entirely to Laos—while Ban Me Thuot–based CCS simply closed down. The best CCS recon teams were transferred to CCC and to CCN.

As quickly as they withdrew from Cambodia, the U.S. 4th Infantry Division, the last major American combat unit in the Central Highlands, departed from Vietnam. Their empty base camp at Pleiku was stripped by ARVN officers, whose agents peddled truckloads of plywood, pipe, and electrical wire on the black market.

In hopes of scrounging some leftover 4th Division matériel for our camp, the day after Independence Day 1970, our club manager, Master Sergeant Richard Smith, our camp engineer, Sergeant First Class Jan Novy, and Sergeant First Class George Lischynski left for Pleiku in a jeep. A proud Czech, Novy had fought in the underground against the Germans during World War II, then tried to resist the Soviet occupation until he had to flee to the West.

Halfway to Pleiku, their jeep rolled into an ambush and spun out of control. All three men were hit. Lischynski never made it out of his seat—a rushing Vietcong finished him off. Smith dived under the jeep. More Communist soldiers dashed along the roadside ditch and closed on the disabled jeep, peppering the unarmed Smith with AK bursts. He died instantly.

Knocked unconscious by an AK slug that grazed his skull, Jan Novy appeared dead. After tugging off his wedding band and wristwatch, the Vietcong stole his wallet. By the time he awoke, the VC were long gone.

Their damaged jeep was towed back to our compound and eventually repaired. While repainting it, our motor sergeant stenciled a message to those who'd murdered Smith and Lischynski: "FYMC I've Returned."

The initials stood for "Fuck Your Mother, Charlie."

With Rex Jaco hospitalized for malaria and not likely to return, I needed a new man on RT California. I received the finest human being I ever knew in Special Forces, Sergeant First Class David Hayes. Standing six foot four with a lumberjack's build, Hayes bore such a pleasant demeanor that he'd long ago been nicknamed "Baby Huey" after the comic book character. A talented commo man, he was on his third Vietnam tour but had never seen combat.

Baby Huey was no shirker and hardly a coward, but his commo expertise always got him sidetracked into rear echelon jobs. With the war winding down, he'd begun to wonder if, as a career Green Beret NCO, he had carried his own weight. For months he'd had mixed feelings. Six months earlier, he'd tried to convince Robert Masterjoseph not to volunteer for CCN, telling him it was too late in the war to justify such extraordinary risks.

Then Baby Huey himself volunteered for SOG. And for recon.

A family man with three children and a wife, Dave wasn't much of a drinker. His greatest passion was the ham radio station in his basement at home.

Upon Dave's arrival, the recon company commander decided it was high time to let John Yancey take out the team. Besides, I had to go down to SOG headquarters in Saigon.

Yancey's first mission as One-Zero was a local training operation, only about a dozen miles from our compound, in an area not known to contain any enemy forces.

Two hours after landing, Yancey paused the team for a break. They'd just stopped when three RPGs crashed among them. While his teammates rushed to cover, Baby Huey, the biggest target there, stood his ground to fire at the NVA—*another RPG crashed, almost at his feet.*

Rushing to his side, Yancey saw that Hayes had lost a leg and was bleeding profusely. Galen Musselman couldn't reach anyone by radio because they were on low ground. Yancey sent him and the rest of the team to a nearby hilltop and, alone, defended Baby Huey, fighting off repeated attacks. Unable to stop the severe bleeding, John stood guard over David Hayes as he died.

Later, a Hatchet Force platoon landed, relieved Yancey, and loaded Baby Huey's body aboard an extraction rig dropped from a hovering helicopter.

Back at our compound, most men stopped what they were doing at the sound of that returning chopper, looked up, and watched it bring in Hayes's body dangling from a rope. "It took forever to lower his body down to the ground," thought Covey Rider Lloyd O'Daniels, tormented by the sight. "And this guy had a wife and three kids."

"God Almighty," O'Daniels asked himself. "Is this worth it?"

It was a good question. My six-month extension was at an end. Along with Glenn Uemura, I was free to rotate home. I could have extended for another six months, but that was no longer administratively possible with so imminent a departure.

While Yancey was leading his first mission, I was at a ceremony at SOG headquarters, in Chief SOG Cavanaugh's office. In recognition for leading Operation Ashtray Two, Colonel Cavanaugh presented me SOG's highest award, a chromed Browning 9mm pistol in a velvet-lined presentation case, engraved with my name.

Later, at SOG's Saigon safe house, I saw Uemura. We said goodbye and shook hands. I waved as he drove off, thankful that he was safe, returning to his family. Then a SOG staff car arrived to drive me to Long Binh, to the U.S. Army, Vietnam, headquarters. There, hand-carrying my personnel file, I was able to extend for another six months. Instead of rotating home I went home on extension leave.

This time, though, instead of partying, high school friend Joe Remarke and

I canoed the Boundary Waters Canoe Area, a magnificent wilderness in northern Minnesota. In that tranquil setting I forgot about the war, except at night.

Convince myself as I might, as our campfire burned to embers, I felt a rising anxiety, realizing we had no claymore mines out there. In the blackness I sensed enemies, trying to creep up. Over and over, I told myself, this was the Canadian border, far from Vietnam, yet I could not rest.

Then I loaded a pistol, laid it beside me in the sleeping bag, and finally drifted to sleep.

Chapter Twelve

As I was riding a truck from Kontum airfield to the compound, an unwelcome sentiment swept over me, a melancholy born of a kind of loneliness. I would not see any of my old comrades—not Glenn Uemura, George Bacon, Ben Thompson, or Franklin Miller or dozens of others. Rolling through the gate, I realized that not one Special Forces soldier who had been there in late '68 when I arrived still served at CCC. Killed, Missing in Action, medevaced, or rotated home, by late August 1970 every single one was gone, replaced by another Green Beret. I had become the old man.

Why did I extend again? I wasn't sure other than that I knew I still belonged there, and could not accept leaving unfinished what so many others had begun and were not there to see through—all those names we recited in "Hey, Blue." That thought depressed me more.

Then, as I walked to the club, my mood spun around with one shout— "Hey, John!"

A lanky figure ambled toward me. *Could it be?* Damn!

"Joe!" I hollered, and he grinned back, showing a mouthful of teeth. *Joe Walker!* Just like he promised, be damned, Joe Walker was back.

Joe pumped my hand. "Thanks for takin' good care a' my team, John."

I had to chuckle—Walker already had reclaimed RT California and there was no contesting that ownership. He'd decided to keep Galen Musselman and had brought aboard two replacements, Sergeants Mike Vermillion and Laughlin "Toby" Todd. Rex Jaco, I learned, had stayed in Saigon after his bout with malaria, finishing his tour working at SOG headquarters. John Yancey, meanwhile, had become RT Delaware's One-Zero and he was about to go home, too.

In the club, Joe described his year with the CIA in Laos, training the Royal Laotian Army, a task at which, he confessed, he'd failed. The nattily uniformed Laotians, Joe said, proved a spineless, parade ground army, unwilling to fight the NVA. "If it wasn't for the Hmong and Vang Pao," he said, referring to the CIA-supported mountain people and their feisty commander, "the North Vietnamese would overrun the whole miserable country." But pacifism wasn't unique to the anti-Communist side. "We had this NVA colonel defect. Shows up at one of our camps. Turns out he was my counterpart, trainin' the commie Pathet Lao.

"So I'm talkin' to this NVA colonel. His bosses warned him, 'Shape these Pathet Lao into soldiers or else.' " To the enemy colonel's complete frustration, he found his Laotians equally fainthearted, their leaders preferring political debates to down-and-out battles.

"So what could I do?" the colonel moaned. "I defected." Through an interpreter he cursed, "Hell with them!"

"I shook his hand," Joe finished, "and told him, 'Damn right! Hell with 'em all!' "

I was still laughing when, from the doorway, boomed, "Wine for my troops!" It was the ever ebullient Fat Albert!—Pete Wilson—the compound's newest One-Zero. I waved him over, congratulated him, and ordered a round of drinks. Fat Albert was robust and enthusiastic, though as rotund as when Bill Spencer and I had recruited him last fall. Having served as Ed Wolcoff's assistant team leader on RT New York, he recently had become One-Zero of RT South Carolina. A couple of weeks after that he'd fought his first firefight as a team leader, in which One-One John Baker suffered a minor wound. Pete got them out OK, proving his mettle.

I looked around the room and noticed two dozen recon men swapping war stories and jokes and plotting ambushes or arguing tactics, just the way it had always been. I was glad to be home.

During my absence, with an end to Cambodian operations, you'd have thought there would be a decline in missions but the opposite was true—we were more active than ever in Laos. At any time, CCC tried to keep six teams roaming the Laotian Ho Chi Minh Trail, and for good reason: With the enemy no longer able covertly to deliver shiploads of supplies through Cambodia's port at Sihanoukville, virtually all NVA ammunition, food, and personnel had to come down the Laotian highway system. Further, by late summer 1970, the U.S. had reached a critical phase in the troop withdrawal: More than half our combat forces had left, including both Marine divisions, along with the U.S. Army's 1st, 4th, 9th, and 25th Divisions, plus many smaller units. The remaining three divisions had shifted from the interior to coastal enclaves and bases near Saigon; the war would never see another major American ground offensive. Thus, gathering intelligence along the Trail—especially keeping track of the North Vietnamese Army—was essential to protect America's diminishing and ever more vulnerable forces.

The job was not without cost. While I was home, CCC Hatchet Force soldier Peter Vander Weg was killed in Laos despite the valorous attempts of a Special Forces medic, Sergeant Lee Garland, to save his life. Before that, another Hatchet Force man, First Lieutenant Mark Rivest, had been killed in action. Among our recon teams, the closest call had been for RT Arizona, whose three Americans—One-Zero Newman Ruff, One-One Mike Wilson, and One-Two Dave Honeycutt—all had suffered shrapnel wounds, though they shot their way clear.

Well, I was back, ready and willing, and asked the recon first sergeant which team I would lead. That took care of itself because RT Hawaii One-Zero Larry White had been selected to ride Covey. This was Larry's second tour at CCC. Only two weeks before I got there in '68, he'd been badly wounded, hit three times by AK fire while landing on a Laotian LZ with Bob Howard. Medevaced, he'd spent months in military hospitals, then served at Fort Bragg. Like many SOG vets, White had grown bored with Stateside garrison duty and volunteered to return to the men and mission he most loved.

So I found myself One-Zero of RT Hawaii—Glenn Uemura's old team—one of the best, with excellent, experienced Montagnards, including Sui Pup, interpreter, Nao on point, and Pleo, Tung, Leh, Gong, Pok, Biuh, Nhit, Disur, and Je. My new One-One was Staff Sergeant Emmet "Les" Dover, and Sergeants Regis Gmitter and John Justice, One-Two and One-Three. Like most of our teams, RT Hawaii now had four Americans, a luxury brought about by an influx of experienced recon men and even whole teams from the disbanded CCS. These included some truly fine Green Berets like Jim "Fred" Morse, Jack Damoth, Brendan Lyons, Carl Franquet, John Gunnison, and Pete Neamtz, to name a few.

One more major change—an outgrowth of the "Vietnamization" that transferred more and more combat to the South Vietnamese Army—was a dramatic increase in South Vietnamese Special Forces recon teams. Unaffected by President Nixon's ending ground operations in Cambodia, these ten South Vietnamese teams picked up the mission to do recon in Cambodia, supported by Vietnamese and American helicopters. Unlike American-led teams, the Vietnamese teams contained military personnel only—no Yard civilians—and had Vietnamese names—varieties of lightning—such as Team Mountain Lightning and Team Sea Lightning. Some Vietnamese teams would display great courage and bring back intelligence as effectively as any American team; but others were led by uninspired, politically appointed officers, whose primary goal was protecting their own miserable skins. And like American teams, their best men and teams were assigned the most hazardous missions.

RT Hawaii was given two weeks to train before receiving our first assignment. By now I knew this process well, teaching or refreshing tactics, immediate action drills, formations, and such. While this training was underway, I was sniffing around for a special mission, something that would let me outdo even Ashtray Two. Immediately after that prisoner snatch, SOG planners had considered RT California so capable that there was talk of putting us on a 500-foot butte way up north of the DMZ, overlooking the Mu Gia Pass, where enemy convoys entered Laos from North Vietnam. The first laser-guided "smart" bombs had arrived in Southeast Asia a little earlier. As far as the world knew, the laser designators that marked targets were sizable devices installed in support aircraft. But down in Saigon, I was informed, SOG had available a man-portable laser designator similar in size and weight to an M-60 machine gun. One planner even suggested inserting us by parachute from an OV-10 forward air control aircraft to deceive the enemy. Would I be interested?

Wow!—what a perfect way to direct air strikes—lazing from a 500-foot butte!

Wow!—what a perfect way to get killed—trapped on a 500-foot butte!

I didn't say no, but the mission didn't pan out, though I had the lingering impression that there was more concern over losing the prototype laser designator than losing my team. Still, that episode got me thinking: What kinds of things hadn't SOG ever attempted? For the first time I had enough stature to suggest missions.

My first idea was to lead a thirty-day mission in which RT Hawaii would insert, lie low for five days, then have the helicopters fake an extraction some distance away. Resupplying our food from a cache hidden near our insert LZ, we'd then walk into an area previously not explored. It was an interesting concept but SOG headquarters didn't buy it.

Then I thought about a river watch, that is, eyeballing where Highway 92 crossed the Dak Sou River in southern Laos. That ford usually was unapproachable because concentric belts of patrols and sentries held us at bay. Not since Ralph Rodd had sneaked in there a year earlier had any of our teams been able to surveil that crossing.

"Why not build a covert watercraft," I suggested to our acting commander, Lieutenant Colonel Serafino Scalise, "disguised to look like a large tree trunk?" Smash it and streak it with burns to make it appear it had been uprooted by a B-52 strike. Inside its hollowed core, we'd conceal two men with cameras, night vision devices, and radios. Fly it in at night slung beneath a CH-47 Chinook helicopter, drop it in the Dak Sou upstream from Highway 92's river ford, then steer it downstream with battery-powered propellers. We could anchor upstream from the crossing site and watch it for days.

Fascinated, Scalise listened, nodding. Then he said, "John, if this was 1967, I'd say, 'Let's go for it.' But it's 1970. It probably can't happen." Another no-go.

I didn't give up.

My next inspiration evolved from an O-1 visual reconnaissance flight over southern Laos with a pilot we nicknamed "Fat SPAF." This army captain—a Seminole Indian, as I recall—bore such a healthy girth that he had to squeeze into that front seat. "SPAF" came from the 219th Aviation Company's nickname, the Sneaky Pete Air Force. Riding Fat SPAF's back seat, I was watching Highway 110 slip past 200 feet below, when we overflew startlingly fresh vehicle tracks. At first we thought these were tank tracks, but flying on we found a site where a bulldozer had repaired the road. By then we were at one of the heaviest bombed spots in southern Laos, "the Falls," where repeated B-52 strikes had vaporized every tree, every twig, and every blade of grass, leaving bright orange, naked hills, pockmarked by overlapping bomb craters. Approximately a half-mile square, it looked like the surface of the moon. And right through the center, curving around those craters, ran Highway 110 and those fresh 'dozer tracks.

After snapping a few photos we saw where the 'dozer had left the road to spend the daytime hours hiding from American aircraft. For the hell of it we decided to follow the tracks and see if we could find the 'dozer. Cruising on the treetops, we banked and turned and banked, losing, then refinding, then again losing the trail. In about ten minutes, sure enough, we came upon a large camouflaged hooch hidden in dense jungle. The tracks dead-ended there. Got him! It was time to radio Covey and get an air strike on it.

Gaining altitude to use the radio, as we reached the height of the surrounding hills—*chug-chug-chug-chug-chug!*—antiaircraft fire! Fiery blobs of 12.7mm arced gracefully at our nose, then—*ZING! ZING! ZING!*—slugs snapped past, right-left, right-left, the nearest not ten feet away. Fat SPAF jerked us right—*chug-chug-chug-chug-chug! Chug-chug-chug-chug-chug!* Two more enemy 12.7s opened fire, filling our sky with intersecting, hostile fireflies. The pilot rolled radically from one line of tracers toward another—*Chug-chug-chug-chug-chug!*—then dived, dropping us so low the guns couldn't touch us. Hugging the trees, we escaped the valley, then called in a USAF Covey. We turned it over to him, marking the hooch with a smoke grenade so he could direct an air strike in hopes of destroying the hidden 'dozer.

Riding back to Kontum, I digested what we'd seen. Here we were bombing the Falls day after day after day, digging up dirt with explosives so the NVA could put it back with their bulldozer. There was no shortage of dirt in Laos. If you really wanted to slow down the enemy, to disrupt his convoys and keep the road closed after a heavy air strike, knock out that bulldozer!

Couldn't a recon team do that? Think of it—a lone recon team could close Highway 110 for weeks, achieving what a 100-man Hatchet Force had done before. Now that was a mission.

And when I proposed it, SOG accepted.

My concept was simple: Under the cover of a heavy strike on the Falls—while enemy soldiers hid in subterranean shelters—two Hueys would slip in, low-level, dropping off RT Hawaii in a couple of hilltop craters. All day we'd stay hidden.

After dark, enemy engineers would arrive to repair the cratered road, accompanied by their bulldozer. Firing an antitank weapon, we'd disable the 'dozer. Then, reinforced with a 60mm mortar and two M-60 machine guns, we'd pin the repair troops in the open and call in a Spectre AC-130 gunship. All night we would repel assaults and extract the following morning, then have fighters finish off the disabled bulldozer. A hell of an operation, I was certain.

Dover, Gmitter, Justice, and I began our preparation by studying how best to disable a 'dozer with an antitank weapon. Checking reference books and speaking to an American engineer, we selected its diesel engine as the most vulnerable point we could hit reliably. Then we test-fired an array of weapons—recoilless rifles, RPGs, and the U.S. M-72 Light Antitank Weapon. Hands down, the RPG-7 won overall for blast effect, accuracy, and range—it would be handy, too, for repelling the human assaults we expected to follow. To confuse the enemy, I developed a night diversion: time-delay star clusters, to make it appear someone was firing bright pyrotechnics some distance from the Falls and draw the enemy away. They worked perfectly.

As we had achieved combat-ready status and completed pre-mission training, our 'dozer mission was about to be scheduled when unexpectedly it was delayed: The Air Force had dropped magnetically detonated Mk-24 antivehicle mines at the Falls to disrupt road repairs and destroy trucks. The mines would not self-destruct for thirty days, preventing us from entering the area for a full month. It was frustrating, especially because, for all we knew, the enemy had found and disposed of the 500-pound mines within one day. All we could do was wait.

That delay proved fortunate.

A couple days after the mines were dropped, a Saigon intelligence NCO confided to me, "You realize, John, even if you kill a 'dozer, they're going to re-place it overnight?"

"That's bullshit," I quipped.

"Oh, no," the intel analyst replied. "They'll replace that bulldozer overnight."

"What?"

"The NVA use a push system for replacing important matériel, like that 'dozer. You knock out a 'dozer at the Falls, and up the road system, maybe ten miles, the next engineer unit sends down their 'dozer to replace it. Next engi-neer unit northward does the same, all the way up the Trail, into North Viet-nam, all the way to Haiphong Harbor. That's where they offload a spanking-new 'dozer, a gift of the Russian people." What a system!—simple, efficient, brilliant.

"Jesus," I responded, "I was ready to risk everybody's lives, get in this in-credible firefight—Sitting Bull and 7,000 Sioux screaming up that hill to come and get us—for a 'dozer they can replace overnight?"

"That is correct. No matter how much we bomb them, they replace lost earthmoving equipment overnight."

The 'dozer mission quietly went away, causing me to appreciate that I was doing exactly what the sagacious Squirrel Sprouse had advised against—almost getting myself run to death. Long ago I'd accepted that I'd meet the Grim Reaper running recon, but I surely didn't have to hasten the encounter. I re-solved to shut up and just take the missions that came my way. For the first time, though, I also understood that Saigon was sitting on considerable intelli-gence and not sharing it with the field. What else weren't we being told?

For several weeks after the scrubbed ambush mission we trained and shot live fire, then, at last, my American teammates and I were called into the Tacti-cal Operations Center, where we were briefed for a recon mission in Laos. Ac-cording to an agent report—apparently a Vietnamese spy recruited by the CIA—a dozen or more Russian-built tanks were hidden in the jungle north of Highway 110, on a ridge above the Dak Sou River. RT Hawaii was to explore that ridge to confirm or deny the information.

There was no firm intelligence on other enemy forces in the area. It was un-usual to encounter trucks or supply dumps or major forces that far north—about four miles—from Highway 110. Still, given the enemy's continuous game of relocating base camps to evade B-52 strikes, the area could have been empty last week and contain 2,000 NVA this week. I always assumed the worst.

Except for a few vegetable gardens nestled in creek bottoms, we saw no sign of any enemy presence as we flew low-level into our LZ. Riding the lead Huey, I went in with Regis Gmitter and three Yards, while Les Dover and John Justice and two Yards followed in a second ship. We landed without ground fire.

For four days we crisscrossed the appointed mile-long ridge. Not only did we discover no tanks, but no trail or road by which tanks could have got there. The CIA's operative had fed them a big one. Our greatest find was artistic rather than military: a four-foot-high ceremonial drum, its carved hardwood surface displaying hundreds of intricately crafted dancing figures. It appeared very old and certainly belonged in a museum. I hoped no bombs ever found it.

Despite the absence of tanks, we could tell troops were nearby. Crossing the ridge's eastern slope we came upon a knee-high, woven fence, with an eight-inch opening every twenty feet to funnel small animals into snares. From one snare hung a huge bullfrog, still wet. We lay near the fence for an hour in hopes of snatching a prisoner as he came down to snatch that frog. Then a gunshot rang out 200 hundred yards behind us—*tracker!* With enemy forces near—I guessed a platoon to have built so elaborate a trapping system—it was time for a bold move. Instead of evading by moving stealthily for hours, I took a calculated risk: We hurried down a water-carved chasm, beneath vertical, twenty-foot walls; a single NVA could have massacred us, but this fast, unhindered route put us on the valley floor in ten minutes flat. That shook off our tracker.

Our mission complete, we found an LZ and were extracted that afternoon with no ground fire.

SOG's intelligence files didn't benefit much from our mission, but, significantly, it told the CIA that their agent was a fraud or a double. Either way, that was worth knowing.

One morning at the end of our stand-down, as I crossed the compound a rumble in the sky drew my eye. I looked up to see four huge CH-53 Sikorsky helicopters escorted by a wide wedge of twelve Cobra gunships and a half-dozen Hueys headed northwest, toward Dak To. All those choppers humming rhythmically made me wish I was up there, with the Hatchet Force's Company B, en route to Laos for SOG's greatest raid. Though I hadn't been formally briefed, I knew by scuttlebutt that Captain Eugene McCarley was leading sixteen Americans and 110 Yards deeper behind enemy lines than had ever been permitted. Their objective was somewhere along the always bustling Highway 165 at the northern extremity of our area of operations, so far away that SOG went to the Marine Corps's HMM 463 Squadron to obtain long-range CH-53s to support them.

I silently wished McCarley and his men well, then reported to the S-3 operations office for a warning order, to learn where RT Hawaii next would deploy.

"You've got Target Alpha-One." The assistant S-3's words churned my stomach. Alpha-One was on Highway 165, perhaps ten miles east of McCarley's Hatchet Force raid. This was the same ominous northern target where, fifteen months earlier, John Allen and I had spotted numerous antiaircraft gun positions, and found almost no terrain that lent itself to concealment or maneuver. Back then, the weather never broke long enough to insert us, causing the S-3 officer to scrub our mission after a week.

"Well," I told myself, "maybe it's better now." I went into the S-2 intelligence shop and studied the Alpha-One target folder, then a USAF stereoscopic photo, shot by an RF-4 reconnaissance jet flying low-level over Highway 165. I eyed it through a magnifying glass. This was bad, very bad, as bad as ever.

"Lots and lots of shit," I warned my One-One, Les Dover, the next morning as we stood beside two O-1 Bird Dogs at Kontum airfield. Momentarily we were airborne, riding the two back seats for a pre-mission aerial recon over Alpha-One.

An hour later, as we neared Highway 165, my pilot suggested, "Let's take a look at how the Hatchet Force is doing." Earlier that morning, a CH-53 carrying two of our medics, John Padgett and John Browne, had extracted several seriously wounded Yards. As the big Sikorsky lumbered away, intense machine gun fire and one RPG struck it, compelling the pilot to crash-land nearby. Amazingly, everyone aboard survived and made it into a second Sikorsky. As it lifted away, more antiaircraft fire filled the sky, downing that chopper, too, again without killing anyone. Then a third chopper arrived, and everyone made it safely away.

Our O-1s slowly circled the second disabled CH-53, deep in a gully along a creek. Already fighters had bombed the first downed chopper, and soon would destroy this second bird. About five miles away, a USAF FAC plane carrying a Covey Rider—Master Sergeant Bill "Country" Grimes—overflew Captain McCarley's Hatchet Force, bringing in continuous air strikes to support them. By monitoring the radio we could hear that it was a real hornet's nest down there.

Knowing that patch of sky was too busy for gawkers, our O-1s turned east, and soon we flew above Alpha-One and the southeast spur off Highway 165. Last year's 37mm antiaircraft gun positions were no longer visible. Had they been reoccupied and camouflaged, or had the jungle simply overgrown the gun pits? I couldn't tell. Other enemy sign abounded—especially foot trails and vegetable fields.

The road's condition told me much. Though hundreds of craters pockmarked the valley floor, the highway was open, perfectly maintained, and bore fresh tracks. I calculated that the workforce it took to keep that road open—not to mention security troops and antiaircraft crews—had to number in the thousands.

The terrain had not changed, either, offering us little advantage: For a half-mile either side of the road, there was only knee-high stubble and elephant grass, and above that, thinly jungled hills. Where could we go, where could we hide?

When we returned to Kontum airfield, I climbed from my O-1 and saw Dover shaking his head. He'd seen the same signs. "I know, boss. There's one hell of a lot of NVA up there." That was half the equation. The other half was that Captain McCarley's Hatchet Force would be extracted before we went in, so there wouldn't be another SOG element within thirty miles, nothing to draw the enemy or occupy his forces. All those troops operating and defending Highway 165 would have just one team to contend with, one team to concentrate against, RT Hawaii.

Two days later, as expected, the Hatchet Force was extracted after achieving a total, stunning success. Fighting westward along Highway 165, they'd overrun a major NVA headquarters and captured the most important documents ever to come out of the Ho Chi Minh Trail. Though suffering forty-nine wounded—with all sixteen Americans hit—and three Yards killed, they had inflicted five times as many casualties on the NVA. Their mission, code-named Operation Tailwind, had created such disruption in NVA rear areas that the enemy was compelled to bring in troops from deeper in Laos, allowing a CIA-trained force to recapture two critical airfields. This diversion was their ultimate mission.

During our aerial recon, Dover and I had noted many open spaces in Alpha-One large enough to land a chopper, but not one good place to land. Every LZ seemed too big, too close to the road, or too exposed to nearby hilltops. I decided to place our fate in the hands of our Covey Rider, Country Grimes. "You pick the LZ, Country," I told him the night before we were to insert. "We'll insert anywhere you say."

An old hand and highly respected, Country Grimes was on his second SOG tour, having previously served in recon and the Hatchet Force. On a 1967 mission in Laos, Grimes had led a platoon that captured one of the war's largest caches, some 250 tons of rice, enough to feed an entire NVA division for six weeks. I trusted his experience and his wisdom.

Country Grimes shared my concern about sending us so far north, especially with helicopters based forty-five miles away at Dak To. "John, I don't know why the fuck we're trying this with this nasty fucking weather. You're liable to get rained in up there." Further, he said, he didn't like having my team so far away, what with all the other teams down around Highway 110. Much of the day no aircraft would be close enough to hear us if we called on the radio.

The following day RT Hawaii flew to Dak To and stood by there all day to insert. Heavy overcast and rain precluded inserting.

The next morning was much the same. But late that second afternoon, the launch officer stuck his head from the radio shack and called, "Weather's a go, Covey has an LZ. Launch."

Because the H-34 helicopter offered longer station time and quicker descent than a Huey, we would insert by a Vietnamese-flown Kingbee. Our smiling pilot waved from the cockpit as all eight of us climbed aboard. Taking off, I rode in the open doorway, the Vietnamese door gunner beside me. Les Dover sat in a canvas seat next to me, with Gmitter, Justice, and the rest of the team arrayed deeper in the Kingbee.

The Cobras led our formation past Ben Het, then fifteen miles later, past Dak Seang, then another twenty miles and barely visible beyond a ridge to our east, I saw Dak Pek. There went my stomach again. I knew I'd feel better once we got on the ground. I smiled to Dover, then gave a thumbs-up to the Yards, who grinned back. Ahead I saw that long, familiar valley take shape, and I knew we were crossing over into Laos. Way off in the distant haze I could make out a thin brown line, which I knew was the southern spur off Highway 165.

As we began orbiting, I psyched myself for the mission. I knew my anxiety and fear would be gone as quick as my feet touched the ground. Let's just be done with it, I told myself.

Centered inside the Cobra's racetrack pattern I saw an immense slash-and-burn area—big as ten football fields—the best LZ Country Grimes could find, given even worse alternatives. To reduce our exposure to antiaircraft fire the Kingbee pilot put us in a radical, nose-down, spiral descent almost to the tree-tops.

As we leveled off, I eased out on the Kingbee's steel steps. A fresh, wide trail came into view, betrayed by slanting afternoon sunlight. *Damn, that's not good.* We passed it, I swung my CAR-15 back and forth, leaning out as the helicopter neared a wood line—just fifty feet to go—I'm out, fanning my CAR-15—*crack! crack! crack!* Were the blades striking bamboo? SMACK!—a slug hit our chopper—SMACK!—another barely missed the pilot's head. In the wood line, a muzzle flash. Instantly I shot!—*brrrt! brrrt! brrrt!*—the door gunner opened up—*bo-bo-bo-bo-bo-boom!* Focused on shooting, I ignored the chopper's wild tipping and banking—*brrrt! brrrt!*—out the door I slid as we banked 45 degrees—*Oh, shit!*—Les Dover seized my web gear and, thank God, held me aboard. *Bo-bo-bo-bo-boom!* The H-34 pivoted and climbed, its blades slapping for air, pulling us away from tracers that flashed erratically toward us while Les pulled me back into the aircraft. Then—*KA-BOOM!*—a tremendous midair explosion. The door gunner crumpled back, hit by shrapnel off an antiaircraft round. Then the Cobras raced beneath us, rippling the area with rockets and miniguns and the enemy gunners forgot about us.

Dover and I tore open the door gunner's coverall and put a pressure bandage on his back; he'd be all right. During the long ride back to Dak To, it was hard not to think that had the NVA waited ten more seconds, we'd never have gotten out of there.

Later, after we unloaded at Dak To, the Kingbee pilot showed us where one round had come through the canopy and hit the cushion behind his head—had he not been leaning over, looking out the side window, it would have killed him.

It was too late to attempt another insert that day, so we refueled and flew back to Kontum.

The S-3 officer gave us a one-day break. I had us practice immediate action drills just to keep us fresh and focused, then let everyone rest for the day. In the club that night, Country Grimes suggested, "Plasticman, why don't you just tell that dumb fucking S-3 to do it himself." He didn't think we should put anyone into that target.

"I can't wimp out on a mission, Country. I just can't."

"Are you scared?"

"Fuck yes. It's getting pretty damned hard to go to Dak To, over and over."

But we did go again, the next day. And the next. The weather wouldn't break. I thought back to John Allen and RT Illinois, how bad the stress had become waiting to go into Alpha-One the previous summer. And I thought about sucker holes and my mission with Fat Albert and Bill Spencer. Two days after we landed, the sky had closed and we were stuck there for eleven days with no possibility of air support or extraction. Had that target been Alpha-One, I had no doubt we would have been hunted down and killed.

With each flight to Dak To the psychological pressure grew. Day after day we sat at the launch site, camouflaged, hydrated, ready to go, and all day I thought about that long, dangerous valley.

After three more days, finally the S-3 announced one last day and he'd scrub the idea of sending our team up north. Most of that day Covey was preoccupied in the southern area, supporting teams along Highway 110. Finally, late that afternoon, Country Grimes asked the launch officer to leave the radio shack and put me on the radio. We switched frequencies so the S-3 at Kontum could not hear our exchange. "Plasticman," Grimes radioed, "this area sucks. Weather is doable, but barely. You sure you *really* want to go in there?"

I looked outside to my teammates sitting by the airstrip, loaded up, ready for bear. I glanced up at the map where our target lay, thought of the poor reaction time, the inhospitable terrain, the likelihood of getting rained in, and how narrowly we'd escaped our first insertion attempt.

A moment later I went outside and the launch officer returned. Grimes radioed, then the launch officer announced, "Looks like the weather's closed in. Target Alpha-One's been scratched."

Given a couple of days off, I was lying on my cot a few days later when a runner knocked on the door and hollered, "All One-Zeros to the orderly room, pronto!" I joined Captain Fred Krupa and a half-dozen men who'd already gathered with our new first sergeant, Henry Gainous. RT Illinois One-Zero Steve Keever whispered to me, "Fat Albert is missing."

What!

Another One-Zero asked Gainous, "What about John Baker and Mike Brown?"

"The rest of RT South Carolina is out, at Dak To," Gainous replied. "Covey tried to put in the Bright Light team. They were driven off by ground fire. That's why I need you folks."

The CCC commander had decided not even to attempt another Bright Light rescue unless there was some sign that Pete Wilson was alive and evading. In that event, a platoon from the Hatchet Force's Company A—now commanded by my old Ashtray Two teammate, Captain Krupa—would go in after Fat Albert. Beginning the next morning, Gainous announced, O-1 Bird Dogs would fly dawn to dusk over the area, and he wanted One-Zero volunteers to ride the back seats.

Every One-Zero volunteered.

That evening we learned disturbing details about what had happened to RT South Carolina.

While taking a break at 1115 that morning, the team interpreter, Klung, saw movement and opened fire, bringing on such heavy return fire that Fat Albert believed they'd been hit by a platoon or even a company. They shot their way clear and started running.

Baker reported bitterly that they'd tried to call Covey repeatedly—both on the team radio and on emergency radios—but no one responded. For hours they evaded, made contact, shot their way clear and ran, over and over. *No Covey was there!* Finally, during their fourth contact, one Yard, Djuit, was hit badly in the ankle, slowing down the team. The overweight Fat Albert, ex-hausted after half dragging, half carrying the wounded man, ordered Baker to lead the others to safety while he hung back with Djuit. "If we're split," Wilson ordered, "keep heading east." Baker dutifully led away the rest and minutes later paused in hopes that Wilson and the wounded Yard would catch up. Mo-mentarily they heard a heavy exchange of fire, then Baker heard Fat Albert's desperate voice on his emergency radio calling, "Mayday! Mayday!"

There was more fire. Then no fire.

Fifteen minutes later, Baker and Brown heard Vietnamese voices and the sound of people chopping bamboo—most of us concluded the NVA had rigged a stretcher to transport the immobilized Yard and Fat Albert. Baker at-tempted to radio Wilson but a foreign voice responded, presumably using Fat Albert's captured radio.

After Baker and the survivors were extracted, the Bright Light team and medic Carl Franquet attempted to insert on the same LZ, but heavy ground fire drove away their chopper.

Why the hell wasn't Covey out there? That was the question.

I learned the answer later, from Covey Rider Larry White. That morning, another Covey Rider, Ken "Shoebox" Carpenter, was supposed to be above RT South Carolina, but a senior CCC officer had commandeered his plane for a "familiarization flight" over Laos, leaving our teams exposed, without commu-nications or air support. White seethed, "That dumb motherfucker was out sightseeing." Several recon men were so angry that they wanted to kill the offi-cer, already renowned for his ignorance, incompetence, and obliviousness, but cooler heads controlled them.

Beginning the next morning, a host of One-Zeros—among them Steve Keever, Newman Ruff, Pat Mitchel, and myself—flew shifts aboard a pair of O-1s over the valley where Fat Albert had disappeared, listening for radio sig-nals and watching for smoke or even a waving hand.

The rest of that week we took turns flying that nondescript valley, dawn to dusk, watching and listening and hoping. No one heard or saw a thing.

I flew the last sad shift, on the last day, staying out there until the sun cast long shadows across the valley floor and we knew hope was pretty well gone. Finally, heading back for Vietnam we crossed northeast Cambodia and I looked down on those rolling hills and thought back to the day when it had been Fat Albert in the back seat of an O-1, shooting up the NVA that threatened my team. It had been Fat Albert who named me Plasticman. I smiled, recalling how Bill Spencer and I had plied Pete with liquor to recruit him, and when we got immersion foot, how we'd danced in Nha Trang, swinging our crutches. They were both gone now. As we crossed into South Vietnam it finally hit me that my good friend, my teammate, Peter J. Wilson, had been swallowed whole, forever, by the verdant black hole of Southeast Asia. I wept.

Missions continued, the war continued.

A few days after we lost Fat Albert, RT Hawaii again was at Dak To, ready to insert into another target, this time into the same area as my first mission with RT Illinois, when we'd called an air strike on NVA constructing a base camp. Again our operation was driven by a CIA operative's report, a claim that the NVA had built a major trail out of Laos, northwest of Dak Seang Special Forces Camp. Further, the agent said, the NVA were transporting supplies on it using elephants as beasts of burden. RT Hawaii's mission was to find the trail and to mine it. For this I packed a tin can with a pound of plastic explosive to place beneath an M-14 mine, boosting it from anti-personnel to anti-elephant.

Our insertion began routinely enough. After loading aboard two Hueys at Dak To, we flew northwest and passed through a rain squall to little effect except that my boots now dripped with water. Shortly after we passed Dak Seang a big green hillside shone reflectively from the fresh rain. Straddling the border, its elephant grass–covered eastern slope was our LZ.

As my Huey descended I raised my CAR-15 to my shoulder, exactly as Gmitter was doing in the other doorway. Then, nearing the LZ, our Huey turned sideways to nestle against the slope and went into a hover.

We just hovered there, some fifteen feet over the elephant grass, too high to jump without likely leg and ankle injuries. There was plenty of clearance between the main rotor and the hillside so I signaled the crew chief with my hand, "Go lower." He spoke into his microphone, then shook his head—the pilot wouldn't go lower. *Damn, must be new.* There was no time to waste. I gestured to Gmitter to unsnap and extend the aluminum ladders. In the few seconds that took, the pilot, instead of holding at his original fifteen-foot hover, rose to the full length of the ladders—equal to the height of a three-story building. Weighted down with the radio operator's rucksack, I had to shift my body and swing my legs around, then lower my right foot to the first rung below the skid. Hovering imperfectly, the Huey shifted as I put my weight on the first rung—my wet boot slid off.

Ahhhhh!

I lay sprawled on my back, my rucksack beneath me. Upon impact, my head had snapped back and my spine hyperextended concavely across the rucksack.

I scrambled to the woods a few yards away, shaking my head to try to clear stars and gray blobs. A camouflaged face materialized before my own and asked, "Boss—you all right?"

"I know you," I replied to Dover but couldn't quite place him. "Who are you?" I demanded.

"Hey," he replied, "you kidding me?"

Where the hell was I? Heavy greenery everywhere. And armed men. Lots of noise—helicopters? Something dangerous, I sensed, and instinctively drew a pistol that I didn't even know I had. Twenty feet away my CAR-15 lay in the dirt where I'd unthinkingly abandoned it. Someone recovered it.

A man relieved me of the heavy rucksack, taking control of the radio. I was happy to be rid of it. All I wanted to do was sit down and try to make my head stop pounding.

In a minute another helicopter was overhead. "We're extracting," the camouflaged man told me and led me to the hovering bird. I climbed aboard, along with several little brown men I believed to be friendly despite their dirty faces and weapons. As we flew, pain pulsed and throbbed, pounding my brain until tears formed in my eyes. I held my head with both hands, trying to squeeze out the beast gnawing the inside of my skull.

We landed someplace, our blades buffeting red dust. A clean-faced man met us. I could tell he knew me, and somehow, I thought I knew him. He held my shoulders and demanded, "Who am I?"

What a silly question! "You're—*I know you!* You're . . ." I tried and tried but couldn't get past forming his name on my tongue.

"It's me," he insisted, "Jim Storter!" I tried to say it, but each time his name wisped away, like the memory of a forgotten dream by midday. Grasping for anything, I blurted out my Social Security number but couldn't get beyond half the digits. I saw other men I must have known but could not recall their names. I kept trying, testing, forcing myself. *Dammit, I could not remember!*

Then pain spasmed my back and I had to sit down.

At some point I noticed I was aboard a helicopter, and after that, people with medical uniforms talked to me. Pain throbbed and throbbed but it was worse losing my memory, lying in a hospital ward not knowing who I was, or where I was, or why I was there. That day and the two that followed forever remain a blur; my medical file records X-rays and cranial tests. The doctors diagnosed temporary amnesia, a brain concussion, and back injuries from spinal hyperextension. A sympathetic nurse eventually assured me that this was Pleiku, the 71st Evacuation Hospital. She said my name a few times and as it began to make sense, the amnesia began to wear off. Somehow I got back to

Kontum, though I cannot remember that trip. Paradoxically, I wondered, how would I ever know whether my memory was completely restored?

Just one day after returning to CCC, I was with my team, back at Dak To awaiting insertion into the same target. I'd actually expected a couple of days rest, at least until my back felt better, but a disingenuous S-3 officer—who'd never been on a recon mission himself—offered, "You don't have to go if you didn't want to." The alternative, he said, was to send my team without me. Les Dover was willing to lead the team, and I'm sure he'd have done an admirable job, but I was the One-Zero who started that mission, and I was determined to be the one who finished it. I would rather have died than quit my team, and the S-3 officer knew it.

So four days after falling thirty-four feet from one Huey, I was in another Huey doorway, looking down on the Cobras in a racetrack pattern and descending into an LZ just inside Laos. This time we settled at a low-hover, jumping about five feet to the ground.

It took two days of steady, stealthy movement to reach our objective, the valley bottom where, this time, this agent was correct. We found a major trail exactly where the agent told his CIA handler it would be. Wide, smooth, and flat, and large enough to accommodate jeeps, it was plenty big for the elephants he'd reported.

I photographed it, then it was time to mine it. First, I sent Dover and Justice, each with two Yards, up and down the path as security. Then, with Gmitter covering me, I knelt and removed my hat, laying it on the trail. I used my banana-shaped machete to scrape aside light-colored surface soil. That done, I dug into the darker subsurface dirt just enough to hold the beer-can-size mine, carefully placing every bit of excess soil in my hat. Next I readied a thumb-size, self-destruct blasting cap, cracking an acid ampule to activate it. In the current ambient temperature, it would take about five days for the acid to dissolve a copper wire inside the cap, harmlessly detonating the mine—if an elephant or NVA didn't set it off first. Arming the mine, I delicately placed it atop the self-destruct cap, then covered both with the lighter surface soil, blowing it smooth to match the similarly colored trail surface. From any direction, I confirmed, it would be visually impossible to detect the mine. Standing, I tossed the excess soil into the jungle and signaled the team to re-form. Hardly three minutes had passed. We had not spoken one word.

Then we were off, crossing the trail and climbing the next jungle hill.

That evening at dusk as we sat in our overnight position spooning down rice—B-O-O-O-M!—the mine exploded, its blast reverberating among the hills and setting birds to flight. For a second we looked to each other, then went back to eating, neither celebrating nor regretting, perhaps privately contemplating, "Thank God that wasn't me."

Another two days and we were out. We could tell our debriefer that we discovered no enemy encampments, but clearly the NVA had been transiting the area and carrying supplies into South Vietnam. And this CIA source was the real thing.

Two weeks later RT Hawaii had a short-notice mission, just one day's warning before we inserted aboard a resupply helicopter into Company B of the Hatchet Force. Captain McCarley's men, who'd so dramatically fought along Highway 165 six weeks earlier, had been walking the Laotian border northwest of Ben Het Special Forces Camp, sweeping for any sign of the enemy. They'd not made any contact, but they thought an enemy element of unknown size had been shadowing them. Company B was to extract in one day, and we would secretly stay behind in hopes of ambushing the shadowers.

That one day with Company B confirmed forever my desire not to serve on the Hatchet Force. They actually talked—*talked in a normal voice*—during an operation. Speaking above a whisper set my heart palpitating and boosted my respiration. Even worse, they actually lit cooking fires. That scared the hell out of me. Don't you know that smell will carry with the wind, I wanted to scream. Eventually Captain McCarley calmed me and the rest of RT Hawaii.

When the choppers began extracting Company B the next morning, Dover, Gmitter, Justice, and I sang them adieu with the Roy Rogers and Dale Evans theme song, "Happy Trails to You." We weren't whispering, either. But twenty minutes later the sound of noisy choppers and planes had abated, so we reverted to stealth and silence, hiding near the LZ in hopes of ambushing some shadowing NVA. None showed up.

We hung in that area most of the day, and over the next four days walked the north–south ridge that demarcated the Vietnam-Laos border. Our march revealed no useful intelligence—only the negative fact that no NVA were there. It was only the second time in two years running recon that I'd found no sign of an enemy presence in a target.

Tired, my back aching, as our chopper descended onto the CCC helipad I looked forward to a cold beer, then a hot shower—but I never expected what I saw beside our Huey. There, standing with Recon First Sergeant Gainous as he handed out cold beers, was Bob Howard. When our eyes met, Howard flashed his trademark squint and "aw shucks" grin. We gripped hands. "Well my eyes ain't playin' tricks," Howard said, "it's really you. John, I can't believe you're still here."

Instead of a cold beer Howard offered me a fifth of Jack Daniel's. I chugged on it and handed it back. I'd never tasted better spring water. And I was never happier. The whiskey was OK, but seeing Bob Howard, damn, that was spectacular. I introduced him to Dover and Justice and Gmitter.

Then I noticed his sergeant's stripes were gone, replaced by a first lieutenant's bar on his collar, a direct commission. I stood at attention and saluted him, I was so proud of him. Howard returned my salute though later he confessed he was embarrassed to be a shavetail lieutenant and could hardly wait to make captain. He was in a captain's slot—as our new recon company commander—but he'd never be allowed to go along on another mission. His Medal of Honor had been approved; he was just waiting for the ceremony with President Nixon, sometime in the next four or five months. He didn't like that price of glory—no more combat—but he'd decided at least he could spend those months back here with us at Kontum.

He walked with us from the helipad. I told him about finding the trail and planting the mine. He asked, "John, how many missions have you run?" I couldn't say, hadn't kept count. Eventually, it was tallied: I'd been on twenty-two missions behind enemy lines in Laos or Cambodia, leading four different teams, plus another seven or eight short operations inside South Vietnam.

That night I spent a half-hour in the shower, letting the hot water massage my back while I chugged down two beers. Life was good.

A few days later I was walking across the compound on stand-down when I encountered Larry White, the former RT Hawaii One-Zero, now a Covey Rider.

He smiled. "Well, there, Plasticman—you know folks have been talkin' about you."

"Really, Larry? About what?"

"All that time you've got running recon. Isn't it time you joined us?"

I wasn't sure what he meant.

He put a hand on my shoulder. "We think you should be a Covey Rider."

PART THREE

Covey

Chapter Thirteen

Sitting beside me in a jeep at Kontum airfield, Larry White yawned and stretched. Though in late November 1970, Larry already was an old hand flying Covey, this was all new to me, from my unmarked gray flight suit to my bulky survival vest and shiny new aviator's helmet. Today would be my first flight.

An OV-10 Bronco buzzed past, then landed and taxied toward us. It arrived bigger than I had imagined, a beautiful gray bird with a twin-boom tail reminiscent of the World War II P-38 Lightning. This plane even felt like a fighter. The pilot, a young Air Force captain, shut down the right engine, then Larry flipped down a booster step so I could climb into the empty back seat.

Lowering myself into that slim cockpit I felt like I was climbing into a pen to mount a bull. From the booster step Larry helped me snap into the ejection seat harness, then pointed between my legs to a yellow and black, fist-size ring behind the control stick. "If you've gotta punch out," he hollered over the noisy left engine, "pull this." I nodded. He shut the plexiglass canopy, stepped away, gave me a thumbs-up, and the pilot restarted the right engine.

My head swam with earphone chatter from five conversations; somewhere in that din my mind heard the pilot's intercom voice say, "Hi, my name's Corky." I couldn't shake his hand; the console between us was jammed with instruments, but I noticed his eyes in a small mirror over his head.

I nodded. "I'm Plasticman."

Momentarily he revved the engines on the runway, released the brakes, and off we rolled, a smooth, powerful acceleration, then an effortless climb into the sky. My seat put me forward of the engines with the bubble-shaped canopy extending to my waist providing an unhindered view of Kontum as it slipped quickly behind us.

Examining the console, I beheld a bewildering cluster of instruments, gauges and switches, and radios—*radios upon radios.* As we sped toward Ben Het—faster than I'd ever made that journey—I pushed the intercom button and asked, "How do I monitor six radios?"

"Memorizing call signs helps," he offered, "but I listen to the voices. Somebody whispers—that's a recon team, they're on FM-1. We talk to choppers on UHF; vibrations shake the pilot's voice so he sounds quivery, like Johnny Cash—'This-s-s is-s-s Wh-i-i-i-te Le-e-e-ad.' Fighter pilots wear oxygen masks—boosts their voices a couple octaves. Sound like they're talking with their noses pinched. They'll be on VHF. I usually handle them myself."

Corky wondered how well I could handle Gs, and inverted flight. Before I could speculate we were flying upside down, then dipped into a steep dive and a body-crushing multi-G turn, so hard I saw gray when the blood rushed from my brain. "If you feel like you're graying out," he advised, "flex your stomach muscles to push blood into your head." That helped and I could see again, though his dives, ascents, and rolls tested my stomach to its limits. I didn't puke but the world spun long after we'd leveled off.

"You'll be OK," Corky decided as we crossed into Laos.

Within the hour we had our first emergency. "Covey! Covey!" RT Texas One-Two Don Green's voice cried, gunfire in the background. "Contact! Contact!" As we sped toward them, One-Zero John Good executed an effective immediate action drill, broke contact, and got them running with One-One Lynn Moss defending their backtrail. They'd suffered no wounded, though Green reported they were being pursued by an estimated forty-man platoon.

Only a few months earlier the OV-10 had arrived in Vietnam, revolutionizing support for our teams; unlike previous FAC aircraft, the OV-10 was armed with four M-60 machine guns and four rocket pods, two of them loaded with high-explosive rounds. Arriving over RT Texas, I had them wave an orange panel, then we made gun runs behind them to slow their pursuers. "Nearest LZ is 300 meters, due east," I radioed the team. "Head 90 degrees."

While they headed east, Corky radioed Hillsborough, the USAF airborne control C-130 that orbited over central Laos, and got a pair of fighters diverted from another strike. "We'll have no time to waste," Corky announced. "The fighters have only ten minutes' station time."

I alerted our choppers at Dak To, estimating I'd call for a launch in fifteen minutes.

Five minutes later a high-pitched voice chirped on VHF, "Covey 533, this is Gunfighter 34." Corky asked, "Plasticman, get this for me." I pulled a grease pencil and jotted data on the plexiglass canopy. Fighter lead continued, "This is Mission Two-Three-Three-Six. Gunfighter Three-Four is a pair of Fox-Fours, wall-to-wall snake and nape."

Corky asked, "Any 20mm?"

"Lead has a pod, 1,000 rounds, 20mm."

Momentarily we spotted the F-4s high overhead. Corky rocked our wings until they saw us. As the Phantoms descended he briefed the situation, identified the target, warned of antiaircraft guns in the area, and recommended emergency bailout at Ben Het Special Forces Camp, twenty-five miles to our southeast. "Let's start with 20mm strafing runs, north to south," he finished. "I will mark the target with a rocket, then orbit south."

After RT Texas waved an orange panel, we dived and fired a white phosphorus rocket 100 yards on their backtrail, then wiggled our wings. "If you have me, and have my smoke," Corky told the fighters, "you're cleared, hot."

"Roger Covey, got you," the F-4 pilot announced. "Gunfighter lead is hot." The camouflage-painted Phantom raced beneath us, spewing his six-barreled Vulcan cannon across RT Texas's backtrail, then kicked in the afterburner to outrun any antiaircraft fire. His aim was perfect.

"Shit-hot!" Corky called. "Number two, napalm, same spot."

While the strike occupied their pursuers, I monitored the team's movement—they were taking forever to travel 300 meters. The choppers were ready to launch but I dared not bring them out too soon or they'd run out of station time before we could extract the team.

Corky had to do something with the Phantoms' 500-pound bombs—too powerful to be dropped near the team. He had them bomb a hillside overlooking the prospective LZ, their shock waves rippling through the foliage, blasting away whatever was hidden beneath the trees. As the F-4s finished, a pair of A-1s arrived from Thailand.

RT Texas was hardly halfway to their LZ. The problem, I realized, was my estimate: Instead of 300 meters, the distance turned out to be 800 because I had not grasped the subtleties of terrain that can fool your eye flying at 3,000 feet. Instead of getting there in fifteen minutes it took them almost an hour. Still, though, I'd correctly gauged their pace and got the helicopters launched to arrive just after the team got there.

When all those aircraft arrived—four Cobra gunships, six Hueys, five Kingbees, and two A-1s—I faced an intense ten minutes. Everything happened simultaneously at warp speed—radio messages, decisions, actions by the team, the Hueys, the Cobras, the fighters—each with his own call sign—all while Corky was directing the A-1s and dodging ground fire. There was no time to slow down or sort anything out or ask questions. At last, I saw the dull green Cobras and Hueys on the treetops, invisible but for the spinning circles of their white and yellow main rotors. Despite enemy ground fire, we got RT Texas out safely. I was drenched in sweat.

I flew away resolved to develop an eye for perspective. That afternoon I looked down at two streams in a valley and estimated they were 300 meters apart, then checked my map to gauge my accuracy. I repeated that exercise for several days until, whether flying at 2,000 or 5,000 feet, I could look at any kind of terrain, and say, "That's 300 meters," and it *was* 300 meters. There was much to learn those first few weeks.

Flying was tough enough, but my toughest early challenge was back at Kontum dealing with my three Covey Rider roommates. Larry White, Ken Carpenter, and Lowell Wesley Stevens had pooled their money for a stereo component system and let me know my music would never make it on their tape deck. "You'll learn to love country music," Lowell Stevens promised, convinced this was for my own good. "Dammit," he insisted, "country's genuinely American and entirely understandable. Why, every country song's about cryin' or dyin' or goin' someplace." Larry White and Ken Carpenter just grinned. At least we had Glen Campbell in common—but Waylon Jennings, Merle Haggard, Charley Pride? Eventually Lowell proved right and somehow I got to singing along with Bill Anderson, even Hank Williams, Jr., God help me.

Despite our differing musical tastes, however, I had nothing but respect for these superb Special Forces NCOs, each with a distinguished combat record. Sergeant First Class Ken "Shoebox" Carpenter had served a previous SOG tour, 1967–68, running recon with Stevens, then came back in 1970, initially to the Hatchet Force. Back in June, Ken had been platoon sergeant when his platoon leader, First Lieutenant Mark Rivest, was killed in a surprise attack. Ken took command, called in air strikes danger-close, then got them out without further losses. Sporting a flattop haircut as thick as a brush, Ken had a dry sense of humor that took time to appreciate. For instance, Ken once took out a local training patrol to acquaint new men with recon. Eyeing it like some great find, Carpenter grabbed a handful of elephant dung and handed it to the new guy behind him, whispering, "Elephant shit. Pass it back." The new guy beheld it like the Holy Grail, relayed it to the following man, and each of the new guys passed it back, repeating Carpenter's words. Ken forgot about it until days later when, back from the field, the tail gunner came to him, presented the elephant turd, and asked, "Sergeant, should I take this to the intel officer?" You just know Kenny said, "Right away, dammit!"

Carpenter's old recon buddy, Sergeant First Class Lowell Wesley "Round-eye" Stevens, was on his fourth Vietnam tour, all in Special Forces. Back in '64 he'd served on an A-Camp, then come back to run recon in SOG, 1967–68, and, in his words, "took a break" by leading a Mike Force Company of Montagnards, 1969–70. A streak of silver accented Stevens's dark hair, and within five minutes of meeting him, if you didn't realize he was from West Virginia, he'd tell you. Raised in a coal mining family that esteemed self-reliance, Lowell was a quick study, self-taught, and, reflecting Appalachian tradition, one of the most gifted storytellers I ever met. He found inspiration in the bedrock of humble patriotism and memorized the words of great Americans. "Make sure you're right, then go ahead," he'd recite, one of the principles he lived by. "Davy Crockett." Though he shunned personal recognition, Stevens had been awarded three Silver Stars, six Bronze Stars, and several Purple Hearts.

I'd already known my third roommate, Sergeant First Class Larry "Six-Pack" White, for some time, having inherited RT Hawaii from him. What I didn't know was that President Eisenhower had recruited Larry to the paratroops. In 1957 Eisenhower had sent in the 101st Airborne Division to escort African-American students into Larry's newly integrated Central High School in Little Rock, Arkansas. Larry didn't pay much attention to the politics, but he sure noticed those tough paratroopers and their spit-shined jump boots. A couple years later, he was spit-shining his own jump boots in the 101st, after which he volunteered for Special Forces.

Like Carpenter and Stevens, White had done an earlier tour in SOG recon, cut short by three AK slugs that almost killed him. By the time he began flying Covey, Larry's awards included three Bronze Stars, two Air Medals for Valor, and the Purple Heart. A fatalist like all of us, Larry knew all the angles and played them cagily. When he flew Covey, he carried a pair of major's leaves in his pocket, to pin on if he was shot down, believing the NVA would less likely kill a field grade officer. As well, though, his standing reward for the Bright Light rescue team that brought him back (preferably alive) was the gold Rolex wristwatch that he left locked in a safe.

Larry appreciated the subtleties of flying Covey, and taught me how to talk to a team in contact. "You'll hear that guy screaming, 'Prairie Fire! Oh, my God!' " White explained. "First thing, calm him down, be that reassuring Great Father in the Sky voice." Larry had me practice lowering my voice an octave and speaking slower. "Your goal is to instill calm and reasonable thinking in a man who's got every right to be excited. If you're up there unable to control yourself, there's no use having you ride Covey, no matter how much you know about tactics or aircraft or anything else." He was absolutely right.

All of us preferred flying Covey in the OV-10, but due to a shortage of aircraft, one third of the time we flew aboard the O-2, a militarized version of the twin-engine civilian Cessna Skymaster. If the OV-10 was the Ferrari of the FAC world, the O-2 was the Ford, a practical, economical plane that functioned adequately in its role. In the smaller O-2, the Covey Rider sat to the pilot's right, sharing instruments and gauges though he had his own steering yoke. The O-2 flew slower, its wings could not tolerate as many Gs, and it lacked ejection seats, requiring both men to wear bulky parachutes. Its biggest shortcomings were a lack of armament and that side-by-side seating arrangement: When the pilot banked left to look at the ground, the Covey Rider was looking to the sky, and vice versa, a problem not encountered with tandem seating in the OV-10.

The next lesson I learned as a Covey Rider was how to pick an LZ. We were in southern Laos and my eyes followed a stream that crossed Highway 110, then meandered southeast among low hills that could mask the choppers from antiaircraft guns. I knew the kind of LZ I needed—not too big, at least one ridge beyond the highway system, plenty of jungle for the team to disappear into, no visible sign of the NVA. That's what RT Ohio One-Zero Jim Fry had requested.

I spotted it—a patch of elephant grass just big enough to land a Huey. It would be easy to find because a nearby bomb crater contained strikingly green water. An hour later I sat back at Kontum with Covey Rider Ken Carpenter and unfolded my map, announcing, "Got a perfect LZ in Hotel-Six [the name we'd given this target zone], a nice grassy spot by that stream—"

He interrupted, "A hundred meters west of that bomb crater with the green water."

My jaw dropped. How the hell did he know?

"After a while, enough flyin', you'll get to know southern Laos like you did your neighborhood when you were a kid." He poured me a cup of coffee. "Problem is, John, your LZ is too good—we've used it a half-dozen times, so the enemy has to have it pegged. Look at the hills east or west, where a bomb has scraped away some jungle, just big enough for a short ladder LZ."

"But the pilots don't like using hillside LZs," I said.

Carpenter smiled. "They always like an LZ where nobody's shootin' at 'em."

A few days later we lost the first recon man since I'd begun flying. The afternoon of 28 November, Lowell Stevens flew over RT Kentucky, a mile south of Highway 110, to learn the five-man team had barely fought off a company-size NVA attack. Sergeant First Class Ronald E. Smith, the One-One, had been killed, and his team leader had been hit by RPG fragments and knocked unconscious. The Yards pushed back the NVA long enough to carry away their One-Zero, but had to leave behind Smith's body. Stevens brought A-1s and Cobras danger-close around the team and, in waning daylight, called in White Lead, a Huey flown by Warrant Officer Mark Feinberg, of the 170th Assault Helicopter Company.

Despite intense ground fire, Feinberg trolled the treetops, looking for the besieged RT Kentucky men but could not find them in the dense foliage. Hearing his chopper, many NVA soldiers peppered the sky with AK and machine gun fire, engulfing Feinberg's Huey with tracers. He was compelled to pull out while Stevens hit the area again with gunships and A-1s, placing fire within fifty yards of RT Kentucky. The team reported they were encircled, they had just one smoke grenade left, with two men seriously wounded.

Realizing that the team faced annihilation, Feinberg had them pop the smoke grenade and went back in. Oblivious to the heavy enemy fire, he hovered at the treetops until he spotted a wisp of smoke, then shifted above the men and held the Huey steady while the four snapped into extraction harnesses. As Feinberg's chopper lifted them above the trees, enemy fire erupted anew. Several rounds slammed into his Huey, including a 12.7mm slug that struck the transmission. Feinberg nursed his crippled bird back across the border, and by the time he gently lowered the men to a hilltop near Ben Het, his oil pressure gauge read zero.

Ron Smith had been lost, but the others had been saved, largely due to Warrant Officer Feinberg. For his heroic flying, Mark Feinberg was awarded the Distinguished Service Cross and received the 5th Annual Avco-Aviation/Space Writers Association Helicopter Heroism award, presented at a dinner honoring him in Wichita, Kansas, the following June.

That same day I had a close call with a Hatchet Force platoon. My OV-10 was overflying a Vietnamese team just across the border when a radio voice called, "Covey! Covey! Any fucking Covey!" My pilot banked east and sped full throttle as I learned their situation from Sergeant First Class John Bean, who'd called in several sets of fighters a day earlier to fight off an NVA company. One squad leader, Sergeant Chester Zaborowski, had been wounded, Bean reported, while another, Sergeant Ed Ziobron, had taken RPG shrapnel for the second time in three days, hit so badly this time that he could barely walk. A large enemy force was assaulting them.

Five minutes later we were overhead twenty miles northwest of Ben Het, and already my pilot had a pair of F-100s inbound; we rolled in and rocketed and strafed, even as the gallant Ed Ziobron led his squad to assault the enemy. At one point, unable to stand on his wounded legs, Ziobron crawled forward and tossed grenades, single-handedly wiping out several machine gun nests. Between our gun runs, Ziobron's aggressive assault, and the F-100s, we pushed back the NVA. The platoon was slated for extraction the following morning.

Ken Carpenter flew the first mission that day, 29 November, and had to bring in fighters immediately to help the platoon reach an LZ. Sergeant First Class Bean, whose expertly directed air strikes had proven so critical the day before, again manned the radio, and that's what he was doing, talking to Carpenter, when he was shot and killed, our second American lost in two days. Despite his worsening condition, Ed Ziobron took command, called in air, secured the wounded and dead, and got them to an LZ for extraction. His spectacular heroism had saved that platoon. Ziobron would receive the Distinguished Service Cross.

By noon that day—the platoon safely back at Dak To—our choppers were refueled, rearmed, and on strip alert just as I arrived in an O-2 to take the midday Covey Rider shift. I began flying a circuit of our recon teams, starting with RT Alabama, about twelve miles northwest of Ben Het. The team was led by a former CCS man, Staff Sergeant Jim "Fred" Morse. His One-One was a relatively new captain, Kent Marshall, and as One-Two, an experienced CCC recon man, Specialist Five Sam Helland, known for being serious but down-to-earth.

My O-2 had just passed Ben Het when I heard Helland's desperate voice call, "Covey, Covey!—Prairie Fire! Prairie Fire!" We flew full speed as Helland reported that both he and Marshall had been wounded, and Morse was dead, their team overrun so fast that they had had to leave his body behind. An RPG had detonated right in front of Morse, blasting his body with multiple lethal wounds, and now several dozen NVA were pursuing them. Immediately I scrambled a pair of Cobras from Dak To while my pilot called for a set of A-1s. Minutes later we buzzed their hilltop and fired marking rockets at least to preoccupy the enemy.

This was to have been Fred Morse's last mission, after which he'd begin a thirty-day, around-the-world extension leave, the trip of a lifetime for an Oklahoma boy. A former CCS man, Fred had been in recon a year and a half and had run so many missions that his old CCS recon buddy Frank Burkhart had talked him into taking a desk job in Saigon. But now Fred was dead, the third Green Beret we'd lost in as many days, and the first man I'd lost flying Covey. What a damn shame.

Now I had to focus on getting his teammates out alive.

As quickly as we got the Cobras overhead, Helland expertly directed them, and I called for a full launch, bringing out all the helicopters. Momentarily the A-1s arrived and we began pounding the area in preparation for extracting the men on ropes. With the Cobras and the A-1s, we managed to hold off the NVA long enough to get the Hueys there; then we all held our breath as the choppers went in to extract RT Alabama. Despite occasional ground fire we got them all, and now, I told my pilot, we'd make the NVA pay for killing Fred; as soon as we got the helicopters clear, we'd pound that hilltop with bombs and rockets and napalm.

What's that buzzing sound? Fred Morse shook his head and lifted to his knees. Blood blurred his vision. He wiped his eyes until he could see, then wrapped a bandanna across his head to stem the flow. In one direction he heard AKs shooting—can't go that way. He'd take his chances and walk a trail the other way. Ever the devoted One-Zero, he retrieved a wiretap device he'd planted earlier and stumbled away. Hardly a hundred yards farther, too weak to continue, he found a clearing where he hoped someone would see him. He slumped to the ground. Morse's survival radio was broken and his mouth was too full of blood to talk. He felt the pain melting away and grew faint. "I guess this is it," he thought, "I'm about out of luck." Then he heard the buzz again, turned his eyes skyward and saw Covey's O-2 circling, and that gave him a final jolt of adrenaline. He remembered a flare gun, given him just before the mission by an old friend, Allyn Waggle. Morse mustered enough strength to pull the flare gun and fire a round.

A thousand feet above him, I asked my pilot, "Did you see that?" He shook his head. It could have been a tracer round, but enemy tracer usually was green, not red. "Wiggle your wings," I said, "just in case." I radioed the last Huey still down on the deck, "White Two, this is Plasticman. Did you see a flare?"

The Huey banked, its pilot radioing, "Wait one, Plasticman." For twenty tense seconds I held my breath. Then Fred fired a second pen flare. "Roger, Plasticman! Roger! We've got him!"

Morse was exhausted but still managed to climb into the extraction harness that was lowered to him. Slowly the Huey lifted him through the trees, then broke clear and climbed skyward.

We flew our O-2 past Fred as he dangled 100 feet below the Huey. We wiggled our wings and sped ahead to Dak To so we could greet him when he came in. Damn, what a day. The team had been overrun, but all those guys came out—despite Marshall and Helland being wounded—and now we got Fred, too. It was a triumphant moment when everyone at the launch site walked out on the Dak To runway, watching the approaching chopper descend with Fred swinging beneath it. Fred coming back from the dead was the happiest day of my life.

Pendulum-like, he swung lower and lower, his back to us, fifty feet, then thirty, then twenty-five. As he neared I noticed caked blood and wounds on his back and legs and wrists. Then Fred swung around and I gasped: His eyeballs were rolled up, his teeth chattering spasmodically, a horrible gap in his skull where I saw his exposed brain. Fred didn't recognize anybody and could not talk. We grabbed him and lowered him to the ground as a medic checked his wrist. "No pulse!" he yelled, and immediately started an IV. Several men carried Fred to a medevac helicopter that rushed him away. Looking at his condi-

tion, I understood why Morse's teammates had thought he was dead—fortunately, so had the NVA, who had run past his unconscious body to pursue the
others. I feared that having survived so much, he was about to die.

At Pleiku's 71st Evacuation Hospital, Fred slipped into a coma. Several days
passed as he hovered between life and death. Finally he opened his eyes, looked
over, and saw a nurse bending to tend another patient. He sighed, entranced by
the prettiest butt he'd ever seen, convinced that this must be heaven. Fred
would make it, but years of surgery and therapy lay before him.

Back at Kontum we celebrated news of Fred's survival in the brand-new
Covey Country Club, a ten-foot-by-twenty addition to our Covey Rider billet.
Incorporating scrounged, swapped, and stolen building materials, the Country
Club was essentially a screened porch whose "luxurious" padded booth
demonstrated the magic a Vietnamese seamstress could achieve from cut-up
GI mattresses and nylon camouflage poncho liners. Lowell Stevens—who'd
just left on his thirty-day extension leave—had even found us a full-size refrigerator, a hot plate, and a popcorn popper, which, combined with the stereo system and several Thai nudes painted on black velvet, made for the finest private
club in Kontum Province.

The Covey Country Club became the gathering place for recon men to de-
compress and discuss that day's narrow escape with the Covey Rider who'd
been on the other end of their radio. The official debrief may have taken place
in the S-2 intelligence office, but the unvarnished "no-shit" version was in the
Country Club, where booze and beer flowed for free. Captain Bob Howard
was a regular patron, but he seldom drank and didn't talk much, preferring to
just sit and absorb men's combat accounts, unable to go into combat himself as
he awaited his forthcoming Medal of Honor.

The Covey Country Club also was where we Covey Riders exchanged lessons learned, much as I'd earlier gleaned a great deal about running recon in
the NCO club. One night in early December, Larry White returned from a long
day of flying, poured a stiff drink, and sat with us at the padded booth to tell
about his most harrowing day ever flying Covey.

That afternoon, RT Washington had been surrounded and nearly overrun
by a tenacious enemy that assaulted right through exploding cluster bombs,
bursting napalm, and streaming cannon fire. "I couldn't believe it," Larry said,
"they just kept coming." The One-Zero, Captain Steve Wallace, had been badly
wounded and One-Two Sergeant George "Curt" Green shot to death. One-
One Jeff Mauceri held the team together, called air strikes, and at a critical moment single-handedly fought off an entire NVA squad. From overhead, White
had spotted ten NVA sneaking around one side of the knoll where RT Wash-

ington was trapped. With practiced calm, he radioed Mauceri, "Don't get excited, partner, but they're comin' around your right flank. I want ya'll to get out a couple hand grenades, 'n get y'self over there."

He watched Mauceri trot, then crawl to where the hill dropped off. "A little farther," White urged, then announced, "There, right there, just to your front." Mauceri hurled down three grenades, killing several NVA and sending the rest running.

Repeatedly, White sent in a Huey only to have ground fire drive it away, even as more NVA assaulted RT Washington. Mauceri's CAR-15 grew so hot that the sling burned off; after expending his own ammo, he had to get more off the wounded and dead.

Finally, after fifty-five minutes of continuous shooting and strafing and bombing, a Huey made it in, door gunners blasting away, and Mauceri managed to get everyone aboard except Green, whose body could not be recovered. Despite multiple hits, their chopper made it away. Later, a Huey pilot radioed Larry that while flying out, on just one flank his crew had counted twenty-seven NVA bodies.

After flying that desperate mission, Larry had a much deserved break, a thirty-day extension leave in the States. White and Lowell Stevens were both gone for a month, leaving only Ken Carpenter and myself to fly Covey. For the next four weeks, we'd fly every single day, some days up to three sorties. Unlike our Covey pilots, we were not on official aircrew status; therefore we faced no limitations and no regulatory rest periods. We flew prodigious numbers of flights.

At this heightened pace I soon knew our area of operations well, and learned a lot about aircraft and air-dropped ordnance. Cobra gunships were nimble, on-a-dime accurate, and responsive because they belonged to us, sitting on strip alert at Dak To. Their limitation: A Cobra could lift about one eighth the ordnance load of a fighter plane—that's why fighter support was crucial. Further, many kinds of ordnance simply were not carried by gunships, such as cluster bombs and napalm and heavy bombs. The propeller-driven A-1, with its hour-long loiter time and ordnance load—cluster bombs, cannons, and napalm—made it our finest supporting aircraft.

When it came to jet fighters, the more high-performance the aircraft the quicker it sucked fuel and the faster we had to use it or lose it. When fighters were out of time, they were gone. For the F-4 Phantom that meant about ten minutes, while F-100s could hang overhead about twenty-five minutes, with similar time for A-7s. These high-speed jets weren't nearly as consistently accurate as A-1s, adding a degree of risk whenever you brought them close to a team. Further, the jets were likely to have been diverted from another mission, and often arrived with 500-pound bombs, which could not be dropped closer than 200 meters without endangering a team.

Timing, I came to see, was the critical factor. We called in gunships and fighters to delay, weaken, and knock the enemy off balance and help the team break contact and make it to an LZ just as the extraction choppers got there. To make that work, my toughest, riskiest decision was when to call for a full launch of helicopters. Call them too soon and they might run out of station time before the team got to the LZ or before we'd sufficiently pounded the enemy to allow the birds to land; call them too late, and the team could be so totally surrounded that you'd never get them out, or you'd face such heavy antiaircraft fire that you'd lose choppers.

Every time you put in an air strike near a team you were testing the limits of ordnance, pilots, and aircraft; regularly we were compelled to put rockets, cluster bombs, napalm, and machine gun and cannon fire a fraction of the book minimums. This was dangerous work, performed in dangerous circumstances, and it didn't always come out perfectly. On one occasion Ken Carpenter's OV-10 was strafing for RT West Virginia when One-Zero Ronnie Knight radioed, "Bring it closer!" On the next pass Carpenter's pilot strafed a few yards nearer the team's panel. "Closer!" Knight repeated. The OV-10 machine-gunned closer, but that still wasn't close enough. Finally a bullet nicked a Yard's boot and Knight radioed, "That's close enough." When Knight told the story in the Covey Country Club we all laughed, but such near-run things were not always humorous, as was the case of RT New Mexico.

I inserted RT New Mexico just across the border, due west of Ben Het, on 13 December. They drew no ground fire, and about ten minutes after landing, One-Zero Richard McNatt radioed a "Team OK." Sergeant First Class McNatt had transferred to Kontum from Ban Me Thuot when CCS had closed down a few months earlier. His One-One was Specialist Five Mark "Jingles" Devine. Both had received Purple Hearts a month earlier when they fought off an attack by forty NVA and managed to reach an LZ, fighting all the way there.

After his "Team OK" McNatt heard our aircraft depart and headed into the jungle. His men had traveled hardly 100 yards when they came across a freshly dug trench line. As quickly as they crossed it, a large NVA force swarmed toward them. Fortunately, my OV-10 was still nearby; while I turned around the departing choppers, my pilot briefed the A-1s.

Hard-pressed by many NVA, One-One Devine knew he had to bring the air strike danger-close—less than 100 yards. Lacking white phosphorus grenades, a Yard popped a colored-smoke grenade that seemed to take forever to reach the treetops. Finally my pilot spotted a wisp of red and directed the A-1s to rocket the hillside, "Seventy-five yards south of the smoke," just as the team requested. What no one realized—neither the men on the ground nor those of us in the air—was that the slow-burning red smoke had drifted seventy-five yards downwind by the time it broke through the trees.

That would put the air strike directly atop RT New Mexico.

In his first pass, the lead A-1 rippled a dozen rockets, decapitating one Yard and wounding every member of the team—severely in the case of One-Zero McNatt, who suffered a painful abdominal wound. As quickly as Devine shouted, we pulled away the A-1s until we spotted him waving a panel, then continued gun runs with the Cobras.

Despite his serious wound McNatt kept his wits and worked with Devine to fight off the NVA, treat his wounded Yards, and adjust the Cobras. McNatt insisted on a rope extraction because he realized so many NVA were there that any Huey that sat down would be shot down. It took ten minutes for the Cobras to push back the NVA and to silence one 12.7mm machine gun, then I sent in the Hueys. The first bird got out without any hits, but as the second Huey hovered and McNatt and his last men snapped on to the ropes, ground fire erupted. As the men lifted away, a slug deflected off McNatt's CAR-15 into his left lung, his second life-threatening wound. At Dak To our medic managed to stabilize him, then McNatt was rushed to Pleiku.

With One-Zero McNatt medevaced and everyone wounded, RT New Mexico was disbanded. I thanked God we had gotten them out, and also thanked God it had not been my error that killed one Yard and wounded everyone else. Though no one was at fault, that incident confirmed my reliance upon white phosphorus grenades; had that Yard tossed a phosphorus grenade, a mushroom cloud would have shot straight up and there'd have been no bombing accident.

There was hardly time to digest what was happening, Carpenter and I were flying so much. A week after the bombing accident, Ken flew a 3:30 A.M. mission, supporting a night parachute jump by RT Arizona. Bundled in U.S. Forest Service smoke jumper suits, One-Zero Newman Ruff and four men parachuted on a ridge one mile east of Highway 92. Ruff and One-One Mike Wilson landed just fine, but First Lieutenant Jack Barton had a dead tree fall on him, dislocating his kneecaps. Both Yards got hung up in the trees; one freed himself and fell sixty feet to his death.

Carpenter extracted RT Arizona just after dawn.

A couple days later it was Christmas and we had only one team still in Laos, RT New York. That morning I took off from Pleiku before dawn in an OV-10 with Captain Bill Hartsell, call sign Covey 556. The choppers flew to Dak To, but the teams slated for insertion remained at Kontum on a one-day holiday stand-down so they could partake in Mess Sergeant Malen "Fat Cat" King's elaborate Christmas feast.

Now into his fourth day in Laos, RT New York One-Zero Ed Wolcoff had been his typical part wolf and part jackrabbit, alternately stalking the enemy or evading or ambushing, as the situation dictated. That morning we overflew his team just east of Highway 92, where'd they'd passed an uneventful night. The previous afternoon they'd heard a few signal shots and glimpsed a handful of passing NVA. Since they were the only team afield, I told his radio operator, Sergeant John Blaauw, we'd stay within radio range and fly the highway looking for enemy activity.

A half-hour later, our OV-10 was ten miles away when Sergeant Blaauw radioed: An estimated NVA platoon was shadowing RT New York, though One-Zero Wolcoff hoped to lose them. We tightened our orbit to five miles, just far enough that the NVA wouldn't hear our engines. Then we learned the enemy had almost closed upon Wolcoff's men. With contact imminent, Blaauw radioed that the bad guys were now seventy-five meters away, at 84 degrees. I instructed him to ready a white phosphorus grenade, and the instant a shot was fired, to throw it.

A minute went by. We closed to two miles. A minute later a white mushroom cloud burst through the trees and Blaauw's voice called, "Contact! Contact!" It had to stun the NVA—*twenty seconds after their first shot,* we pounced upon them, Hartsell rolling in to pepper their ranks with machine gun fire. Between RT New York's immediate action drill and our strafing, that platoon was sent running, and within the hour we safely extracted the team.

Now everyone could go home for a Christmas meal.

That night at the Covey Country Club, I learned from Blaauw that enemy ground fire had tracked our OV-10 as we strafed that morning. Like our Covey pilots, I didn't give ground fire much thought—miss by an inch, miss by a mile. Rarely could we hear enemy guns, and usually we were simply too busy to notice tracers. Unless a team radioed a warning, such concerns didn't even register. On the ground the enemy's malevolence was ubiquitous. But up in the sky that threat seemed distant and impersonal—it was not people that might kill us but things—arcing tracers, bursting flak, exploding RPGs. We didn't pay much heed unless a tracer screamed past our canopy or a slug hit our plane.

Yet the possibility of being shot down could not be ignored. A Covey Rider could bail out of an O-2 or eject from an OV-10, but what if his pilot was disabled? Could you just leave him? It was more than an academic question. The previous January, USAF Captain John Lehacka was flying an O-2 with Covey Rider Sam Zumbrun when enemy fire struck their windshield. Sam knew nothing about flying, so when his pilot was hit there was no hope in taking the controls. Both men died. Wisely, then, after that tragedy the Covey pilots went out of their way to teach Covey Riders how to fly.

With only the most preliminary instruction, I started to get stick time. That was the best perk of being a Covey Rider, flying the OV-10 or O-2 while my pilot coached or, after I'd gained his confidence, napped. Many a quiet afternoon, we monitored the radios and cruised the azure sky, listening for the teams while exploring the Laotian wilderness. Occasionally we drifted west to the mysterious edge of SOG's area of operations, where the mountains melted away and a great, grassy plain began. One day that December, beneath a clear sky, I gazed far to the west and saw a sheer rock face that had to be twenty miles wide. From maps I knew it was the Bolovens Plateau, jutting 3,000 feet above the grassland, and beneath it lay the populous town of Attapeu.

It was like looking beyond the end of the earth. What happened out there, we'd seldom, almost never, heard. But we'd often been told someone else was out there, a shadowy CIA secret army, fighting its own war, just as we were fighting ours. In recon we didn't get the details.

By contrast, considerable Laotian war information was supplied to the Air Force, and to the Pleiku-based Covey squadron's intelligence shop, to which we Covey Riders had full access. In a single hour I learned more about what was happening in Laos than I'd learned in two years at Kontum, from the exact location of friendly airfields and outposts, to those that had recently been overrun. The big picture was right there, on the wall-size intelligence map. The Royal Laotian Army had abandoned Attapeu months earlier, without firing a shot, when an NVA force neared the town. Rumors of Chinese troops in Laos? There they were, some 10,000 Chinese soldiers in northern Laos, constructing a new highway from southern China to expedite war supplies to North Vietnam. U.S. aircraft were forbidden from bombing that road. Thousands more Chinese soldiers were in North Vietnam, a top secret report disclosed, to run the railway system and man antiaircraft guns, so Hanoi could send more troops into Laos and Cambodia.

Interesting as it was, that month I had little spare time to be studying intelligence, though I was gradually acquiring enough experience to improvise my own Covey Rider tactics. One of them was a little deception I called the "Old Willy Pete Trick."

RT Colorado, led by One-Zero Pat Mitchel, had been in Laos three days when one morning their radio operator whispered, "Covey! Covey!—got a

Tac-E!" A tactical emergency meant they were not yet in contact, but needed immediate air support. "Got bad guys all around us," the radio operator, Sergeant Lyn St. Laurent, explained. Apparently a major NVA unit had moved in during the night and deployed around them without knowing Mitchel's team was there.

A Special Forces medic, One-Zero Mitchel had kept his cool and shifted his men a bit, but with every passing minute, odds were they'd be discovered. An adept team leader, Mitchel had learned his craft well from Shephard Patton, RT Colorado's past One-Zero, and had run a half-dozen missions without making contact. His One-One, Sergeant David Mixter—nicknamed "Lurch" after the butler on *The Addams Family* TV comedy—towered over his teammates, twice the size of Mitchel or One-Two Lyn St. Laurent. Competent and quiet by nature, St. Laurent never made it a subject of discussion, but tragically, his twin brother, Lance, had been killed in combat a year earlier, when his chopper was shot down on the 4th of July.

By the time we were over them, my pilot had a pair of F-4s a few minutes out. First I needed a visual, provided by Lurch flashing a mirror from a bomb crater. "Oh, shit!" I hissed to myself—they were hardly 200 yards from Highway 110, right beside the most heavily bombed hilltops for twenty miles, the very spot I'd wanted to take RT Hawaii last summer to ambush an NVA bulldozer.

Things did not look good for RT Colorado. How the hell were we going to help them slip away and extract in this godforsaken area? While I started thinking through the options, the Phantoms arrived and began orbiting overhead.

"Covey! Covey!" St. Laurent's voice whispered. "The planes are being shot at! Taking fire!"

Sure enough, gray smudges were puffing the sky behind the F-4s—the enemy was firing 37mm antiaircraft guns. Even worse, *the guns were right around RT Colorado.* They had been encircled by an antiaircraft unit that had moved in under the cover of darkness. How could the situation be worse? The 37mm guns were so close that we couldn't bomb without hitting the team.

In this terrible situation, I recalled Larry White's advice, lowered my voice an octave and confidently announced, "Partner, we're going to try the Old Willy Pete Trick"—military phonetic alphabet slang for white phosphorus. I told St. Laurent to ready a phosphorus grenade. "I'll give you a countdown, buddy, then I want you to throw it and give me an azimuth and distance to the enemy." When St. Laurent was ready, I had my pilot dive and—as I said "Zero"—we fired a rocket barely over their hill just as St. Laurent tossed his grenade. Our rocket soared off God knew where, *but the enemy mistakenly*

*thought St. Laurent's bursting grenade was our rocket, and concluded we'd spotted
their guns and were going to bomb them.*

The NVA ducked into trenches and crawled into bunkers, allowing RT Colorado to slip away undetected. Half the problem was solved. But I still had to extract Mitchel and his men.

Hundreds of NVA were nearby and the closest usable LZ was 400 yards away—right down Highway 110. I held RT Colorado at the edge of the jungle, then, as the Cobra gunships and A-1s arrived, I told Mitchel to get on the road and run east. Dashing past fresh tire tracks they were about to run into the clearing when I radioed, "Stop! Get back on the road! There are people in that field!" While our fighters strafed the first clearing, they kept going, expecting any second to see trucks roll up loaded with NVA, but our strafing Cobras blasted the road ahead and behind them. Then a Huey materialized right over them, banked hard, and landed. They flew out low, staying on the treetops while the fighters pounded the surrounding hills, and got clean away.

Not a single aircraft was hit.

That night, Mitchel, Mixter, and St. Laurent had complimentary drinks in the Covey Country Club. After talking through that close-run day, Mitchel asked, "Say, Plasticman, how many times have you used that Old Willy Pete Trick?"

I smiled. "Counting today? Once."

Those last days of 1970, Ken Carpenter and I spent in constant emergencies, extracting teams from seemingly impossible situations. On 26 December, Ken attempted to insert a team twice, on both its primary and secondary LZs, only to have to retrieve them when they made contact as quickly as they landed. The next day I inserted a team and had the same thing happen, but this time we had to bomb and strafe for two and a half hours to get them out. We did, with no losses. On 28 December, Ken put in another team that lasted just forty minutes before they had to shoot their way out. Then, on 29 December, a team was ready to leap from their insertion chopper when they spotted NVA near the LZ and aborted, withdrawing barely in the nick of time. That afternoon a team landed despite taking fire against their choppers, not far from the LZ. The One-Zero requested extraction but the S-3 operations officer did not want them withdrawn unless they made contact, an asinine call, I thought, since obviously the enemy knew they had inserted. They made it through the night, then made contact, shot their way clear, and we got them out OK.

Facing pressure from Saigon to keep teams on the ground, the S-3 sometimes made bad calls, second-guessing a One-Zero and refusing to have his team extracted. That put the Covey Rider in the middle, since he worked for the S-3 but empathized with the One-Zero. Hearing his extraction request denied, the angry One-Zero often would radio the Covey Rider, "Tell that stupid motherfucker to get us out *now*, or I will cut out his guts and strangle him with his own stinking entrails!"

When the Covey Rider relayed this message to the S-3 it became, "Team leader requests reconsideration while we still have good weather. He's being pursued to exhaustion, contact is inevitable, and right now he's near a usable LZ." After the restated request was approved, the One-Zero could tell his teammates, "All you gotta do is know how to talk to that bastard."

In that he was exactly correct.

New Year's Day 1971 found RT Iowa sneaking along Highway 110, attempting to verify a CIA agent's report that the NVA were bringing tanks close to the border of South Vietnam. Led by my old Operation Ashtray Two comrade, Sergeant Paul Kennicott, in addition to Iowa's normal complement of Sergeants Ralph Munson and Jim Doggett, he'd brought along two volunteers, Sergeants John Gunnison and Phillip "Woody" Wood. There had not been a confirmed tank sighting in southern Laos in two years, not since the failed tank attack on Ben Het.

Boldly walking the highway that afternoon, looking for any distinctive signs of tracked vehicle passage, it felt spooky, like they were being watched, shadowed, stalked. The surface was so hard that they couldn't discern any distinct wheeled or tracked vehicle prints. They walked silently past dozens of foxholes just off the road, probably to protect truck drivers and sentries during air strikes. They found an abandoned military truck, its engine apparently burned out.

After a half-hour, Kennicott decided they'd taken enough risk, it was time to disappear back into the jungle. One American happened to glance down on the roadbed—he waved over Ralph Munson and together they brushed dust from the highway surface. Be damned, it was a two-foot section of tank track, run over by vehicles and pressed into the clay! Kennicott knew that intelligence experts could figure out exactly the kind of vehicle it had come from; dig it out and they'd have accomplished their mission.

Munson knelt and scraped hurriedly at the track edges, lifting and tugging and finally freeing it. Only two feet long, the track section weighed almost ninety pounds. All five Americans circled their hefty prize, almost too good to be true—mission accomplished.

BOOM!—an RPG exploded between them, throwing all five to the ground—followed by full-auto bursts of three dozen AKs. One-Zero Kennicott struggled to his feet, firing his CAR-15 at shadows down the road. Shrapnel had shattered Kennicott's glasses and left blood spots all over his face and hands.

Gunnison, also seriously wounded, opened fire, as did the wounded Doggett. Dazed and bleeding from both ears, Woody shook his head and couldn't hear a thing. Munson had only a bit of shrapnel in one knee, the steel track having deflected the blast.

Taking heavy fire from three sides, the recon men shot and ran for the jungle, taking cover among tree stumps and ant mounds. They heard shouting as the NVA closed a circle around them. Munson called into his radio handset, "Covey! Covey! Prairie Fire! Prairie Fire!"

Less than five miles away, I heard his shout—and luckily, damned luckily, our helicopters had just launched from Dak To for a late afternoon resupply flight to the Leghorn radio relay site. Hearing their critical situation, I led our Cobras to them and turned the Hueys back to Dak To to reserve their station time. Meanwhile, my FAC pilot had called Hillsborough, and got two sets of F-100s diverted from another target up north. The fighters would be over us in less than ten minutes. The problem was waning daylight. It would be dark in thirty minutes.

As we reached RT Iowa, they were still locked in a desperate gun battle, outnumbered more than three to one. With so many wounded I knew I couldn't move them far—therefore, we had to pulverize the NVA and extract them right there. But already the afternoon shadows had cast so deep that the Cobras' rockets looked like fireworks when they exploded in the trees.

Momentarily the F-100s got there, an Air National Guard unit from Phang Rang, known as the Bobcats and Yellow Jackets. Learning of the critical situation, the F-100 pilots pressed dangerously low to put their 20mm strafing runs right alongside the endangered team. One flier whisked past so low that Munson could see the nickname "Tex" on his helmet.

As the Hueys approached, my pilot put in the F-100s' napalm and bombs. Some of the 500-pounders detonated so close that it lifted the recon men off the ground. They didn't mind.

The NVA were still there, but enough had pulled back from our heavy fire that it was time to bring in the Hueys. Covered by a pair of Cobras, White Lead went in, dropped ladders, and safely carried away the first load. Moderate ground fire followed him, but there were no hits. I spoke with Kennicott, letting him know the second Huey was inbound. I watched that bird hover while Doggett climbed the ladder, followed by Munson; a door gunner stopped firing to tug him aboard.

"Taking fire, nine o'clock," the Huey pilot calmly reported, holding his ship steady. A Cobra banked and riddled the trees to his left. It was Kennicott's turn to climb, last man on the ground.

Halfway up, a burst of AK fire hit him, dropping him off the ladder. "Taking fire," the calm pilot repeated, "nine o'clock," and again the Cobras let loose. Hit in his stomach, chest, and one arm, Kennicott struggled to his feet and reached for the ladder. Blazing away, the desperate door gunners covered him but there was no time for anyone to crawl down the ladder to help him. Again Kennicott fell. Instinct begged for the pilot to pull away, but he didn't, holding it right there while the door gunners and Kennicott's teammates fired, and the Cobras strafed, and one last time the One-Zero tried to climb.

Kennicott was too weak to make it—he hooked his legs on a rung, snapped his harness to the ladder, and waved the Huey away. Under intense ground fire, the bird lifted out, Kennicott riding the ladder, bleeding profusely. They made it out.

By the time a medic got to him at Ben Het, Kennicott had almost bled to death. Medevaced back to the States, he was gone by the time Saigon analysts determined the track he'd brought back was from a Russian-built PT-76 tank, a major intelligence find that bode ill for what was coming to South Vietnam.

With Paul gone, that left just Captain Fred Krupa and myself as the last Ashtray Two veterans still in Vietnam.

Chapter Fourteen

Damn, another Prairie Fire Emergency!

RT Illinois had just shot its way clear of an NVA patrol. Sergeant Dan Ross, their radio operator, said the enemy was searching high and low for them. Close calls were nothing new to them or their One-Zero, Steve Keever. Two months earlier a Huey carrying Keever and Sergeants Larry Predmore and John Grant had lifted off an LZ just as ground fire erupted, compelling their pilot to bank toward some immense trees. Too late to turn away, their Huey flew right into the treetops only to *bounce* into the sky, as if off a trampoline.

Today, looking down at their flickering signal mirror, the danger was no less. They were just 100 yards south of Highway 110, in an area usually swarming with North Vietnamese—who knew by now that a team was down there somewhere, and probably were rushing troops to every suitable LZ within a mile to lie in wait for an extraction attempt.

My OV-10 pilot, Captain James "Mike" Cryer, requested fighters, then we rolled in to strafe and buy time until the planes could get there. Hardly five minutes passed and a pair of F-4 Phantoms appeared with two dozen 500-pound bombs—not useful here—but each plane also had a 20mm Vulcan cannon pod. We put them to work, firing up the team's rear and flanks and the area where they'd had the gunfight. After the Phantoms expended their 20mm we had them make noisy passes with afterburners to keep the enemy off balance and buy more time.

When the A-1s got overhead our Cobras, too, arrived, followed by the extraction choppers. Cryer had the F-4s "pickle" their bombs—dumping all twenty-four in one pass atop a nearby ridge—and scat. Then, after the Cobras got down and sprayed a length of road, I had Keever run his men to the last LZ the enemy expected us to use: Highway 110. A minute later a Huey from the 57th Assault Helicopter Company swooped down to the roadbed, they jumped aboard, and off they flew, the Cobras mowing down NVA troops that rushed out of the jungle after them.

It was a close-run thing but not a chopper was hit and we got everyone out safely.

By then it was late afternoon. Our OV-10 overflew the only other team in Laos for their daily situation report, then headed back to Vietnam. As we passed over Dak To all fifteen helicopters rose beneath us in one long trail, outbound for Kontum. Spotting us, Cobra Lead radioed, "Hey, Covey, what about a parade?" Cryer thought it a splendid idea. Our OV-10 led, followed close by the four Cobras, then six Hueys carrying RT Illinois in a wide V, with five H-34 Kingbees in a single line between the Hueys. It was a thing of choreographed beauty. Our formation passed the Kontum compound in a wide circle, then as they landed on the south pad, Cryer gave me the controls. As he'd taught me, I dived at 45 degrees, got our airspeed up to 180 knots, streaked toward the compound's radio antennas, then lifted the nose, kicked hard left rudder, and spun round and round in an aileron roll—*Ya-hoo!* The good guys won today.

Even better, when Keever and his men came by the Country Club that evening, not only was my fellow Covey Rider Larry White back from leave, but so was Lowell Wesley Stevens. We had a fine time that night, especially listening to Stevens, who was more entertaining than any TV show.

That night he told us about his "Monkey in Space" project, instigated by the 1969 moon landing. "When I told the Yards Americans were walkin' on the moon they just stared at me. If a Yard couldn't see it he didn't understand," Lowell explained. "Finally they sez, 'OK, maybe they're up on the American moon. But that's a Vietnamese moon and they ain't up there.' "

Stevens decided to demonstrate just how it was done, selecting a volunteer spider monkey from among several that stole cigarettes and constantly masturbated at his Mike Force base. Like NASA, he advanced in graduated steps, first putting the monkey in a handmade harness and connecting him to a miniature parachute salvaged off a mortar illumination round. "So I dropped him from a helicopter 'n' his little chute deployed just fine but, I swear, that monkey got so damned excited it climbed the lines, collapsing his own canopy."

Lowell shook his head regretfully. "The Yards ate that one."

Pressing on, he got another monkey and fashioned another miniature harness from a piece of elastic cord, then attached the cord to an 81mm mortar round. "Now, I figured, six seconds after leavin' the tube, that round's at its apogee, the peak of its trajectory. So I taped a blasting cap to the cord with a six-second time fuse to cut him free from the mortar round."

The moment of truth had arrived. "There he is, little harness on, lines attached to the parachute, just lookin' around." One second the monkey sat beside the mortar tube chewing on a cigarette butt, the next he was flying away at

875 feet per second. "That son-of-a-bitch went into orbit, way, way high, and all of a sudden, *POP!*—he cut free from the mortar round and his li'l chute opened. The Yards was clappin' 'n' jumpin'." The monkey drifted to the ground, safe and sound, and now the Yards grasped how Project Apollo had worked.

"Now I've got to tell you the truth, my friends," Lowell confessed. "That monkey was never right after that." We laughed so hard beer came out our noses.

It was great having Larry and Lowell back, and the timing was perfect because, at last, I was ready to attempt something I'd been calculating and practicing for weeks, a great way to welcome a fellow Covey Rider back to Laos. A few days later Stevens flew aboard an O-2 to relieve my OV-10 at noontime. "Say there, Roundeye," I radioed, "could you come alongside? I've got something to show you."

It was tough in that cramped cockpit, not eight inches' clearance over my head, but I unsnapped my ejection seat harness and worked my shoulders out of my flight suit. It was hard, twisting my body in such a contorted way. Then I squatted down on the seat, bent forward, and crammed my head down beside the stick. It was difficult breathing.

At last Stevens's O-2 appeared off our left wing.

"Welcome back, Roundeye," I radioed. He looked over, stared hard at the OV-10 canopy, did a double take, then laughed too hard to talk. It may have been a Guinness World Record, for in addition to mooning Stevens I had simultaneously mooned Laos, Cambodia, and Vietnam.

Just being around Lowell improved your outlook. In another man humor may have masked despair, but for Lowell Wesley Stevens it reflected the positive energy of an effervescent personality. No matter how grim the situation, Lowell looked for comic relief; I'm not sure which saved more men, his combat prowess or his mirth. Indeed, however, he did save men. In November 1969, in the black of night, he led a Mike Force company through entrenched NVA to rescue American soldiers at a hopelessly surrounded artillery firebase. For days the enemy had shelled their hilltop near Bu Prang, wounding a dozen GIs and driving away rescue helicopters. It totally surprised the more numerous NVA when Stevens and his Montagnards punched open an escape corridor and whisked away in the darkness some seventy-five Americans, including a number of wounded men they had to carry. Stevens was as courageous as he was humorous.

And he was cunning. One afternoon he was flying along in an O-2 with nothing going on, so he challenged his pilot to see which of them could more accurately fire a 2.75-inch marking rocket. "Just to make it fair," Lowell offered, "you can use the plane's gunsight 'n' I'll just eyeball it." It seemed like a sure thing to the pilot. They selected a water-filled crater as their target, then the pilot rolled in and fired. His rocket burst about thirty yards long and a dozen yards right.

Now it was Stevens's turn. What the pilot didn't realize was that in 1963 Lowell Stevens had won the title as the best mortar gunner in the 101st Airborne Division, possibly the best mortarman in the whole U.S. Army. This simple West Virginia country boy thrived on ballistics; he had placed a grease pencil dot on the windshield to mark where the crater had appeared when the pilot fired, then carefully tracked the rocket's path. Seeing where it hit, he simply adjusted with a second dot—just like adjusting a mortar round—and when he dived and fired—be damned!—his rocket splashed into the crater. Incredibly, the pilot did not realize how he had done it, so afterward, anytime a Covey Rider wanted a free beer, we had a shooting contest in an O-2.

With Stevens and White back, Carpenter and I could reduce our grueling flying schedules to a more palatable pace, with two days off per week. Still, though, you never knew when an emergency might arise and it was those stressful moments—not the number of hours you flew—that drained body and mind.

Getting teams out was tough enough, but now we were having almost as much difficulty getting them in. About half of our inserting teams encountered the enemy right at their LZ or shortly thereafter. Many recon men believed there was a mole—an enemy spy—somewhere in SOG, probably in Saigon, who was compromising our operations. To counter that possibility, some One-Zeros, such as Steve Keever, reported a false official location by prearrangement with the Covey Rider, who alone knew his true location.

Another counter-tactic was prepping the insertion LZ area, that is, hitting it with a preparatory air strike to kill or send running anyone that might be hiding there. Many One-Zeros didn't want a prep because it drew attention to the LZ, but other One-Zeros believed in them. As a minimum, a prep employed Cobras with nails—thousands of nail-size steel flechettes—delivered by 2.75-inch rockets that spewed across a wide area. Some teams wanted heavier ordnance such as cluster bombs and 20mm cannons, anything but napalm lest it set the LZ afire.

Our use of preps got SOG planners in Saigon to take the concept a dramatic magnitude higher. When RT Texas was scheduled to land in the Dak Ralong Valley to search for the NVA 6th Infantry Regiment—whose transmitter had been pinpointed by electronic triangulation—they arranged with the Seventh Air Force for the most impressive LZ prep in SOG history. God help them if the

NVA were tipped off about this insertion, for it would be prepped with the biggest nonnuclear bomb in the world.

That morning of 11 January, my OV-10, piloted by Captain Bill Hartsell, Covey 556, orbited northwest of Dak Seang Special Forces Camp, while we listened to the radar ground controller at faraway Pleiku direct the drop aircraft, a C-130 from the 463rd Tactical Airlift Wing. Inside its cavernous hold the plane carried a 15,000-pound bomb the size of a VW bus, code-named Commando Vault.

While RT Texas, led by One-Zero Charlie Walker with One-One Owen McDonald, rode choppers ten miles to our south, Hartsell and I circled west of the LZ. On cue, the C-130 approached at 11,000 feet, airspeed exactly 150 knots, the ground controller telling the pilot to adjust altitude and bearing as he neared. Then came the final countdown, "5, 4, 3, 2, 1, *MARK!*"

The loadmaster released a cargo lock lever, and a chute jerked the palletized bomb out the tailgate. We watched it plummet for twenty-six seconds, trailing a stabilizing drogue chute. Amazingly, it impacted within 100 yards of its designated grid coordinate, its three-foot fuse extender detonating the huge bomb exactly one yard above the earth.

I saw a bright burst, like an atomic bomb, a massive shock wave, then a vertical column of churning, angry smoke that climbed slow-motion to 2,000 feet and spread into a mushroom. We flew through the dissipating cloud, its acrid vapors almost overwhelming us. I gagged but kept from vomiting. Soon the dust settled and we saw the results: a clearing as big as a football field, large enough to land five Hueys, its circular edge heaped twenty feet high with stacked tree trunks as neat as if a gigantic broom had swept them aside, leaving behind broken-off stumps. For an additional 100 yards, the explosive flash had burned leaves off trees, while the blast pressure, according to the Air Force, would destroy booby traps or mines out to 700 yards and inflict "significant injuries" just shy of a mile.

Unsurprisingly, the Hueys inserting RT Texas took no ground fire. It was the strangest LZ Walker and McDonald had ever seen, with scorched soil and ash-colored tree stumps surrounded by a twenty-foot wall of logs. Climbing over the wall, the RT Texas men found blood smears at several locations but not one body, human or animal. They thought the blood was from enemy soldiers blasted to bits but, McDonald later told me, they couldn't tell for sure.

The rest of the day they encountered no enemy, but the next morning an NVA force—following their trail across the ash-covered ground—tried to attack them. RT Texas blasted them with claymore mines, opened fire, and broke free. Another Covey Rider extracted them.

"That bomb really rang their ears," McDonald told us over a drink that night in the Country Club. "If they were there when it hit on top of that radio antenna," he said, "there would have been nothing left, nobody." SOG planners hoped that would deter other NVA from lying in wait beside LZs.

With all the Covey Riders back, the popularity of the Covey Country Club soared. Soon we were going through ten cases of beer each week, not to mention liquor and food. Unconcerned, we pooled our money and even hosted parties, constructing an enormous awning from a cargo parachute and a telephone pole. While Fat Cat King grilled T-bone steaks for 100 men, our big stereo speakers blared tunes from Waylon Jennings, Country Charley Pride, and Porter Waggoner. Damn, those were fine times, with everyone invited— recon and Hatchet Force men, plus Cobra and Huey pilots, even Covey pilots from Pleiku who showed us how to line up tables, pour beer over them, and do "carrier landings" by running and belly-flopping and sliding. After one party, Covey pilots Mike Cryer, Jim Roper, George Degovanni, and Wesley Groves rode back to Pleiku suspended from extraction rigs beneath a Huey.

On less elaborate occasions, we fed up to a dozen guests home-cooked beans, thanks to a relative that kept Stevens supplied with great northerns he'd slow-cook with onions and ham hocks, and season with Tabasco sauce, which he called "Mexican Kool-Aid." It was fine eating, but the after effects could be agonizing. After one late-night party, a recon man showed up at the door in terrible shape. I welcomed him in for a cup of coffee. Meanwhile another man attempted to restore his precious bodily balance by helping himself to Stevens's leftovers—a boiled egg, sauerkraut, and a jalapeño pepper sandwich. Like radioactive neutrons bouncing around, that began a chain reaction of compressed kinetic energy, until suddenly he let loose the most noxious human odor I'd ever confronted. It was too much for our hungover guest, who twisted his face and shook as tears filled his eyes, then he gagged, ran for the door, and vomited on our sidewalk.

That's what Lowell Stevens's beans could do.

Recon company needed a new first sergeant, so our boss in the launch site, Billy Greenwood, was tapped for the job. A fine NCO and recon veteran with a previous tour in Project Omega, he was not too shy to let superiors know if they were wrong. When a new launch site officer tried to change combat-tested procedures just to demonstrate that he was in charge, Greenwood pulled him aside, pointed to a wall locker, and advised, "Sir, you get in that wall locker, stay out of our way, and in one year you'll come out a lieutenant colonel."

That solved that problem.

One of Greenwood's biggest fans was a young recon sergeant, Phillip "Woody" Wood. Twice the size of Greenwood, Woody was lethal in combat but a big teddy bear the rest of the time. One morning while First Sergeant Greenwood was pacing before a formation, chewing asses over some small infraction, Woody sneaked up behind him, grabbed him under his arm like a football, and ran off. Once he had him, Woody dare not let go of the grizzled old Greenwood, whose vitriol could melt steel. As Woody ran past the front gate, Greenwood tried to wrest away the guard's rifle, so angry he swore he was going to shoot Woody. But Woody loved old Greenwood, and that was just his peculiar way of showing it. Greenwood understood that such antics resulted from the strain of dangerous missions, and he interceded when superiors tried to impose serious penalties for men blowing off steam. He once confronted a SOG lieutenant colonel and warned, "Sir, you better give these recon men room to breathe. Or tomorrow morning, when you want to get these missions run, you'll be putting on your own rucksack." The officer backed off.

The amazing thing was that these recon men kept at it, day in, day out, despite the inanities of sometimes unappreciative leaders and the reality that the war was winding down. They were always ready to go. Only about a week after we detonated the 15,000-pound bomb, RT California, now back in the hands of Joe Walker, fought a tough, toe-to-toe engagement when some fifteen NVA got the drop on them—at least, it *seemed* they got the drop on Walker's men. As quickly as the enemy opened fire, RT California let loose such an all-out barrage that it temporarily stunned the NVA. One-Zero Walker, One-One Donald Davidson, and One-Two Toby Todd and their Yards out-shot and out-maneuvered the enemy, allowing them to break free of what could have been a catastrophic ambush. While the rest got a head start, Todd hung back to shoot and delay any pursuit. Incredibly, the NVA ambushers suffered severe casualties, while among the ambushees, only Walker suffered a minor wound.

Soon afterward, RT California figured in one of the strangest incidents in SOG history. The same three Americans—Walker, Davidson, and Todd—were exploring a side road off Highway 110 when Walker heard chain saws and people chopping. Creeping forward, he and Davidson peered down a hillside where they saw NVA engineers building storage bunkers. They radioed a Covey Rider only to learn no tactical air was available.

Then Davidson spotted one NVA climbing the hillside toward them, unaware they were there. "Give me a hand grenade," he whispered. Walker tossed him a baseball-size M-33 grenade. Before he joined the Army, Davidson had played semipro baseball and even competed for a major league pitching position—he was damned good with a grenade. "He eased up on one knee," Walker recalled, "stuck his left foot out in front of him, and he hauled off and threw a hand grenade and hit the guy in the side of the chest so hard that I could hear his breath leave and bones break." The NVA soldier collapsed as the grenade bounced downhill and exploded, igniting a sharp fight that RT California won in two minutes, thanks to the 60mm mortar Walker had brought along. "They were absolutely devastated," he said. "They just died or ran in every direction."

After the firing ceased, Walker climbed down to the enemy soldier Davidson had knocked down. "The guy didn't have any holes in him," Walker discovered. The force of that half-pound grenade, whipped through the air by Davidson's powerful pitching arm, had struck him dead. "It killed the son of a gun," Walker reported, hardly believing it himself.

That January had been fairly wet over southern Laos, but late in the month the weather turned and early one afternoon I couldn't believe the perfect skies. Flying in an OV-10 with Captain Mike Cryer, returning after lunch at Pleiku, we found stunningly clear heavens, horizon to horizon, like one of those dreamy days when you were a kid and lived to play baseball. As we neared Ben Het, Cryer switched our radio frequency so I could check in with Ken Carpenter, flying the midday shift in an O-2.

We caught him in mid-transmission, asking, ". . . and where's the fire coming from?" I sat up, craned my neck, and looked far ahead in that perfect sky to where little dots flitted like mosquitoes. A tense voice whispered, "Northwest, Covey, hit northwest seventy-five meters." I knew that voice—Regis Gmitter. *It was my old team, RT Hawaii.*

Clear weather, thank God, I thought. We'll need it for bombing.

Cryer shoved the throttles full forward, heading directly toward that distant, little storm amid a perfect sky, where aircraft dived and smoke arose from bursting rockets. I will never forget the following hour, not only because of what happened but because, unknowingly, our radio transmissions were recorded by a Huey crew, a complete account that would reach me almost thirty years later.

As our OV-10 overtook the Hueys, Carpenter quickly briefed me: "We got the team to a short ladder LZ, Hueys are almost here, Cobras already on-station, firing. A-1s about ten minutes out. They had contact forty minutes ago, been running ever since. An RPG hit one Yard. No fire yet at the LZ. It's yours if you're ready, Plasticman."

I radioed, "Got it, Shoebox." His O-2 turned away.

I had great faith in my old teammates, Les Dover, John Justice, and Regis Gmitter, and in our air team of Cobras, Hueys, and Covey. The most critical factor was speed, getting them out quick before the enemy could rush dozens, maybe hundreds of soldiers to the scene, to assault the team or shoot down helicopters. Eyeing high ground just beyond where I saw RT Hawaii's orange panel, I warned the Lead Cobra—Panther 36—"You can expect possible ground fire on those hillsides to the north."

At almost the same instant, Gmitter called, "You guys are taking ground fire!"

"I'm bringing the Cobras in right now," I replied, "a heavy gun team. Give us an azimuth and distance." As Panther 36 turned inbound, I relayed from Gmitter, "Ground fire is generally north and northwest."

Panther 36 reported, "We're to the south, we'll make south-to-north gun runs, with right-hand breaks." To reduce the time gap between the Cobras and the Hueys—led by White Lead—I had his birds immediately begin descending.

Everyone stayed off the radios those crucial seconds, listening for any report of ground fire. I saw White Lead level off just above the trees a mile south, as two Cobras pummeled the northern hillside with rockets and minigun fire.

Panther 36 radioed, "White Lead. No fire down here. We're ready for you."

Then a breathless voice cried my formal call sign: "Delta Papa Three! Delta Papa Three! Tango Pa—"—cut out by White Lead on the same frequency. I radioed Gmitter, "White Lead will be down in a moment, get your people together and let's get out of there, quick."

A desperate voice shrieked, "Covey-Covey! Covey-Covey!"—this time cut out by Panther 36 transmitting as he vectored the approaching Huey into the LZ.

I radioed Gmitter, "Did you attempt to call me?"

"Negative-negative."

I looked at the other call signs and immediately I knew, a terrible stab in my guts: *It was RT Colorado, Pat Mitchel's team, ten miles southwest.* More than anything in this world I wanted to be two places at once, rescuing two teams. Here below me, in great danger, was my old team, and that other beseeching voice was RT Colorado. No matter how bad it was, he had to wait.

I saw White Lead on the treetops, nearing RT Hawaii's yellow smoke— Mitchel's breathless voice interrupted, *"Plasticman! Plasticman!"* I could not ignore him again and warned, "I have a team in a Prairie Fire right now. As quickly as possible I'll send you a light gun team."

Those first minutes in a gunfight can be life and death, I reminded Mike Cryer on the intercom. Our OV-10 had a full load of fourteen high explosive rockets and 2,000 rounds of 7.62 mm; we agreed to rush to RT Colorado as soon as we got RT Hawaii on the choppers. I radioed Mitchel, "I will attempt to send aid as quickly as possible. What is your situation right now?"

"Prairie Fire! Prairie Fire! Prairie Fire!"

"Roger, I copy." That's all I could do. Each passing second, I knew, meant more shots, more RPGs, maybe more lost men. We had two teams in Prairie Fire, the assets already committed to one, all the choppers on-station, gunships on the deck. I had to focus here, get this right, first.

A Cobra turned in front of the Huey as it neared RT Hawaii. "Taking fire!" White Lead called. Door gunners opened up and a Cobra riddled the treetops. In danger of being shot down, White Lead's Huey pulled out. This was going to take some time. I radioed Panther 36: "I've got another team in Prairie Fire, can you take over this extraction?"

Coming out of a gun run, he responded, "Negative. If you leave, we won't get A-1s." One Huey had almost been shot down, the A-1s were at least five minutes out, and all we had were four Cobras. I understood and looked southwest, to the hills where I knew RT Colorado was fighting for its life and silently urged, Hold out, guys, hold out.

White Lead came around. Mitchel, breathless from carrying a wounded teammate, gasped again into the radio. All I could do was repeat, "I have a Prairie Fire in progress. If possible, evade, evade." The gunships were lined up again and White Lead shifted his approach to put more trees between him and the earlier ground fire. Lead spotted the team's panel and flared to land.

I radioed Mitchel again, "I cannot depart yet. Do your best to hold out."

I watched White Lead ease down into a hole in the treetops and kick out ladders. Gmitter shouted, "Taking ground fire!" The door gunners blasted with their M-60s, and the Cobras fired rockets and miniguns danger-close. That brave son-of-a-bitch White Lead stayed right there until he got half the team. Momentarily the second Huey went in to get the rest. I radioed Panther 36, "Sayonara, I'm departing with the OV-10." I told him to meet me at RT Colorado as soon as he was finished here, then told White Lead to take his Hueys back to Dak To, rearm, refuel, and prepare to launch immediately.

Mike Cryer shoved the OV-10 throttles full forward. I radioed Mitchel, "I am en route your location, will be there in three minutes."

For the first time in twenty minutes, Pat Mitchel thought there was a chance he'd get his men out—at least his badly wounded One-Two, Lyn St. Laurent. It was too late already for David Mixter, who lay dead a dozen feet away. Mitchel and St. Laurent were alone. The NVA were less than fifty yards away and Mitchel could hear them calling to one another.

It had all begun forty minutes earlier. Just after eating lunch RT Colorado had climbed a ridge and come upon a new sandbag bunker with freshly cut bamboo and footprints everywhere. Their approach had sent the NVA running, Mitchel suspected. Walking at the rear of the column, Sergeant Mixter and a Yard, Wdot, noticed a whole line of fresh bunkers in the distance.

Mitchel signaled to get away, fast, but they were in a bamboo grove, the ground covered with husks crunchier than dried leaves. To move quietly they followed a narrow dirt path, and had traveled five minutes when Sergeant St. Laurent, RT Colorado's radio operator, heard Covey Rider Carpenter reacting to RT Hawaii's emergency. St. Laurent alerted Mitchel, who decided it was best to lay up and hide until that was resolved. They crept off the trail and down a little ledge, put out claymores and got in a semicircle. St. Laurent sat in the middle with the radio.

For a few minutes they sat there silently while St. Laurent monitored the radio. Then Pin, a Yard lying beside Mitchel, leaned over, eyes wide, and whispered, "VC." Everyone lay flat, hoping the NVA would pass them by. St. Laurent heard brush breaking.

KA-BOOM!—an RPG exploded—then five claymores—*BOOM! BOOM! BOOM! BOOM! BOOM!* AKs and CAR-15s blended into one wild intermix of close-range fire. St. Laurent tried to call Covey, then looked over his shoulder at an NVA running directly at him, aiming an AK—*No time to shoot!*—he closed his eyes—Mixter shoved him down and shot dead the charging NVA with a solid burst from his sawed-off RPD machine gun. St. Laurent couldn't believe he was still alive. The fire peaked, then dropped.

Queerly, it was quiet again.

RT Colorado's bursting claymores and concentrated fire had repulsed the assault, leaving dead and wounded NVA scattered in the jungle before them. Mitchel waved his hand to withdraw before the enemy could reorganize for a second attack. Dave Mixter rolled to his knees, spotted an NVA raising an RPG—they fired simultaneously—*Ba-ba-ba-bang!*—*KA-BOOM!*—the gunner fell dead and his rocket exploded at Mixter's knees. Mixter crumpled forward, riddled with terrible wounds. He was dead, One-Zero Mitchel could see.

Then St. Laurent gasped, "I'm hit." RPG fragments had torn into his chest and a leg, along with an AK slug that had hit his right forearm and biceps, leaving his arm hanging uselessly. Worse yet, as Mitchel knelt beside St. Laurent, all their Yards ran off, abandoning them.

KA-BOOM! KA-BOOM! Two more RPGs exploded. They had to get to better cover.

Mitchel threw St. Laurent down a six-foot embankment, then rolled after him and, peeking over the top every twenty seconds, began treating his wounds and pausing to shoot his CAR-15 or 40mm grenade launcher at the enemy. The NVA would have swarmed over them already, Mitchel thought, except they were busy treating and carrying off their own wounded. That could end any second, especially when NVA reinforcements arrived. Unable to both fight and carry St. Laurent, Mitchel knew his only hope was to get Covey overhead and start putting air on the NVA. Taking over the radio, Mitchel spoke with me, then injected St. Laurent with morphine, and waited. In those lonely minutes, he and St. Laurent made a pact: Rather than be taken alive, they would kill each other.

As the groan of OV-10 engines sounded overhead, Mitchel finished stemming the worst of St. Laurent's bleeding. He looked over the embankment again and saw David Mixter's body, not ten yards away. Mixter's biggest fault had always been his size—six foot five. Other One-Zeros didn't want him because they worried about what would happen if he were severely wounded; how would they carry him? Despite their disparate sizes—as dramatically different as Mutt and Jeff—Mitchel so admired Lurch's spirit that he took him anyhow. And now, what could he do?

I radioed, "This is Plasticman. Pop smoke. Where do you want our fire?"

The NVA were still so close that Mitchel could hear their voices. "No can talk," he whispered. "Two of us together. Charlie is dead on our ass." But he did pop a grenade, and I saw his smoke on the treetops. Then Mitchel whispered, "Hit fifty meters south."

As Cryer positioned our OV-10 for the first run, Mitchel warned that his Yards had run off and he was afraid we might hit them. I did not share his compassion. "The Yards made their choice. Now get your heads down. We're coming in hot."

Cryer rolled in, nearly touching the treetops as we strafed and fired four rockets. "Bring it closer, closer," Mitchel requested. I warned, "Get your head down, we're doing it again." With that pass the NVA began firing at our plane, but Cryer performed magnificently, pressing low and disregarding ground fire to put those rockets and tracers where RT Colorado needed them.

For the first time I heard animation in Mitchel's voice. "That was Number One! Now do it 360 degrees."

As we finished our next series of passes, Panther 36 arrived with his Cobra wingman, adding their considerable firepower to the effort. Momentarily, pounded by rockets and miniguns, the enemy pulled off just a bit. If we stood any chance of getting Mitchel and St. Laurent out alive, we had to exploit that break and move right away. I radioed, "Are you capable of carrying your wounded?"

Mitchel realized St. Laurent was badly hit and he'd need help to walk but Lurch was there, too, only a few yards away. David Mixter had died saving their lives. "I'm with Lurch," Mitchel radioed. "I can still see Lurch. I can't leave him."

I shared the anguish in Mitchel's voice and dreaded the idea of leaving Mixter's body, but the last thing Pat needed was to hear my grief. I pounded my fist hard on the canopy, then, regaining control, put on a calm, almost fatherly tone. "You can't be worried about the dead right now. We've got to be concerned about the living. Now get moving." With great regret, Mitchel turned away from Mixter's body, put an arm around St. Laurent and led him south while the Cobras and our OV-10 rocketed and strafed their backtrail, hitting it as hard as we could.

Already I'd contacted the Bright Light team at Dak To and had them board two chase helicopters, putting our Special Forces medic in White Lead so he could begin treating St. Laurent immediately—if Pat could make it to the LZ. If that proved impossible, I'd have the Bright Light team land and fight their way through to what remained of RT Colorado.

Then three Vietnamese A-1s arrived and I sent Panther 36 back to refuel and rearm. Cryer put half the A-1 ordnance in the area where RT Colorado had fought, then used the fighters sparingly to preoccupy the enemy while Mitchel carried St. Laurent 500 yards to the extraction LZ.

Forty minutes later all the choppers were back, ready to extract Mitchel and St. Laurent, who had reached the LZ. Mitchel was composed though exhausted. When Cryer began using a fresh pair of USAF A-1s to prep the area around the LZ, all seven of the missing Yards showed up, drawn to the sound of aircraft engines. Mitchel put them to work, helping him carry St. Laurent to the first extraction Huey. Living by the recon ethic, Mitchel was the last man to leave the LZ. Thanks to our heavy prep, we got them out with almost no ground fire.

The badly wounded St. Laurent was medevaced. Mitchel would lead two more missions, then serve as a medic in the dispensary.

The next morning my pilot, Captain Cryer, flew with Larry White to insert the Bright Light team to look for Lurch. They found Mixter's hat and a huge pool of blood. That was all. The NVA had even gathered all the expended cartridges.

That night a dozen young recon men showed up at the Country Club. They talked and laughed and showed no respect when I began to sing "Hey, Blue." I jumped to my feet to attack their insolence—then I realized they had no idea what that song meant. Hardly four months had passed since I'd left recon, and the turnover was such that these men simply didn't know. This had to be corrected.

I led them all to the NCO club, then stood in the very spot where Captain Lesesne, my old recon company commander, had stood in 1968, when I'd first heard those verses. To the silent club I retold the story of "Hey, Blue," then together, everyone in the club stood, and we all sang, adding David Mixter's name at the end. "Those verses, those names," I finished, "we can never forget them. Or everything we've done was for nothing."

We were still in the gloom of Lurch's loss a few days later when more bad news arrived. We were entertaining my roommate's old friend and a Project Delta recon legend, Jay Graves, in the Country Club. Jay had arrived in Vietnam in the early days and forgotten to go home. Now, with Project Delta gone, he'd become an instructor at SOG's recon school near Saigon. Bob Howard came by and we had quite a party going when a recon man carried in the latest *Stars and Stripes* newspaper. Its headline announced a dramatic reduction in Special Forces, the first since JFK had called the green beret "a symbol of excellence." One full Special Forces Group—2,000-plus slots—was being disbanded, and that was just the first of several cutbacks. The Green Berets had been the symbol of America's fight in Vietnam, and now our long jealous enemies in the military bureaucracy had declared open season. Already we'd begun to feel the effect, with some of our finest, most decorated NCOs rotating home to be drug counselors or guards at Leavenworth Prison, which we considered the worst assignments in the Army. Jay Graves pinned the *Stars and Stripes* to the window screen over our heads. We all glared at it.

Disgusted, Captain Howard turned and left.

Five minutes later we were still commiserating when Howard pulled open the door, lifted an AK and—*KA-KA-KA-KA-KA-KA-KA-KA-KA-KA-KA-KA-KA-KA!* He emptied the magazine in one long burst over our heads, riddling that *Stars and Stripes,* shooting off bits of newsprint that floated away like snow. Howard said nothing, just turned and walked away. A few days later he was en route to Washington to meet President Nixon and receive the Medal of Honor. Then I left, too, going home for yet another thirty-day extension leave.

Just as I reached Minnesota, the South Vietnamese Army invaded Laos, advancing west from the old Marine base at Khe Sanh. Called Operation Lam Son 719, it soon became a debacle, and I watched the sad televised spectacle of South Vietnamese soldiers so panicked that they wrapped their arms around Huey skids to get out of Laos. It proved a costly defeat.

At least I had Howard's medal ceremony to look forward to.

The day that President Nixon draped the Medal of Honor's pale blue ribbon around Howard's neck, I sat before the TV in my parents' living room watching the evening news. Coming on top of his previous decorations—the Distinguished Service Cross and multiple Silver and Bronze Stars, plus eight Purple Hearts—Howard's combat awards exceeded those of Audie Murphy, America's legendary World War II hero, until then our most highly decorated serviceman. At last, Howard would get his due. I flipped station to station, but not one of the networks—not CBS or NBC or ABC—could find ten seconds to mention Captain Robert Howard or his indomitable courage. I found nothing about him in the newspapers. Twisted by the antiwar politics of that era, many in the media believed that to recognize a heroic act was to glorify war. They simply chose not to cover the ceremony. It might as well not have happened.

As I prepared to go back to Vietnam, a neighbor woman asked why I'd volunteered for yet another six months. "I'm paid $625 a month tax-free," I replied flippantly, "and the weather's great." It was an inane thing to say but it made more sense to her than if I'd tried to explain why men fight in combat and what comradeship means.

Going back this time, instantly I could see changes. While I was home the 5th Special Forces Group had folded its colors and withdrawn, so that technically, my unit, Command and Control Central, no longer existed. I defiantly wore my beret, as did the other returning SOG veterans I encountered in Nha Trang. There I learned that all the old Special Forces A-Camps had been transferred to the South Vietnamese Army, while the Mike Forces had been disbanded, a sorry thing, for they had been the most effective indigenous unit in the entire war.

When I reached Kontum I found our compound just as I'd left it, except our name had changed. Instead of belonging to the departed 5th Special Forces Group, we were now "advisors" assigned to the innocuously titled Task Force Two, Advisory Element, our green berets replaced by black baseball caps, and our Special Forces patches replaced by U.S. Army Vietnam patches. The same had happened at CCN, except they were called Task Force One, Advisory Element.

That wasn't the most substantive change.

President Nixon had taken such heavy political heat when the South Vietnamese Army invaded Laos—and mindful that Congress had passed the Cooper-Church Amendment a year earlier forbidding American ground troops in Laos—that he secretly ordered our operations ended. Thus, U.S. Special Forces recon and Hatchet Force missions into Laos ceased on 7 February

1971. Laos operations would continue, as had been the case earlier with Cambodia, to the extent that they could be performed by South Vietnamese recon teams.

Were we out of business? Hardly.

Months earlier SOG intelligence had noticed a trend that we confirmed in the field: With most U.S. combat units withdrawn and almost no South Vietnamese forces opposing the NVA along the Laotian border, the North Vietnamese had begun shifting their units, their logistics—virtually the Ho Chi Minh Trail system itself—inside South Vietnam. Highways that had ended in Laos now snaked their way secretively into South Vietnam, belts of antiaircraft guns crept eastward, and where once there had been a single NVA bastion inside South Vietnam—the Ashau Valley—similar redoubts were taking shape in a half-dozen remote border valleys. Immense territory had been conceded to the enemy without a shot fired.

With ever fewer Americans in Vietnam, and more NVA nearby, the danger to our remaining units was great. Someone had to penetrate these new haunts and monitor that growing threat. Thus our new area of recon operations was a ten-mile strip the length of South Vietnam's border with Laos, from the Demilitarized Zone in the north to the Ia Drang Valley, southwest of Pleiku. We no longer had to go across the border to explore the Ho Chi Minh Trail, for it had come to us.

Among our recon teams, not a whole lot had transpired during my leave because we were readjusting to the new area of operations, and most air support had been diverted to the South Vietnamese invasion of Laos. Though they practically had to hog-tie him, SOG headquarters persuaded Joe Walker to leave RT California and become a recon tactics instructor at SOG's recon school near Saigon. He'd hardly turned over the team to its new One-Zero, Staff Sergeant Charles Clayton, when it became embroiled in a heavy firefight that wounded all three Americans—Clayton, Galen Musselman, and Toby Todd. A volunteer who accompanied them, Captain Robert Camors, Jr., was wounded, too.

Mercifully, during my absence we had not lost any more men.

On my first Covey flight on my return, with Captain Gary Armentrout, we flew over Dak To and though I'd been gone only five weeks it looked like a ghost town, its wooden buildings stripped, tents gone, the entire base almost deserted but for our launch site. Yet fifteen miles away, the NVA looked stronger than ever. The war was changing in an unsettling, troubling way.

For us, though, it was a quiet day. We had no teams to insert or extract, and the teams afield had nothing of consequence to report. All day we flew in wide circles, talking and listening to music from Armed Forces Radio. In mid-afternoon Armentrout asked, "John, you ever ski?"

"A bit," I said, "in Minnesota."

"But have you ever skied the clouds?" To show me, he put the OV-10 in a lazy, climbing turn, going up, up, up until we topped a puffy cumulus mountain. "You'll love this," he promised as we nosed down a wispy slope, riding its edge just close enough to stay in sunlight, turning and banking and riding it down, down, down until we jumped its final knoll and looked for another mountain. That's how we spent the rest of the day, taking turns skiing the skies, riding ethereal slopes beyond the antiaircraft fire, far above any thought of war.

A few days later another OV-10 pilot, known as "Eagle Eyes" for his ability to find even heavily camouflaged targets for air strikes, proved quite the opposite of Armentrout. I asked him, did he have any secret technique to share?

Eagle Eyes hesitated, then announced, "I'll show you how I do it."

We spiraled downward and when we leveled off we were on the trees—*right on the trees*—dipping and banking among threatening hills that towered over us. A Seventh Air Force directive required FACs to fly no lower than 2,500 feet AGL (above ground level) with reprimands and even Article 15 punishments for violators, but here we were, 100 feet above the jungle, so low, Eagle Eyes explained, that he could see through most NVA camouflage. "I can't find a damned thing from 2,500 feet," he complained, "so I risk ground fire and reprimands but I do find the bastards." It wasn't danger to pilots that so concerned the Air Force bureaucracy, he said, but damage to aircraft. What would he do if his plane were hit by AK fire—proof he'd been below 2,500 feet? "Then I'll lie and tell the desk jockeys that I was shooting for one of your recon teams." That was the sole justification for a FAC taking an AK hit. Then all he faced was buying the crew chiefs a case of beer for each bullet hole—if they found the holes before he did.

To some extent we all sidestepped or violated rules. When fighters had ordnance left after inserting or extracting a team, we had to dump it somewhere because it was unsafe to send them home with fused bombs and napalm. Oftentimes there wasn't a worthwhile target in the team's official six-kilometer area of operations, which had been cleared with the U.S. ambassador in Vientiane. The choice then was blindly dumping it there to satisfy the ambassador, or reporting it as having been dropped in this authorized area but actually expending it where it might hit something. Most of the time, frankly, we did the latter—we lied. So, for example, we'd lead the fighters ten miles from a reported target, and instead bomb a spot where a week before I'd seen a glint off what could have been a truck windshield, or we'd pound a ridge where we'd taken antiaircraft fire. Sometimes it was only for personal satisfaction: For three months after David Mixter was killed, when I had tactical air to spare I bombed the lonely hillside where he'd died.

Some days we had no teams on the ground and the area so socked in that we knew we wouldn't insert any. Then we'd go exploring, aerial tourists wandering wherever we wished across northeast Cambodia or southern Laos. On one such expedition, a pilot flew our OV-10 just fifty feet above the Se Kong River, a major tributary of the mighty Mekong, at times dropping below the treetops. Rounding a curve, we stumbled upon a supply boat that had run aground on a sandbar, stacked high with 100-kilo rice bags. As we flashed past, three NVA leaped headfirst into the water, swimming for their lives. My pilot turned around, lined up and fired rockets that skipped across the water like tossed stones, then slammed into the boat, blowing it sky-high. Enemy soldiers opened fire but we were gone before they got a good aim. We continued downriver to Attapeu, the largest town in southern Laos and the farthest west I'd ever been. Nestled in a mile-wide river bend beneath the Bolovens Plateau, Attapeu was smaller than Kontum, with perhaps 5,000 residents. As we circled at 2,500 feet, I looked down at the old French provincial headquarters, looking like a Southern plantation house, and at NVA trucks that boldly drove its streets in broad daylight. I'd never seen better defensive terrain: a river barrier beneath a plateau, with eastern, northern, and southern approaches of open grassland for ten miles. A single tank battalion supported by artillery or air should have been able to hold Attapeu forever.

How in the hell had the Royal Laotian Army lost this town?

While exploring Laos that day I missed General Creighton Abrams, the commander of U.S. forces in Vietnam, when he visited our compound to present the Distinguished Service Cross to Sergeant Gary "Mike" Rose, a medic who'd performed gallantly on Operation Tailwind.

Before the ceremony, General Abrams toured a layout of recon gear and weapons, and met RT West Virginia, escorted by One-Zero Ron Knight. Abrams asked a few questions of One-One Larry Kramer. Impressed by his gung ho responses, Abrams turned to Knight. "I see such great esprit and morale here," the four-star general said. "What are you doing to encourage your young people to take such chances on getting killed this late in the war?"

The answer was obvious to Knight. "Shucks, sir, we don't have to do nothin' to motivate people. These ain't nothin' but regular old run-of-the-mill Special Forces soldiers."

Standing nearby, Covey Rider Lowell Stevens could not believe the general's reaction. The veins stood out on Abrams's head as he barked, "Goddamn it, Sergeant, I didn't ask what you think . . ." The rest was incoherent, crammed with expletives. It astonished Stevens.

After Abrams pinned the medal on Rose's chest, Stevens went back to the Country Club and found Carpenter, drunk on his day off, wearing a pair of baggy old GI undershorts pulled high over his belly. When Stevens described what he'd just seen, Carpenter shouted, "That son-of-a-bitch!" Carp indignantly pulled on flip-flop shower shoes and hung around his neck a Crown Royal bottle in its blue sack and announced, "I wanna see this damn general who's sayin' bad things about Special Forces!"

Meanwhile, Abrams had gone to the camp theater and was addressing the entire unit. Reaching the theater's screen door, Carpenter paused, his good sense temporarily restored. But the devil materialized beside him in the figure of Lowell Stevens, who whispered, "Carpenter, you ain't got a hair on your airborne ass if you don't go in there and show that bastard what a *real* Green Beret looks like."

Carp pulled up his shorts and strolled onto the stage within twenty feet of Abrams—the astonished audience watched the drunken, half-naked Carpenter bow and grin and wave. God smiled on SOG that day, for every man in the theater saw Carpenter, *except* Abrams, who was so wrapped up in his speech that he didn't turn his head and didn't see Stevens pull Carp away.

A few days later I inserted a Hatchet Force platoon along the Cambodian border. Led by Sergeant First Class Gerald Denison, a SOG old hand on his second tour, the platoon found no enemy until the fifth day, when a brief exchange of fire killed Staff Sergeant Kevin Grogan. Larry White flew that day and extracted them without further casualties.

As April came to a close, a company-size Hatchet Force raid was being readied for a suspected enemy logistics site on the Cambodian border. The night before the mission, the raid commander came by the Covey Country Club to talk about air support. It was Captain Fred Krupa, the last of my Ashtray Two comrades still in Vietnam.

What he had to say troubled me.

Chapter Fifteen

Krupa's company raid evolved from a close-run recon mission a few days earlier.

Larry White had flown Covey for that extraction, and told me about it over a drink in the Country Club. In the northern Plei Trap Valley, almost due west from Kontum, a six-man team had observed some 100 NVA rolling three-wheeled supply bicycles from Cambodia to an apparent way station just inside South Vietnam. Creeping closer to investigate, the team made contact and had to run for it. Flying with Captain Mike Cryer, White put in two sets of A-1s to get the team out. It was estimated that the bombing and team's fire had killed at least fifty NVA—quite a hot engagement and an indicator of how highly the enemy valued their supply dump.

SOG headquarters concluded this was a target worthy of a 100-man Hatchet Force raid, to be led by my old friend and Ashtray Two teammate Captain Fred Krupa.

Sitting with me in the Country Club the night before his raid, Krupa declined a drink but wanted to discuss his insertion. "Actually," I told him, "I won't be inserting you." Our newest Covey Rider, Steve "Jade" Keever—former One-Zero of RT Illinois—was flying the next day's first shift. I had the midday shift, by which time Fred's company should have landed.

"Maybe so," Krupa agreed. "But in case things run late, I don't want any prep." I could understand no preparatory air strike for a recon team insertion, but landing 100 men in a spot known to be heavily occupied? Surprise, Krupa declared, was key to his raid, and even a delay of five or ten minutes for an aerial bombardment would jeopardize the shock of his sudden, unanticipated landing. Besides, he'd have double the normal complement of helicopters, so his entire force could land at once. Practicing the ethic that a leader leads from the front, Krupa announced he'd be the first man off the first helicopter. I still recommended a prep but, like Keever, respected that this was Krupa's call. In case of trouble, a set of A-1s would be orbiting overhead.

There was another matter, though, that concerned me as much as the prep.

"Why are you taking Robideaux along?" I asked. Gene Robideaux is a pseudonym.

"I think he was railroaded for being too aggressive," Krupa said. "So I'm giving him a chance." I disagreed mightily and told him so. Sergeant First Class Gene Robideaux, a former One-Zero, was physically impressive but his eyes shifted when you looked into them. An incessant talker, during a previous Mike Force tour he'd been called "Motor Mouth." Instinctively I did not trust him. But the case against Robideaux was more than my instinct.

Most recon men blamed Robideaux for getting his One-One killed four months earlier by unnecessarily blowing up an easily repaired bamboo water pipeline, which told every NVA for miles where they were, instigating a bloody firefight. On another mission he'd blown up ordinary termite mounds and called them "underground caches." On still another operation, Robideaux's Yards told debriefers, he'd faked a firefight to get his team extracted.

He may have been delusory, too, for Robideaux saw imaginary objects in photos he'd snapped while overflying prospective targets, drawing grease pencil circles around what he claimed were weapons or trenches or men. The photo lab supervisor, Ted Wicorek, told him the photo paper was too grainy to resolve anything so small, sparking an angry shouting match.

Because we were short of men, Robideaux remained until Recon First Sergeant Billy Greenwood finally threw him out, but then Fred Krupa recruited him as his new Hatchet Force first sergeant.

Since the Ashtray Two operation, Krupa had evolved into an aggressive Hatchet Force leader, even changing his code name to "Mad Dog," not to insult the memory of the MIA Jerry "Mad Dog" Shriver, but to reincarnate his daring spirit. Therefore, he saw Robideaux's boisterousness as dynamic leadership akin to his own.

"I wouldn't put any faith in Robideaux," I warned.

"Listen, John, Robideaux will be right beside me. I can watch him. And don't forget, I have 100 men," Krupa reasoned. "Robideaux punks out?—I still have ninety-nine." I shook Fred's hand and wished I could go along. Under his leadership it would be a hell of an operation.

Late the next morning at Kontum airfield, an O-2 flown by Captain Wesley Groves, Covey 598, picked me up. After we'd gained altitude, I radioed Covey Rider Jade Keever to learn how Krupa's raid was going. He reported there had been several delays in getting Krupa's company to the launch site, Polei Kleng Special Forces Camp, selected because it was closer to the Plei Trap Valley than our Dak To launch site.

"The choppers are now refueling," Keever finished. "So I guess it's your game."

It was good that Fred had briefed me, for otherwise I'd have put in a prep for him. As it was, as quickly as our O-2 reached the Plei Trap Valley and I confirmed the correct landing zone—an old slash-and-burn field large enough to land a dozen Hueys—and got the A-1s overhead, I radioed Polei Kleng for a launch.

Larry White had told me that the team he'd extracted had taken heavy fire from ridges on the north and northwest, and the suspected supply dump lay only about 300 yards west of the LZ. I scanned the area with binoculars but could detect no sign of the enemy.

Minutes later I spotted Cobra Lead arriving from the southwest with the entire flight behind him, some four gunships and twelve Hueys. The Hueys, from the 57th Assault Helicopter Company, were led by an experienced pilot, call sign Yellow Lead. To make sure the Cobras and Hueys recognized the correct LZ, my pilot, Captain Groves, dived on it while calling, "Bingo-bingo-bingo."

Now everyone was ready.

Cobra Lead and his wingman buzzed the LZ to see if they'd draw ground fire. There was none. Nor did he see anyone, he radioed. Therefore we'd keep the pair of A-1s in high orbit and only bring them in if necessary.

I OK'd Huey Lead—with Captain Krupa aboard—to take his flight in. Six Hueys dropped down low to follow Cobra Lead to the LZ. The other half-dozen Hueys held in orbit. My O-2 flew directly overhead as we watched Fred's chopper cross the last tree line, then drop down and hover on the LZ, another five Hueys close behind it.

Over the radio I heard a burst of machine gun fire—*then nothing.*

Yellow Lead suddenly lifted, turned his nose east, and flew away—but no radio message. He poured on speed, heading toward Polei Kleng, not rejoining his formation.

"Yellow Lead," I radioed, "say status, over."

There was no response. Apparently gunfire must have knocked out his radios. Cobra Lead raced away to fly alongside the Huey and assess the damage. Momentarily the Cobra returned, reporting he'd observed several bullet holes, while those aboard the chopper had waved their arms and pointed back toward the LZ.

As best Cobra Lead could tell, that fire had come from the north, so while Captain Groves, my pilot, brought down the A-1s, I told all the choppers to return to Polei Kleng and refuel while we sorted out the situation.

Ten minutes later we were bombing a hillside facing the LZ when I got a frantic message from Polei Kleng: *"Krupa's on the LZ! Mad Dog was shot, he fell out, he's on the ground!"*

Instantly we suspended bombing and dived to the LZ. We buzzed low across the slash-and-burn and tried to spot Fred among the brush and logs; all we could see were green tracers that followed us across the sky. Groves didn't give a damn about ground fire, we just flew back and forth and back and forth. We could not see him. Nor did we hear Krupa's emergency radio.

He's next to a log, was all that anyone knew. A mahogany log lay near where Fred's bird had hovered, but try as I might I could not make out anything in the shadow beside it.

The raid was forgotten; this was now a rescue mission. I told the choppers to shut down at Polei Kleng while we brought in a massive prep, which Captain Groves already was requesting from Hillsborough, the C-130 airborne control center for tactical air. While fighters rushed to our location, I planned a strategy: Fred Krupa, alone and wounded, was somewhere below us, either on or near the original LZ. Instead of landing the company where he'd fallen—which is what the NVA probably expected and already had covered by fire—I selected another large LZ, only 500 yards south. That way I could bombard the new LZ with little risk of accidentally hitting Krupa.

Not five minutes later the first set of F-4 Phantoms arrived, carrying two dozen 500-pound bombs. I had Groves put their bombs along one edge of the new LZ and their 20mm cannon fire on the route the company would use to go after Fred. Before they were expended, another set of Phantoms was overhead, and Groves did the same thing. Then a third pair got there, and a fourth, a fifth, a sixth pair, until we had expended twelve F-4 Phantoms—half-again the payload of a B-52 bomber, some 144 bombs. Bomb blasts had completely encircled the new LZ, while thousands of 20mm rounds had peppered the route the rescuers would take to reach Krupa. We stood a decent chance, acting fast, before the enemy could come back. Time was of the essence.

Even before this tremendous prep finished I radioed for the choppers to launch; not until they were en route did I learn that leading the company was Robideaux. I felt a sickening knot in my stomach.

When finally Billy Greenwood had run Robideaux out of recon, it was after he'd refused to get off a chopper because he claimed to have seen enemy on the LZ. This so incensed the Covey Rider, Lowell Stevens, that he'd told our acting commander, "I am not going to insert that man anymore. He's going to get people killed who don't deserve to be killed."

I hoped that with Krupa's fate at stake, and after such a heavy prep, Robideaux would seize this chance to redeem himself, just as Fred had hoped. Hell, he'd probably be awarded a medal. And getting Fred back, alive or dead, he'd deserve it in my book.

As the Cobras descended into the new LZ, I held my breath. I watched the gunships race back and forth across the field. Then Cobra Lead radioed, "Negative ground fire." The bombs had done their job. The lead Cobra called in the Hueys.

Six Hueys went in, flared and hovered.

And hovered.

And hovered.

"What's wrong?" I radioed the lead Huey.

"The ground leader says he can see enemy. Says he cannot go in." In heavy static I heard Robideaux's voice, "Uh, Plasticman, we can't do this. There's bunkers here, enemy. We can't go."

I shouted, *"Get out!"*

Robideaux kept chattering away.

I screamed, *"Get out, you motherfucker!"* Robideaux pretended not to hear me and kept babbling excuses. I flipped to a UHF frequency and called his pilot, "Tell him to get out."

"Roger, Plasticman." There was a pause, then Lead came back, contempt in his voice, "The team leader says he sees people. He won't go."

Crazily, I thought, maybe I could parachute from our O-2 and take command. But that couldn't work, not now. The Hueys just hovered and hovered. The NVA had to be out of their bunkers by now, rushing toward the sound of our helicopters, our advantage declining by the second. The copters had been there hovering at least four minutes—begging for trouble. Robideaux kept babbling away purposely, so he could not hear me ordering him to get out.

I could not risk the aircraft any longer. "Withdraw, Yellow Lead," I directed.

The Hueys dipped their noses and climbed over the trees, taking not one hostile shot.

Immediately I radioed Kontum and requested authority to send the choppers back to Polei Kleng, so I could land there, relieve Robideaux, and personally take command of the Hatchet Force for another rescue attempt. We had several hours of daylight left.

Five minutes later came the response: Denied, with no further discussion. All the aircraft were to return to Kontum and call it a day.

Groves and I circled the LZ another few minutes while, one last time, I held binoculars to my eyes and searched for any sign of my friend and fellow veteran of that night-long run through the jungle on Ashtray Two. Then we, too, had to leave.

As we flew away, a horrible dread overwhelmed me—minutes already had become tens of minutes, then hours, and soon would follow days, then years. I thought back to Fred in Bangkok, when Yancey played the John Lennon song and we fooled him into thinking the lyric was, "Give war a chance." *And he jumped from his hotel window and missed the pool and* . . . I slammed my fist against the windshield. Fred was gone, there was nothing more I could do. Fred Krupa, a brave man who led from the front was now Missing in Action. I broke down.

As our O-2 approached Kontum airfield I radioed ahead, requesting a meeting with our acting commander. Minutes later I stood before him and in vivid detail described exactly what had happened. Then I requested that Robideaux be court-martialed for cowardice in the face of the enemy, He assured me he would see that the proper thing was done.

Nothing was done. Not one blasted thing. Every recon man I'd ever known would not have hesitated to leap off that chopper; every Hatchet Force man I'd ever met would have stormed into that jungle—all would have risked their lives going after Fred Krupa—except Robideaux, the miserable, craven coward, made all the worse because he wore the green beret. But who was worse? The coward Robideaux or our commander who failed to punish him? In the world of covert operations, security and deniability exceed concerns about justice and the fate of lost men, providing the perfect shield for an unscrupulous dreg like Robideaux. Cloaked behind SOG's curtain of secrecy, his postwar reputation suffered not in the slightest. I was not asked to contribute to the official incident report, never even saw it, but it must not have hinted at Robideaux's culpability, for in later years he was promoted to sergeant major.

As for Fred Krupa, we did not know whether he was alive or dead. The Montagnard company commander, Ayom, who'd been sitting in the doorway beside Krupa, told debriefers he had grabbed Fred's right shoulder, then lost hold of him when a bullet struck his hand. The Huey crew chief, Specialist Four Melvin Lew, reported he saw Krupa fall, then lie on his back next to a log, not moving or making a sound.

Krupa's loss drained me, an emotional blow that left me nearly empty.

That night I sat in the Covey Country Club alone in the dark, drinking and thinking. So long ago I had toasted my lost teammates on RT New Mexico—Stephens, Bullard, and Simmons—followed by more teammates—Bill Spencer, Fat Albert, Baby Huey. I recited my personal version of "Hey, Blue," with still more names, too many names. All those fine men—David Mixter, Chuck Hein, Ken Worthley, Jim Ripanti, Ricardo Davis, Ron Bozikis, Wayne Anderson, the entire RT Pennsylvania, Ron Goulet, Dennis Bingham, Mike Kuropas, Bill Stubbs, Greg Harrigan, Sam Zumbrun, and a dozen more, so many more.

And now, Fred Krupa. How many times had I sung "Hey, Blue"? I didn't know, didn't want to know. I was numb, empty, overwhelmed, and I felt terrible for all their families. Fat Albert and Bill Spencer and Baby Huey had wives, the latter two had children, as well. A "limited war" this had been called. Limited? To the men giving their all, fighting and dying, how can death be limited? The fine distinctions so understandable in Washington made no sense in the field.

I drank late into the night.

Following Fred's loss everything seemed to begin coming apart.

Only a few weeks later came word that our Hatchet Forces were being disbanded—inconceivable! There had been Hatchet Forces long before I arrived in SOG—Mad Dog had run his last mission in the Hatchet Force, Bob Howard had gone in with a platoon to try to recover Bob Scherdin on his Medal of Honor mission. They *couldn't* disband the Hatchet Forces! Who would block the Laotian highways? Hadn't anyone noticed that there were more NVA than ever?

But disband the forces they did, giving each Yard two months' pay, a ten-kilo bag of rice, and transportation back to his home village. That was that.

Chief SOG had attempted to retain one Hatchet Force company at Da Nang and another at our compound, as an emergency rescue force for POWs and downed pilots, but MACV headquarters and the Joint Chiefs would authorize only one forty-man platoon at each location. Because individual skill levels would be critical for such small, specialized rescue forces, Chief SOG decided to organize new platoons, each composed of three recon teams, called Combat Recon Platoons One and Two. At Kontum, CRP-2 contained two of my old teams—RT California under Donald Davidson and RT Hawaii under Les Dover—plus Larry Kramer's RT West Virginia. The platoon was led by Sergeant First Class Donald "Ranger" Melvin, who trained them long and hard before they assumed rescue responsibilities that summer.

Meanwhile the normal pace of recon operations continued but, I began to wonder, to what end? One afternoon I prepared to insert a team north of Ben Het, ten miles west of the old Dak Seang Special Forces Camp, now a South Vietnamese Army Ranger camp. As the Cobras got down to eyeball the LZ, Panther Lead spotted dozens of uniformed soldiers waving hands and running for cover. The target area had been cleared by province headquarters, which said no friendlies were anywhere nearby. I told Panther Lead, "Shoot 'em up."

He made a gun run but didn't fire because red smoke grenades began popping, the universal signal to cease fire. I radioed our compound, where our S-3 confirmed with Kontum Province, no friendlies were out there. Again, I told Panther Lead, "Shoot 'em up," but he wouldn't because it didn't feel right. Thank God for his instincts, for minutes later the Dak Seang commander finally admitted that he had lied to the province chief, it was his Ranger company, many miles from where he'd claimed it was, hiding in the jungle to avoid fighting the NVA. This was the same South Vietnamese commander made notorious a year earlier for selling water and rations to his own soldiers during a siege.

That was the largest South Vietnamese operation near the border in many months, and it had been a complete fraud.

The situation was no better in Laos. At the Covey intelligence office in Pleiku, I read a report about the NVA seizure of Attapeu, which I'd overflown a few weeks earlier. There had been no desperate fight, not even a real engagement: When the NVA showed up, the Royal Laotian Army had simply run away.

It was also through Covey intelligence that, for the first time, I understood the big picture of Laos, a realization that tore at me as much as the loss of Fred Krupa. For years we had been told that the limit to SOG's penetration in Laos was an operational boundary, that "someone else" was attacking the enemy from the other side, a blatant hint that secret forces were waging a parallel covert war deeper in Laos. That, I learned, was hardly true. Yes, the boundary existed, and yes, the U.S. ambassador to Laos controlled that area, which included hundreds of miles of highways and hundreds of enemy truck parks, supply dumps, and base camps—but *nothing* was happening on the ground out there.

What about the guerrilla chief, Vang Pao, and his hearty Hmong warriors fighting the CIA's secret war? Vang Pao and his mountain people, indeed, were carrying the brunt of the war in Laos; however, they were hundreds of miles north of the Ho Chi Minh Trail corridor, defending the traditional invasion approach to the capital city of Vientiane. The ambassador might boast that his secret army was tying down thousands of North Vietnamese soldiers that could have joined the war in South Vietnam; to me, now, it seemed the opposite, that a few thousand NVA were tying down excellent Hmong troops far in the north, so they would not endanger what Hanoi really valued—its logistical lifeline for the entire war, the Ho Chi Minh Trail. In the bureaucratic rivalry that substituted for strategy, the ambassador thought it better to allow a sanctuary for the enemy than to lose authority to SOG and the military. No matter how closely I studied the situation maps in the Covey operations center, I found not a single

Laotian unit anywhere along the Ho Chi Minh Trail. The only force truly disrupting the Trail always had been SOG and SOG alone.

The single breath of optimism that spring came with the arrival of our new commander, Lieutenant Colonel Galen "Mike" Radke. A rugged man, six foot four and solidly built, he bore a misshapen nose, a token perhaps from youthful boxing, which projected physical courage. Here was a leader, I knew, who lived by the code and lived for Special Forces. He would have court-martialed Robideaux, I had no doubt. Yet, like Colonel Abt, he possessed both confidence and self-deprecating humor, a good balance for a combat leader.

This was Radke's second Vietnam tour in Special Forces. Before that he'd served on loan to the CIA to advise classified Nationalist Chinese special operations from Taiwan. His current tour had begun as a staff assignment at SOG headquarters, so he was already well aware of our operations before he arrived.

Under Radke's leadership the fight continued but every day it became more apparent that we were the only Americans still fighting the ground war. Already both Marine divisions were gone, along with most Army divisions—the 9th, 4th, 1st, 23rd, and 25th—and now logistical and support units were packing up and departing, too, sometimes with detrimental effects. Our mail was disrupted, the little Kontum PX temporarily stocked just one brand of cigarettes—Kool menthols—then food distribution simply stopped. For weeks our mess hall featured cold cuts, rice, and gristly Vietnamese beef, which our cook, Fat Cat King, did his best to render palatable.

Then, suddenly, ammunition shortfalls became critical. In particular, we had so few 40mm rounds that when extracted recon teams reached Dak To, they turned over their unfired rounds to teams going to the field so the latter could have a basic load. Live fire training had to be cut back. But food and ammo shortages were only irritants compared to combat losses, felt severely that month of May at our sister unit, CCN, now Task Force One, Advisory Element.

Those were difficult times, that summer of 1971, reconciling our warrior's ethic with the American disengagement, continuing to run dangerous missions despite the world beyond us slowly turning upside-down. Trained to fight and never quit, living an ethic that put mission and comrades above self, how could we withdraw—run away—with the war still underway and the enemy undefeated? What of honor, commitment, duty? At a private level, each of us thought about it but didn't say much, though we talked a great deal about a new motion picture, Sam Peckinpah's *The Wild Bunch*, which violently depicted the final days of an outlaw gang led by William Holden. Coincidentally, his gang was the same size as a recon team, and like us, the world about them had changed too much, too fast. By unconscious agreement, Holden's men purposely provoked an impossible fight with hundreds of Mexicans and went down fighting in a final frenzied gunfight, the bloodiest ever recorded on film.

Every one of us watched *The Wild Bunch* once, some twice.

Almost universally, we fantasized—*that's the way to go.* Strap on our guns, load our magazines, one final confrontation to prove we were not afraid to die and not about to quit. They wanted us, they could come and get us. Some of SOG's most dangerous missions of the whole war were launched in 1971, when men knowingly pitted themselves against masses of NVA, daring them, beckoning the enemy to fight. Earlier that year, CCN's RT Python, led by Captain Jim Butler, had occupied the abandoned hilltop Firebase Thor in the Ashau Valley, to block a major enemy highway. Heavily armed with M-60 machine guns and a 60mm mortar, Butler's fourteen men fought day and night, supported by fighters and AC-130 Spectre gunships. Escaping just as an NVA battalion swept over the hilltop, RT Python was credited with killing nearly 350 NVA, including those hit by air strikes.

In late May RT Indigo inserted in the Ashau Valley and, like Butler's men, occupied a hilltop overlooking Highway 548. Led by Sergeant First Class Eckard Carnett, One-Zero, and First Lieutenant Gary Dunnam, One-One, the team included Sergeants Kevin Smith, Jesse Campbell, and Douglas Thomas. Employing a recoilless rifle and 81mm mortar and supported by AC-130s, they killed masses of NVA and destroyed fifteen trucks before being extracted.

These impossibly lopsided fights came to a final crescendo on 7 August, when RT Kansas occupied an old hilltop firebase near the abandoned Marine fortress at Khe Sanh, and faced a 2,000-man human wave assault by a reinforced NVA regiment. In what was undoubtedly the war's most violent half-hour, this handful of SOG men killed more than 100 NVA and wounded another sixty, at extreme cost: The One-Zero, First Lieutenant Loren Hagen, was killed and posthumously awarded the U.S. Army's final Medal of Honor in the war; One-One Tony Anderson suffered multiple wounds; the One-Two, Sergeant Bruce Berg, was MIA and presumed dead; of the three volunteers who accompanied them, Sergeant Oran Bingham was killed, and Sergeant Bill Queen was wounded. Sergeant William Rimondi alone was not hit. Of their eight Yards, six were killed and two wounded.

The impulse to accept great risk in SOG's waning days was not unique to CCN. A number of our teams at Kontum abandoned any pretense of recon for more men and more heavy weapons, and instead of breaking contact and evading, they ambushed, assaulted, and startled the NVA.

This embrace of ever more boldness spread even to the Covey Riders, with Lowell Stevens and me deciding to do what no one had done before: run a two-man recon mission, just the two of us. Over drinks in the club we convinced ourselves we could hide so well and move so quietly that the NVA wouldn't find us. Off to Colonel Radke's room we went, woke him up, and explained our plan: We'd go in aboard an OH-6, a small observation chopper, and land in a fifty-foot LZ.

"Nobody's done it before," Stevens said, "the enemy wouldn't expect it."

I added, "I'm sure we could do it, sir."

Colonel Radke listened but promised nothing. Were we trying to be the Wild Bunch?

Colonel Radke finally dismissed our proposal as talk generated by alcohol and let it go, but years later he admitted, "The only thing the matter with either one of you was the fact that you knew it was drawing down. It was almost time that you were going to have to leave. You didn't want to do that. You felt like you'd lied, that you'd lied to people, it was a great guilt feeling—I understood that. There wasn't anything I could tell you that would make you feel any better, but I understood it. And you just had to talk it out and get ready to come home because you didn't have any choice."

A few nights later Steve Keever and I sat in the Country Club with Lowell Stevens, all of us drinking too much. With great anguish I listened to Stevens, who quoted Davy Crockett and lived selflessly and fought bravely, at last confront what was ailing him. "Back in '64, I told the Yards, 'We ain't the French. America doesn't run off and leave people.'" Lowell shook his head. "I promised 'em. I promised the Yards," he sobbed. "My God, *don't they know,* I promised the Yards."

Ken Carpenter wasn't immune from introspection, either. I walked into the Country Club one night and found Ken sitting there alone in the dark, drinking, listening to an old country song. His eyes glistened, reflected in the dull light on the stereo deck. I asked, "Kenny, what's wrong?"

He looked away, shook his head, then mumbled, "Aw, just gettin' sentimental."

"I'll come back later," I offered.

Instead Ken turned on the lights, poured Crown Royal in two glasses, and passed me one. "To our guys," he offered. "Fuck everybody else."

We downed it and never said another word about it.

Though I flew Covey as carefully and wisely as ever, it was becoming increasingly difficult. For a while it seemed a blur of flying, bombing, and extracting teams. Although pilot records disclose I flew several Prairie Fire Emergencies that summer, I cannot remember much detail.

Losses among Covey pilots and Covey Riders peaked in SOG's final year. Back in February, a Covey bird supporting CCN went down in the Ashau Valley, killing USAF Captain Larry Hull and his Covey Rider, Sergeant First Class William "Jose" Fernandez. Two months earlier, another Da Nang–based Covey plane had been shot down carrying a CCN Covey Rider, Staff Sergeant Roger "Buff" Teeters, and pilot, USAF Captain James L. Smith. Both were MIA.

The luckiest Covey pilot flying the summer of '71 had to be Captain Art Moxon. The young Air Force Academy graduate was putting an air strike on NVA trucks near Laotian Highway 92 on 4 June when a suspected shoulder-fired missile—the first in the war—hit his plane. He and his back-seater, an Air Force major, punched out and, shortly after Lowell Stevens's OV-10 got there, a Jolly Green chopper arrived to extract them. Just two weeks later, on 20 June, the same two were flying the same stretch of Highway 92 when enemy fire knocked out one engine. This time it was Larry White's OV-10 that responded and followed Moxon as he nursed his plane closer to the border. Unable to maintain altitude, Moxon and his back-seater punched out, again recovered by Jolly Green.

When they got back to Pleiku this time, however, their squadron commander met them and announced, "Gentlemen, pack your bags—you've just completed your tour in Vietnam." For Moxon it was quite a relief to go home after six months of combat, but his back-seater had been there only seventeen days.

The outcome was not so joyous two weeks later when yet another OV-10 was shot down over southern Laos. This plane was based at Nakhon Phanom, Thailand, and carried a SOG officer, Captain Donald "Butch" Carr, and his pilot, USAF Lieutenant Daniel Thomas. Hardly ten miles from where Moxon had been hit twice, the Thailand-based OV-10 was in radio contact with a Vietnamese recon team when there was a sudden barrage from antiaircraft guns. Then the team lost radio contact with Carr. A search-and-rescue effort found no wreckage and we heard no emergency radios. Their plane simply disappeared, with Carr and Thomas carried as MIA.

Not long after that, I was inserting another Vietnamese recon team about ten miles east of there when a quiet landing became a hellacious fight. The team had set down in a rather wide slash-and-burn field and just reached a wood line when ground fire hit their departing Huey. I sent another chopper in

to pull the team but an enormous volume of fire erupted from three directions—that helicopter barely made it out.

The team was trapped on the LZ, surrounded by hundreds of NVA. We
brought down the A-1s while I sent the choppers back to Dak To to rearm, refuel, and wait for another attempt to extract them. My pilot stretched out coverage by the A-1s long enough to get more fighters so we could keep up a
relentless aerial bombardment. It did not help things that no one on the team
spoke good English; impatient, I told them just to keep their heads down.

As the A-1s finished we had our first radio contact from a diverted flight of
Navy fighters off a carrier in the Tonkin Gulf. A high-pitched voice called,
"Covey, this is Liberty Two-Seven."

"Roger," my pilot responded. "Say type aircraft."

"We're a flight of Alpha-Sevens."

A-7s—that was good, lots of bombs, sixteen apiece. "Covey rogers. Say
number of aircraft."

"Two-four."

That had to be his mission number. My FAC pilot repeated, "Say again,
number of aircraft."

"Roger, Covey. We are two-four, twenty-four-each, A-7s, hot to trot and almost at your location."

My pilot looked at me, incredulous—*twenty-four fighter-bombers, each laden
with bombs!*

How could we use them quickly? They had only twenty minutes' station
time and all those bombs—how could we drop so many bombs close to a team
without blasting them to bits? Then I spotted a tall dead tree in the middle of
the LZ. I radioed the Vietnamese team leader and told him to have his men
crawl to the base of that tree, lie around it, cover their ears, and open their
mouths wide to protect their eardrums from the pounding concussion.

Then we unleashed a fury like no recon team had ever seen. My pilot
brought the A-7s in two at a time, flying side by side, bombing tree lines on the
LZ, and each time donut-shaped concussion waves snapped past that dead tree.
A Vietnamese screamed on the radio but when he confirmed no one had been
hurt, I told him just to get down and open his mouth again. For almost a half-
hour, we dumped plane after plane of bombs, danger-close, virtually bouncing
the Vietnamese in the air amid unending shock waves. They took it without
further complaint.

In the end, we brought back the choppers and got the team out with almost
no ground fire.

That evening I learned several of the Vietnamese had suffered broken eardrums from the bombs, and I felt remorseful—not for having exposed them to danger, for there was little else I could have done—but for having ordered them about as less than the brave men they were.

Outside the recon company orderly room I saw a half-dozen Vietnamese waiting for me, the team I'd supported that afternoon. I expected them to blame me for their injuries. They stood there, stiff, formal. Then one shook my hand and offered, "Thank you, Truong Si. Maybe we be dead, but not now." I told them I was sorry about their hearing injuries. One motioned to a deaf man who could not hear my words. He smiled and nodded. "No sweat," he translated. "Is OK."

I felt shamed, for so casually had I risked their lives without even consulting them.

A few days later my O-2 had to land at Dak To because we'd flown too long and needed fuel to reach Pleiku. The Vietnamese pump operator was nowhere in sight. As our engines shut down I noticed all the choppers were gone. While my pilot dragged out the hose, I climbed on the wing to open the fuel tank, then heard a dull *Ka-rump!*—an incoming 82mm mortar round impacted across the strip, about 200 yards away.

Standing on the wing I was unhurried, unconcerned and continued filling the tank. I didn't give a damn. My pilot displayed a bit more interest but not enough to do anything. *Ka-rump!* Another round detonated, fifty yards closer. The enemy was adjusting fire, walking them toward us. The pilot looked to me; I shrugged. The tank was almost full, and I wasn't in the mood to be run off by some bastard with a mortar, I thought foolishly.

Only when the tank was entirely full and we were good and ready, finally did we taxi out and take off, as normally as ever, the mortar rounds never quite catching up with us. It seemed all unremarkable to me—but in reality, it had been extremely dangerous.

Perhaps my new boss in the launch site, Master Sergeant Walter Shumate, learned of my incaution at Dak To, or maybe he'd noticed my growing listlessness. "Some people burn out after one mission," Lowell Stevens once told me. "Some people can last a year, some last a year and a half. But we all burn out in this game, I don't care who you are." Shumate told me he was sending me down to guest-lecture at SOG's recon school near Saigon. "After that, take a few days off," he said. "Just come back here when you're ready."

Arriving at SOG's Camp Long Thanh school, I saw Joe Walker, now a staff instructor on the recon course. Together we stood at the back of the classroom while an Air Force major from Saigon addressed two dozen Special Forces recon students on close air support. The major gave a generic airpower briefing that was worthless. As I stood there listening, I grew angrier and angrier until I was seething when I got to the podium. Within days, these men would be leaving for the most dangerous assignments in Southeast Asia, and that stupid major was too busy playing handball—or whatever rear echelon staffers did in Saigon—to prepare a proper briefing. I tried to be tactful but I told them they should unlearn most of what they'd just heard: "Forget about the book minimum safe distances for air-dropped ordnance—in most cases that won't be close enough to help you." And, "F-4s make lots of noise with their afterburners but their only useful ordnance for a recon team is 20mm Vulcan cannon fire." The major had spoken highly of the A-37, but we had never used A-37s to support recon teams. They were too slow and vulnerable. I told them about how an OV-10 could save their lives by strafing and rocketing, then urged them to master passive ways of signaling, like mirrors and panels, and always, always to bring white phosphorus grenades. By then I had contradicted most of what the staff officer had said but I didn't care. He'd slunk from the room long before then.

Afterward I caught a lift to SOG's Saigon safe house, where I found Ken Carpenter in the bar. He had just two weeks left in Vietnam, and he noted, regretfully, it was too late to extend his tour. "I'm sure going to miss you guys," he lamented.

"But it's not too late," I declared and explained how a letter from SOG headquarters, hand-carried to U.S. Army Vietnam headquarters in Long Binh, would do the trick. "I did it myself last year." It would be great to have Ken there, flying Covey for another six months.

"I don't know," Ken said, "I'm already on orders for an assignment at Fort Bragg."

I bought him another Crown Royal and Coke and assured him we could do it.

The next morning we got chief SOG's signature on a classified letter, explaining why it was essential to the war effort that Ken be allowed to extend. Then a SOG sedan took us to Long Binh, where Ken presented his classified letter to the master sergeant in charge of personnel. The master sergeant took one look at where he had to sign for the letter labeled "Secret," and announced, "I don't sign for classified materials. I won't sign for anything."

A perfect bureaucrat, he didn't want to be on the hook to protect what he learned. But unless he read the letter, Ken wouldn't get his waiver and he'd have to go home. I pulled Ken aside and whispered, "We'll bypass this silly ass and find an officer. There's got to be a major or colonel with clearance who isn't afraid to be SOG-briefed."

Ken put the classified letter back in his briefcase and snapped it shut. "I guess that's that," he said as if he hadn't heard me.

More emphatically, I repeated, "But we can bypass—" I stopped in mid-sentence as my eyes met Ken's—and I knew. *How could I have been so stupid?* Ken didn't really want to extend, but he didn't want his friends to think he wouldn't extend to stay with them and fight. My God, he'd already served two and a half years in combat and finally had a chance to survive this war and go home to his family, and I almost took that away.

I put my arm around Ken's shoulder and said, "Well, fuck these sorry moth-erfuckers. Let's just go back to Saigon and have a Crown Royal and Coke."

We spent that afternoon and evening in the safe house bar.

Then the next morning Ken flew back to Kontum, and I rode the Blackbird to Nha Trang, where the 5th Special Forces Group had been headquartered. Now it housed just a small Special Forces administrative detachment. The old NCO club was gone, replaced by a one-room bar in an empty barracks. Alone, I sat there all day, drinking, brooding, and thinking. How long, I wondered, be-fore corrupt Vietnamese officers stripped this place like a carcass beside a road, as they'd already done to the 4th Infantry Division base camp at Pleiku?

I played the jukebox and kept to myself, thinking. What began as coherent thoughts melded with alcohol into depressing flashes of recollections, things you shouldn't think when you're alone. Mostly I remembered Fred Krupa and wondered what would become of him. And Fat Albert? How could we just leave our men here, alive or dead, not knowing? And what of all those ghosts, good men, fine men—all those names from "Hey, Blue." I thought about the day in 1969 when I carried Jim Ripanti from the chopper only to learn he was dead. And my whole lost team. And the day Chuck Hein died. I kept drinking. Over and over the jukebox played Glen Campbell singing "I'm So Lonesome I Could Cry," Bill Spencer's favorite song. Suicide music, Lowell Stevens called it.

I drank and thought all the more, but I couldn't blame anyone else, for I played that song myself, over and over. At midnight the bar closed. I staggered back to my bunk in the former B-55 Mike Force barracks—transient rooms now—and found a bottle of vodka. Alone I walked outside, across the deserted parade ground where the proud Mike Force once had stood formations. I sat on the ground and tried to imagine all those ranks of cheery Montagnards, and their Special Forces leaders, all now ghosts. I chugged on the bottle.

The night sky was clear. The stars went on forever. I closed my eyes.

Then it was daylight. I sat up, my back soaked with dew, face mosquito-bitten, a bad taste in my mouth. A stray dog had lain beside me and stirred when I stood, someone's pet from the Mike Force, hoping like me that things would again be like before. He followed me back to the barracks and waited at the door while I showered and packed, and tried to follow me when I left for the airfield. But he had to stay there.

By noon I was back in Kontum. I'd been gone a week but felt no different. I knew I'd pretty well had it, I'd done all I could. Maybe I'd been here too long. Maybe it was time I just went home. I was scheduled to rotate in a few weeks, on 12 September. That would be it. I was running on empty, drained. I could do no more.

That afternoon I sat in the Country Club, drinking a cup of coffee and nursing my latest hangover when a voice called, "Hey, Plasticman, got a minute?" It was Colonel Radke.

"Sure, sir." I poured a cup for him as he sat at the booth.

He wasn't a man who wasted time with pleasantries, but when he spoke I wasn't sure where he was going. "I'm a lot smarter than a lot of people that are out here. I want to save as many lives as I can. That's why I extended, John."

I said nothing, waiting to hear his point.

"Well, Plasticman, that's the way it is for me—and I think that's the way it is for you, too. I think it's up to us to save lives. That's why we're here. That's our job. We've got missions to run, but we've got to do this in such a way that we save as many lives as possible."

I hadn't thought of it that way but agreed, "Yes, sir. I think you're right."

"Well, John, I found out you're going home." He looked long at me, thinking about his words. "How would you like to stay?"

"What?"

"Our job isn't done. We've got guys running missions. In four or five months it's all going to be over. There'll be no more SOG, no more missions to run. I think you're doing a pretty good job, and I'd like you to help me. Well, John, what do you think?"

How could he ask that? Damn him! Four more months? Not even a leave? I've been here too long. Someone else—ask anyone else!

Then I thought about what he'd said, *really thought*—and all the frustration and anger swept away. No one had asked me to stay before except this man, who looked me straight in the eye. In that moment I was new, fresh. What we must do, what was worth fighting for and risking our lives for, was clear again. I began to feel like my old self.

There was only one response. "Yes, sir. Yes I will."

"I'll get the S-1 to write up your extension." We shook hands. He left.

Colonel Radke had it right. Washington's failed strategy didn't matter anymore; what the U.S. ambassador in Laos said or did didn't matter either. Special

Forces had come into this war with honor, its men had fought with distinction, and now that's all we had left—our honor. Fighting to the end would preserve that honor, for all who'd been there earlier, and all our lost comrades. That was worth fighting for. In these final months we Green Berets still in combat could allow no letup. But more than ever before, we'd be fighting for one another. We would never quit. I would never quit.

My turmoil was over. It all made sense again.

Chapter Sixteen

As I continued flying that summer of 1971, the NVA began building roads at a pace never before seen in the war. In August, just before he left, Ken Carpenter had discovered about fifteen miles west of Dak To a new road coming out of Cambodia hidden under elaborate bamboo lattices. Each of the Covey Riders studied it with binoculars and agreed there was a major road under there, snaking its way into the Plei Trap Valley. Paralleling the border, the valley ran south some thirty miles until it emptied into a grassy plain west of Pleiku, the most critical allied base in the Central Highlands. The new road grew at an amazing rate—several miles in a single night.

So dramatic was its growth that our commander, Colonel Radke, had an airborne radar mission flown over it, which detected trucks and bulldozers operating in the dark. A few nights later a B-52 strike straddled the new highway for almost two miles but that hardly slowed them down. As on the Laotian Ho Chi Minh Trail, construction crews repaired it overnight and soon passed the area where we'd lost Fred Krupa, continuing southward at an astonishing pace.

This perplexed Colonel Radke and our intelligence analysts, who knew U.S. Army engineers could not cut roads that fast through dense jungle. Theories abounded, but eventually our S-2 intelligence officer found the answer in South Vietnam's National Library in Saigon. He brought back a map he'd found of colonial Indochina and, sure enough, a long overgrown French road ran down the valley floor. "They were just clearing off the jungle," Radke realized. "That road was already there."

Across the border in Laos, too, enemy activity was expanding as never before. For the first time ever, U.S. aircraft began to detect enemy radar near Chavane, the area of Operation Tailwind just one year earlier. American analysts determined that the radars were linked to heavy 85mm and 100mm antiaircraft guns, the first time they'd been detected so far south. North of there, surface-to-air missiles, too, began to appear, with four sites near the North Vietnamese border firing forty-nine missiles that downed three U.S. aircraft.

All signs indicated more enemy, operating at a heightened pace—except for truck sightings on the Ho Chi Minh Trail. Here there was a dramatic decline over the previous year; sensor detections disclosed a surprising drop from 32,000 vehicle contacts in January 1971, to just 382 in October. Had night-flying USAF AC-130 Spectre gunships made life unbearable for trucks? Had the enemy shifted to some new means of shipping supplies?

That mystery was solved one sunny noonday when a pilot and I flew along Highway 92 to radio a Vietnamese recon team. Our OV-10 banked and the angle of light was just right as I glanced eastward, when I saw a flash of orange, a bright, ribbonlike strip tucked in the hills two miles away. Flying closer, we circled and banked and circled, catching glimpses and connecting them until we saw enough: *Unbelievably, the North Vietnamese had completely replaced Highway 92 with a new, heavily camouflaged road.* For an hour we traced it on a map, and that night plotted it on the Covey squadron's wall-size intelligence map. We had discovered the enemy's greatest engineering feat of the war, an entirely fresh parallel highway system that constituted a new Ho Chi Minh Trail.

It wasn't only Highway 92. Air Force photo analysts spotted a new highway hewn through heavy jungle, parallel to the well-exposed Highway 16, leading to Attapeu and the Bolovens Plateau. In 1966, the enemy's Laotian road network had included 820 miles of usable highways; now, in August 1971, this had tripled to 2,500 miles.

Untold numbers of B-52 strikes had stripped away the jungle from the old highways, leaving night convoys exposed and vulnerable to air attacks; now it was 1965 again, with highways, trucks, and convoys all reenshrouded in verdant mystery. Worse yet, as a 1971 Air Force intelligence report noted, this road expansion would "further dilute the intensity of our air strikes," which had been declining due to the withdrawal of Air Force and USMC fighter squadrons. Compared to 1970, air attacks along the Trail had fallen 30 percent in 1971, to just 320 sorties per day.

In such declining numbers, individual strikes came under closer scrutiny. When Covey Rider Steve Keever put a strike on a Laotian hilltop, a teletype message arrived the next day from the U.S. ambassador in Laos, angrily demanding to know who had authorized the attack. Keever didn't realize the rest of us kept two sets of books—we sometimes bombed worthwhile targets outside approved areas, but *reported* them inside areas cleared by the embassy. Keever told Colonel Radke he had bombed the hill because he knew it to be heavily occupied by NVA forces. This information was relayed to Vientiane. "How," the embassy shot back, "did he know the NVA were there?"

Keever suggested to SOG headquarters that they forward the ambassador a copy of his debrief of September 1970, when his RT Illinois fought a heavy engagement against numerous NVA on that very hill. There were no further tele-types, and from that time, Steve, too, kept two books.

A more pressing problem than bombing records was learning what was happening in the suddenly bustling Plei Trap Valley. Here, Colonel Radke de-cided, was a perfect place to employ HALO—military skydiving, or, High Alti-tude, Low Opening parachuting—as an infiltration technique. A HALO insertion offered real stealth, for the team would jump at night from such high altitude—more than 10,000 feet—that the enemy would hardly even hear the C-130's engines. Further, because helicopters of that era couldn't land safely in darkness, the enemy did not employ LZ watchers at night, almost insuring our men would avoid detection.

Just nine months earlier, SOG recon men had performed the world's first-ever combat HALO jump when a CCN team leaped into Laos just north of our area of operations. Led by Staff Sergeant Cliff Newman, the six-man team in-cluded Sergeants First Class Sammy Hernandez and Melvin Hill, a South Viet-namese officer, and two Montagnards. Jumping from 18,000 feet, they were split by darkness and rain, landing in three groups far from their intended drop zone (DZ). Nevertheless, they reconned for five days and apparently went un-detected by the enemy.

Two more CCN HALO missions had followed, on 7 May and 22 June 1971, and in both cases men were split during the free fall, and injured upon landing. Captain Larry Manes, a respected two-tour SOG veteran, led the all-American second team, which included Specialist Six Noel Gast, Staff Sergeant Robert Castillo, and Sergeant John Trantanella. The third team, led by Sergeant Major Billy Waugh, included Staff Sergeant James "J.D." Bath and Sergeants Jesse Campbell and Madison Strohlein. Losing sight of the others during descent, Bath landed hard, hurting his back and knees, while Strohlein broke his right arm landing in a tree.

A Bright Light rescue team, with Sergeants Lemuel McGlothern, Jr., and James Woodham, Jr., rappelled in at first light and got J.D. Bath. Another Bright Light element, with Sergeants Robert Cook, Richard "Nick" Brokhausen, Dave Daugherty, and Robert Woodham, found the tree where Strohlein's parachute had been pulled to the ground, and discovered 40mm casings, apparently fired from Strohlein's weapon, and scattered AK brass. But the twenty-three-year-old Green Beret was gone, apparently captured, though the North Vietnamese would never admit holding him.

Despite the loss of Madison Strohlein, Colonel Radke believed HALO of-fered such great potential that when our recon company commander, Captain

James Storter, offered to lead a fourth HALO jump, Radke immediately phoned chief SOG and got it approved.

Captain Storter recruited three experienced skydivers from among his recon men—Sergeant First Class Newman Ruff and Sergeants Millard Moye and Michael Bentley—then attended a HALO refresher course at SOG's training facility near Saigon. All were experienced skydivers except Storter, who had exaggerated his qualifications—his only HALO training was this refresher course, but the former NCO proved a quick study.

After two weeks' training, Storter's men were targeted into the northern Plei Trap Valley, where thousands of NVA had made daylight helicopter landings especially difficult. The Covey Rider slated to support their jump was Sergeant First Class Gerry Denison, and here was a touch of irony: Denison, who had replaced Ken Carpenter, had led a recon mission into almost the same spot during a previous SOG tour, in February 1968, when he and Staff Sergeant Robert Kotin and four Yards ambushed and destroyed four trucks on a road that had since been absorbed by the jungle. After that mission he was selected to fly Covey and on 5 October 1968, while he was flying low-level looking for a split team, an antiaircraft machine gun opened fire. The feisty Alaskan was hanging out the window shooting back when a bullet hit his face, then his plane slammed into the treetops. Denison was thrown through the trees, suffering severe injuries. Everything was a blur until he awoke in a hospital bed where a recon buddy, Sergeant Paul Poole, examined his stitched, purple face, and quipped, "Gee, Gerry, you're sure pretty."

Thus ended his first SOG tour. It took him years to recover. Now, ironically, on 22 September 1971, Denison was flying in darkness above the very valley where he'd ambushed those trucks so long ago.

The weather looked good, Denison radioed to the approaching Blackbird.

High above Denison's O-2, the C-130 cruised at 16,000 feet, with Colonel Radke—acting as jumpmaster—at its open tailgate. When the green jump light flashed, Radke slapped Storter's backside and out went the four men, swallowed instantly by the tropical night. In a sliver of moonlight, they stayed in sight of each other and landed just thirty yards apart, right in their appointed DZ. Not a man had been injured. For four days they roamed the valley, unseen by an enemy who had no idea they'd landed.

Colonel Radke also rode their extraction Huey, and when he saw their faces, "I was damned happy." Storter's HALO jump was SOG's most successful, with the entire team landing together, without injury, and conducting an entire recon mission without detection.

"It was picture perfect," Storter said.

Fortunately for Storter's team, they'd been extracted on 26 September, because the following morning, when I next flew, a fifty-mile storm front extended across southern Laos and over the Plei Trap Valley. No teams were on the ground and one look at the thunderheads near Ben Het told me we'd be inserting no teams that day. I couldn't even see the ground at Dak To.

What to do? I suggested to my OV-10 pilot, "Let's go look for Stormy Zero-Three."

That morning over steaming coffee in the Covey intel office, like every aircrew in Southeast Asia, we'd been briefed that an RF-4 photo bird—call sign Stormy Zero-Three—from the 421st Tactical Reconnaissance Squadron was missing somewhere between its base at Da Nang and the Laotian highway structure. We were told to monitor the "Guard" emergency radio frequency for any sign of the missing pilot and copilot.

The odds of finding anyone were poor, but we had nothing better to do. If that plane made it out of Laos, Stormy Zero-Three had to have crossed the border somewhere north of us, so that's the direction we turned. As our OV-10 sliced through heavy overcast, rain pelted our canopy. Then it cleared somewhat as we passed hazy valleys where the sweet stench of burning cassava root hung in the air. Cassava—or manioc—is second only to rice as a source of starch in Southeast Asia, where its harvested fields are burned in the eternal cycle of slash-and-burn agriculture. Though it stunk like smoky tapioca, it reminded me of home and burning elm leaves in the fall.

As we were leisurely flying north, a CCN recon team, RT Kansas, was soaked and tired. They had spent a day looking for a suspected enemy camp. They'd been psyched, eager to raid the camp and seize prisoners. Now, instead, huddled at dawn, the men of RT Kansas were miserable. At least the rain that had pelted them all night was easing with the dawn.

The CCN men had landed in good weather the previous day in a remote valley forty-five miles southwest of Da Nang, near the Laotian border. Their plan was to land a mile away, then sneak up to the NVA camp—discovered by a CCN Covey Rider—and raid it, capturing several prisoners. It was supposed to take just a couple of hours.

RT Kansas One-Zero George Cottrell and One-One Sergeant Mark McPherson had asked several men to come along. Staff Sergeant Eldon Bargewell, One-Zero of RT Sidewinder, had volunteered, a welcome addition due to his prowess with a sawed-off RPD machine gun and two years' experience running recon. Bargewell brought along his friend and teammate, Staff Sergeant Jean-Paul Castagna. Rounding them off was RT Habu's radio operator, Sergeant Robert Cook. With eleven Yards and five Americans, Cottrell was loaded for bear.

It had been only six weeks since Lieutenant Loren Hagen had been killed and RT Kansas almost annihilated, yet Cottrell, the new One-Zero, quickly had rebuilt the team with fresh Yards and Americans and readied them for this, their first major operation. After landing, they'd hurried to the suspected camp, then crossed and recrossed the coordinates but didn't find a thing. Well, Cottrell and Bargewell agreed, another prisoner would have to do. The rest of the day they looked high and low but encountered no enemy, not even a trail.

Then just before dark, their Yard tail gunner reported movement, probably trackers, behind them. Soon they heard signal shots. Cottrell sat them on a hilltop almost until dark; then, to throw off any trackers, in steady rain he relocated them to another hill. All night the rain pounded and poured, an unending deluge that washed away their senses; none of the men heard or saw a thing in the darkness.

Now at first light they were sitting, drying out, eating rice, facing outward. Soon they'd make their morning radio check, then be on their way and maybe still snatch a prisoner. By habit, Eldon Bargewell rested his sawed-off RPD machine gun on his lap.

Ka-Boom! Ka-Boom!—RPGs!—*Ka-Boom! Ka-Boom!*—Bargewell collapsed, seriously wounded—*a shout!*—100 North Vietnamese soldiers rushed forward. *Ka-Boom!* Castagna was hit, too. *Ka-Boom!* An RPG blasted a Yard next to Cook, killing him instantly and flipping Cook sideways as shrapnel tore into his shoulder, knocking him unconscious. McPherson thought Cook was dead.

Then AKs chattered along a wide front, advancing on Bargewell's side of the perimeter.

Knocked to the ground by an RPG, Bargewell shook his head, wiped blood from his eyes, and snatched a claymore firing device—*BOOM!*—the explosion smashed the nearest attackers, buying him five seconds. Ignoring the blood squirting from his face, he lifted his RPD machine gun and opened up as the enemy launched an all-out assault. Despite heavy AK fire all around him, Bargewell sprayed long bursts into rows of NVA rushing madly at him. Backed by CAR-15 fire from the wounded Castagna and three Yards, he knocked back the enemy, leaving bodies scattered on the jungle floor, the closest just three yards away.

Hurriedly, Bargewell replaced his gun's empty 100-round drum as Cottrell rushed men over to reinforce him. Seconds later the NVA launched a third assault, with rockets blasting everywhere, wounding more men. Stunned, Cook crawled to check the nearest Yard—an RPG had detonated almost in the man's face, killing him instantly. Then Cook saw an NVA machine gunner trying to flank the team and dropped him with his CAR-15.

They barely fought off the third assault.

Taking over the radio from the wounded Cook, McPherson called, "Prairie Fire! Prairie Fire!"

But no Covey's voice answered him.

By 8:30 A.M. that day our OV-10 had passed the old Dak Pek Special Forces Camp, as far north as I'd ever ventured. In the distance we saw the weather breaking while below we could see the ground again. Before us lay NVA territory, more than 100 miles of remote borderlands running all the way to the DMZ, conceded as indefensible by the South Vietnamese. I could almost feel these valleys teeming with enemy forces, as free of interference as if they were in Laos.

We continued northward in hopes of overflying Stormy Zero-Three.

Just ahead I saw a dirt airstrip take shape. I knew it was the old Kham Duc Special Forces Camp, which had been overrun in May 1968. Our intel map at Kontum, reflecting radio intercepts and triangulations, had plotted a 10,000-man North Vietnamese division headquarters somewhere just north of here. Both ends of the dirt runway, I noticed, were blocked by tall pyramids of stacked 55-gallon drums, erected by the enemy so damaged planes could not make emergency landings there. Along the north side of the runway, almost ghostlike, fresh truck tracks accented the red dirt though there was not a known enemy road for twenty miles.

We'd flown almost within sight of Da Nang, which my pilot said lay northeast on the blue horizon that was the South China Sea, about forty miles away. It was time to turn back.

As we were preparing to turn south, Bargewell had barely succeeded in breaking the assault and forcing back the enemy. In fierce, close-range gunfights, he and the men around him had killed or wounded an estimated fifty NVA. For the moment firing ceased.

Taking stock, Cottrell saw that one Yard had been killed, two more gutshot, and every American wounded, too, with Bargewell's injuries the most severe. To stand there and fight, Cottrell knew, was hopeless. Forming up to withdraw, he was compelled to leave the Yard's body and scuttle a 60mm mortar. Somehow Bargewell mustered the strength to carry his machine gun. Cook dumped his rucksack so he could drag a wounded Montagnard.

As they limped along, just beyond their vision the NVA followed, firing intermittently, then falling back when Cottrell's men returned fire. They could not move fast enough to break away. That was Cottrell's gravest concern.

Then they heard the distant buzz of aircraft engines.

McPherson called on the team radio, "Covey, Covey, any Covey!" Again no response. He pulled his emergency radio, pre-set to the emergency Guard frequency, 243.00 megahertz. "Covey, Covey, Prairie Fire, Prairie Fire!" Nothing.

Hoping it would carry his signal farther, he switched the radio to beeper mode.

Bbbbzzz-uppp!—bbbbzz-uppp!—bbbbzzz-uppp!

We could barely make out the beeper. Keen to listen for the missing Stormy Zero-Three, my pilot immediately tuned his TACAN direction finder to 243.00. "He's north of us," he reported, banking hard and pushing the throttles full-forward.

Momentarily the signal grew stronger. "Beeper, beeper," my pilot radioed, "come up voice. Are you Stormy Zero-Three?"

A desperate voice sounded familiar. "Prairie Fire! Prairie Fire!"

It had to be a SOG team—up here that meant a CCN team.

We had no call signs, no frequencies, no maps for anyone up here—we didn't have any choppers, didn't even have the authority to be here. But that didn't stop us. While my pilot scrambled fighters, I had Cottrell's men toss a smoke grenade. Momentarily our OV-10 rolled in hot, strafing and rocketing their backtrail while I directed them uphill toward a usable LZ.

Somewhere a helicopter pilot radioed, "Get off Guard, get off Guard."

I came back, "We have a tactical emergency on Guard. Be advised, *we must use Guard.*"

We heard another voice, another pilot. "Covey, this is Widowmaker Two-Seven, a flight of four Cobras, on Guard. Could you use some help?"

Pulling out of a strafing dive, our tracers bouncing between the trees, my pilot asked me, "Why not?"

"Shit yes," I agreed. "Let's do it."

"Widowmaker, this is Covey. We're on the 192 radial out of Da Nang, at forty-one miles. We'd welcome you folks out here."

For twenty minutes Cottrell's men climbed, tossing grenades and shooting downhill at the NVA while we fired for them and brought in Cobra gunships. Reaching the LZ, Cottrell set up a perimeter and began treating wounds, at last stopping the severe bleeding from Bargewell's face.

Then, magically, just as a pair of A-1s arrived, here came still another voice on Guard, announcing, "Covey, this is Blue Flight. We're west of Da Nang, a flight of four Hueys—could you use us?" We told them to come on out—we were going to play this as a regular extraction despite assembling a hodgepodge of helicopters from aviation units we'd never encountered before, who didn't even work for SOG.

Amazingly, I had to turn down still more chopper pilots who offered to come out.

Momentarily the Hueys arrived, we had the Cobras on the deck eyeballing the LZ, and a pair of A-1 Skyraiders in orbit overhead. "Let's play ball," I told my pilot.

With no warning, a Da Nang–based OV-10 buzzed below us, announced he was the Covey for this area, and thanked us for our help. So, while the Hueys went in, we pulled off to the west and watched until the final helicopter lifted away. As the line of choppers faded toward Da Nang carrying Cottrell and his teammates to safety, we turned south for Kontum.

That moment was the proudest of all my time in Vietnam. From out of the blue, complete strangers had come together and braved enemy fire to save voices they'd heard over a radio, genuine heroes risking their own lives for other Americans. In my book, theirs was the highest form of valor.

As for Stormy Zero-Three, we never learned his fate. But Eldon Bargewell's great courage was recognized: After healing from his wounds, he was awarded the Distinguished Service Cross, while One-Zero George Cottrell received the Silver Star.

To this day, I have no idea who all those chopper pilots were.

Down in our area of operations, intelligence continued to pour in concerning new roads and fresh tank trails crossing from Laos; this news put Colonel Radke at loggerheads with the American civilian advisor to the Central Highlands region, John Paul Vann. Famous for his flamboyant if aggravating style, Vann refused to believe the enemy was massing tanks along the border. "What's this crap, Radke!" Vann snapped. "There are tanks in the tri-border area?"

"There are," Radke assured him. Vann said that was "a lot of horseshit."

Just after that confrontation, I was flying along Laotian Highway 110 one afternoon, when my pilot and I spotted an odd-looking stack of wood on the road. At first we thought it might be bait to draw us into the sights of antiaircraft guns, but examining it minutely with binoculars, hidden beneath the heap of logs we detected the distinctive boatlike hull of a PT-76 tank, apparently broken down. Despite marginal weather, we bombed it with a pair of F-4 Phantoms.

Only a few days later, Sergeant First Class Fred Zabitosky dropped by to visit his old buddies, Larry White and Gerry Denison. "Zab," a former One-Zero who'd been awarded the Medal of Honor for a 1968 mission, was now first sergeant of a 75th Ranger Long-Range Reconnaissance Company, which had just run several operations near Ben Het. Over a drink, he told us that his men, too, had found fresh tank trails and several artillery caches well inside South Vietnam. Our own teams had discovered two more tank trails aimed toward Ben Het and Dak To. Clearly, the enemy was preparing to bring sizable numbers of tanks into South Vietnam's Central Highlands.

Incredibly, Vann still refused to acknowledge the growing tank threat.

Then one morning I was flying along the road in the northern Plei Trap Valley, and spotted vehicle tracks glistening in the sun. I called Lowell Stevens to come over in his O-2 and take a look. We didn't think the pattern looked as flat and smooth as that of 'dozer tracks; they seemed to chew up soil more like tank tracks. But we couldn't be certain.

That report instigated a Saigon request for detailed photos and ground measurements so that analysts could determine whether it was tank tracks. Rather than insert a team some distance away, then have them try to sneak into this heavily occupied area, I urged that we land them directly on the road—quick and dirty—photograph the tracks, get in and out in less than twenty minutes. I was so certain this would succeed that I told Colonel Radke that I would lead the mission.

Radke chuckled, reminded me I was a Covey Rider not a One-Zero, and approved the concept. A few days later we inserted a recon team right on the road without a hitch, and Saigon got its photos and measurements. Word came back: definitely PT-76 tank tracks.

Eventually, Radke presented all this evidence to Vann—along with the track section carried out by Paul Kennicott's team some months earlier. At last, Vann had to admit the tank threat was real. Soon after that, Covey Rider Gerry Denison photographed a suspicious pile beside a road, which photo analysts determined to be a tarp-covered Soviet T-54 tank.

The growing danger of a tank attack inspired wacky humor among some recon men. At CCN Sergeants Richard "Nick" Brokhausen and Robert Cook donned World War I leather flying helmets and long, black overcoats with lugers on their hips, then borrowed a black civilian jeep, and launched "tank patrols" in Da Nang. Imagine the effect when they'd roll up to a Marine or USAF compound, tell the gate guard they were on "tank patrol" and ask, "Haff yu zeen any tanks?"

This unsettled the gate guards and launched so many scary rumors that the CCN commander had to order them to stop. Instead, Brokhausen—who spoke fluent German and carried a German identity card—scrounged a motorcycle and sidecar that he and Lemuel McGlothern rode to a German hospital ship in Da Nang harbor, the *Helgoland*. An American MP on the dock pretended he could read Brokhausen's identity papers, then waved them through. Once they were aboard, the German nurses were happy to share their excellent beer and wine with the crazy Americans. "They had a great wine cellar," Brokhausen reported.

Early that fall, our new special rescue force—Combat Recon Platoon Two or CRP-2—was fully trained and ready for its first mission. In Saigon, it was decided to insert CRP-2 on the LZ where Fred Krupa had been lost, in hopes of discovering some sign of him. Two HH-53 Jolly Greens from the Air Force's Thailand-based 21st Special Operations Squadron inserted Donald "Ranger" Melvin and his thirty-seven-man force. I flew Covey for the operation.

Hardly had they landed, though, than a fast-moving storm threatened to roll across a ridge just west of them, which would have engulfed their area, possibly for hours. I radioed a warning to Melvin, then to Colonel Radke back at Kontum. What did he want me to do? Radke radioed, "Plasticman, that's your call."

There wasn't a man in SOG who wanted Fred Krupa back more than I but I refused to let that cloud my judgment. We'd had tank sightings two miles away and massive numbers of enemy nearby. The threatening weather could block extraction or air support for hours. If Krupa had been taken alive, the enemy would have hustled him away months ago. If he were dead, our men might find his remains. How much should I risk living men for the remains of a friend?

I radioed Ranger Melvin, "Get your folks ready. We're extracting you."

I pulled them out, ending the operation. It is a decision I live with.

A few weeks later CRP-2 deployed again, this time 100 miles away, near the central coast, where a passing aircrew had spotted an evasion symbol in tall grass along a river. Lowell Stevens flew Covey, and this time Melvin's men found absolute evidence that, indeed, the symbol was real, apparently made by an American pilot who'd escaped captivity. Whether he was recaptured or simply wandered away, they could not determine. It would forever be a mystery.

Meanwhile, buoyed by the success of Captain Storter's HALO mission, another Kontum recon team readied for SOG's fifth HALO jump, for which I would be the Covey Rider. This time the drop zone was thirty-five miles west of Pleiku, right on the Cambodian border.

Designated RT Wisconsin, the team was led by Sergeant First Class Richard "Moose" Gross, an old friend and fellow former RT California One-Zero now on his third SOG tour. His team included Sergeants First Class Mark Gentry and Bob McNeir, Staff Sergeant Howard Sugar, Master Sergeant Charles Behler, and five Yards—Not, Biu, Hluih, Hmoi, and Kai. At ten men, they would be SOG's largest HALO team.

Just after 2:30 A.M. on 11 October, I took off from Pleiku with Captain Glenn

Wright, Covey 593, aboard an O-2. Minutes later we were orbiting ten miles from the drop zone, over the old Duc Co Special Forces Camp, where a pre-arranged bonfire was roaring. Keying off that visual beacon, a SOG Blackbird approached unseen at 17,000 feet. Momentarily we received a radio code word that the men had jumped, waited five minutes to insure the descending sky-divers were clear, then flew west the final ten miles.

Bbbbzzz-uppp!—bbbbzz-uppp!—bbbbzzz-uppp!

I called, "Beeper, Beeper, come up voice." It was One-Zero Gross, alone and unsure where everyone else had landed. Another beeper turned out to be Howard Sugar, in the same situation, not far away. Then a third and a fourth. In forty-five minutes I'd accounted for everyone; all ten had landed separately, though fortunately there had been no injuries. After daylight—one and a half hours away—I'd have them flash mirrors or wave signal panels, then herd them together. Until then Wright and I would cut holes in the black sky.

A half-hour later Gross and Sugar got together, then heard enemy soldiers shouting and moving in the brush—the NVA must have found a parachute. "Shit!" Gross whispered. Then Gentry radioed, reporting that he was going to try to link up with them and that he, too, had heard NVA calling and moving in the dark, searching for their teammates.

I cannot express our frustration, flying directly over them and talking to them, but not being able to do a thing to help. All we could do was wait for day-light and listen to their tense voices, whispering, "Plasticman, I've got move-ment," and, "Enemy movement fifty meters away."

At last dawn broke, and with it ground fog blossomed and met heavy rain clouds hanging on the hilltops, smothering the valley in an opaque sheet. Fly-ing above the clouds at 3,000 feet, I looked down and knew that in these condi-tions we could neither extract them nor bring in fighters and gunships to help them. Here and there small holes opened—sucker holes that closed minutes later. If we dived down we might never get back out, not without plowing into a hillside. Then Mark Gentry radioed that he heard NVA talking and maneu-vering toward him. Gross told Gentry to join him and Sugar, but Gentry pur-posely went the opposite direction, to draw the NVA away. Five minutes later Gentry stumbled into an NVA squad eating breakfast and the chase was on. He dumped his rucksack, threw several grenades, ran some ways, then ambushed his pursuers, killing two. Then he was up again, running, but the NVA kept close behind him. He ambushed them a second time, then dashed down a dry streambed, found a bomb crater, jumped into it, stacked magazines and that was it—he'd fight or die right there. At least, Gentry radioed us, the NVA hadn't yet found him in the crater.

My pilot, Glenn Wright, radioed the 361st Attack Helicopter Company, our Cobra unit, and told them they'd have to stand by at Pleiku until the weather broke. But Gentry was in grave danger—as were Gross, Sugar, and the whole team. What could we do? There were no good options, each risking someone else's life, except one, in which Wright and I risked only our own lives: Fly back to Pleiku, get an M-16 rifle, find our way back *under* the heavy clouds, then I'd shoot from the right window while Wright orbited. "Fuck it, let's do it," Wright agreed.

The weather was so bad that we flew by instruments back to Pleiku, then the approach radar guided us until we finally broke through overcast just 200 feet above the runway. A van raced out from Covey Operations with the requested M-16 and twenty-five loaded magazines. "Good luck," the Air Force sergeant wished us. We'd need it.

While we were picking up the M-16, another Covey flying the border, Lieutenant Paul Curs, heard Gentry's emergency radio and dove his O-2 into a sucker hole. Finding Gentry, Curs fired marking rockets and made low-level passes to knock the NVA off balance. Here and there, AKs fired up at Curs as he flashed along the treetops. Before the hole closed Curs climbed away.

Meanwhile our O-2 was en route, ten miles west of Pleiku, where the cloud bottoms dropped to just 200 feet above the ground. Contrary to every flying rule, every instinct, even good sense, we dove beneath the clouds; in my lap lay the map we'd follow, using landmarks to avoid the hidden hills. Initially we flew the dirt road heading to Plei Djereng Special Forces Camp, following it due west, hugging the bottom of the overcast. Right and left we saw hills disappear into the clouds, but so long as we kept to the road, I knew we were safe.

In three minutes the road turned south—Wright banked northwest, then we skimmed over miles of flat grassland. Two more minutes—a wall of green hills took shape ahead—*and there it was, the river!*—Wright banked hard left over the water, we descended a few feet and looked up at the passing trees, fifty feet off the deck. *It felt claustrophobic, like flying down a tunnel*—no room left or right or up, just riding above the water and making the curves, staying below the clouds. Even flying as slowly as possible we went too fast to make the tighter curves and we almost hit the trees, missing them by a dozen yards. Wright never hesitated, never uttered a word about turning back or giving up, he just kept us going west, determined to make it.

Then the river curved again and the clouds fell to 100 feet, then what we'd feared most—*200 yards ahead, wispy clouds hung all the way to the water*—no room to turn, not enough time to climb. Wright pushed forward the throttles, we whisked past treetops by ten feet—damn, ten feet! I tried but couldn't remember the words for the Catholic Act of Contrition—then we were enveloped in clouds and swirling mist, completely blind, a split second from plowing into trees, clouds all around us. We could see nothing, absolutely fucking nothing, knowing we were among trees waiting to grab us and throw us to the ground. We held our breath, speechless.

His knuckles white on the steering yoke, Wright knew there was nothing left but to run the gauntlet and hope for the best. Over and over, treetops poked toward us, almost touching our wingtips, then solid clouds, a blinding, white wall. I prayed there wasn't a mountain ahead of us—and then the ceiling lifted and we roared down a shallow fifty-foot opening over the river, where we saw it turn distinctly south. This was the border with Cambodia, where our men were.

Right there, the fog broke into a mile-wide hole of clear sky. We were safe, again, right over the team. I cranked open the window and hefted the M-16 as Wright lined up to shoot. I was about to have Gentry wave a panel when our radio crackled, "This is Panther Two-Seven. I've got a heavy gun team, west of Duc Co." Unable to sit on their hands knowing a team was in danger—and appreciating that Wright and I had risked it all to fly out there—the Cobras had launched on the chance the clouds would open. What was my M-16 compared to a Cobra's firepower? We climbed high up the hole, poked above the clouds, then stayed there until the Cobras reached us, and led them down the rabbit hole. In a moment they were shooting for Gentry and Gross, and I radioed Pleiku, calling for our Hueys to launch quickly, while there was still a hole out there.

The weather improved long enough to find everyone, get the choppers in position, then extract them. We did not lose a single man, did not suffer a single casualty.

That was SOG's final combat HALO jump.

Back at Kontum I welcomed a new roommate and Covey Rider, Staff Sergeant Ken McMullin, who replaced Steve Keever when he rotated home. A longtime Special Forces veteran, McMullin had made a Mike Force combat parachute jump in 1967. He had landed with the assault force at Son Tay, North Vietnam, the previous November in an attempt to rescue American POWs. Though the prisoners were not there, everyone in the Special Ops community admired the raid's brilliance and audacity. An all-around superb soldier, McMullin had been One-Zero of RT Delaware before being selected to fly Covey. But there was a bit of the devil in him, too.

Soon after McMullin moved into the Covey Country Club, a visiting general from U.S. Army Pacific was invited by for a drink. Quite a VIP, the general had been wined and dined at SOG headquarters, then briefed at our compound with special layouts of gear and live fire demonstrations. He had all the senior officers on eggshells with his every question.

The general nodded approvingly at our liquor cabinet—Tanqueray gin, Chivas Silver Label, Wild Turkey bourbon, Napoleon cognac, Stolichnaya vodka—varieties not found anywhere in Southeast Asia. "Only the best for the best," we boasted to visitors. What our visitors didn't know was that Lowell Stevens kept the real booze in the back, and each morning, for example, he refilled the Stoli bottle with ordinary red label Smirnoff.

A scotch man, the general took it on the rocks. Puffing an oversize cigar and sipping a water glass of our economy liquor, he practically held court—not totally pompous but quite impressed by himself. After an hour of this, and after several drinks, Ken McMullin leaned shyly toward him and asked, "Sir? Would you mind telling me? What's your first name?"

The general was a bit surprised but also flattered. He smiled, knocked an ash off his cigar and said, "Why, my name—is Ralph."

McMullin clinked his glass to the general's and admonished, "Well, *fuck you,* Ralph!" Everyone gasped, not least the general, who almost dropped his drink. He looked around at all of us, wide-eyed, and glared at Ken. Then he blinked, shook his head and laughed. "Nobody's—*ha-ha*—told me—*ha-ha*—to *fuck myself*—*ha-ha*—in years!"

Then all of us lifted our glasses and hollered, "Well, fuck you, Ralph!"

The general lifted his glass and retorted, "And fuck you, too!"

For the rest of the evening we talked about pheasant hunting, hound dogs, growing up on farms—anything but the war. And he genuinely loved it.

A few days later I was again flying with Captain Glenn Wright on a routine mission, crossing into Laos to find an LZ for a Vietnamese team, listening to Top 40 songs on Armed Forces Radio, and watching the countryside slip past. As we overflew a section of Highway 110, I noticed clumps of bushes on the road, a parallel line of leafy clusters for quite a ways. I didn't say a word to Wright and he didn't say a thing to me—we flew another twenty seconds, then looked to each other and asked, "Did you see what I just saw?"

Wright turned the O-2 around and, sure enough, some of the bushes moved—soldiers, heavily camouflaged NVA squatting on the road. If they'd taken one step sideways into the jungle, we'd have never seen them. Quickly, I calculated, the column ran two kilometers, down both sides of the road. With one man each two meters, that meant about 2,000 men.

While I flipped on the secure radio, Wright held us just far enough away that the NVA would not hear our engines. Momentarily I reached Colonel

Radke and requested that he contact Saigon and get a B-52 strike diverted to hit the exposed troops. "I'll do everything I can," he promised. For fifteen minutes we orbited ten miles from the road, letting the enemy believe we had left. I worked up coordinates so the B-52s could bracket that stretch of road.

Then came Colonel Radke's response. "Plasticman, Seventh Air Force says we cannot divert a strike."

Damn! What a missed opportunity.

Then, Radke added, "They said you may simulate a B-52 strike."

Preposterous! Asinine! Wright asked, "How the hell do we *simulate* a B-52 strike?"

We should not have lacked such faith in Seventh Air Force. A minute later, the airborne control center, Hillsborough, radioed and announced we had priority for all U.S. strike aircraft in Southeast Asia. It was astonishing. With Seventh Air Force's order, Hillsborough began sending us wave after wave of fighters—like nothing we'd ever seen—jets stacked to 40,000 feet, ready to go in. Every ten minutes another set of fighters arrived.

Within an hour we had the NVA running for their lives, but we could barely keep up with all the fighters swarming to us, a flow that never slowed.

Colonel Radke canceled all other operations and put the choppers and the O-1 Bird Dogs at our disposal. Our replacement Covey and Covey Rider—Lowell Stevens—launched early, so we held a quick radio brainstorming session. To expend so much air effectively, we split the area between us, right across a prominent ridgeline. Then we divided the aerial assets into identical task forces: Each of us had a pair of O-1 Bird Dogs to get down low in the weeds and find the enemy, a pair of Cobra gunships to cover the O-1s and pin the enemy whenever he was spotted. And just to our south, I had our flight of Hueys orbit, ready to come in and extract instantly anyone who was shot down. Now we were ready to roll.

That endless supply of bomb-laden fighters kept coming, carrying every kind of ordnance available. A plane up there had cluster bombs—we had a target for that; another showed up with 500-pound bombs—there was a target for that; napalm—a target for that, too. Whenever a pair of fighters ran out of station time, we had them dump their remaining load at the last place the O-1s had spotted any enemy. Every ten minutes, another set of planes arrived—USAF F-4s, Navy A-7s, South Vietnamese A-1s—a continuous aerial bombardment without precedent in the war. Our aerial task force pounced and pounded relentlessly along that stretch of highway until it was too dark to see.

Then at daylight we were back, doing it again, with Larry White joining us. Our initial strikes had split the NVA, sending them running in every direction.

Their leaders had lost control of their troops. There were little clusters of soldiers all over that didn't know where to go or what to do. They drifted back to the road to re-form, and that's where our O-1s and Cobras caught them, and we bombed them again.

And the more we bombed, the more we peeled back the onion, exposing hidden camps and supply stockpiles and truck parks, which, in turn, brought on more air strikes. Back at Dak To, the Bright Light team hustled all day to rearm the Cobras and turn them around, which required a quick resupply of rockets and 40mm ammunition from Pleiku, airlifted by Chinook helicopters.

That afternoon Colonel Radke got a message that a brigadier general was flying in to Kontum to see him. Climbing from his chopper on the helipad, the gruff officer demanded, "I'd like to know what the hell's been going on up here the last two days!"

Radke escorted him to our operations office and thoroughly briefed him, only to have the general snap, "Do you realize that you've fired up all the goddamn ammunition for my aviation units for the next thirty days?"

Radke was unshaken. "Is that right, sir?"

"Not only that, but you know this damned war is starting to wind down and you're overstressing my helicopters, endangering my pilots' lives." He tapped the table. "I don't like that."

Radke nodded thoughtfully.

The general ended, "I just wanted to let you know how I felt."

Back at the helipad, the general asked, "Did you understand what I said?"

With everyone beyond earshot, Radke at last could speak forthrightly. "I understood, General, but let me tell you something. None of the ammunition we fired was *your* ammunition. That's an allocation to support *our* operations, it has nothing to do with your unit. Secondly, all the helicopters and all the aircraft that were sent to us were allocated by General Abrams to support *his* operation, which is *our* operation. The third thing, from a personal observation, I'm over here, this is my third tour, and I thought the object of the war was to kill the enemy. If we get the opportunity tomorrow to do the same thing again, we're going to do it again. And I hope to Christ that you don't try to stand in my way. Do you understand, sir?"

The general's eyes flared. "I'll remember that, Colonel."

Radke snapped his sharpest salute. "Yes, sir."

He never heard another thing from the general.

By the time we wrapped up the three days of bombing, we must have expended more than 500 sorties—a thousand planes. "And that night," Colonel Radke would later recall, "old General Abrams himself diverted B-52 strikes into that area, and then they sent in the infrared [surveillance planes] and detected thousands of fires and smoke billowing up thousands of feet." Colonel Roger Pezzelle, who headed SOG's covert cross-border operations, later wrote a study that concluded that our devastating strikes, because they hit right on the nose of the North Vietnamese moving into South Vietnam, set back plans for the 1972 Easter Offensive by six months.

SOG's secret war may have been drawing to a close, but none of our men were watching the clock. In late October, RT Washington ran a close-run mission near Ben Het, in which One-Zero Bob McNeir initiated contact with a forty-man NVA platoon, badly bloodied them, then escaped. His One-One, Specialist Four Frank Dyl, called in Cobras and fighters to cover their extraction. Only McNeir had been hit, suffering a minor shrapnel wound. During October, according to SOG records, four American-led teams fought firefights near Ben Het, and remarkably, all shot their way clear.

The award for late-war audacity, though, must go to Sergeant Will Curry, One-Zero of RT New Hampshire. In late November—only three weeks before SOG recon ceased operations—he led a mission into the Plei Trap Valley and spent six days observing groups of passing enemy soldiers. Determined to seize a prisoner, on the morning of 19 November he ambushed a large body of NVA troops. His One-One, Sergeant James Giaco III, blew claymores and Curry shot two NVA; they came away with three AKs but no prisoners. Captain Charles Flott, the new recon company commander, had accompanied them to carry their radio, and in that role directed air strikes behind them that inflicted numerous casualties.

It was almost over, but you couldn't tell that by how hard the men were fighting. During the month of November, according to SOG records, five U.S.-led teams ran missions, and all faced such heavy opposition that enemy action forced their extraction, usually under fire. That month our teams had an average stay of eight hours or less per mission.

I flew for one such mission, when RT New York searched the area southwest of Ben Het for tank trails and enemy encampments. While One-Zero Larry Nixon was radioing me his end-of-day situation report, he paused, then reported he'd just heard the distinct metallic clank of mortar tubes snapping into their mounts. Then NVA voices called back and forth uphill. It was nearly dark, too late to extract them, but I could not just wish them good luck and fly away.

I thought about it, then radioed Colonel Radke, recommending that I refuel my plane, and overfly Nixon's men all night in hopes that the sound of our OV-10 engines would deter the enemy from attacking. My pilot was all for it.

"If you want to do it, you do it," Radke responded.

So, all night long our OV-10 buzzed near RT New York, the sound of our engines telling the NVA, "You shoot at them, and we'll shoot at you." Occasionally Nixon radioed that he heard voices uphill, but the enemy never attacked. Later RT New York was extracted without incident.

A few days later I was done.

There was a going-away party for me at recon company, then we drank late into the night at the Covey Country Club. As I packed my bags I regretted leaving just then because Martha Raye was arriving the same day I left, and I'd like to have seen her again. On the other hand, I didn't want to be there when this became a ghost town—I wanted to remember it whole, as the compound had been when I had arrived in 1968.

That morning I wore my green beret, discarding the silly black baseball hat we'd recently been required to wear. I said goodbye to Larry White, who was scheduled to fly the midday shift, then boarded a jeep with Lowell Stevens for the airfield.

Looking back at the compound as I drove away that final time I felt a mixture of regret and hope, thankful that Colonel Radke had asked me to stay to the end. At the airfield Lowell sat in the jeep with me, waiting for the Blackbird, amusing me with stories about a masturbating monkey and some dog licking its own testicles in the hollows of West Virginia. I asked him what he'd do when all those tanks came rolling over the border. "Hell, just give 'em coffee 'n' donuts, 'n' wave 'em through." We laughed.

And then came the big SOG Blackbird. As the C-130 reversed engines and taxied over, I shook Lowell's hand and grabbed my bag. Lowell called, "Goodbye, John." We had fought it hard, to the very end.

I thought for a second, trying to muster something profound to say, but it all seemed trivial for that moment and for a man I so respected. "Watch yourself, Roundeye." He nodded.

In a moment, I was gone.

Afterword

The day after I departed Vietnam, my roommate, Gerry Denison, slept late, having partied the previous night with actress Martha Raye, who'd just arrived on her annual holiday visit. About 8 A.M., he reached to his foot locker for a cigarette—*a blinding flash!*—walls blew out and Gerry fell under the collapsed roof. Confused, half-conscious, he didn't realize that a 122mm rocket had crashed in and detonated on my empty bunk.

Displaying incredible strength, Staff Sergeant Spencer Gregory, Jr., lifted the burning debris, allowing the badly wounded Denison to crawl to safety, as well as Covey Rider Ken McMullin, who'd been hit by shrapnel in the abdomen. Larry White, who was also in the building, escaped with minor wounds.

McMullin and Denison were medevaced.

One week later, just as Colonel Radke had forecast, recon missions ended. A couple of months later, SOG's Saigon headquarters closed down, too. There was no mustering out, no retirement of the colors, no ceremony, no formation, nothing. It was as if SOG had never existed, which was just fine with the security officers who spent days burning SOG's voluminous files.

Though SOG disappeared, its veterans went on to other endeavors, both military and civilian.

My best friend, Glenn Uemura, spent a career with the telephone company in Hawaii and today installs optical fiber cables in Oregon.

Glenn's former RT Vermont One-Zero, Franklin "Doug" Miller, eventually stood in the White House and received his Medal of Honor from President Nixon. After not seeing Doug in twenty years, I saw him twice in 2000, not long before he died of cancer.

My RT Illinois teammate George Bacon became a career CIA officer, serving in northern Laos as General Vang Pao's personal advisor. After the fall of Vietnam, he drifted from the Agency to Africa. George was killed on St. Valentine's Day 1976, when his Land Rover was ambushed by Cuban troops in Angola, the only American to die there.

Our RT Illinois One-Zero, Ben Thompson, retired as a master sergeant and today works in private security.

Richard Woody, who took two AK slugs beside me during our convoy ambush on Highway 110, returned to Vietnam for a tour with the Americal Division. After again being severely wounded, he left the Army and today is the postmaster in Inman, Kansas.

John Yancey, who grabbed the truck driver and later did his all to save the mortally wounded David "Baby Huey" Hayes, eventually became a counterterrorist on the elite Delta Force. John was in the Iranian desert during the failed rescue attempt of American hostages in April 1980. A decade later he was accidentally shot to death in a Delta Force training exercise.

Rex Jaco, my RT California One-One, was interviewed by the FBI in the 1971 hijacking of a Northwest Airlines plane. Rex was not the notorious "D.B. Cooper," who parachuted with a $200,000 ransom and has never been found. Today he serves on the board for the David Crockett VFW Post in Lawrenceburg, Tennessee.

Covey Rider Lloyd O'Daniels retired from the Army, earned an accounting degree, and today directs audits for the U.S. Special Operations Command.

The man whose life Captain Edward Lesesne saved by pulling a pistol and commandeering a Huey, Morris "Mo" Worley, retired in 1977. Today the ever active Worley is information manager for the Center for Oral and Systemic Diseases at the University of North Carolina School of Dentistry. Lesesne retired, too, and now lives in Panama.

After Vietnam, Medal of Honor recipient Bob Howard commanded Special Forces training at Camp Mackall, then headed the Mountain Ranger Training Camp at Dahlonega, Georgia, inspiring another generation of Green Berets and Rangers. He retired as a full colonel. He has since undergone a dozen surgeries to repair his many wartime injuries, reflecting his eight Purple Hearts. Bob Howard remains America's greatest little-known hero.

Our commander at Kontum, Colonel Frederick Abt, a combat veteran of World War II, Korea, and Vietnam, retired and became a fifth-grade teacher where, I've been told, his fatherly character brought out the best in his students. He passed away a decade ago.

The phenomenal Joe Walker spent another year in Vietnam after SOG, training Cambodian soldiers. Retiring from Special Forces, the former RT California One-Zero continued his special operations service in a civilian capacity, then, ten years ago, almost died when he fell while rappelling from a helicopter. After extensive surgery and spinal fusion, he went right back to work. Everywhere he goes today, I suspect, he still brings a 60mm mortar.

Eleven months after a mortar fragment shattered Frank Belletire's skull during a Hatchet Force operation, he finished physical therapy and left the Army on a medical disability. Frank graduated from college in 1976, and today he and his wife restore houses in the Chicago area.

Captain Neil "Wild Bill" Coady left the Army and now teaches at a Florida junior college, also operating a massage therapy business. He never received any award for his heroic rescue of the badly wounded sergeant during the 1970 Qui Nhon sapper attack.

Two years after One-Zero Ricardo Davis's death, his teammate Jim Lamotte visited his widow in New Mexico to help the family collect his life insurance, denied until then because no body had been recovered. Lamotte succeeded. Despite serious health problems in recent years, Jim continues to teach the martial art of aikido and to counsel troubled youths.

Another CCN veteran, Captain Chuck Pfeifer, whose phenomenal grenade-throwing saved lives during the 1968 sapper attack, achieved a degree of fame after SOG. In the 1970s he appeared on billboards nationwide as the Winston Man, then acted in the movie *Wall Street* and on NBC-TV's *Law and Order.* Two years ago Chuck received a much belated Silver Star for his courage that night in 1968, presented at his alma mater, West Point.

Pfeifer's fellow New Yorker Robert Masterjoseph, badly wounded when he captured a North Vietnamese officer, left the Army on a 100 percent disability. Today he still laughs when retelling the story of how he swore, "I'd give my left nut for a prisoner."

Another severely wounded recon man, RT New York One-Zero John St. Martin, spent many months in recovery. Despite his right leg being shorter than the left, back injuries, and hepatitis contracted from a blood transfusion, he earned a civil engineering degree and today works on major construction projects in California.

Ed Wolcoff, the assistant team leader who saved St. Martin's life, went on to earn a college degree and a commission as an ordnance officer. His final active duty assignment, as a lieutenant colonel, was heading a special bomb disposal unit at the White House. Today Ed develops defenses against possible terrorist use of chemical and biological weapons.

Funny, courageous, compassionate, Covey Rider Ken Carpenter made it safely back to the States. Then, two years later, Ken was in a bar in Alaska when a total stranger smashed a whiskey bottle over his head, killing him instantly. Former One-Zero Carl Franquet served on Ken's burial honor guard.

Fellow Covey Rider and RT Hawaii One-Zero Larry White spent his final active duty days with the 101st Airborne Division. Larry went on to a second career as an auctioneer in Louisville, Kentucky.

Another Covey Rider, Lowell Wesley Stevens, eventually became sergeant major of Blue Light, the classified counter-terrorist unit that preceded Delta Force. Although retired, today he operates the Camp Mackall shooting ranges used to train Special Operations units.

Seriously wounded by the 122mm rocket that hit my empty bunk, Gerry Denison healed sufficiently to finish his Army career, then served with distinction in the Alaska state troopers. Three years ago we fly-fished on the Talkeetna River near his retirement dream home.

Wounded by the same rocket, Ken McMullin recovered and later retired as a sergeant major. We sometimes cross paths when I speak about SOG and Ken speaks about the Son Tay Raid—the 1970 attempt to rescue POWs in North Vietnam—of which he's also a veteran.

The Covey Rider who flew dangerously low-level beneath the clouds to lead choppers to my rained-in RT Illinois, Captain Jim Young, left Special Forces, graduated from college, and started an insurance agency in Virginia.

One-Zero Jim "Fred" Morse, who had almost lost consciousness when he saw my passing Covey plane, survived his life-threatening wounds and today represents a pharmaceutical company. In that capacity he's had a few saves of his own, helping doctors find drugs to treat their patients. One physician told Fred that his information saved a patient's life. "So maybe that's what I was put here for," he philosophizes.

RT New Mexico One-Zero Richard McNatt, whose entire team was wounded because their signal smoke had drifted laterally, recovered from his wounds and retired from Special Forces in 1978. His small scuba shop grew into a regional chain, then a mail order business and his own line of scuba gear. Despite serious wounds and recurring pneumonia from having been shot through the lungs, today he walks, swims, pumps iron, and still instructs scuba diving.

On Veterans Day 1995, I spoke with David Mixter's parents almost a quarter-century after his loss. They found comfort knowing there was no question that he'd died and appreciated that One-Zero Pat Mitchel was ready to give his own life rather than abandon their son's body.

Mixter's courageous team leader, Pat Mitchel, today is a physician and a professor of medicine at the University of North Dakota.

The OV-10 pilot with whom I flew when we strafed and rocketed around Mitchel to help him and Lyn St. Laurent escape, Captain Jim "Mike" Cryer, left the Air Force after Vietnam and today lives in Tempe, Arizona, where he's business manager for the Comanche helicopter engine program.

Another OV-10 pilot, Captain Bill Hartsell, with whom I strafed and rocketed to help Ed Wolcoff's RT New York on Christmas Day 1970, mastered nearly every fixed-wing aircraft in the USAF. His final assignment was flying *Air Force Two* when George Bush was vice-president. After retiring, Hartsell became a pilot for the governor of Oklahoma.

Richard Gross, the RT California One-Zero who later led the HALO night skydive I supported, retired, then served as a State Department security consultant. After a long fight against debilitating diseases, Rich died two years ago.

Howard Sugar, one of Rich's teammates on that night HALO jump, left the Army and founded a thriving real estate appraisal business in Florida.

Another HALO jumper on that mission, Mark Gentry, who fought and evaded the NVA for three hours, continued his career in Special Forces, including several years with the Army skydiving team, the Golden Knights. Later Mark joined Delta Force and went on to be that unit's much respected command sergeant major.

The Covey pilot I flew with to support that night HALO jump, who somehow kept us from plowing into a mountain, Captain Glenn Wright, put in another Vietnam tour, eventually accumulating 275 combat missions. Glenn left the Air Force in 1975 and is now an industrial safety engineer in the Caribbean.

Former RT Michigan One-Zero Eldon Bargewell received the Distinguished Service Cross for his heroic actions that bloody morning when my Covey aircraft stumbled upon his team while looking for the missing F-4, Stormy Zero-Three. After being commissioned, he joined the formidable Delta Force, fighting in Iraq and Somalia, eventually becoming the Delta commander. Receiving his first general's star four years ago. Bargewell was appointed the commander of U.S. Special Operations Forces in Europe and today wears two stars as a major general.

Colonel Galen "Mike" Radke, the CCC commander in 1971, spent his final active duty years at Fort Bragg, commanding the Special Forces Training Group. He was a candidate to become founding commander of Delta Force (the job went to Colonel Charles Beckwith). Radke retired as a full colonel and today, married to a retired Army nurse, resides in Palm Harbor, Florida. "I think so much of Vietnam veterans," he likes to quip, "that I married one."

After Vietnam, Martha Raye appeared in the TV series *McMillan and Wife*, followed by semi-retirement (and Poli-Dent commercials). Green Berets were always welcome in her Bel Air home, where she sang for them in the den she'd converted into her own "team room," containing the Special Forces memorabilia she'd collected during almost two and a half years in Vietnam. When Raye passed away in 1994, she bequeathed this room to Fort Bragg's JFK Special Warfare Center Museum, where it has been reconstructed.

My two missing friends and teammates Peter "Fat Albert" Wilson and Captain Fred Krupa remain unaccounted for, as do SOG's four dozen other MIAs. The government of Vietnam claims it has no idea what happened to them.

But I remember Pete and Fred and all the men I served with. As the years pass and the controversies that swirled around Vietnam fade into insignificance, what still shines for me with stunning, lasting clarity are the devotion and courage of those beside whom I had the privilege to serve. I came away richer and stronger for having been among these finest of men, and if I ever forget any of them, all I have to do is sing "Hey, Blue."

Index

A-1 Skyraiders, 150–51, 159, 168, 279
Abrams, Creighton, 54, 121, 186, 214,
   306–7, 342
Abt, Frederick, 130, 133, 137, 159, 169, 184,
   208, 213, 316, 346
   leadership style of, 135–36
   on RT Hawaii mission in Laos, 136
A-Camps, 20, 21
   transfer to South Vietnamese Army of,
   303, 314, 323
Airborne-Infantry, 5
Air Force, U.S., 101
Air Force Two, 239
air horn fight, 232–33, 243
Air Medal for Valor, 152, 273
Air National Guard, 287
Alexander, Mrs. Billy, 22, 116
Allen, John, 139–41, 142–43, 145, 155, 164,
   218, 255, 258
   Camp Lang Vei mission led by, 138, 140,
   141, 149
Alphin, Talmadge, Jr., 76
Ambrose, Floyd, 55, 57, 73–74, 157, 166,
   187
ambushes, 61, 132, 317–18
Americal Division, 346
ammunition:
   accidents, 234–35, 314
   sabotaged, 64
   shortages, 316
Anderson, Bill, 272
Anderson, Harry A., 181
Anderson, Tony, 317

Anderson, Wayne, 170, 172, 181, 184,
   314
Angao, 200, 233, 239
Angola, 345
AN/GRC-109 radio, 17–18
Armed Forces Radio, 155, 305, 340
Armentrout, Gary, 304–5
artillery, 102, 103
Ashau Valley, 232, 317, 319
A-Teams, 9, 20
Attapeu, 283, 306, 315, 327
Avco-Aviation/Space Writers Association
   Helicopter Heroism Award, 275
Ayom, 313

B-52's, 156, 158, 169
   "simulation" of strike by, 341–42
Bacon, George W., III, 58, 61–62, 73, 74–75,
   76, 78, 79–80, 89, 113, 136, 247, 345
   bomb damage assessment and, 122–23,
   126–27, 129
   Bright Light duty of, 81–83, 85, 88
   counter-artillery mission of, 104–6, 108,
   110
   first RT Illinois mission of, 63–71
Baez, Joan, 142
Bahr, Roy, 44, 63, 130
Baker, David, 84, 86–87, 155
Baker, John, 248, 259–60
Ballard, Asa, 103
Bamboo Lounge, 95, 100
bangalore torpedoes, 113
Bangkok, 224–25, 226, 313

Ban Me Thuot, *see* Command and Control
    South
Bargewell, Eldon, 330–34, 349
Barnes, "Big Bob," 35
Barras, Sam, 146–48
Barthelme, Art, 226
Barton, Jack, 281
Batchelor, Tommy, 199
Bath, James "J. D.," 328
Batman, Sherman, 89–90
BDA missions (bomb damage assessment),
    119, 121, 122–29, 136, 192–96
Bean, John, 275
Becerra, Rudy, 209
Beckwith, Charles, 349
Behler, Charles, 336
Belletire, Frank, 57, 73, 170–72, 247
Ben Het Special Forces Camp, 1, 65, 73,
    103, 105, 155, 198, 210, 215, 257, 269,
    271, 275, 288, 314, 334, 335
  NVA attacks on, 83, 92, 101–2, 123–24,
    139–40, 286
Bentley, Michael, 329
Berg, Bruce, 317
Bessor, Bruce, 132
Bich, Mama, 178
Bingham, Dennis, 143, 144, 145, 147, 150,
    314
Bingham, Klaus, 145
Bingham, Oran, Jr., 145, 317
Binh, 59, 105, 124–25
Birchim, Jim, 57, 104
Bittle, Gary, 178–79
Biu, 336
Biuh, 249
Blaauw, John, 137, 150–52, 168, 186, 282
"Blackbird," 28
"black propaganda," 64
blackwater fever, 240
Blatherwick, Robert, 78–79
Bless, Charlie, 240–42
Blythe, Edward, 187–88
Bobcats, 287
body count mentality, 73
Bolivia, 36

Bolovens Plateau, 283, 306, 327
book codes, 18
Boronski, John, 208–10
Boui, 161, 163, 173, 184
Boundary Waters Canoe Area, 246
Boyle, William, 198
Bozikis, Ron, 170, 172, 184, 314
Bric, William, III, 77
Bright Light rescue teams, 47, 48, 81–94,
    170, 178, 180, 259, 273, 301, 328, 342
Brock, Dave, 170
Brock, Jim, 171–72
Brokhausen, Richard "Nick," 328, 335–36
Bronze Star for Valor, 152, 181, 273, 303
Brook, Bill, 224
Brown, Andrew, 188
Brown, Mike, 259
Brown, Robert, 187–89
Browne, John, 255
Bru tribe, 75
Buchanan, Michael, 145–46
Bu Dop, 183
Bui, 161, 163, 184
Bullard, Charles, 46, 47, 65, 313
Bunker, Ellsworth, 121
Bu Prang, 291
Burkhart, Frank, 276
Burkins, Lee, 214
Bush, George H. W., 349
Butler, Jim, 317

C-4 explosive, 105
Callaway, George, 16
Cambodia, 29, 32, 83, 102, 104, 105–6, 136,
    154, 240, 306
  bomb damage assessment in, 192–96
  Fishhook region of, 118–20, 232, 238
  neutrality of, 232
  as "neutral" territory, 33, 101, 119
  NVA in, 101, 231–33
  Parrot's Beak region of, 232
  RT California missions in, 232–33,
    237–39
  RT Illinois's mission into, 155–59
  RT Level mission in, 236

RT Vermont's mission into, 187–89
secret bombings of, 116, 119–25, 130
U.S. invasion of, 232, 237–38, 243
U.S. withdrawal from, 243, 248
Camors, Robert, Jr., 304
Campbell, Glen, 272, 323
Campbell, Jesse, 317, 328
Camp Crockett, 5, 7
Camp Long Thanh, 137, 321–22
Camp Mackall, 10–11, 20, 346, 348
CAR-15s, 36, 42, 60, 151, 156–57, 159, 163, 165
Carnett, Eckard, 317
Carpenter, Ken "Shoebox," 272, 274, 307, 318, 322–23, 329, 347
missions as Covey of, 260, 275, 279, 280, 281, 285, 292, 296, 326
Carr, Donald "Butch," 319
Castagna, Jean-Paul, 330–31
Castillo, Robert, 328
Cavanaugh, Steve, 122, 186, 208, 214, 216, 245
CCC, see Command and Control Central
CCN, see Command and Control North
CCS, see Command and Control South
Central Intelligence Agency, 8, 253, 256, 286, 316, 345
Central Office for South Vietnam (COSVN), 121
Chaine Annamatique, 65
chase medic, 85–86
Chavane, 326
China, 283
CIA, 136, 166
claymore, 67–68, 105
Clayton, Charles, 304
cluster bombs, 70–71, 150
Coady, Neil "Wild Bill," 166, 215, 347
in Qui Nhon sniper attack, 227–31, 347
Cobra gunships, 35, 85, 151, 158, 233–34, 279
rearming of, 91
Cobra Lead, 310, 312
code numbers, 36
codes, 18–19, 36

Combat Recon Platoon One (CRP-1), 314
Combat Recon Platoon Two (CRP-2), 314, 336
Command and Control Central (CCC), 154, 164, 174, 177, 180, 196, 200, 231, 243, 247–48, 249, 251, 258, 263, 272, 274, 280, 290, 303, 312, 323, 324
Christmas feast at, 282
communication failures at, 213
Covey barracks at, 272
Covey Country Club at, 278, 280, 282, 285, 290, 294, 301, 307, 308, 313–14, 318, 324, 339–40, 344
debriefings at, 196
elimination of unit at, 303
establishment of, 131
NCO club at, 34, 50, 220
sapper attack at, 215
supply shortages at, 316
Command and Control North (CCN), 27, 30, 95, 131, 145, 169, 243
August 1968 attack on, 75–81
barbed wire compound of, 28, 30
FOB-2 of, see Forward Operating Base Two
Kontum operating base of, 29, 31–32, 34, 122
Command and Control South (CCS), 32–33, 53, 118, 131, 232, 235–36, 240, 242
rocket attack on barracks at, 345
shut down of operations at, 243, 280
Commando Vault, 293
communications training, 16–19
"Conversation, The," 111
Cook, Robert, 328, 330–32, 335–36
Cooper-Church Amendment, 303
Cooper, D. B., 346
Copley, Bill, 13, 16, 20, 41, 57, 104
Corky (pilot), 269–71
Cornish, Judson, 16
COSVN, see Central Office for South Vietnam
Cottrell, George, 330–34
counter-guerrilla operations, 22

Country Joe and the Fish, 141
Covey Country Club, 278, 280, 282, 285,
    290, 294, 301, 307, 308, 313–14, 318,
    324, 339–40, 344
Covey Riders, 63–64, 87, 146–48, 155, 157,
    158, 265
  increased boldness of, 318
  increasing pressure on, 285–86
  losses of, 319
  missions logs kept by, 327–28
  timing as critical to, 280
  training for, 269–70, 273–74, 283–84
Crofton, Dave, 236
Cryer, James "Mike," 289–90, 294, 296–301,
    308, 348–49
Cunningham, Tom, 89–90
Curry, Will, 196–97, 343

D-48 Soviet 85mm gun, 103
Dak Klong River Valley, 105
Dak Pek Special Forces Camp, 168, 180,
    257, 332
Dak Ralong Valley, 292–93
Dak Seang Special Forces Camp, 215, 257,
    261–64, 293, 314
  rescues near, 225, 226–27
Dak Sou River, 250–51, 253
Dak To, 45–46, 64–65, 81, 83–84, 87, 88, 92,
    93, 105, 113, 143, 150, 169, 192, 209,
    215, 219, 225–26, 254, 256–58, 261–64,
    270, 276, 277, 279, 282, 287, 298, 300,
    304–5, 321, 335
Dalley, Richard "Dirty Dick," 191
Damoth, Jack, 16, 236, 249
Da Nang, 95, 131, 332, 333
  CCN compound at, 75–81, 314,
    330
  harbor of, 335–36
  see also Command and Control North
Da Nang airbase, 28
Daugherty, Dave, 328
Davidson, Donald, 295–96, 314
Davidson, Jon, 38
Davis, Clint, 170
Davis, Craig, 38, 104, 111

Davis, Howard "Karate," 63–64, 65, 68,
    150, 152, 155–59, 170–71, 175,
    188–89
Davis, Ricardo, 20, 21, 23, 30, 95–100, 111,
    165, 314, 347
Deacy, Bill, 236–37
dead letter drops, 9
Dean, Kyle, 177
Degovanni, George, 294
Delima, Bill, 33, 37, 62, 84, 93, 94, 136–37,
    143–45, 166
Delta Force, 346, 348, 349
demilitarized zone (DMZ), 250, 332
demolitions training, 19
deniability, 43, 48, 105, 124, 313
Denison, Gerald, 89, 133, 239, 307, 334,
    335, 345, 348
Devine, Mark "Jingles," 280–81
Dias, George, 114
Digiovanni, Dennis, 170
Dilger, Joe, 240–41
Disur, 249
Djuit, 259–60
Doggett, Jim, 286
Doney, Norm, 134, 137, 143, 149, 152, 155,
    167, 183, 187, 199, 201
Donlon, Roger H. C., 6
Dorff, Tony, 89
Dove, Luthor "Luke," 48, 69, 94, 132
Dover, Emmet "Les," 2, 249, 252, 254, 255,
    257–58, 262–65, 297, 314
Duc Co Special Forces Camp, 242, 337,
    339
Duggan, Mike, 189–91
Dunnam, Gary, 317
duress codes, 19
dysentery, 149, 240

"Eagle Eyes," 305
Easter Offensive (1972), 343
Eisenhower, Dwight D., 273
"Eldest Son," 64
equipment, 61–62
Erickson, Charles, 174
Evans, William, 118

F-4 Phantoms, 151, 279, 322
Fails, George, 86–87
false trails, 54
Fant, Ernie, 10
Farrell, Allan, 113
"Fat SPAF," 251
fear, succumbing to, 111
Federal Bureau of Investigation, 346
Feinberg, Mark, 274–75
Felker, Rick, 151
Fernandez, Margarito, Jr., 120
Fernandez, William "Jose," 319
5th Special Forces Group, 20, 22, 27, 52,
    179, 303, 323
    see also Task Force Two, Advisory
    Element
57th Assault Helicopter Company, 85, 289,
    310
Firebase Mary Lou, 35
Firebase Thor, 317
1st Air Cavalry Division, 103, 187, 202, 238,
    240, 242–43
1st Infantry Division, 316
first aid training, 82
Fishhook region, of Cambodia, 118–20,
    232, 238
Fleming, Jim, 118
Flott, Charles, 343
foot trails, 50–51
Fort Belvoir, Va., 19
Fort Benning, Ga., 5, 7
Fort Bragg, N.C., 6–7, 116, 145, 152, 236,
    322, 349, 350
Fort Campbell, Ga., 5
Fort Gordon, Ga., 5
Fort Lewis, Wash., 23
Fort Sam Houston, Tex., 19
Forward Operating Base Two (FOB-2),
    31–32, 33
4th Infantry Division, 34, 46, 92, 244, 316,
    323
14th Field Artillery, 101–2
40th Artillery Regiment (NVA), 83
46th Special Forces Company,
    149

421st Tactical Reconnaissance Squadron,
    330
463rd Tactical Airlift Wing, 293
Franke, Bob, 8, 114–15
Franklin, Louis, 214
Franquet, Carl, 249, 260, 347
French and Indian War, 50
French Indochina War, 103
French Resistance, 6
friendly fire, 281
Fry, Jim, 274
Fulton, Don, 124, 147–48, 150–52

Gabbard, Bill, 27, 30–31, 54
Gai, 187–89
Gainous, Henry, 259, 264
Galasso, Jim, 203, 212
Gande, Berman, 209
Garcia, Geoffrey, 139–40, 149, 154
Garland, Lee, 249
Gentry, Mark, 336–38, 349
"ghosting," 20
"Ghost Riders," 40
Giaco, James, III, 343
Gilmer, David, 60–61, 102, 132–34
Gim, 161
"Give Peace a Chance," 224, 313
Glashauser, Gregory, 84, 93, 113, 133, 166,
    225–26
Glass, Wendell, 184
Gmitter, Regis, 2, 249, 252, 254, 257–58,
    261, 263–65, 296–98
Godwin, Jim, 14
Golden Knights, 349
Gong, 249
Good, John, 270
Goodwin, Ray, 225–26
Goulet, Ronald, 113, 166, 227, 314
Grace, A. Michael, 203
Grant, John, 186, 205, 289
Graves, Jay, 302
Gravett, Rob, 88, 90, 91, 92
Green, Don, 270
Green, Gary, 210
Green, George, 278–79

Green Berets, *see* Special Forces
Greenwood, Billy, 294–95, 309, 311
Gregory, Spencer, Jr., 345
Greko, Frank, 174
grenades, 141
Griffin, Jerome, 40
Grimes, Bill "Country," 255, 256–59
Grogan, Kevin, 307
Gron, Robert, 40
Gross, Richard "Moose," 51, 102, 103,
  167–68, 199, 336–39, 349
Groupe Mobile 100, 228
Groves, Wesley, 294, 309–10, 312
guerrilla warfare, 6, 9
Guevara, Che, 36
Gunnison, John, 249, 286–87
Guns & Ammo, 216
gunship pilots, 85
Guzzetta, Jerry, 187, 192–95, 197, 199

Hagen, Loren, 317, 331
Haggard, Merle, 272
Hai, 59–60, 65, 66, 69, 105, 126, 129–30,
  157–58
Haiphong Harbor, 253
Hamburger Hill, 232
Hamric, Terry, 40
Hanson, Bill, 54, 67, 82
Hanson, Dale, 154
Hanson rig, 82
Harned, Gary, 208, 210
Harrigan, Greg, 121–23, 314
Harris, Ray, 186
Harrison, Randy, 118–20
Hartsell, Bill, 282, 293, 349
Hartwig, Oliver, 133, 186
Harvey, Dan, 104
Hatchet Force, 33, 39–40, 93–94, 113, 152,
  158–59, 166, 169, 181, 185, 188, 204,
  227, 240, 249, 252, 272, 275, 307,
  346
  Company A of, 259
  Company B of, 254–56, 264
  disbanding of, 314
  Montagnard, 114

  Plei Trap Valley raid by, 308–13
  roadblock by, 197–98
Hatchett, William, 170
Hayes, David "Baby Huey," 244–45, 313,
  314, 346
Hein, Chuck, 216–23, 234–35, 314, 323
"Helen," 34
Helgoland, 335–36
helicopters:
  assault companies of U.S. Army, 40, 45,
   85, 120, 209, 236–37, 274, 338
  Kingbee H-34, 124, 148, 166
  pilots of, 84–85
Helland, Sam, 276–77
Herald, Charles "Weird," 155, 157–60,
  174
Hernandez, Sammy, 328
Hetzler, Walter "Jerry," 215
"Hey, Blue," 41, 48, 95, 154, 166, 168, 172,
  181, 186, 210, 226, 235, 247, 301–2,
  313–14, 323, 350
Higgins, David, 20, 34, 82, 130–31
High Altitude, Low Opening (HALO)
  parachuting, 328–30, 336–39, 349
"High Hopes," parody of, 197
Highway 14, 31, 163, 180
Highway 16, 327
Highway 92, 250–51, 281, 282, 319, 327
Highway 110, 53, 65, 93–94, 133, 150, 184,
  192, 202, 203–5, 207, 210–11, 241, 258,
  289, 346
  NVA along, 251–54, 274–75, 285–88,
   295–96, 340–43
  NVA tank movements on, 334–35
Highway 165, 96, 142, 148, 254–59, 264
Highway 548, 317
Highway 613, 192
Hill, Melvin, 328
Hill 875, 105
Hillsborough, 270, 287, 311, 341
Hlien, 161
Hluih, 336
Hmoi, 200, 336
Hmong people, 247, 315
Ho Chi Minh, death of, 155, 157

Ho Chi Minh Trail, 1, 29, 36, 55, 187, 204, 248, 304, 327
  see also Laotian Ho Chi Minh Trail
Holden, William, 316–17
Honeycutt, Dave, 249
Horion, Walter, 20
Hosken, John, 209
House 22, 30
Howard, Robert, 47, 53, 54, 57–58, 72, 74, 90, 94, 109, 111–12, 132, 134, 137–38, 141, 149, 154–55, 163, 166, 222–23, 249, 264–65, 278, 302, 314, 346
  Medal of Honor for, 88–89, 154, 265, 278, 302, 303, 314
  medals awarded to, 38, 43, 265, 303, 346
  personality of, 38–40
  return after injury of, 43
  training overseen by, 38
Hull, Larry, 319
Humphrey, Hubert, 23
Huynh, 59, 124, 126
Hyuk, 187–88

Ia Drang Valley, 242–43
"I-Feel-Like-I'm-Fixing-to-Die Rag," 141
Ilyushin 718 plane, 73
immediate action drills, 82, 141, 163
"I'm So Lonesome I Could Cry," 186, 323
interrogation, 22
Iraq, 349
Ireland Army Hospital, 115–16

Jaco, Rex, 200, 225, 242, 244, 247, 346
  in Cambodia, 232, 234–35, 239–40
  Operation Ashtray Two role of, 203, 206, 211, 212
Jaks, Frank, 43–44, 49, 184, 186, 196, 201–2, 205, 208
Jamison, Ernest, 122
Je, 249
Jennings, Waylon, 272, 294
Jerson, Jim, 40, 41
Joecken, Richard, 166
Johnson, Lyndon B., 17, 23, 101
Johnson, Pete, 132

Jones, Bob, 8
Jones, Sergeant, 135
Jump School, 5
Justice, John, 2, 249, 252, 254, 257–58, 263–65, 297

Kai, 336
Kedenburg, John, 89–90
Keefer, Barry, 51, 141
Keever, Steve "Jade," 199, 259–60, 289–90, 292, 308, 309–10, 318, 327–28, 339
Kelley, Francis, 198–99
Kennedy, John F., 6, 11
Kennicott, Paul, 203, 206, 211, 286–88, 335
Kepczuk, Tadeusz, 77
Kerns, Donald, 77
Keyton, Cecil, 166
Kham Duc Special Forces Camp, 76, 142, 332
Khe Sanh, 9, 44, 76, 83, 142, 302, 317
Kickliter, James, 77
King, Malen "Fat Cat," 282, 294, 316
Kingbee H-34 helicopter, 124, 148, 166
king cobra, 239
Kinnear, Mike, 86–87
Kirschbaum, Dave, 88, 90, 91, 92
Kissinger, Henry, 119
Klung, 259
Knight, Ronnie, 280, 306–7
Knot, 187, 194–95
Kontum, 81
  CCC established at, 131
  CCN operating base at, 29, 31–32, 34, 122
  supply shortages in, 316
  see also Command and Control Central
Kotin, Robert, 329
Kramer, Larry, 306–7, 314
Kramps, Henry, 113
Kratie, 238
Krupa, Fred, 202, 203, 204, 206–8, 210–13, 224–25, 259, 288, 307, 308–14, 315, 323, 326, 336, 350
  Plei Trap Valley raid led by, 308–14
Kuropas, Mike, 133, 225–26, 314

Laird, Melvin, 119
Lake, Jim, 209, 226
Lam, 59, 105, 106–7
Lamotte, Jim, 30, 95–100, 111, 347
Lamphier, Roy, 169
land navigation, 12
Lang Vei Special Forces Camp, 9, 21, 76, 92,
    138
Laos, 28–29, 32, 37, 43–44, 63, 83, 88, 96,
    114, 136, 145, 159, 166, 169, 227, 238,
    239, 243, 282–88, 319, 332, 345
  cessation of U.S. recon missions into,
    303–4, 345
  CIA in, 247–48, 315–16
  HALO jumps into, 328
  highway system in, 43, 110, 248, 250–51,
    281, 282, 314, 319; see also specific
    highways
  Ho Chi Minh trail in, 65–66, 101, 248,
    256, 315–16, 326
  increase of recon missions in,
    248
  increasing NVA presence in, 326–27
  mining missions in, 263
  Operation Ashtray Two into, 209–13,
    236, 245, 250, 286, 288, 307
  RT Hawaii recon in, 253–54, 257–58,
    261–64, 296–98
  RT Illinois recon in, 169–72, 289–90
  RT Moccasin recon in, 187–89
  RT Ohio recon in, 241–42, 274
  RT Vermont recon in, 216–22
  security concerns of recon missions in,
    292
  South Vietnamese Army invasion of,
    302–4
  tank movements in, 286, 334–35
Laotian Ho Chi Minh Trail, 65–66, 101,
    248, 256, 315–16, 326
Larsen, Stanley, 231–32
laser designator, 250
Lechner, David, 185
Leh, 249
Lehacka, John, 185, 283
Lennon, John, 224, 313

Lesesne, Edward, 36, 40, 41, 43, 47, 48, 72,
    77, 78–79, 80, 94, 113–14, 115, 302, 346
Lew, Melvin, 313
Lischynski, George, 244
Lively, Jim, 114
Loi, 59, 105, 106–7, 124–26
Lok, 97, 99
Long, Clarence, 60–61, 102
Longaker, Frank, 166
Long Binh, 245, 322
long-range rocket attack, 83–84
Long Thanh, 149
Lon Nol, 231
Louks, Bryon, 90
luck, 52, 56
Lun, 161, 184
Lynch, Tim, 133, 186
Lyons, Brendan, 249

M-16 machine guns, 159
M-60 machine guns, 82
M-79 grenade launcher, 59, 165
McCarley, Eugene, 254–56, 264
McClelland, Barre, 93, 166
McDonald, Owen, 293–94
mace, 133–34
McGirt, John, 115
McGlothern, Lemuel, Jr., 328, 335
McGuire extraction rigs, 45, 57, 59, 91
McLeod, Willie, 174, 184, 186
McMullin, Ken, 339–40, 345, 348
McNamara, Robert, 232
McNatt, Richard, 280–81, 348
McNeir, Bob, 336, 343
McPherson, Mark, 330–31, 333
MACV, see Military Assistance Command,
    Vietnam
Maggio, Louis, 43
Malone, Bob, 236–37
Manes, Larry, 328
Mang Yang Pass, 228
Mann, Bob, 213
Manning, Nick, 179–80
Manz, Bob, 177–78
Marble Mountain, 75, 76

Marines, U.S., 9, 316
    HMM 463 Squadron of, 254
Marshall, Kent, 276–77
Masci, Ernie, 236–37
Masterjoseph, Robert, 189–92, 244, 347
Mauceri, Jeff, 278–79
May, Michael, 118
Meadows, Dick, 54
media, war coverage of, 303
medic training, 19
Mekong Delta, 200
Melvin, Donald "Ranger," 314, 336
Memot, RT California recon in, 239
Meou, 199
Merkerson, Willie, 184
Mertz, Ken, 237
message encryption, 18–19
methods of instruction (MOI), 7–8
Mike Force, see Mobile Strike Force
Military Assistance Command, Vietnam, 122
Miller, Franklin "Doug," 187–89, 215, 216–23, 222–23, 234, 247, 345
Miller, John, 132
Miller, Robert K., 116
Miller, Roger, 226
Mills, Travis, 78
Mims, Bernie, 187, 240–42
Minnicks, Skip, 21
Minnihan, Terry, 166
Mitchel, Pat, 1, 260, 283–85, 297–301, 348
Mixter, David "Lurch," 1, 284, 298–302, 306, 314, 348
Mobile Strike Force, 21, 23, 33, 183, 272, 303, 309, 323, 339
Mohs, Bob "Patches," 167–68
"Monkey in Space" project, 290–91
Monroe, Moose, 21
Montagnards, 8, 20, 21, 31–32, 36, 55, 58, 161–62, 249, 323, 328, 332
    training of, 162–63
Montgomery, Marvin "Monty," 84, 86–87
Moore, Jim, 78–79, 80
Morgan, Rheuban, 187

Morris, Joe, 134, 143, 145
Morse, Jim "Fred," 249, 276–78, 348
Morse code, 16–17
Moss, Lynn, 270
Moss, Richard, 146
Mountain Ranger Training Camp, Ga., 346
Moxon, Art, 319
Moye, Millard, 329
Mu Gia Pass, 250
Munson, Ralph, 286–87
Murchinson, Roary, 80
Murphy, Audie, 303
Murphy, Barry, 118, 120, 123
Musselman, Galen, 231, 232, 235, 242, 245, 247, 304

Nakhon Phanom (NKP) Air Force Base, 96, 319
Nao, 249
napalm, 70, 150, 159
Neal, Dennis, 225–26
Neamtz, Pete, 249
Newman, Cliff, 328
Nguang, 39
Nha Trang, 27, 261, 303, 323
Nhit, 249
Nigon, 199
95th Field Hospital, 229, 230–31
9th Infantry Division, 316
Nixon, Larry, 343–44
Nixon, Richard M., 89, 119, 121, 122, 232, 243, 265, 302, 303
Non-Commissioned Officers (NCOs), 7, 17, 34, 38, 50, 220, 323
Norodom Sihanouk, Prince of Cambodia, 33, 119, 121, 231, 234
Norris, Charles, 76
North Carolina, University of 346
North Dakota, University of 348
North Vietnam, 250
    bombing halt on, 101
    Chinese support of, 283
    see also North Vietnamese Army
North Vietnamese Air Force, 73

North Vietnamese Army (NVA), 39, 44,
        50–51, 70, 119–20, 145–48, 151,
        154–59, 247–48, 261–64, 273, 304, 314
    along Highway 110, 251–54, 274–75,
        285–88, 289, 295–96, 340–43
    along Highway 165, 256, 264
    artillery in Cambodia of, 101
    Attapeu seized by, 315
    Ben Het siege by, 92, 139–40
    in Bu Prang, 291
    in Cambodia, 101, 231–33
    captured member of, 212–15
    "City" near Snuol of, 238
    commandos of, 31
    counter-recon unit of, 55, 156, 204
    in Fishhook region, 118–20, 238
    Hatchet force encounters with, 198,
        308–13
    Laotian highway system of, 248, 314
    push system used by, 253
    Qui Nhon tank farm attack by, 229–31
    recon teams' encounters with, see specific
        teams
    roadbuilding of, 326–27
    6th Infantry Division of, 292
    SOG ambushes of, 317–18
    Special Operations Brigade of, 75
    SVA recon teams and, 320–21
    trackers of, 54–55, 60, 104
    withdrawal into Laos of, 29
Norwegian Resistance, 6, 30
Not, 336
November-One, as target, 63, 66
Novy, Jan, 244
Nowak, Richard, 60–61, 102, 133
Nungs, 21
NVA, see North Vietnamese Army

O-1 Bird Dogs, 158–59, 169
O'Conner, Mike, 136
O'Daniels, Lloyd "O.D.," 198, 199, 209–10,
        213, 215, 241–42, 245, 346
O'Donnell, Mike, 209
Office of Strategic Services, 8–9
O'Kelly, Terry, 237

"Old Willy Pete Trick," 283–84
On, 97–98
101st Airborne Division, 140, 232, 273, 292
122mm rocket launchers, 83
175mm guns, 102
155th Assault Helicopter Company, 236–37
170th Assault Helicopter Company, 209,
        274
173rd Airborne Brigade, 46
175th Ranger Long-Range Reconnaissance
        Company, 334
189th Assault Helicopter Company, 40, 45
    see also "Ghost Riders"
195th Assault Helicopter Company, 120
One-Ones, 66, 137–38
one-time pads, 18
One-Zeros, 51–52, 54, 56–57, 137–38
One-Zero School, 36
Opera Hotel, 224–25
Operation Ashtray, 186, 203, 205
Operation Ashtray Two, 202, 208–14, 224,
        236, 245, 250, 286, 288, 307
    planning of, 203–8
Operation Lam Son, 302–4
Operation Tailwind, 254–56, 306, 326
O'Rourke, Bill, 121
Ortman, Bill, III, 118–20, 123
OV-10 airplane, 273–74, 322

Padgett, John, 255
paratroopers, 5, 235
Parker, Carlos, 170
Parnar, Joe, 85–86, 88–90, 104
Parrot's Beak region, of Cambodia, 232
Pathet Lao, 174, 248
Patton, Shephard, 284
Paulaskis, Ed, 233–34
Peacock radar center, 124
Peacock restaurant, 240
Peckinpah, Sam, 316
Pegram, Richard, Jr., 76
Pesten, Charlie, 12
Peterson, John, 102
Pezzelle, Roger, 343
Pfeifer, Chuck, 75–81, 347

Phang Rang, 287
Pheng, 203
Pher, 161
Phung, 203, 204–5
Phyit, 161, 163, 165
Pin, 299
Pinn, Lionel "Choo-Choo," 33, 35, 36, 37,
     38, 43, 47, 72
Pisgah National Forest, 19
Plei Djereng Special Forces Camp, 338
Pleiku, 124, 152, 228, 242, 244, 262, 281,
     293, 315, 319, 323
   HALO jumps into, 336–39
Plei Trap Valley, 308–13, 326–27, 328,
     329–30, 335, 343
Pleo, 249
Pok, 249
"Pok Time," 68–69
Polei Kleng Special Forces Camp,
     309–12
Pool, Jerry, 208–10
Poole, Paul, 329
Pope, Reinald, 27–28, 30–33, 166
Pope Air Force Base, 10
Potter, Paul, 77
Pouih, 161
prairie fire, 1–2, 44, 56, 91
Predmore, Larry, 289
prep, 187–88
Presley, Eulius "Camel," 197–99, 204
Pride, Charley, 272, 294
Prin, 168, 200
prisoner snatches, 60–61, 124, 133–34,
     149–52, 185–86, 204, 236
Project Delta, 21, 23, 52, 137, 149, 302
Project Omega, 294
Project Popeye, 136
promotions, 112–13
Pruitt, Jim "Mule Skinner," 16, 30, 145–46,
     155
psychological warfare, 64
Pulliam, Lonnie, 37, 166
Purple Hearts, 146, 166, 273, 280, 303,
     346
"Pusher, The," 141

Quamo, George, 21
Quang, 59, 124, 126, 129–30
Quan Loi launch site, 118–19, 238–39
Queen, Bill, 317
Qui Nhon, 227–31
Quiroz, Joe, 187, 192–95, 197

racism, 58
Radio Hanoi, 121
Radke, Galen "Mike," 316, 318, 324, 326,
     327, 328–29, 334–36, 340–44, 345, 349
RAND corporation, 6
rappelling, 81
Ray, Ron, 181
Raye, Martha, 62–63, 95, 100, 177, 344, 345,
     349–50
recon cocktail, 74
Recon One-Zero School, 149
recon teams, 33, 36–37
   disbanding of, 345
   leader code names of, 36
   multiple insertions by, 123–24
   prisoner snatches by, 60–61, 124, 133–34,
        149–52, 185–86, 204, 236
   rank in, 37
   return from missions of, 72
   tactics of, 42, 50–51, 56, 292
   training NCO's of, 38
   see also specific recon teams
Remarke, Joe, 245–46
Rhade tribe, 161–62
Rhea, Randy, 146, 180–81
Rickmers, Rolf, 77
Riders, Covey, 63–64
Riffe, Jimmy, 179–80
Rimondi, William, 317
Ripanti, Jim, 86–87, 94, 314, 323
Rivest, Mark, 249, 272
roadblocks, 197–98
Robideaux, Gene, 309, 311–12, 313, 316
Roche, Steve, 89
rocket-propelled grenades (RPGs), 48
Rock Island East, 239
Rodd, Ralph, 37, 52, 104, 146–48, 155, 250
Rogers, William, 119

RON (rest overnight-position), 67
Roper, Jim, 294
Rose, Al, 94
Rose, Gary "Mike," 306–7
Ross, Dan, 289
Royal Laotian Army, 247–48, 283, 306, 315
RT Alabama, 138, 140, 141, 149, 276–78
RT Arizona, 55–56, 199, 249, 281
RT Arkansas, 146–48
RT Asp, 30, 145–48
RT California, 37, 42–43, 52, 60, 102–3, 167,
    199, 200, 208, 240–42, 247, 250, 304,
    314, 336, 349
  Cambodian insertions of, 232–33,
    237–39
  Ia Drang Valley mission of, 242–43
  Memot mission of, 239
  NVA encounters of, 167–68, 232–33,
    295–96
  Snuol mission of, 238–39
  training of, 200–201, 227
RT Colorado, 1–2, 37, 52, 104, 174
  NVA encounters of, 283–85, 297–300
RT Copperhead, 30, 96, 99
RT Delaware, 37, 48, 247, 339
RT Florida, 134, 143, 144
RT Habu, 330
RT Hawaii, 2, 33, 37, 93, 112, 136–37, 143,
    145–47, 150, 225–26, 249–59, 273, 314
  in Cambodia, 225–26
  'dozer mission of, 251–53, 284
  encounters with NVA of, 226, 253–54,
    257–58, 261–64, 296–98
  Juliet-Nine mission of, 143–44
  Laos recon by, 253–54, 257–58, 261–64,
    296–98
  psychological pressure on, 258
  recon of "the Falls" by, 251–53
  Target Alpha One mission of, 254–59
  training of, 250, 252, 258
RT Illinois, 58, 59, 62, 81, 117, 136, 139–40,
    149, 152, 160, 161, 180, 183–84, 258,
    259, 327–28
  BDA assessment mission by, 123–29
  Bright Light duty of, 81–94

Cambodia mission of, 155–59
counter-artillery mission of, 101–12
debriefing of, 72–73
first mission of, 63–71
Laos missions of, 169–72, 289–90
second Laos mission of, 173–78
and sniper hunt, 163–65
Target Alpha-One Mission of, 142, 148
Vietnamese members of, 58, 59
RT Indigo, 317
RT Iowa, 286–88
RT Kansas, 145, 317, 330–34
RT Kentucky, 38, 88, 90–92, 274–75
RT Level, 236
RT Maine, 73, 84, 86–89, 155
RT Moccasin, 189–91
RT Montana, 225–26
RT Nevada, 73, 89, 114
RT New Hampshire, 86–88, 143, 343
RT New Mexico, 36, 38, 47, 50, 55, 56, 64,
    67, 88, 104, 108, 141, 313
  NVA encounters of, 241, 280–81
RT New York, 42, 104, 137, 248, 349
  NVA encounters of, 281–82, 343–44
  prisoner snatch of, 149–52
RT Ohio, 55, 57, 73, 133, 240–42
  Laos recon by, 241–42, 274
  NVA encounters of, 241–42
RT Pennsylvania, 209–10, 213, 220,
    314
RT Python, 317
RT Sidewinder, 330
RT South Carolina, 93, 248, 259–61
RT Texas, 60, 102, 133, 270–71, 292–93
RT Vermont, 57, 187–89, 216–22
RT Washington, 144, 187, 197–98, 278–79,
    343
RT West Virginia, 280, 306, 314
RT Wisconsin, 336–39
RT Wyoming, 38, 102–3, 123
rucksacks, 62, 156
Ruff, Newman, 249, 260, 281, 329
Russia, ambassador to Thailand of,
    225
Ryan, Rich, 240–42

S-2 intelligence office, 103, 163, 168–69
S-3 intelligence office, 168–69, 174, 196, 209
Saga magazine, 137
Saigon, 227, 240, 245, 247, 276, 285, 292, 304, 321, 345
St. Laurent, Lance, 284
St. Laurent, Lyn, 1, 284–85, 298–301, 348
St. Martin, John, 42, 56, 104, 137, 150, 151–52, 155, 347
Sample, Joe, 225–26
Sang, 98–99
Santana, Anthony, 77
sappers, 30–31, 75–81
Savage, Earl, 20
Scalise, Serafino, 250–51
Scherdin, Bob, rescue of, 39–40, 41, 314
Scott, Mike, 132
Secor, Gilbert, 77
Se Kong Rover, 306
Seper, Bob, 181
Septer, Charlie "Putter," 207, 210
serum albumin, 61
Seventh Air Force, 292, 341
7th Special Forces Group, 22
71st Evacuation Hospital, 129, 235, 262, 278
77th Special Forces Group, 10
Sheppard, Mike, 166, 225–26
Shriver, Jerry "Mad Dog," 21, 53–54, 121–23, 187, 236, 309
Shumate, Walter, 321
signal security, 18
Sihanoukville, 248
Silver Star, 180, 189, 273, 303, 334, 347
Simmons, Billy, 36, 38–39, 43, 46, 47, 48, 65, 313
Sinyard, Cletis, 14
Sisler, George K., 89
situational awareness, 131
6th Battalion, 101–2
66th regiment (NVA), 83, 103, 155, 192–96
"smart bombs," 250
Smith, James L., 319
Smith, Kevin, 317
Smith, Richard, 234–35, 244
Smith, Ronald E., 274–75

"Smith, Sergeant," 112
smoke grenades, 62, 64
Snuol, RT California recon in, 238–39
Snyder, Ken, 166
soap chip, 64
SOG, *see* Studies and Observations Group
Somalia, 349
Son Tay Raid, 339, 348
South China Sea, 228, 332
South Vietnam:
  National Library of, 326
  NVA roadbuilding in, 326–27
  NVA tanks in, 287, 288, 334–35
  recon ops in, 314–15
South Vietnamese Army, 332
  A-Camps transferred to, 303, 314, 323
  invasion of Laos by, 302–4
  recon undertaken by, 249, 319–21
Soviet Union, 9, 73
SPAF, 158
Special Forces, 5–6
  A-Team of, 9, 20
  communications training in, 16–19
  land navigation training for, 12
  memorial stone for, 22
  Phase One training for, 7–15
  Phase Two training for, 19–22
  qualifications for, 5–6
  seven-day field exercise for, 10–15
  "snake eaters" as nickname for, 11
  specialty training in, 16–22
  survival instruction for, 11–12
  training as constant in, 17
  Unconventional Warfare training in, 8–9
  see also Studies and Observations Group, *specific recon teams*
Special Forces Qualification Test, 6
Special Operations Brigade (NVA), 75
Special Operations Command, U.S., 346
Special Operations Forces, U.S., 349
Spencer, Bill, 149, 152–53, 155–59, 161, 163–64, 168, 172, 174–75, 178, 182, 183, 186, 248, 260–61, 313, 314, 323
Sprouse, Robert "Squirrel," 38, 50–51, 102, 123, 142, 182

Spurgeon, Bill, 186
stand-down, 73–74
Stars and Stripes, 302
State Department, U.S., 48, 105, 119, 124, 349
Sten gun, 30, 54
Stephens, Larry, 36, 37, 38, 40, 43, 44–45, 46, 47, 48, 65, 313
Steppenwolf, 141
Ster, Daniel, 186
Stevens, Lowell Wesley, 272–73, 274–75, 278, 279, 290–92, 294, 306–7, 311, 318, 319, 321, 323, 335, 336, 340, 341, 344, 348
Stevenson, Jim, 58
Stormy Zero-Three, loss of, 330, 332, 333, 334, 349
Storter, James, 111, 162, 262, 328–30, 336
Straussfogel, Adolph, 181, 187
"string" training, 59
Strohlein, Madison, 328
Stubbs, Bill, 167–69, 200, 314
Studies and Observations Group (SOG), 1, 8, 21, 23, 27, 30, 95, 100, 131, 145, 154, 182, 211
  air support for, 53
  bomb damage assessment by, 119–20
  Cambodian withdrawal of, 243
  Camp Mackall training of, 10–11, 20, 346, 348
  cross-border missions of, 102
  first MIA in Cambodia of, 115
  HALO training for, 329
  infiltration of Cambodia of, 33
  Long Thanh recon school for, 321–22
  manpower shortages of, 240–41
  Naval Advisory Detachment base of, 186
  NVA ambushes of 1971 by, 317–18
  possible mole at, 216
  recon school of, 137
  reduction of, 302, 314, 324, 345
  safe houses of, 73, 179
  secret launch site of, 96
  security inside, 122

unique equipment of, 34
  see also specific recon teams
Subelsky, Barry, 1
Suber, Randy, 181
Sugar, Howard, 336–38, 349
Sui Pup, 249
Surfaris, 34
survival instruction, 11–12
Suu, 59–60, 65, 105, 140, 155, 157, 159
Swedish K9mm submachine gun, 60, 62
Swiss seat, 59, 61, 81

Tactical Operations Center, 32, 63, 149, 215, 227, 241, 253
  see also Command and Control Central
tactile sense, 131
tail gunner, 106
Taiwan, 316
Talkeetna River, 348
Tandy, Peter, 166
tanks:
  as increased threat, 335
  NVA movements in Laos of, 286, 334–35
  NVA movements in South Vietnam of, 287, 288, 334–35
  in Plei Trap Valley, 335
Target Alpha-One:
  RT Hawaii mission, 254–59
  RT Illinois mission, 142, 148
Target Juliet-Nine, 84, 93
Task Force One, Advisory Element, 303, 316
Task Force Two, Advisory Element, 303
  see also 5th Special Forces Group
Taylor, Floyd, 170
Taylor, Mike, 85
Tay Ninh Province, 240
Team Mountain Lightning, 249
Team Sea Lightning, 249
Teeters, Roger "Buff," 319
Tet Offensive, 9, 31
Thailand, 96, 225, 271, 319
Third Army Field Hospital, 240
Thomas, Daniel, 319
Thomas, Douglas, 317

Thompson, Ben, 58–59, 61, 72, 73, 100,
101–2, 113, 122, 124–26, 128–29, 131,
136, 141, 173, 176, 247, 346
  bomb damage assessment and, 122–23
  Bright Light duty of, 81–83, 85, 87, 91
  counter artillery mission of, 105–8, 110
  first RT Illinois mission of, 63–71
361st Attack Helicopter Company, 85,
338
Todd, Forrest, 186, 241
Todd, Laughlin "Toby," 247, 295, 304
Todd, Richard, 187
Torres, Manuel, 11, 13, 14, 15, 20
tracker dogs, 54
Tramel, Jim, 89–90
Transportation Corps, 230, 231
Trantanella, John, 328
treachery, 55–56
tree charges, 82
truck mining, 132–33
trucks, Russian, 203–4
Trung, 59
Truong Nhu Tang, 238
Tung, 249
20th Special Operations Squadron, 242
21st Special Operations Squadron, 336
23rd Infantry Regiment, 316
24th division (NVA), 83
27th Infantry Regiment, 122–23
28th division (NVA), 83
219th Aviation Company, 100–101,
251

Uemura, Glenn, 16, 27–28, 37, 62, 81, 84,
86, 94, 113, 136–37, 149, 155, 181–82,
189, 245, 247, 249, 345
  awarded Bronze Star for Valor, 93
  joining of SOG by, 30–33
  Juliet-Nine fight of, 93, 143–45
  in Laos, 216–22
  as One-One, 187
  promotion of, 112
Unconventional Warfare, 8–9
Uwharrie National Forest, 22
Uyesaka, Robert, 77

Vander Weg, Peter, 249
Van Diver, Joe, 38
Vang Po, 247, 315, 345
Van Hall, Robert, 38
Vann, John Paul, 334–35
Varni, Howard, 76
Vei, Lang, 77
Vermillion, Mike, 247
Vientiane, 305, 315, 327
Vietcong Memoir, A (Truong), 238
"Vietnamization," of operations, 249
Vietnam War, 1, 9
  bombing halt in, 23
  first Medal of Honor awarded in, 6
  partial bombing halt in, 17
  peace talks in, 22
  slow down of, 342–43
  U.S. withdrawal from, 244, 316, 318
Virachey, 234
visual reconnaissance (VR), 100–101
Voorheis, Harold, 77

Waggle, Allyn, 277
Waggoner, Porter, 294
Walker, Al, 220
Walker, Charlie, 293
Walker, Joe "Gladiator," 37, 42–43, 48,
52–53, 60, 102–3, 131, 132, 141, 200,
247, 295–96, 304, 321, 346–47
  advice of, 51, 67, 193, 207
  tactical judgment of, 53
Wallace, Robert, 166
Wallace, Steve, 278
Walter, Albert, 77
Warren, Jack, 28, 30, 80, 95
Waskovich, Tom, 93–94
Watkins, Pat, Jr., 77
Waugh, Billy, 21, 328
Wayne, John, 22
Wdot, 299
weapons, *see specific weapons*
Weapons School, 16, 19
web harness, 61–62
Weems, Ronald, 184
Weet, 200–201, 208, 239

Welch, Don, 77
"Wendell," 152–54
Westmoreland, William, 54
West Point, 347
We Were Soldiers, 103
Wheeler, Earle, 119
Whelan, Joseph, 170–72
White, Charlie, 115
White, Larry "Six Pack," 111, 243, 249, 260,
     265, 272, 273, 278–79, 284, 290–91,
     292, 301, 307, 308, 310, 334, 341, 344,
     345, 348
White Lead, 274–75, 287, 297, 298
white phosphorus grenades, 62, 64
Wicorek, Ted, 309
Widowmaker Two-Seven, 333
Wild Bunch, The, 316–17
Williams, Hank, Jr., 186, 272
Wilson, Mike, 56, 177, 249, 281
Wilson, Peter J. "Fat Albert," 160, 161,
     163–65, 168, 172–74, 176, 178–79, 183,
     184, 248, 259–61, 313, 314, 323, 350
"With God on Our Side," 142
Wo ("Wo-One"), 161, 200, 203
Wo ("Wo-Two"), 200, 203, 239
Wolcoff, Ed, 137, 151–52, 248, 282, 347,
     349
Wood, Phillip "Woody," 286–87, 295
Woodham, James, Jr., 328

Woodham, Robert, 328
Woodworth, Jason T., 21
Woody, Richard, 200, 203, 206, 211–13, 227,
     346
World War II, 73, 244, 346
Worley, Morris, 7–8, 113–16, 346
Worthley, Ken, 104, 154, 155, 314
Worthley Hall, 154
Wright, Glenn, 336–38, 340–41, 349

Yancey, John, 200, 224–25, 242, 245, 247,
     313, 346
   in Cambodia, 232, 234–35
   Operation Ashtray Two role of, 203,
     205–6, 208, 210–12
Yard Camp, 42, 48, 113–14
Yards, *see* Montagnards
Yellow Jackets, 287
Yellow Lead, 310, 312
Yeo, 161, 173
Young, Jim "King Arthur," 55–56, 177–78,
     208–9, 348
Yube, 187

Zabitosky, Fred, 89, 115, 334–35
Zaborowski, Chester, 275
Zaika, Larry, 179–80
Ziobron, Ed, 275–76
Zumbrun, James "Sam," 185, 283, 314